OPERA INDIGENE: RE/PRESENTING FIRST NATIONS AND INDIGENOUS CULTURES

ASHGATE INTERDISCIPLINARY STUDIES IN OPERA

Series Editor
Roberta Montemorra Marvin
University of Iowa

Advisory Board
Linda Hutcheon, *University of Toronto, Canada*
David Levin, *University of Chicago, USA*
Herbert Lindenberger, Emeritus Professor, *Stanford University, USA*
Julian Rushton, Emeritus Professor, *University of Leeds, UK*

The *Ashgate Interdisciplinary Studies in Opera* series provides a centralized and prominent forum for the presentation of cutting-edge scholarship that draws on numerous disciplinary approaches to a wide range of subjects associated with the creation, performance, and reception of opera (and related genres) in various historical and social contexts. There is great need for a broader approach to scholarship about opera. In recent years, the course of study has developed significantly, going beyond traditional musicological approaches to reflect new perspectives from literary criticism and comparative literature, cultural history, philosophy, art history, theatre history, gender studies, film studies, political science, philology, psycho-analysis, and medicine. The new brands of scholarship have allowed a more comprehensive interrogation of the complex nexus of means of artistic expression operative in opera, one that has meaningfully challenged prevalent historicist and formalist musical approaches. The *Ashgate Interdisciplinary Studies in Opera* series continues to move this important trend forward by including essay collections and monographs that reflect the ever-increasing interest in opera in non-musical contexts. Books in the series will be linked by their emphasis on the study of a single genre – opera – yet will be distinguished by their individualized and novel approaches by scholars from various disciplines/fields of inquiry. The remit of the series welcomes studies of seventeenth century to contemporary opera from all geographical locations, including non-Western topics.

Opera Indigene: Re/presenting First Nations and Indigenous Cultures

Edited by

PAMELA KARANTONIS
University of Greenwich, UK

and

DYLAN ROBINSON
University of Toronto, Canada

LONDON AND NEW YORK

First published 2011 by Ashgate Publishing

Published 2016 by Routledge
2 Park Square, Milton Park, Abingdon, Oxon OX14 4RN
711 Third Avenue, New York, NY 10017, USA

Routledge is an imprint of the Taylor & Francis Group, an informa business

Copyright © Pamela Karantonis, Dylan Robinson, and the Contributors 2011

Pamela Karantonis and Dylan Robinson have asserted their right under the Copyright, Designs and Patents Act, 1988, to be identified as the editors of this work.

All rights reserved. No part of this book may be reprinted or reproduced or utilised in any form or by any electronic, mechanical, or other means, now known or hereafter invented, including photocopying and recording, or in any information storage or retrieval system, without permission in writing from the publishers.

Notice:
Product or corporate names may be trademarks or registered trademarks, and are used only for identification and explanation without intent to infringe.

British Library Cataloguing in Publication Data
Opera Indigene: Re/presenting First Nations and Indigenous Cultures. – (Ashgate interdisciplinary studies in opera)
   1. Opera – Anthropological aspects. 2. Opera – Australia. 3. Opera – Canada. 4. Indigenous peoples in popular culture – Australia. 5. Indigenous peoples in popular culture – Canada.
   I. Series II. Karantonis, Pamela. III. Robinson, Dylan.
   782.1'089-dc22

Library of Congress Cataloging-in-Publication Data
Opera Indigene : Re/presenting First Nations and Indigenous Cultures / [edited by] Pamela Karantonis and Dylan Robinson.
   p. cm. – (Ashgate interdisciplinary studies in opera)
   Includes bibliographical references and index.
   ISBN 978-0-7546-6989-0 (hardcover : alk. paper) – ISBN 978-1-4094-2406-2 (ebook) 1. Indigenous peoples in opera. I. Karantonis, Pamela. II. Robinson, Dylan.
   ML1700.O67 2010
   782.1089–dc22

2010038450

Bach musicological font developed by © Yo Tomita

ISBN 13 : 978-0-7546-6989-0 (hbk)

In Memory of Catherine Parsons Smith

Contents

List of Figures	*xi*
List of Tables	*xiii*
List of Music Examples	*xv*
Notes on Contributors	*xix*
Series Editor's Preface	*xxv*
Acknowledgments	*xxvii*

Introduction   1
Pamela Karantonis and *Dylan Robinson*

PART I CRITICAL AND COMPARATIVE CONTEXTS: OPERA'S COLONIZING FORCE AND DECOLONIZING POTENTIAL

1   Orpheus Conquistador   15
    Nicholas Till

2   Decentering Opera: Early Twenty-First-Century Indigenous Production   31
    Beverley Diamond

3   "Singing from The Margins": Postcolonial Themes in *Voss* and *Waiting for the Barbarians*   57
    Michael Halliwell

4   Performativity, Mimesis, and Indigenous Opera   73
    Pamela Karantonis

PART II AUSTRALIAN PERSPECTIVES

5   "To Didj or Not to Didj": Exploring Indigenous Representation in Australian Music Theater Works by Margaret Sutherland and Andrew Schultz   93
    Anne Boyd

6   Giving Voice to the Un-voiced "Witch" and the "Heart of Nothingness": Moya Henderson's *Lindy*   115
    Linda Kouvaras

viii *Opera Indigene: Re/presenting First Nations and Indigenous Cultures*

| 7 | *The Eighth Wonder*: Explorations of Place and Voice
Anne Power | 141 |

PART III INDIANISM IN THE AMERICAS

| 8 | *Indianismo* in Brazilian Romantic Opera: Shifting Ideologies of
National Foundation
Maria Alice Volpe | 159 |

| 9 | Native Songs, Indianist Styles, and the Processes of Music
Idealization
Tara Browner | 173 |

| 10 | Composed and Produced in the American West, 1912–1913:
Two Operatic Portrayals of First Nations Cultures
Catherine Parsons Smith | 187 |

PART IV CANADIAN PERSPECTIVES

| 11 | Assimilation, Integration and Individuation: The Evolution of
First Nations Musical Citizenship in Canadian Opera
Mary I. Ingraham | 211 |

| 12 | "Too Much White Man In It": Aesthetic Colonization in
Tzinquaw
Alison Greene | 231 |

| 13 | Peaceful Surface, Monstrous Depths: Barbara Pentland and
Dorothy Livesay's *The Lake*
Dylan Robinson | 245 |

| 14 | The Politics of Genre: Exposing Historical Tensions in Harry
Somers's *Louis Riel*
Colleen L. Renihan | 259 |

PART V NEW CREATION AND COLLABORATIVE PROCESSES

| 15 | Creating *Pimooteewin*
Robin Elliott | 279 |

| 16 | After McPhee: Evan Ziporyn's *A House in Bali*
Victoria Vaughan | 295 |

17	West Coast First Peoples and *The Magic Flute*: Tracing the Journey of a Cross-Cultural Collaboration	309
	Robert McQueen Interviewed by Dylan Robinson, with Responses by Cathi Charles Wherry and Tracey Herbert, Lorna Williams, and Marion Newman	
18	*Pecan Summer*: The Process of Making New Indigenous Opera in Australia	325
	Deborah Cheetham and Daniel Browning, interviewed by Pamela Karantonis	

| *Bibliography* | *337* |
| *Index* | *347* |

List of Figures

1.1   Amerigo Vespucci discovers America, Theodore Galle (after Jan van der Straet), *Nova Reperta*, Antwerp, c.1588–1612. Courtesy of the British Museum   22

2.1   *Skuvle Nejla*, Scene 5. Two worlds: the mountain where Maria (Anna Kråik) goes to have her child, on the upper tier, and von Westen (Jan Nilsson) with converts on the lower tier.
Photo permission: Frode Fjellheim and Estrad Norr   39

2.2   *Skuvle Nejla*, Prologue. Inga-Marit Gaup Juuso as Allaq, at one with nature. Photo permission: Frode Fjellheim and Estrad Norr   45

2.3   *BONES*: The tiered worlds of humans below (first family played by Carlos Rivera, Cherith Mark, and Santee Smith) and spirits above (Kalani Queypo as Fire Man, Jani Lauzon as Wind Woman, and Faron Johns as Rattle Man). Photo credit: Don Lee. By permission of Don Lee and the Banff Centre for the Arts   47

9.1   Artwork from Charles Cadman's personal *Shanewis* stationery, 1926. Courtesy of the Braun Research Library, Autry National Center of the American West, Los Angeles, MS.1.1.620, Mr. Charles Wakefield Cadman Correspondence, 1916–1927   183

15.1   From the Toronto premiere production of *Pimooteewin* at the Jane Mallet Theatre, February 2008: Tenor Bud Roach as Weesageechak, soprano Xin Wang as Migisoo, and two *kuroko* figures, with the Elmer Iseler Singers in the background. Photo credit: Cylla von Tiedemann for Soundstreams Canada   288

16.1   Photo of Cloud Fabric used in production of *A House in Bali*. Photo credit: Victoria Vaughan   307

17.1   *The Magic Flute*, produced by Vancouver Opera, Sarastro and his men, costumes designed by John Powell. Each of the nations on the coastal land of British Columbia was represented in costumes designed and created by John Powell.
Photo credit: Tim Matheson   317

17.2   *The Magic Flute*, produced by Vancouver Opera, The Queen of the Night, costume designed by Christine Reimer. Photo credit: Tim Matheson   318

18.1   Deborah Cheetham. Photo credit: Jorge de Araujo   326

List of Tables

7.1	Chronology of scenes	145
8.1	The myth of national foundation: system of (sub-)myths	161
8.2	The myth of national foundation: mythical structure: rite of passage (tripartite)	164
8.3	Comparative analysis of the myth of national foundation in Indianist operas	165
10.1	Indianist operas produced in the USA, 1907–1918	189
10.2	Plot summary of *Narcissa: or, The Cost of Empire*	192
10.3	*The Sun Dance Opera*: two versions	200
11.1	Canadian operas incorporating First Nations characters and events, 1867 to 1967	216
11.2	Related events in Canadian history and politics, 1867–1967	218
11.3	Selected First Nations cultural signifiers in the texts of Canadian operas	224

List of Music Examples

2.1 *Skuvle Nejla*, Scene 14: The bear hunt. The church warden and
Quartet respond to improvised vocal and keyboard sounds:
"A monster rises from the snow. Watch out! Watch out!".
Permission: Frode Fjellheim 41

2.2 *Skuvle Nejla*, The "bear joik" recorded in 1910 by Karl Tiren,
used as a Leitmotif for Allaq. 42

2.3 *Skuvle Nejla*, Scene 1. Thomas von Westen's prayer: "Lord give
me strength to be able to cope with this mission. You Creator who
gave me this task to turn the gaze of heathens from darkness." 43

2.4 *BONES*, the lullaby "Oma Bema" used in several scenes:
"Earth Baby / With me exist / in love." 50

2.5 *BONES*, Act II, Scene 4: Excerpt from the antiphonal choral
singing during the building of the "big house": "Carry, carry the
words / raise, raise the words..." 51

5.1 *The Young Kabbarli*, Daisy, the young Kabbarli, singing an Irish
folk melody. Composed by M Sutherland and M Casey © 1972
J Albert & Son Pty Limited. Used with permission by Albert Music. 103

5.2 *Karrerrai worlamparinyai*, "Wachet Auf" ("Sleepers Awake"),
from J.S. Bach, Cantata 140. © Andrew Schultz: *Journey to
Horseshoe Bend* Bars 36–61. Chorale Melody sung by the
Ntaria Ladies Choir. 107

6.1 *Lindy*, Dingo music. Courtesy of Moya Henderson 128

6.2 *Lindy*, "What end? What end?", CD 1, Track 15. Courtesy of
Moya Henderson 131

6.3 *Lindy*, "Where Butcherbirds Sing", CD 1, Track 5. Courtesy of
Moya Henderson 136

7.1 *The Eighth Wonder*, the Prologue – Earth and Sky.
Permission: Alan John 147

7.2 *The Eighth Wonder*, the rising step motif.
Permission: Alan John 147

7.3 *The Eighth Wonder*, buried alive motif.
Permission: Alan John 150

7.4 *The Eighth Wonder*, Alex's aria in Act I, Scene 4:
"The dream awakens." Permission: Alan John 151

xvi   *Opera Indigene: Re/presenting First Nations and Indigenous Cultures*

7.5	*The Eighth Wonder*, Act I, Scene 7, Alex and Ken, "Why must it wait?" Permission: Alan John	151
7.6	*The Eighth Wonder*, Act 2, Scene 1, Alex, "It watched a city grow and treaded time." Permission: Alan John	153
9.1	Excerpt from Charles Wakefield Cadman, *The Robin Woman (Shanewis)* (Boston: White Smith Publishing Co., 1918), p. 95	181
10.1	*Narcissa*, excerpt from the Act I love/commitment duet between Marcus and Narcissa	194
10.2	*Narcissa*, Act IV, dirge at end of opera. Ostinato fades away. The end of a way of life and of entire race as well as that of the missionaries. "The final brotherhood of all mankind" is to be achieved only in the afterlife	195
10.3	*The Sun Dance Opera*, "Ohiya's Serenade" and "Ink-pa-ta" from Act II, Scene 2, 1912 version	204
10.4	*The Sun Dance Opera*, chorus concluding Act I	205
13.1	*The Lake*, Susan's opening aria. Courtesy the estate of Barbara Pentland and BC Region, Canadian Music Centre	252
13.2	*The Lake*, conclusion to Susan's opening aria. Courtesy the estate of Barbara Pentland and BC Region, Canadian Music Centre	253
13.3	*The Lake*, "Up rose Na'aitka." Courtesy the estate of Barbara Pentland and BC Region, Canadian Music Centre	256
14.1	*Louis Riel* Introduction ("Riel sits in his chamber o'state"). Permission: Barbara Chilcott Somers	266
14.2	*Louis Riel* Act II, Scene 6 (Dance: "The Buffalo Hunt"). Permission: Barbara Chilcott Somers	267
14.3	*Louis Riel* Act I, Scene 4 (Aria: "Dieu! O mon Dieu!"). Permission: Barbara Chilcott Somers	269
14.4	Riel Row 1. Permission: Barbara Chilcott Somers	273
14.5	*Louis Riel* Act I, Scene 2 (Aria: "Au Milieu de la foule"). Permission: Barbara Chilcott Somers	274
14.6	*Louis Riel* Act I, Scene 3 (Aria: Macdonald's "Sugar Aria"). Permission: Barbara Chilcott Somers	275
16.1a	McPhee's score of *Kinesis*, mm. 1–5 © Master Music Publications	300
16.1b	Ziporyn, *A House in Bali*, Act I, Scene 1, mm 1–7 © Airplane Ears Music (ASCAP) 2009	300
16.2	Ziporyn, *A House in Bali*, McPhee composing in vain, Act I, Scene 1, mm. 36–44 © Airplane Ears Music (ASCAP) 2009	301

16.3	Ziporyn, *A House in Bali*, Realization of McPhee's writer's block, Act I, Scene 1, mm. 112–122 © Airplane Ears Music (ASCAP) 2009	301
16.4	Ziporyn, *A House in Bali*, The "hammering" rhythms, Act I, Scene 3. © Airplane Ears Music (ASCAP) 2009	302

Notes on Contributors

Anne Boyd enjoys a distinguished career as a composer and music educator. In 1990, she became the first Australian and the first woman to be appointed Professor of Music at the University of Sydney, where her research work focuses upon the influence of landscape and of Asian music upon Australian composers. In 1996, Anne Boyd was honored with the award of an AM in the Order of Australia for her service to Music. In 2003, she was conferred Honorary Doctor of the University by the University of York (UK).

Tara Browner is professor of Ethnomusicology at the University of California, Los Angeles. She is the author of *Heartbeat of the People: Music and Dance of the Northern Pow-Wow* (University of Illinois Press, 2002), editor of *Music of the First Nations: Tradition and Innovation in Native North American Music* (University of Illinois Press, 2009), and editor of Songs from *"A New Circle of Voices": The 16th Annual Pow-wow at UCLA* (Music of the United States of America, A-R Editions, 2009).

Daniel Browning is from the Minjungbal clan of the Bundjalung nation in Australia. He is a film-maker, radio broadcaster and producer of the *Awaye!* arts and culture program for the Australian Broadcasting Corporation. The program also showcases documentaries produced by diverse Indigenous peoples including Maori, Polynesian, native American and South African broadcasters. In 2008 and 2009, Daniel Browning produced radio documentaries following Deborah Cheetham's creative process in making and rehearsing *Pecan Summer* in anticipation of its 2010 premiere, and aims to continue his documentary work on the project.

Deborah Cheetham is an Indigenous Australian soprano, actor and author of the internationally acclaimed play *White Baptist Abba Fan*, has worked as classical singer since the early 1990s and currently teaches voice at the University of Melbourne. Since her international debut in 1997, Ms Cheetham has performed in the United States, Europe, the United Kingdom, New Zealand and throughout Australia. She is currently working on *Pecan Summer*, a newly commissioned opera about the Yorta Yorta and Indigenous people of southeastern Australia and the summer of 1939 which changed the lives of the people of Cummeragunja mission forever.

Beverley Diamond holds the Canada Research Chair in Ethnomusicology at Memorial University. She established and directs the Research Centre for the

Study of Music, Media, and Place (MMaP). She has worked with Inuit and First Nations elders and musicians, focusing recently on aspects of Indigenous modernity: recording studio practices, Indigenous awards, film soundtracks, and Indigenous opera. Her newest book is *Native American Music of Eastern North America* (Oxford University Press, 2008). She was named a Trudeau Fellow in 2009.

Robin Elliott was on the faculty at University College Dublin for six years before returning to Canada in 2002. He is currently a professor of musicology and Associate Dean, Undergraduate Education at the Faculty of Music at the University of Toronto, where he also holds the Jean A. Chalmers Chair in Canadian Music, is the Director of the Institute for Canadian Music, and is a Senior Fellow of Massey College.

Alison Greene received her Bachelor's degree in music from the University of Western Ontario, and her MA in theater history from the University of Victoria, British Columbia. As an opera director, she has been associated with the opera companies of Victoria, Vancouver, Edmonton, and Ottawa, Opera Ontario, the National Arts Centre, Mobile Opera Alabama, and the Geneva Grand Opera. Alison is currently on faculty with the Pacific Opera Victoria Young Artists' Program.

Michael Halliwell was born in South Africa, studied music and literature at the University of the Witwatersrand in Johannesburg and at the London Opera Centre with Otakar Kraus, as well as with Tito Gobbi in Florence. He was principal baritone for many years with the Netherlands Opera, the Nuremberg Municipal Opera; and the Hamburg State Opera, and he sang in many European opera houses. He was Chair of Vocal Studies and Opera and Associate Dean (Research) at the University of Sydney Conservatorium of Music. His book, *Opera and the Novel: The Case of Henry James*, was published by Rodopi Press in 2005.

Tracey Herbert, BFA, (Shuswap, Bonaparte) is Executive Director of the First Peoples' Heritage, Language, and Culture Council. She has a degree in fine arts, and a strong community development background based in 16 years administering First Nations community programs in British Columbia.

Mary I. Ingraham is Professor of Musicology at the University of Alberta. Her current research examines issues of cultural politics, identity, and representation in Canadian opera. She has published a catalogue of Canadian operas and created several web-based educational projects for the Canadian Music Centre, and, with Dylan Robinson, she initiated and co-ordinates a national working group on interdisciplinary perspectives on the music of Canada. Additionally, she has presented widely and published on Brahms's cantata *Rinaldo*.

Pamela Karantonis is a Lecturer in Drama at the University of Greenwich in London and gained her PhD from the University of New South Wales, Sydney. She has published in *Studies in Musical Theatre* and is a convenor of the International

Federation for Theatre Research (IFTR) Music Theatre Working Group. In 2009, she was invited to speak at an Oxford University European Humanities Research Council Colloquium on the politics of opera.

Linda Kouvaras is a musicologist, composer and pianist. She holds a Senior Lectureship in music at the University of Melbourne and publishes in contemporary music, both classical and popular, focusing especially on Australian music, postmodernism and gender issues. Her latest book chapter appears in Ashgate's *Soundscapes of Australia: Music, Place, and Spirituality* (ed. Fiona Richards, 2007). She is Co-Chief Investigator on an Australian Research Council Discovery Project Grant to research issues of postmodernism in contemporary Australian art-music (2005–2008).

Robert McQueen's recent directorial work includes the new music theater piece *Where Elephants Weep*, which had its world premiere in Phnom Penh, Cambodia and the Japanese-language production of *Carousel* at the Galaxy Theatre in Tokyo, as well as opera and theater productions in the USA and Canada. Born in Vancouver, Canada, Robert now lives in New York City.

Marion Newman is a Kwagiulth and Coast Salish First Nations mezzo-soprano interested in projects that make it possible for her to mix her First Nations culture with her classical vocal training. Recent appearances include Third Lady in Vancouver Opera's North West Coast production of *Die Zauberflöte* and the world premiere of *Bigiiwe*, by Barbara Croall (Odawa), and she has recorded *The Huron Carol* in Wendat for Naxos records. Marion has appeared as a soloist on the National Aboriginal Achievement Awards for CBC television four times.

Catherine Parsons Smith (1933–2009) was Professor Emerita at the University of Nevada, Reno. Specializing on American music and musicians of the late nineteenth and first half of the twentieth centuries, she is the author of several books, among them *Making Music in Los Angeles: Transforming the Popular* (University of California Press, 2007) and *William Grant Still: A Study in Contradictions* (University of California Press, 1999), which won the ASCAP Deems Taylor Award.

Anne Power is Senior Lecturer at the University of Western Sydney in the School of Education. Her musicological expertise is in the field of contemporary Australian opera. In 2002, she devised the Secondary Schools Music Australian Opera Series with the Australian Music Centre. Anne Power is also Deputy Chair of the NSW Chapter of Australian Society for Music Education. She is on the Editorial Board of the national journal and is a representative to the Australian National Council of Orff Schulwerk and the editor of its journal *Musicworks*.

Colleen L. Renihan is a PhD Candidate in Musicology at the Faculty of Music, University of Toronto. She is working on a dissertation that examines historical and musical narrative elements in historical Canadian operas by Harry Somers, Istvan Anhalt, and John Estacio. Other research interests include twentieth- and twenty-first-century opera and musical aesthetics. Her research is generously supported by the Social Sciences and Humanities Research Council of Canada.

Dylan Robinson has held positions as a postdoctoral fellow at the University of Toronto's Faculty of Music and as a Visiting Scholar in Canadian Studies at the University of California Berkeley. He is currently working on a book that investigates the degree to which musical reconciliation in Canada conveys the necessarily agonistic process of restorative justice. Addressing Indigenous art music projects that feature Indigenous musicians as soloists or members of ensembles, as well as art music by First Nations composers, his research theorizes how Indigenous epistemology and worldviews might impact upon the re-telling of music history in North America.

Nicholas Till is Professor of Opera and Music Theatre in the School of Media, Film and Music at the University of Sussex, where he is Director of the Centre for Research in Opera and Music Theatre. He works as a historian, critic, theorist, and practitioner in opera and music theater. Nick has also taught at institutions such as the Royal College of Music, Britten–Pears School Aldeburgh, and Stanford University. In 2001 he was Visiting Professor in Opera at UCLA (Los Angeles). He is the author of *Mozart and the Enlightenment: Truth, Virtue and Beauty in Mozart's Operas* (Faber, 1992; W.W. Norton, 1994), and is currently editing *The Cambridge Companion to Opera Studies*.

Victoria Vaughan is Director of Productions for Real Time Opera and the Assistant Director of Opera Theatre at the Oberlin College Conservatory of Music. A specialist in the staging of new works, she has devised and developed numerous world premiere productions, in addition to producing standard operatic repertory and some recent directorial forays into French court opera. Vaughan trained as an opera director at the Indiana University Opera Theater and also holds a PhD in Musicology from the University of Southampton. Originally from South London, she now freelances in the USA.

Maria Alice Volpe earned her doctoral degree in Musicology/Ethnomusicology from the University of Texas, Austin and her master's degree in Musicology from the Universidade Estadual Paulista-UNESP, Brazil in 1994. Volpe is Professor/ Chair of Musicology at the Universidade Federal do Rio de Janeiro, and is currently on commission as the Head of the Graduate Studies Program in Music at the Universidade de Brasília. She was awarded research grants from Brazilian government foundations, and is currently ad hoc consultant for the Ministry of Education, and the Ministry of Science and Technology.

Cathi Charles Wherry BFA (Anishnabeque, Rama Mnjikaning), is a visual artist, curator and writer. As Arts Program Coordinator for the First Peoples' Council she supports Aboriginal artists and cultural workers through development and delivery of funding, resources, and training.

Lorna Williams is Lil'wat from the St'at'yem'c First Nation; she holds the Canada Research Chair in Indigenous Knowledge and Learning in the Faculty of Education and Department of Linguistics at the University of Victoria. Dr. Williams is board chair of First Peoples Heritage, Language, and Culture Council. Lorna was a CCL Minerva Lecturer in 2007 and was invested into the Order of British Columbia for her work in education in 1992.

Series Editor's Preface

The *Ashgate Interdisciplinary Studies in Opera* provides a centralized and prominent forum for the presentation of cutting-edge scholarship that draws on numerous disciplinary approaches on a wide range of subjects associated with the creation, performance, dissemination, and reception of opera and related genres in various historical and social contexts. The series includes topics from the seventeenth century to the present and from all geographical locations, including non-Western traditions.

In recent years, the field of opera studies has not only come into its own but has developed significantly, going beyond traditional musicological approaches to reflect new perspectives from literary criticism and comparative literature, cultural history, philosophy, art history, theater history, gender studies, film studies, political science, philology, psycho-analysis, and even medicine. The new brands of scholarship have allowed a more comprehensive and intensive interrogation of the complex nexus of means of artistic expression operative in opera, one that has meaningfully challenged prevalent historicist and formalist musical approaches. Today, interdisciplinary, or as some prefer cross-disciplinary, opera studies are receiving increasingly widespread attention, and the ways in which scholars, practitioners, and the public think about the artform known as opera continue to change and expand. The *Ashgate Interdisciplinary Studies in Opera* seeks to move this important trend forward by including essay collections and monographs that reflect the ever-increasing interest in opera in non-musical contexts.

Opera Indigene: Critical Perspectives on Re/presenting First Nations and Indigenous Cultures, the first volume to be issued in the *Ashgate Interdisciplinary Studies in Opera*, aptly fulfills the series' remit. The book's editors, Pamela Karantonis and Dylan Robinson, have brought together a refreshing mixture of essays about the representation of non-Western, specifically indigenous or First Nations, cultures in opera. The volume reflects the varied voices of its international group of contributors: many are members of the ethnic groups about which they write, some are theater professionals and opera practitioners, and others are highly experienced historians in music or other disciplines.

More specifically, as the use of 're/presenting' in the book's title signals, the volume addresses both how representations of indigenous identity have been constructed in opera by non-indigenous artists and how indigenous artists have recently utilized opera as an interface to present and develop their cultural practices. The interdisciplinary nature of this volume is further enhanced by the multiple methodological approaches, including postcolonial theory, ethnomusicology, cultural geography, and critical discourses on nationalism and multiculturalism, that the contributors apply in their explorations of their subjects.

Opera Indigene fills several major gaps in existing scholarship in drama, performance and theater studies; musicology, especially opera studies; postcolonial studies, and aboriginal/indigenous studies. Opera and theater/performance studies have considered a number of issues pertaining to exoticism and Orientalism, but, with few exceptions, scholars have not engaged specifically with musical or dramatic representations of the indigene, especially in national/nationalist narratives of the New World. And postcolonial and aboriginal studies have paid little attention, beyond ethnomusicological detailing, to music/opera. Karantonis and Robinson's collection extends the discourse in all of these fields because of its historical breadth, intercultural scope, theoretical sophistication, broad geographical focus, and dual perspective.

Roberta Montemorra Marvin

Acknowledgments

Deeply felt thanks goes to Nicholas Till, The Centre for Research in Opera and Music Theatre, and Björn Heile, University of Sussex, for feedback and funding assistance in the early stages of this project. For other funding support and assistance, we thank Peter Wilton of the Gregorian Society; Jane Arthurs, Scott Fraser, and Lisa Thrower of the University of the West of England; Ian Henderson of the Menzies Centre; and the technical staff King's College London. Pamela and Dylan would like to thank their families for their support and also the following people for the mentorship and encouragement early on that eventually led to the idea for this volume: Heather Dawkins, Donna Zapf, Jin-Me Yoon, Clemens Risi, Pieter Verstraete, Tereza Havelkova and the Music Theatre Working Group of the International Federation for Theatre Research. We would also like to make particular mention of composers who worked so generously with our authors to provide assistance with musical excerpts: Moya Henderson, Alan John, Andrew Schultz, and Evan Ziporyn.

It has been a pleasure to work with Sara Peacock, whose astute suggestions and copyediting skills have strengthened this collection enormously. We also extend our warmest thanks to Heidi Bishop and Barbara Pretty at Ashgate Publishing for their guidance in bringing this volume to completion.

Introduction

Pamela Karantonis and Dylan Robinson

At the 2005 Talking Stick Festival, an annual event that showcases Indigenous Performance in Vancouver, Canada, the Tsimshian/Cree performance artist Skeena Reece, offered a perspective on the developing performance traditions of First Nations song:

> I figure in like a hundred years our songs are just gonna sound real different ... . They're probably gonna sound something like this:
>
> *Reece begins to sing what sounds like a traditional song with vocables, but performs it with full operatic bravura and excessive vibrato. She concludes the aria with a rising arpeggio, ending on a high note that causes her eyes to roll up toward the back of her head. It is a parody of operatic singing at its best. Thunderous cheers and laughter erupt from audience.*
>
> What? Come on, that's not a good thing, man. That's not good—how're we supposed to dance to that?[1]

Any written transcription of Reece's routine, be it textual or musical, cannot convey the full extent of absurdity in her adaptation of traditional singing, nor the ebullient response of the largely First Nations audience in attendance. The worlds of Indigenous cultural traditions and opera would seem to be diametrically opposed in a large majority of their aspects including performance style, participation, venue, and cultural function. In Reece's parody we see the worlds of opera and First Nations song come together as questionable partners. Yet the conjunction of these worlds has historically been much more common in an international context than one would expect, and has often resulted in productive exchange and the reciprocal growth of both traditions. In striking contrast to what Reece and her audience hear as the incongruous pairing of cultural traditions and operatic practice, there is both a long history of operas that represent First Peoples and a lesser-known history of opera by First Peoples used to express and re-assess cultural traditions. The chapters contained within this volume explore the range of incongruities, synchronicities, and alliances between indigenous cultural practices and operatic traditions. While the representation of non-Western cultures and 'otherness' in opera has long been a

---

[1] Skeena Reece, *Talking Stick Festival 2005*, www.fullcircleperformance.ca/uploads/documents/talking_stick.mov, 2′00″–2′39″ (accessed August 10, 2009).

2   *Opera Indigene: Re/presenting First Nations and Indigenous Cultures*

focus for critical inquiry, the diverse relationships between opera and First Nations and Indigenous cultures[2] have received far less attention. *Opera Indigene* takes these relationships as a focus, addressing the changing historical depictions of Indigenous cultures in opera and the more contemporary uses and adaptations of the form by Indigenous and First Nations artists. The "re/presenting" of our title thus signals an important distinction between how non-Indigenous artists have *represented* the Indigene in opera[3] and how Indigenous artists have more recently utilized opera as an interface to *present* and extend cultural practices.

In the first instance, *Opera Indigene* examines how operatic representations of First Nations and Indigenous cultures are often entwined with ideologies of nation-building and nationalism. A great wealth of research on the construction of Indigenous identity in the visual arts and literature has addressed topics including the role of salvage ethnography in relation to artistic production, the complexities of intercultural collaboration, cultural autonomy, and the roles artistic practice plays in the continuing processes of historical redress. In relation to the varied examination of these topics across the humanities, opera scholarship has left the intersections between such issues and Indigenous re/presentations in opera underexamined.[4] The work contained in *Opera Indigene* builds upon this significant body of research

---

[2]   The capitalization of "Indigenous" throughout this volume denotes the subject status of specific people; in contrast to the more abstract use of "indigenous" in relation to cultural practice.

[3]   Like the double meaning of "re/presenting" we are using the term "Indigene" here and in the title of the collection in two distinct senses. Firstly, Indigene can refer to operas by indigenous peoples of (and often about) the land. In this sense such operas are "Indigene," as in Richard Hakluyt's first use of the word, and "bred upon that very soyle" (*The Principall Navigations, Voiages and Discoueries of the English Nation*, 1589, as quoted in the *Oxford English Dictionary*). Secondly, the 'Indigene' might be understood in terms of representation, as the "homogenised fantasy image of the generic indigenous Other ... a mythic sign fabricated within white culture, projected outwards, and superimposed over indigenous worlds": Elspeth Nina Tilley, *White Vanishing: A Settler Australian Hegemonic Textual Strategy, 1789–2006* (diss. University of Queensland, 2007), pp. 15–16. See Terry Goldie, *Fear and Temptation: The Image of the Indigene in Canadian, Australian, and New Zealand Literatures* (Montreal: McGill-Queen's University Press, 1989).

[4]   Notable exceptions to this include scholarship on more well-known operatic repertoire such as Jean-Philippe Rameau's *Les Indes galantes*. See Roger Savage, "Rameau's American Dancers," *Early Music*, 11/4, Rameau Tercentenary Issue (October, 1983), pp. 441–52; Howard Brofsky, "Rameau and the. Indians: The Popularity of Les Sauvages," in *Music in the Classic. Period: Essays in Honor of Barry S. Brook*, ed. Allan Atlas (New York: Pendragon Press, 1985), pp. 43–60; Joellen A. Meglin, "'Sauvages, Sex Roles, and Semiotics': Representations of Native Americans in the French Ballet, 1736–1837, Part One: The Eighteenth Century," *Dance Chronicle*, 23/2 (2000), pp. 87–132; Michael V. Pisani, *Imagining Native America in Music* (New Haven, CT: Yale University Press, 2005); Timothy Taylor, *Beyond Exoticism: Western Music and the World* (Durham, NC: Duke University Press, 2007); and Olivia Bloechl, *Native American Song at the Frontiers of Early Modern Music* (Cambridge: Cambridge University Press, 2008). See also Carol

Introduction 3

in the humanities that examines artistic representations of Indigenous peoples to compare differences in operatic portrayals of Indigenous subjects across settler-invader colonies. The chapters included here take a variety of perspectives toward their examination of how operas on Indigenous subjects reflect unspoken historical records of the relationships between Indigenous peoples and colonizing powers, convey stories that face up to colonial pasts, and contextualize forms of internal colonization within the construction and maintenance of national identity.[5]

The decidedly interdisciplinary nature of this study is additionally underscored by the multiple methodological frameworks our contributors apply in their examinations of operatic re/presentations of Indigenous and First Nations cultures. Drawing upon postcolonial theory, ethnomusicology, cultural geography, and critical discourses of nationalism and multiculturalism, this collection brings together experts on opera and music in Canada, the Americas, and Australia.[6]

E. Robertson (ed.), *Musical Repercussion of 1492: Encounters in Text and Performance* (Washington, DC: Smithsonian Institution Press, 1992).

[5] Derived from the early Marxist theory, particularly that of Antonio Gramsci, internal colonialization has been defined as "a form of colonialism in which the dominant and subordinate populations are intermingled, so that there is no geographically distinct 'metropolis' separate from the 'colony'" (Mario Barrera, *Race and Class in the Southwest: A Theory of Racial Inequality* (Notre Dame, IN: University of Notre Dame Press, 1979), p. 194). In relation to Canada, one form of internal colonization results from governmental definitions regarding First Nations status. Thomas King's definition of how the Canadian government, rather than First Peoples themselves, impose the legal definition of status (irregardless of cultural identity and First Peoples' definitions of kinship) provides a particularly strong example of internal colonization: "here in Canada we have what is called the 'two-generation cut-off clause.' Marry out of status for two generations, and the children from the last union are non-status. Oh, you can continue to call yourself an Indian, but you can't live on a reserve. You can continue to tell people that you're Cree, or Blackfoot, or Ojibway, or Mohawk, but you can't vote in band elections. You can go to powwows, sing at a drum, sell arts and crafts if you like, but you are no longer eligible for treaty benefits, and neither are your children or their children or their children right down to the end of time … No need to send in the cavalry with guns blazing. Legislation will do just as nicely … No one know knows for sure how long it will take, but according to John Borrows and Leroy Littlebear, two of Canada's leading Aboriginal scholars and teachers … in fifty to seventy-five years there will be no status Indians left in Canada. We'll still have the treaties and we'll still have the treaty land held in trust for status Indians by the government. We just won't have any Indians" (Thomas King, *The Truth about Stories* (Minneapolis, MN: University of Minnesota Press, 2003) pp. 143–4). See also Eva Mackey, *The House of Difference: Cultural Politics and National Identity in Canada* (Toronto, ON: University of Toronto Press, 2002); Ian Hughes, "Dependent Autonomy: A New Phase of Internal Colonialism," *Australian Journal of Social Issues*, 30 (1995), pp. 369–88.

[6] This selection is made with the awareness that there is future scholarship to be conducted on opera's relevance to the postcolonial communities throughout Africa and the Arab world. We have sought to address this diversity by including work outside of these three areas, notably Beverley Diamond's examination of Sámi traditions in *Skuvle Nejla*

Central to the dialogic ethos of collaboration, *Opera Indigene* equally provides a forum for Indigenous opera practitioners—including librettists, composers, directors, and set and costume designers—and non-Indigenous artists working with Indigenous communities to voice their perspectives on the developing form of Indigenous opera creation. The final part of this collection contains interviews that address the potential for forms of Indigenous opera to challenge opera's implication in the history of colonization.[7]

Chapters are here grouped by region, with an opening section that provides theoretical contexts of opera's role in colonization and decolonization, and a concluding section that addresses new work and collaborative processes. In doing so, the opening and concluding sections frame the collection in a way that moves from colonialism and opera as mutual enablers to consider the diversity of Indigenous voices in making the choice to express traditions through operatic expression. While these sections allow primarily for regional and historical comparisons, the chapters also contain points of contact across the sectional divides. To begin, let us for the moment return to the opening aria, and Skeena Reece's rhetorical question "How're we supposed to dance to that?" in all seriousness, and address it through reference to the use of dance in opera by First Peoples.

As evidenced in several of the operas discussed in this collection, dance has a central function in operas created by, or in collaboration with, Indigenous performers and artists. Adaptations including Vancouver Opera's Coast Salish *The Magic Flute* (2007), the participation of the Bangarra Dance Theatre in *Black River* (1989/1993), and Sadie Buck's opera *BONES* (2001) evidence this. As Sadie Buck, the composer of *BONES* describes:

> For Haudenosaunee people music and dance go together. All of our songs have a dance to it. There is not one of our songs that does not have a dance through all our ceremonies including medicine and socials. There is no separation for us.[8]

(2006) within Part II, Michael Halliwell's inclusion of 1970s South Africa in *Waiting for the Barbarians* (2005) in Part I, and Victoria Vaughan's discussion of Balinese culture in *A House In Bali* (2010) in Part V.

[7] Several scholars, including Nicholas Till in this collection, examine the concurrence of colonial exploration with the coalescence of opera, and posit that the form of opera provided a means for addressing these changing notions of modern subjectivity and "otherness." See Slavoj Žižek, "'The Wound Is Healed Only by the Spear that Smote You'," in *Tarrying with the Negative: Kant, Hegel, and the Critique of Ideology* (Durham, NC: Duke University Press, 1993); Edward Said, *Culture and Imperialism* (New York: Vintage, 1994); and Timothy Taylor, *Beyond Exoticism: Western Music and the World* (Durham, NC: Duke University Press, 2007).

[8] Sadie Buck, interviewed by Elma Miller, www.nativedance.ca/index.php/Scholars/Sadie_Buck (accessed October 30, 2009).

Introduction 5

Consequently, it is fitting that some of the operas (including *BONES*) created by Indigenous artists addressed in this collection are specifically defined as "dance operas" by their authors, thus signaling a re-orientation of operatic language that reflects the equality of artistic forms in Indigenous cultural practices. Alternately, the representation of Indigenous peoples exclusively through the medium of dance in the place of sung text in opera is a strategy complicit with colonialism, as may be apparent to audiences of *Voss*, an opera written in the twentieth century but set in the nineteenth-century British colony of New South Wales in which the Indigenous characters, who have no cultural power to the colonizers, do not sing or speak. In a similar vein, *Tzinquaw* places traditional Cowichan dance against a "civilizing" accompaniment of church hymn harmonization and the musical language of early twentieth-century operettas like those of Gilbert and Sullivan. Historically, then, works like *Tzinquaw* (1950) and *Voss* (1986) are linked to exhibitionary codes of colonialism, whereby folkloric quotation of Indigenous choreographies may be presented as fragments, devoid of their narrative contexts and the "voices" (both literal and figurative) of the participants.[9]

Importantly, many of the chapters contained here examine how representations of Indigeneity are mediated by other art forms that intersect within opera. As much of the work in this collection illustrates, First Nations and Indigenous artists have increasingly used the multidisciplinary nature, and interdisciplinary potential, of opera to present the integration of storytelling, dance and song central to their cultural practices. Evidence of such genre shifts are addressed by the chapters this collection through sustained engagement with questions of hybridity in the musico-dramatic languages the works employ. Operas including *Skuvle Nejla* (2006) and *BONES* bear less relation to the musical conventions of contemporary opera but instead amalgamate traditional practices with popular music genres. Other examples include Andrew Schultz's semi-staged cantata *Journey to Horseshoe Bend* (2003) and the place of Yorta Yorta ceremonial storytelling in Deborah Cheetham's *Pecan Summer* (2010).

Conversely, *Opera Indigene* considers how the boundaries of cultural traditions and Indigenous worldviews are stretched by the generic conventions of opera. How do such operas honor the histories of traditions and the diverse worldviews of specific Indigenous groups and First Nations? In the case of *Pimooteewin (The Journey)* (2008), Robin Elliott asks what it is, specifically, that might define this opera as "Cree"? Following upon the discourse of Native nationalism,[10]

---

[9]   The nineteenth-century practices underlying the cultural display of alterity at Expositions, Exhibitions and World's Fairs are discussed in Barbara Kirshenblatt-Gimblett, *Destination Culture: Tourism, Museums and Heritage* (Berkeley: University of California Press, 1998).

[10]   Gerald R. (Taiaiake) Alfred, *Heeding the Voices of Our Ancestors: Kahnawake Mohawk Politics and the Rise of Native Nationalism* (Toronto: Oxford University Press, 1995); Craig S. Womack, *Red on Red: Native American Literary Nationalism* (Minneapolis, MN: University of Minnesota Press, 1999); Jace Weaver, Craig S. Womack, and Robert

6 *Opera Indigene: Re/presenting First Nations and Indigenous Cultures*

we might see such questions framed within a perspective that acknowledges a commitment to addressing the social and political issues and honoring the worldviews of the Indigenous communities these operas are written in association with, as well as presenting such works for the benefit of those very communities. As such, these works might also be seen to take part in the larger field of "post-operatic" work that critically engages genre conventions and the role of opera itself in engagement with communities outside of the traditionally homogeneous opera audience of the twentieth century.[11]

The decolonizing contexts of many of the works in this book witness the questioning of other social inequalities, such as repressive gender politics, the exclusionary nature of official histories, the limits of salvage ethnographies and the pursuit of individual liberation against, or in harmony with, Indigenous communities' self-determination. Among many of the creative works our contributors analyze, the narrative of the libretti often evidence a direct relationship between the abuse of individuals for their gender and sexuality in addition to their Indigeneity by the colonizing authority, as is the case particularly for the operas *Lindy* (1997) and *Waiting for the Barbarians* (2005). Therefore the protagonist's victory over these hardships is complex. At times the individual could be going against a communally defined sense of tradition, as seen in the depiction of a parodic Indigenous character in *The Young Kabbarli* (1965). Furthermore, the potent metaphor of the journey can be situated in the narrative either as a personal quest for the protagonist, as in *Pimooteewin (The Journey)*, or as a means of escape from persecution, as in *Pecan Summer*. Conversely, the metaphor of the journey is also the premise of the colonial project, via the romanticizing of exploration, as in the postcolonial reading of the protagonists in both Monteverdi's *Orfeo* and, more recently, Richard Meale's *Voss*.

Chapter Synopses

Opera Indigene is divided into five parts, beginning with an opening section that contextualizes key theoretical perspectives and recent developments in the representation of, and collaboration with, Indigenous subjects in opera. To begin, Nicholas Till's "Orpheus Conquistador" proposes a reading of Striggio's libretto for *L'Orfeo* as an early modern manifesto for navigation and the colonial project. More specifically, he examines how *L'Orfeo* aligns itself to the spirit of scientific

---

Warrior, *American Indian Literary Nationalism* (Albuquerque: University of New Mexico Press, 2006); Kristina Fagan and Sam McKegney, "Circling the Question of Nationalism in Native Canadian Literature and its Study," *Review: Literature and Arts of the Americas*, 41/1 (2008), pp. 31–42.

[11] See Nicholas Till, "I don't mind if something's operatic, just as long as it's not opera: A Critical Practice for New Opera and Music Theatre," *Contemporary Theatre Review*, 14 (February 2004), pp. 15–24.

and colonial exploitation which lay at the heart of early modernity. Till here presents a reading of *L'Orfeo* through the Galilean lens of the long alternative history of Orpheus as tamer and civilizer, drawing on the writings of contemporaries such as Francis Bacon (in particular his "Orpheus; or Philosophy" of 1609) to show how, as Edward Said once wrote, "the opera form itself ... belongs equally to the history of culture and the historical experience of overseas domination."[12] Beverley Diamond approaches the subject from an opposing cultural and political reality: that of operas created by First Peoples in the twentieth century to the present. Specifically, she examines the agency of First Peoples in opera creation, focusing on the potential that hybrid styles and juxtapositions may have as a decolonizing strategy. Taking a comparative approach, Diamond analyses the language and musical style of Sadie Buck's *BONES* and Frode Fjellheim's *Skuvle Nejla* in relation to narrative and staging, and gender representation. Michael Halliwell's comparative analysis of *Voss* and *Waiting for the Barbarians* explores connections and contradictions between two postcolonial novels and their operatic adaptations. Halliwell examines how both novels by Patrick White and J.M. Coetzee, respectively, and their corresponding operas by Richard Meale and Philip Glass investigate the limits of language and writing in a distinctly postcolonial fashion—particularly in the silencing of the "other". His analysis of *Voss* is an important recognition of the deconstruction of colonial power through the ambitious and ill-fated expeditions of Ludwig Leichhardt into the deserts of central Australia. Drawing on the literary powers of Patrick White and David Malouf's libretto, the title character represents a model of failed masculinity and destabilizes the assurance of the colonial map in an operatic working of themes relevant to Conrad's *Heart of Darkness*. In his analysis of *Waiting for the Barbarians*, Halliwell makes a compelling case for the self-destructive consequences of colonial violence. Pamela Karantonis's chapter, "Performativity, Mimesis, and Indigenous Opera," provokes readers to consider the dramatic or theatrical languages of opera by taking an interdisciplinary approach to her case studies in line with recent performance studies and opera scholarship. Her chapter revises significant moments in Australian operatic history and their relationship to the emergence of a theatrical discourse surrounding Indigenous Australian performance. This includes an acknowledgement of the already performative status of ritual in traditional cultures and the difficulties in negotiating concepts of "authenticity" of expression in new creative forms.

The second part of this collection focuses on Australian perspectives, here taken as perspectives on Australian operas about Indigenous Australians, gender politics, and the abstraction of "indigeneity" itself as an imaginative concept. To begin, Anne Boyd's chapter introduces significant political factors to the debate by contextualizing her analysis in relation to the nationalist and somewhat problematic *Jindyworobak* movement in Australian literature. This is balanced most significantly, with a discussion of the "Two Ways" philosophy of educational theory and cultural interaction between Indigenous and non-

---

[12] Said, *Culture and Imperialism*, p. 114.

8   *Opera Indigene: Re/presenting First Nations and Indigenous Cultures*

Indigenous Australians. Such theoretical perspectives provide a vital context in looking at the groundbreaking work of both Margaret Sutherland and Andrew Schultz. Feminist perspectives are also considered in Sutherland's work about the historical figure of Daisy Bates in *The Young Kabbarli* (1965). Boyd's chapter also includes an analysis of the little-known work *Rites of Passage* (1972–1973) by canonical Australian composer Peter Sculthorpe, whose use of re-staged ritual and the Aranda language paves the way for new staged compositions that recognize Indigenous language and practice, rather than Western attempts to represent them. Ultimately, this chapter advocates a musicology that brings Aboriginal anthropology by Indigenous scholars and activists into the dialogue. To this effect, Boyd accounts for the collaborative practices of Andrew Schultz, whose work is formed in consultation with traditional communities, resulting in the creation of the liminal theatrical form of the concert-opera *Journey to Horseshoe Bend* (2003). In the following chapter, Linda Kouvaras deepens a feminist engagement further by highlighting the important nexus between marginalization of gender and Indigeneity in her work on Moya Henderson's *Lindy* (1997). Her perspective on the demonization of both the historical person of Lindy Chamberlain and Australian Aboriginal knowledge systems by conservative legal and media discourses in Australia makes a convincing and disturbing case for the continuum between the injustice of the criminal trial and the inherent disregard of mainstream Australia for Indigenous Australians in the 1980s and 1990s, particularly. To conclude this section, Anne Power's work illuminates the model of the colonial myth-making that ties the Australian experience to much wider colonial projects. Alan John's *The Eighth Wonder* (1994) places itself within a discourse of the monumentalism of global history of the great "civilizations" with an opera about the opera house in which it was premiered—namely the Sydney Opera House. In this respect, it is quite explicitly a nation-building event that celebrates a sense of place and cultural memory. However, it is most interesting in the context of this volume to read *The Eighth Wonder* in the way it sets itself between the universalizing process of viewing "indigeneity" as a concept in relief against the social realities of Indigenous Australia. Anne Power here examines the complex relationships with Aztec culture in *The Eighth Wonder* (both in the opera and the opera house) in the construction of Australian national identity through the metaphor of both visceral and creative sacrifice. Power's chapter thus explores how Aztec symbolism avoids the immediate socio-political and historical reality of the Dharug people on whose land the Sydney Opera House is built. Instead, in the libretto of *The Eighth Wonder*, the Architect experiences a mythic connection to Aztec culture, which is said to correspond to Jørn Utzon's architectural inspirations in the history of the building's construction.

The development of *Indianism* and *Indianismo* in late nineteenth and early twentieth century "new world" operas becomes the focus of our volume's third part, in Brazil and the United States, respectively. Each chapter in this section examines the work of composers who wished to develop self-consciously nationalist operatic traditions through *Indianist* narratives. To begin the section,

Maria Volpe illustrates how *Indianismo* was an ideological and literary device in Brazilian romantic-era nation-building. Providing a comprehensive comparative analysis of the tropes of *Indianismo* in Latin American literature and opera, Volpe's study proposes an intertextual analysis of how the operatic adaptation of the Indianist novel and epics affected the ideological discourse related to the myth of national foundation, and the issue of interethnic contact and miscegenation. This comparative analysis considers what Indianist myths are maintained, denied, deflated, or omitted in the opera in comparison to the literary work upon which it was based, and how this new setting of mythical relations reconfigures the ideological message conveyed by the operas. Both Tara Browner's and Catherine Parsons Smith's contributions extend the examination of Indianism with case studies of particular operas. Browner's intent is three-fold: first, to examine the relationships between composers and field ethnographers—using Charles Wakefield Cadman's opera *Shanewis* (1918) as a case study—through which composers collaborated with ethnographers in choosing songs for their scores; second, to study the actual process of "idealization" from field ethnography to finished product; and, third, to discuss the repercussions of these choices on the American Indians who served as consultants and collaborators, and their larger communities. Catherine Parsons Smith's chapter concludes this section, discussing two Indianist operas from the West: *Narcissa: Or, The Cost of Empire* by Mary Carr Moore, and *The Sun Dance Opera* by William F. Hanson and Gertrude Simmons Bonin, also known as Zitkala Sa. Smith examines these works as expressions of regional interests and attitudes that expand our perceptions and understanding of the culture of the American West, and notes how both operas are unique in their treatment of religious conviction, and in their status as operas whose music was composed or libretto written by women. As Smith notes, unlike the dominant focus on love triangles in other Indianist operas, *Narcissa* instead depicts missionary passion as the opera's dominant theme, while *The Sun Dance Opera* (though it does center upon the typical love triangle), focuses a post-contact Sioux religious ceremony: the Sun Dance itself. The choice to use this ceremony is notable, considering the outlawing of the Sun Dance by the United States government as early as 1883 for its "great hindrance to the civilization of the Indians."[13]

Prohibitions for performing cultural traditions are further addressed in the fourth part of *Opera Indigene*, which focuses on Canadian operas written before 1967 that represent First Nations and Métis cultures. Mary Ingraham's chapter opens this section with a semiotic analysis of the markers of First Nations culture in Canadian opera from 1867 to 1967 as indexical to political notions of citizenship. From the assimilationist policies of the first Indian Act passed in 1876 to the integrationist strategies of its amendments in 1951 and subsequent multicultural

---

[13]   US Interior Minister Henry M. Teller quoted in Peter Bolz, "The Lakota Sun Dance Between 1883 and 1997: The Outlawing and Revival of a Cultural Symbol," in *Mirror Writing: (Re)constructions of Native American Identity*, ed. Thomas Claviez and Maria Moss (Berlin, Galda + Wilch Verlag, 2000), p. 4.

10   *Opera Indigene: Re/presenting First Nations and Indigenous Cultures*

discussions leading up to the federal policy on multiculturalism adopted in 1971, Ingraham examines how consecutive democratic governments in Canada have attempted to control and institutionalize "difference" vis-à-vis native and non-native culture and how this has manifested itself in Canadian operas. Alison Greene, in the second chapter of this section, examines the development and reception of *Tzinquaw*, an opera written as a result of a collaboration between Abel Joe (Coast Salish, Cowichan Band) and amateur musician Frank Morrison. Greene's chapter investigates the uneasy assimilation of European aesthetic styles of nineteenth-century church music and operetta with the traditional practices of the Cowichan people, which Greene argues constitutes a form of aesthetic colonization. Greene's research here provides a cogent reception study of *Tzinquaw* within the many communities that engaged with the opera, including ethnomusicologists, the larger Cowichan community upon whose traditions the work is based, and the reactions of Barbara Pentland and Dorothy Livesay, respectively the composer and librettist of *The Lake*, a work about native-newcomer relations in the Okanagan region of British Columbia. Indeed, as Dylan Robinson suggests, *The Lake* can be read as an index of Pentland and Livesay's critical views of *Tzinquaw*. Robinson's chapter here provides a discursive analysis of the interaction between the settler and First Nations characters in *The Lake*, and examines how this interaction is mediated through a language of commodity and ownership. As with the settlers' descriptions of the lake's peaceful and placid surface beneath which lurks a monstrous presence (Na'aitka, the lake monster), the dialogues between the settler and Okanagan First Nations characters also present a seemingly peaceful "surface" interaction under which lurks a monstrous exscription of the First Nations voices through the semblance of inclusion. Colleen Renihan concludes this section with an analysis of the ramifications of the operatic genre upon telling the history of Louis Riel. In particular, Renihan reads the opera *Louis Riel* by Harry Somers and Mavor Moore for its sites of tension where expressions of Riel's Métis heritage and the operatic genre's conventions conflict. Renihan here offers a generic analysis of the operatic and a stylistic examination of the musical language, while attending to the problematic use of atonal and serial techniques to represent Riel and his people, as well as the atonal "ground" found in all scenes set in the West. Renihan further notes how Somers and Moore were interested in exploring the conventions of "Grand Opera as a form of nation-building, a platform for discovering who we are." *Louis Riel* thus acted as a forum for the re-assessment of Canadian national identity though an operatic lens.

The final part of this collection concerns new opera creation and collaborative processes. Here a number of international artists and scholars discuss the intricacies of intercultural collaboration in opera. Several of these chapters additionally examine the reception of these works by the Indigenous communities they are developed in conjunction with. To begin this section, Robin Elliott gives an overview of *Pimooteewin (The Journey)*, a work sung in Cree, with an English narrator who provides translations for the audience. The work was created by the librettist Tomson Highway (Cree), the composer Melissa Hui (born in Hong Kong, raised in Vancouver), and the choreographer Michael Greyeyes (Plains Cree). Elliott here picks up on earlier questions of genre, asking whether this opera is more an oratorio rather than opera, and the impact such generic conventions have on understanding this work. Additionally, Elliott examines the different responses to the work as it was received by a cosmopolitan audience in Toronto, and the largely Cree communities while on tour in rural areas of Northern Ontario in 2009. In the second chapter of this section Victoria Vaughan gives an analysis of Evan Ziporyn's opera *A House in Bali*, addressing questions on Colin McPhee's interactions with Balinese culture and how this influenced his music.[14] The third chapter of this section is an interview with director Robert McQueen on the Coast Salish First Nations adaptation of Mozart's *The Magic Flute* that also includes several responses from the First Nations community that was involved in the development and as an audience for the work. The final chapter in this section is an interview with Indigenous singer and composer Deborah Cheetham and film-maker and radio broadcaster Daniel Browning (of the Minjungbal clan of the Bundjalung nation in Australia) with a discussion of Cheetham's new work *Pecan Summer*. The chapters contained in this section demonstrate new directions for opera creation which engage larger Indigenous communities in their development, and provide a fitting conclusion to the collection, returning as they do to the original critical contexts of decolonization and the involvement of Indigenous communities in opera development discussed by Karantonis and Diamond in the first section.

Notably, creative work on topics of First Nations and Indigenous history continue to emerge at an extraordinary pace. One such work currently in development is *Pauline*, an opera by Margaret Atwood and Christopher Hatzis on the Métis poet-performer Pauline Johnson. The cultural Olympiad that coincided with the Vancouver 2010 Olympics supported the revival of *Louis Riel* at the University of British Columbia, and the production of a musical entitled *Beyond Eden*, a work based on the 1957 expedition by Bill Reid and Wilson Duff to Haida Gwaii (Queen Charlotte Islands) on the north-west coast of Canada to "salvage" Haida totem poles. In addition to Deborah Cheetham's *Pecan Summer*,[15] Vancouver Opera's *Magic Flute*, and *Pimooteewin (The Journey)*, other projects by Indigenous artists are also in development. *Giiwedin* is an opera written partially in Anishnawbe Mowin by Algonquin playwright Spy Dénommé-Welch, co-composed with Catherine Magowan, and produced by Native Earth in Toronto, Canada. Another such work is the upcoming Opera Ontario production of an opera on the life of Mohawk chief Joseph Brant by singer-songwriter ElizaBeth Hill (Mohawk) and composer Thomas

---

[14] This opera's premiere was reviewed internationally and can be viewed at http://www.houseinbali.org/ accessed 13 January 2011.

[15] See http://www.abc.net.au/7.30/content/2010/s3069406.htm accessed 30 December 2010.

Dusatko.[16] The ongoing development of these works attests to the continuing interest in exploring relationships between the operatic and First Nations and Indigenous cultural practices.

This introduction began with the light-hearted de-centering of Western musicology's claim to opera criticism through a description of Skeena Reece's parody of the awkward fit between conventional operatic practice and the dance-oriented expression of First Nations traditions. There is much to be said for the role of the trickster and comic discourses within Indigenous and First Nations practices as effecting the decolonizing of many performing arts traditions in settler-invader colonies.[17] However, while Reece's satire makes light of the disjunctions between the operatic and First Nations song, as the work in this collection illustrates, such amalgamations are quite the opposite of a joke; rather they are increasingly seen as relevant to the lives of Indigenous artists and audiences themselves. As the contributors to this volume discuss, Indigenous and non-Indigenous creators have, both individually and in collaboration, turned to opera throughout the 20th and 21st centuries as a form through which to redress the historical record through storytelling and expression of Indigenous worldviews.

---

[16]   What cannot be addressed in this volume are the numerous notable operatic careers of Indigenous and First Nations Peoples in the mainstream of operatic history and the present. However, we have been able to mention a few select artists whose work relates to our case studies.

[17]   Robin Elliot's chapter in particular addresses the role of the trickster in *Pimooteewin*, and points toward some of the complexities surrounding the essentializing tendencies of trickster trope in First Nations literature. For a detailed examination of the historical use and limitations of the trickster figure in First Nations literature, art, and cultural practices, see Deanna Reder and Linda M. Morra (eds), *Troubling Tricksters: Revisioning Critical Conversations*, (Waterloo, ON: Wilfred Laurier Press, 2010).

PART I
Critical and Comparative Contexts: Opera's Colonizing Force and Decolonizing Potential

PART I
Critical and Comparative Contexts: Opera's Colonizing Force and Decolonizing Potential

Chapter 1
Orpheus Conquistador

Nicholas Till

In his discussion of Verdi's *Aida* in *Culture and Imperialism*, Edward Said writes that "*Aida*, like the opera form itself, is a hybrid, radically impure work that belongs equally to the history of culture and the historical experience of overseas domination."[1] This sentence may only mean that opera is like *Aida* in being "hybrid and radically impure." But it could also mean that opera itself is convicted in its very form of being complicit with the project of European imperialism—a breathtaking assertion.

Said says nothing more about this to substantiate his claim. But he does suggest that Verdi's obsession, at the time he was writing *Aida*, with "unified" works, "in which," to quote Verdi, "the idea is ONE, and everything must converge to form this one," and Verdi's dismissal of the idea that singers or conductors might make a creative contribution to the work of opera since there must be "only one creator" should be seen as an assertion of an "imperial notion" of the artist.[2]

Is this use of the term "imperial" really anything more than a metaphor? Certainly for Said, whose main concern as a critic was with the European novel, there is a kind of narrative and epistemological confidence in the novel that he believes is only made possible by an imperialistic attitude to the world.[3] Said also argued that the cavalier treatment of space in the eighteenth-century English novel conveys a consciousness informed by colonial expansion.[4] Musicologists have suggested that the tonal system, developed around 1600, should be identified as a quasi-spatial expansion of the language of music in the same vein, an argument first put forward by Edward Lowinsky, who claimed as long ago as 1941 that "it was the same spirit of adventure, the same desire to open new and unexplored spaces, that lured the sailors across the sea and beckoned the musicians to their discoveries of remote

---

I am extremely grateful to Tim Carter for looking this chapter over for me, and for his invaluable observations, queries and suggestions.

[1]   Edward Said, *Culture and Imperialism* (London: Vintage, 1994), p. 137.

[2]   Said, *Culture and Imperialism*, p. 140. The Verdi quotes are from Hans Busch, *Verdi's Aida: The History of an Opera in Letters and Documents* (Minneapolis: University of Minnesota Press, 1978), pp. 4–5.

[3]   Said, *Culture and Imperialism*, p. 95.

[4]   Said, *Culture and Imperialism*, p. 83.

16   *Opera Indigene: Re/presenting First Nations and Indigenous Cultures*

and distant keys and new harmonic conquests."[5] This analogy of exploration and discovery is now commonplace in accounts of the beginnings of modern music in the hands of Monteverdi and his contemporaries.[6] Recently Timothy Taylor has suggested that such musical developments should also be been seen in relation to the impact that colonialism had upon European notions of selfhood and otherness, arguing that tonality "arose to a long supremacy in western European music in part because it facilitated a concept of spatialization in music that provided for centers and margins, both geographically and psychologically."[7] Both Taylor and Eric Chafe suggest that there was also a close relationship between the development of tonality and the rise of opera as an art form that responded to the "newly awaked desire to extend the human hegemony into hitherto unexplored regions"[8] (although we might wish to rephrase that in less universalizing terms).

In these accounts the precise nature of the relationship between opera and tonality is far from clear, and the association of exploration and colonization with expanded musical spatialities remains largely figurative. This chapter is part of a larger project in which I hope to show that the emergence of opera as an art form around 1600 must indeed be understood as an essential component of the intellectual and cultural project of early modernity, of which colonialism was one of the most distinctive elements. Said went so far as to describe imperialism as "the determining political horizon of modern western culture"[9] and there has been a suggestion by historians of the early modern period that that period should be rebranded as "Early Colonial" to highlight the centrality of colonialism to its outlook.[10] In this chapter I will attempt to make the relationship between early opera and colonialism clearer through an analysis of a little commented-upon passage from Alessandro Striggio's text for Monteverdi's *Orfeo* of 1607.

Along with the European encounter with, and domination of, the Americas, the development of observational and experimental methods in science, which we now call the scientific revolution, is also identified as a crucial aspect of early modernity. In a scene at the end of Act III of *Orfeo* these two axes of early modernity—navigational and scientific exploration—are quite clearly referred to in

---

[5]   Edward Lowinsky, "The Concept of Physical and Musical Space in the Renaissance," *Papers of the American Musicological Society*, ed. Gustave Reese (Minnesota: Minneapolis University Press, 1941), pp. 57–84, p. 81.

[6]   Thus Eric T. Chafe refers to "the qualities of exploration and discovery in Monteverdi's music," Eric T. Chafe, *Monteverdi's Tonal Language* (New York: Schirmer, 1992), p. 2.

[7]   Timothy Taylor, *Beyond Exoticism: Western Music and the World* (Durham, NC, and London: Duke University Press, 2007), p. 25.

[8]   Chafe, *Monteverdi's Tonal Language*, p. 2.

[9]   Said, *Culture and Imperialism*, p. 70.

[10]   Margaret de Grazia, Maureen Quilligan and Peter Stallybrass (eds.), *Subject and Object in Renaissance Culture* (Cambridge: Cambridge University Press, 1999), Introduction pp. 1–13; p. 5.

words sung by a chorus of Infernal Spirits (*Spiriti Infernale*). Orpheus, attempting to cross the river Styx to penetrate into the underworld to rescue Eurydice, has failed to persuade Charon, the ferryman of the dead, to transport him across the river. Instead he lulls Charon to sleep and seizes Charon's barque to ferry himself across the river, thrice repeating the ardent plea "rendetemi 'l mio ben" ("restore my love to me") as he does so, each phrase rising in pitch and passion. It is a striking moment: the musical and dramatic climax of the whole opera, and Orpheus's daring elicits from the Infernal Spirits the following encomium:

> No enterprise is undertaken by man in vain,
> Against him nature can no longer protect herself,
> And on the unsettled plain
> He ploughed the rolling fields, and scattered seed
> With his own efforts reaping golden harvests.
> Hence that the memory of his glory might live on,
> Fame loosed her tongue to sing
> Of he who harnessed the ocean with fragile ships
> Defying the fury of the south wind and of the north.[11]

Those last four lines should be heard as accompanying the visual image of Orpheus navigating the perilous river.

Tim Carter notes that this chorus "has usually been interpreted as a conventional Humanist statement of the power of man,"[12] a latter-day example of the Renaissance encomium[13] in praise of the dignity of man such as those by the fifteenth-century Florentine humanists Marsilio Ficino and Pico della Mirandola. A belated example of the genre can be found in Shakespeare's *Hamlet*, written only a few years before *Orfeo*:

> What a piece of work is a man! how noble in reason! how infinite in faculties!
> in form and moving how express and admirable! in action how like an angel! in
> apprehension how like a god! the beauty of the world! the paragon of animals.[14]

But the Italian historian Lauro Martines suggests that during the sixteenth century the theme of the dignity of man went out of fashion in Italy as the political and social temper of the period darkened during the course of the century after the invasion of Italy by the French in 1494, the Sack of Rome by Habsburg troops in 1527, and the subsequent social and political turmoil of the Reformation and

---

[11] Alessandro Striggio, "La Favola d'Orfeo", Mantova, 1607. Reprinted in Barbara Russano Hanning, *Of Poetry and Music's Power: Humanism and the Creation of Opera* (Ann Arbor: UMI Research Press, 1980), Appendix E, p. 318.

[12] Tim Carter, *Monteverdi's Musical Theatre* (New Haven, CT: Yale, 2002), p. 113.

[13] Encomium: a rhetorical term meaning the praise of a person or thing.

[14] William Shakespeare, *Hamlet*, II, 2, 303–312.

18   *Opera Indigene: Re/presenting First Nations and Indigenous Cultures*

Counter-Reformation.[15] Hamlet's words are, of course, ironic, and the references in the chorus from *Orfeo* are in fact much more specific. The verse cited above is the first of three, of which Monteverdi only set one. Carter suggests that the reference in the first verse is to the voyages of Jason and the Argonauts. This is plausible not only because Orpheus was, by some accounts, one of the Argonauts himself, but also since in the following verse the heroism of Orpheus is explicitly compared to that of Daedalus, the great scientist of Greek mythology, who invented the means of human flight. In the final verse there is an unmistakable reference to Phaeton, who carjacked the chariot of his father Apollo and drove it through the heavens. Carter notes that the verses describe the conquest of each of the elements: Water, Air, Fire and Earth (Orpheus himself), but that as an encomium it is tinged with foreboding since Daedelus's son Icarus fell to his death when he ignored his father's warnings and flew too near the sun, and Phaeton expired when he lost control of the chariot of the sun itself. Citing also the bloody denouement of Jason's relationship with the barbarian princess Medea, Carter sees all three stories as portents of the hubris that will shortly reverse the fortunes of Orpheus too.[16]

If this were the case it would be uncharacteristic of the era in which Monteverdi and Striggio wrote *Orfeo*. The seafaring feats of Jason and the technological inventions of Daedalus were often referred to in literature and imagery of the period. However, I have found only one example of these feats being described as hubristic, in the verse epic *L'Adone* of 1623 by Giambattisto Marino, many of whose poems were set by Monteverdi. In his invocation to the tenth canto of the poem, Marino compares the poetic challenge has he set himself to the dangerous feats of Typhis (the steersman of the Argonauts), Orpheus, Daedalus, and Prometheus

> Typhis first raised sails above the ways,
> Orpheus with his lyre went down to hell,
> Daedelus plied wings through upper air,
> Prometheus to the sphere of fire took flight.
> 'Tis meet that pain should follow recklessness
> Through rash and foolish ventures such as these.[17]

But later in the same canto, in a section that serves as a lengthy encomium to Galileo, Mercury predicts the prowess of Columbus:

---

[15]   Lauro Martines, *Power and Imagination: City-States in Renaissance Italy* (Harmondsworth: Penguin, 1979), p. 299.

[16]   Carter, *Monteverdi's Musical Theatre*, p. 114.

[17]   Giambattista Marino, *Marino* Adonis: *Selections from the l'Adone of Giambattista Marino*, ed. and trans. Harold Martin Priest (Ithaca, NY: Cornell, 1967), Canto X, stanza 3, pp. 182-3.

Cleaving the breast of the ocean, vast and deep,
But not without grave peril and bitter strife,
Liguria's Argonaut down on earth
Will yet discover a new land and sky.

Following which Galileo is described as "a second Typhis, not of sea but of heaven," whose discoveries are even more praiseworthy because they are "without risk"—a comment not without irony given Galileo's fate at the hands of the Inquisition ten years later.[18]

Marino's condemnation of Orpheus and his peers may be no more than a rhetorical flourish, but even if we take it seriously it is nonetheless relative, since Marino's dismissal of classical overreachers serves to offset his later praise for Columbus and Galileo, in which Galileo takes the ultimate crown since his achievements are intellectual and "heavenly" (a distinction that is also, perhaps, present in *Orfeo*, in which, as we shall see, Orpheus conquers Hades but fails to conquer his own affections, a sign of his inability to rise above worldly concerns to more elevated spiritual heights). Marino would seem to be contrasting the failure of the classical adventurers, whose exploits are deemed premature, with the successful ventures of the modern era. Perhaps Marino's ultimate accolade for Galileo is because, at a time when Italy had ceded seafaring prowess to the new colonial powers of Portugal, Spain, England, France, and Holland, Marino is keen to shift attention from geographical to scientific exploration, in which, with Galileo in the ascendant, Italy could claim a new pre-eminence.

It is true that in classical literature the fate of Jason was often adduced as a warning against voyaging into forbidden realms, as in Seneca's play *Medea*, in which the chorus admonishes Jason for his foolhardiness. The injunction against voyaging in foreign parts was also associated with venturing beyond the Pillars of Hercules, upon which Hercules was supposed to have placed the command *ne plus ultra* ("no further," or "nothing beyond"). The Italian historian Carlo Ginzburg has shown that in the Middle Ages and early Renaissance the story of Daedalus and Icarus served similarly as an illustration of St. Paul's warning against the sin of intellectual curiosity.[19] But by the seventeenth century it was far more common for the negative connotations of these stories to have been reversed. In 1516, the year that he became King of Spain, Charles V adopted a new motto: it showed the Pillars of Hercules emblazoned with the words "Plus Oltre" ("Yet Further/More Beyond"), a motto that came to be seen as a reference to the Atlantic voyaging to the New World beyond the Pillars of Hercules in which the Spanish kingdom was already so invested.[20] By the mid-sixteenth century Jason's intrepid steersman

---

[18]   Marino, *Marino* Adonis, Canto X, stanza 45, p. 191.

[19]   Carlo Ginzburg, "High and Low: The Theme of Forbidden Knowledge in the Sixteenth and Seventeenth Centuries," *Past and Present*, 73 (1976), pp. 28–42.

[20]   Earl Rosenthal, "Plus Ultra, Non Plus Ultra and the Columnar Device of Emperor Charles V," *Journal of the Warburg and Courtauld Institute*, 34, (1971), pp. 204–228.

20   *Opera Indigene: Re/presenting First Nations and Indigenous Cultures*

Typhis was often represented as patron of the new breed of exploratory mariners,[21] and Ruben's 1635 designs for The Arch of the Mint in Antwerp show Jason himself as a victorious conquistador standing triumphantly atop Mount Potosi, the richest silver mine in South America.[22]

Similarly, by the sixteenth century the characterization of Icarus as a rash overreacher had often been modified. In one of his allegorical readings of the Greek myths, published as *De sapientia veterum* (*The Wisdom of the Ancients*) in 1609, Francis Bacon suggested that Icarus had chosen the better path if the choice was between ambition or caution (described by Bacon as "defect"), despite his eventual fate:

> And no wonder that excess should prove the bane of Icarus, exulting in juvenile strength and vigour; for excess is the natural vice of youth, as defect is that of old age; and if a man must perish by either, Icarus chose the better of the two; for all defects are justly esteemed more depraved than excesses.[23]

Ginzburg shows that by the seventeenth century the myth of Icarus was regularly being represented in this kind of positive light. In 1635 The Italian Jesuit Daniello Bartoli even compared Icarus to Columbus, concluding "without his boldness, we would have neither American spices, nor American mines," and Ginzburg points to popular emblem books that similarly represented Icarus as a symbol of intellectual courage, one such image carrying the Virgilian motto "Nil linquere inausum" ("leave nothing untried"). As Ginzburg puts it, "the very notions of 'risk' and 'novelty' were now seen as positive values—appropriate, in fact, to a society increasingly based on commerce."[24]

What all of these examples suggest is that when *Orfeo* was written there was a widespread cultural excitement about the still expanding worlds of navigational and scientific discovery, which were almost always seen in a positive light. In Striggio's text for Monteverdi we are presented with an analogy between these two spheres of action, an analogy that was articulated most consistently by Francis Bacon, today recognized as the chief ideologue of the scientific revolution. In *The Advancement of Learning* of 1605 Bacon suggested that "proficience in

---

Rosenthal demonstrates that the origins of the Latin form of the "Ne/Non Plus Ultra" motto are very uncertain, although it is cited in Italian by Dante.

[21]   John Gillies, *Shakespeare and the Geography of Difference* (Cambridge: Cambridge University Press, 1994), p. 171.

[22]   Elizabeth McGrath, "Rubens's Arch of the Mint," *Journal of the Warburg and Courtauld Institute*, 37 (1974), pp. 191–217.

[23]   Bacon, "De sapienta veterum," translated as "On the Wisdom of the Ancients," in James Spedding, Robert Leslie Ellis, and Douglas Denon Heath (eds), *The Works of Francis Bacon* (London: Routledge/Thoemmes Press, 1996; reprint of 1879 edition), Vol. VI, Part II, pp. 754-5.

[24]   Ginzburg, "High and Low," p. 38.

navigation and discoveries may plant also an expectation of further proficience and augmentation of all sciences, because it may seem that they are ordained by God to be coevals, that is, to meet in one age."[25] In *The New Atlantis*, Bacon's vision of a utopian community based upon scientific principles, the first and only named founding father of the state is Columbus.[26] On the title page of what was to have been Bacon's crowning achievement, the incomplete *Instauratio Magna* (1620), Bacon appropriates Charles V's famous emblem to show an image of two proud galleons setting sail across the Atlantic beyond the Pillars of Hercules.

In equating science and exploration Bacon insisted that the aim of science was to dominate nature so that nature could be made to work for the benefit of humankind, in the same way that the conquistador dominated and exploited the new found lands of America. For Bacon knowledge was power, and his metaphors were invariably couched in terms of both patriarchal and colonial domination. In *The Masculine Birth of Time* Bacon writes "I am come in very truth leading you to Nature with all her children, to bind her to your service and make her your slave."[27] The representation of America as a supine female nude in Jan van der Straet's famous image of Vespucci's discovery of continental America might serve equally as an illustration of Bacon's Nature, particularly since we note that Vespucci carries not only the cross of faith, but also, prominently, the scientific instruments of navigation that have made his expedition possible (see Figure 1.1).[28]

But Bacon's equation of colonial and scientific exploration was already a commonplace of thought in the sixteenth century. Just as Bacon and Galileo challenged the Aristotelian natural philosophers' reliance upon textual authority over observation and experiment, for many advocates of the scientific pursuit of truth it was the discovery of the New World that had been the first empirical refutation of the Aristotelian system, confounding the classical and Christian conviction that there could be no inhabited lands beyond the Pillars of Hercules. Thus in 1549 Jacques Cartier, the French mariner credited with the discovery of that part of the North American continent now known as Canada, declared that "the common navigators of our day, making experiments, have learned the opposite of

---

[25]   James Spedding, Robert Leslie Ellis, and Douglas Denon Heath (eds), *The Works of Francis Bacon* (London: Routledge / Thoemmes Press, 1996) (reprint of 1879 edition), Vol. III, Part I, p. 340.

[26]   Spedding, Ellis, and Heath, *The Works of Francis Bacon*, Vol. III, Part I, p. 165.

[27]   Bacon, "Temporis Partus Masculus," translated as "The Masculine Birth of Time," in Benjamin Farrington, *The Philosophy of Francis Bacon: An Essay on its Development from 1603–1609, with new translations of fundamental texts* (Liverpool: Liverpool University Press, 1964), p. 62.

[28]   In the background a second group of women are dismembering and roasting some human victims. We cannot but remember Orpheus's fate at the hands of the female Maenads in most versions of the myth: similarly dismembered, even if Striggio and Monteverdi had the good taste (or good sense) not to try to represent this event in the version of their opera that was actually performed.

Figure 1.1 Amerigo Vespucci discovers America, Theodore Galle (after Jan van der Straet), *Nova Reperta*, Antwerp, c.1588–1612

the opinions of the philosophers."[29] Many thinkers, including the political theorist Jean Bodin, suggested that technological inventions such as the printing press were innovations that could be compared to geographical discovery, and as early as 1532 the geographer Apianus wrote that, without inventions such as printing and instruments of navigation "life would return to the state of the ancient men who lived without laws of civilization, similar to beasts." Those "ancient men" had, of course, been found living when Columbus reached the Americas.[30]

Columbus originated from Genoa. As noted above, although Italian mariners were great navigators, the Italian states themselves were not involved in the discovery or colonization of the New World. But between 1581 and 1596 there were no fewer than three epic poems on the voyages of Columbus published in Italy. At a time of marked economic and political decline in Italy, Columbus was, it seems, being vigorously promoted as an Italian hero in an act of retrospective

---

[29] Paolo Rossi, *Philosophy, Technology and the Arts in the Early Modern Era* (New York, Evanston, IL, and London: Harper and Row, 1970), p. 66.

[30] For Bodin and Apianus, see Rossi, *Philosophy*, p. 71.

mythologizing.[31] And, in 1608, Parigi's spectacular stage sets for the Florentine intermezzo *La notte d'amore*, presented to celebrate the wedding of Prince Cosimo de' Medici, depicted the ship of another Italian seafarer Amerigo Vespucci, reminding those present that the continents of America had been named after a Florentine, an employee of Lorenzo de' Medici, the Magnificent.

Tommaso Campanella, best known as the author of the Christian utopia *Città del sole*, writing during his imprisonment for heresy between 1600 and 1626, compared Columbus's feats directly with those of the heroes of Greek mythology and, like Cartier, declared that Columbus "saw more with his eyes and experienced more with his body than did with their minds the poets, philosophers, and the theologians Augustine and Lactantius, who denied the Antipodes."[32] For Campanella too, inventions such as printing, the compass, and now Galileo's telescope, served as signs of man's new mastery over nature, which Campanella describes in language that is very close to Striggio's verses in *Orfeo*:

A Second God, miracle of the First,
He commands the depths; without wings he mounts to the heavens
And counts its motions, measures and qualities...
He masters the wind and wave; in full-sailed ships he circles the earthly globe,
He beholds and conquers all, trades and plunders.[33]

I have cited these examples so extensively to demonstrate how ubiquitous were the rhetorical tropes linking science and discovery in the era of *Orfeo*, and also to demonstrate that the modern heroes of discovery and science were regularly exemplified by their mythological forbears. Scholars of early opera such as Robert Donington and Gary Tomlinson have made much of the neo-platonic allegorizing of the Orpheus myth that was prevalent in Italian Renaissance culture.[34] But in their desire to embed the opera in the intellectual climate of its era, in Tomlinson's case suggesting that Monteverdi must be understood in relation to Foucault's pre-modern episteme of magic and resemblance, they have overlooked the fact that the early seventeenth century is a very different world from that of the earlier Renaissance humanists and neo-platonists. Foucault himself was curiously uninterested in the influence of scientific thought upon what he call the "classical" episteme, and, like Tomlinson, is inclined to extend the Renaissance episteme right through until the end of the sixteenth century, ignoring the impact of the technologies recognized

---

[31]   Leicester Bradner, "Columbus in Sixteenth-Century Poetry," in *Essays Honoring Lawrence C. Worth* (Portland, ME: Anthoensen Press, 1951), pp. 15–30.

[32]   Tommaso Campanella, *Poesie: a cura di Giovanni Gentile* (Bari: Giuseppe Laterza & Figli, 1915), p. 86.

[33]   Campanella, *Poesie*, pp. 170–71.

[34]   Robert Donington, *The Rise of Opera* (London: Faber, 1981); Gary Tomlinson, *Music in Renaissance Magic: Toward a Historiography of Others* (Chicago, IL: University of Chicago Press, 1993).

24 *Opera Indigene: Re/presenting First Nations and Indigenous Cultures*

long before by scholars such as Apianus, or the new cosmography of Copernicus. For Hegel, typically idealist (and, of course, German), the decisive historical moment of modernity was the Lutheran Reformation, also ignored by Foucault. But it could perhaps be argued that Foucault's most significant oversight was to have failed to recognize the impact of colonialism upon European intellectual culture in the sixteenth century. In Tzvetan Todorov's searching account of the conquest of Mexico by Hernando Cortés between 1519 and 1521, Todorov suggests that Cortés's astonishing victory was as much due to his superior epistemology as to his weapons, horses, or disease. In effect, the Mexicans had no cognitive means of dealing with the intruders since theirs was a truly pre-modern episteme based upon a cyclical, ritualized understanding of the world, whilst Cortés showed himself to be not only a supreme interpreter and manipulator of signs, but an empirical pragmatist willing to adapt his strategies according to the situation rather than according to pre-ordained expectations. In this he is in clear contrast to Columbus, whose encounters with the New World were always over-determined by his essentially medieval expectations.[35] If Columbus came to stand as a synecdoche for modernity to his contemporaries, it is the praxis of conquest represented by Cortés rather than the epistemology of encounter that now seems to mark the modern worldview more decisively. In support of my argument for placing *Orfeo* firmly within the early modern episteme I will offer another reading of the Orpheus myth by Francis Bacon from *De sapientia veterum*, which is known to have been written in the same year as *Orfeo*. In an essay entitled "Orpheus; or Philosophy," Bacon presents Orpheus's descent into the underworld as an allegory of the scientist's attempts to master the secrets of nature, arguing that Orpheus "seems meant for a representation of universal philosophy." Bacon then divides philosophy into two categories—natural and civil:

> The singing of Orpheus is of two kinds; one to propitiate the infernal powers, the other to draw the wild beasts and the woods. The former may be best understood as referring to natural philosophy; the latter to philosophy moral and civil. For natural philosophy proposes to itself; as its noblest work of all, nothing less than the restitution and renovation of things corruptible.[36]

For Bacon, listing in his appendix to *The New Atlantis* the thirty ends to which science could be put, the first and foremost was "the prolongation of life,"[37] which, as "restitution and renovation," is clearly the object of Orpheus's quest to restore Eurydice to life. One question that none of the commentators on *Orfeo* raise is: why did Striggio put the words of his encomium to modern man into the mouths

---

[35] Tzvetan Todorov, *The Conquest of America: The Question of the Other*, trans. Richard Howard (New York: Harper and Row, 1984).

[36] Spedding, Ellis, and Heath, *The Works of Francis Bacon*, Vol. VI, Part II, pp. 720-22.

[37] Spedding, Ellis, and Heath, *The Works of Francis Bacon*, Vol. III, Part 1, p. 167.

of the Infernal Spirits? We might, of course, interpret the words as a dispassionate, authorial proclamation of a universal truth, which had to be put into the mouths of someone. But the Infernal Spirits surely speak as the representatives of that vanquished nature that can no longer arm itself against humankind, the forces of death which Bacon's Orphic natural philosopher seeks to conquer, declaring their own defeat with Orpheus's decisive action of seizing Charon's barque.

So why, if he is apparently so invincible, does Orpheus eventually fail in his mission to rescue Euridice? For Striggio and Monteverdi, in words assigned to a *Choro di Spiriti*, who may or may not be the same as the Infernal Spirits, Orpheus fails because he allows his passions to get the better of him:

> Orpheus defeated Hades, and then was defeated
> By his own affections.
> Worthy of eternal glory
> Is only he who over himself has victory.[38]

Bacon often suggested similar obstacles to successful scientific enquiry: "The government of reason is assailed and disordered ... by violence of passions."[39] But in his reading of the Orpheus story Bacon gives a slightly different explanation for the failure of natural philosophy: "And yet being a thing of all others the most difficult, it commonly fails of effect; and fails (it may be) from no cause more than from curious and premature meddling and impatience,"[40] a condemnation of those who abandon the path of painstaking experiment.

After his failure to rescue Eurydice, Bacon's Orpheus turns to "civil philosophy." And where Striggio makes the equation of science and exploration by analogy, in Bacon's reading of the Orpheus myth the relationship to colonialism is much more explicit, suggesting that Orpheus's ability to tame the beasts, woods, and mountains is an allegory of the effects of law and civilization upon primitive peoples.

> Civil philosophy teaches the peoples to assemble and unite and take upon them
> the yoke of laws and submit to authority, and forget their ungoverned appetites,
> in listening and conforming to precepts and discipline; whereupon soon follows
> the building of houses, the founding of cities, the planting of fields and gardens
> with trees; insomuch that the stones and the woods are not unfitly said to leave
> their places and come about her.[41]

---

[38]   Claudio Monterverdi *L'Orfeo—Favola in Musica; Lamento D'Ariana, Tomo di Monteverdi—XI. XII, Opere*, ed. G. Franscesco Malipiero (Bologna: Ventura, 1930), pp. 107–112.

[39]   Bacon, "De dignitate et augmentis scientiarum," translation in Spedding, Ellis, and Heath, *The Works of Francis Bacon*, Vol. IV, p. 455.

[40]   Spedding, Ellis, and Heath, *The Works of Francis Bacon*, Vol. VI, Part II, p. 714.

[41]   Spedding, Ellis, and Heath, *The Works of Francis Bacon*, Vol. VI, Part II, pp. 720-22.

Bacon's description of the civilizing powers of Orpheus employs precisely the kind of argument that was used by Europeans to justify the appropriation of uncultivated land in the Americas and rule over indigenous American inhabitants. Although many Europeans were at first impressed by the apparently civilized behavior of the native inhabitants that they encountered in the new world, the imperative of domination meant that inevitably native Americans had to be recast as barbarians or savages. As one sixteenth-century European reported, the natives of America "lived like wild beasts without religion nor government, nor town, nor houses, without cultivating the land, nor clothing their bodies," quite clearly serving as ideal subjects for the civilizing effects of Orphic philosophy.[42] And although in several places Bacon himself argued against colonial empire-building in favor of extending the bounds of intellectual "human empire,"[43] as a politician Bacon fully supported the English and Scottish colonization of Ireland. The Irish were often compared to American Indians by Bacon's contemporaries, and in 1617 Bacon himself declared that British colonization had brought the Irish "from savage and barbarous customs to humanity and civility."[44]

Let us consider again the question of why Striggio's encomium is sung by the Infernal Spirits. Historical anthropologist Bernard McGrance argues in relation to the Europeans' earliest encounters with Native Americans that "within the Christian conception of Otherness anthropology did not exist; there was, rather, demonology."[45] De Certeau suggests that early travel literature in general serves as a "displacement of demonology" from Europe to the New World,[46] and Stephen Greenblatt has proposed that the increasing attribution of satanic worship and demonology to Native Americans during the later sixteenth century may have been influenced by Jean Bodin's *De la démonomanie des sorciers* of 1580.[47] The attribution of demonology became particularly prevalent when Europeans discovered how intransigent Native Americans could be about accepting the Christian religion, for which their only explanation was that the natives must be

---

[42] Cited in Carolyn Merchant, *The Death of Nature: Women, Ecology and the Scientific Revolution* (San Francisco, CA: Harper and Row, 1980), p. 132.

[43] Bacon used this phrase in numerous of his writings, as for instance in *The New Atlantis*, Spedding, Ellis, and Heath, *The Works of Francis Bacon*, Vol. III, Part 1, p. 156.

[44] Charles C. Whitney, "Merchants of Light: Science as Colonization in *The New Atlantis*," in William A. Sessions, *Francis Bacon's Legacy of Texts* (New York: AMS Press, 1990), p. 263.

[45] Bernard McGrane, *Beyond Anthropology: Society and the Other* (New York: Columbia University Press, 1989), p. ix.

[46] Michel De Certeau, *The Writing of History*, trans. Tom Conley (New York: Columbia University Press, 1988), p. 242, n. 52.

[47] Stephen Greenblatt, *Marvellous Possessions: The Wonders of the New World* (Chicago, IL: University of Chicago Press, 1991), p. 15. See also Olivia Bloechl, "Protestant Imperialism and the Representation of Native American Song," *Musical Quarterly*, 87/1 (Spring 2004): pp. 44–86.

devil-worshipers. Thus John Smith, he of Pocahontas fame, wrote of the natives that he encountered that the chief god they worshiped was the devil, and that "they say that they have conference with him, and fashion themselves as near his shape as they can imagine."[48] In a rather Bosch-like painting of Hell by a Portuguese painter of c.1550 Satan is depicted as a fearsome Indian in feathered headdress and costume.[49]

Striggio's and Monteverdi's rather dignified Infernal Spirits are not, of course, the devils or demons of Christian mythology, although no Italian could ignore the resonances of Dante in the adjective "infernal." But the Infernal Spirits are, nonetheless, alien beings; quite clearly, we may say, "Other."[50] And, moreover, an Other that acknowledges its subjugation in this moment to the power of Orpheus Conquistador.

Francis Bacon's interpretation of the Orpheus myth in terms of scientific enquiry and colonial subjugation provides grounds for suggesting that the references to science and exploration in Striggio's chorus are more than incidental, particularly since they can also be shown to relate to some of Monteverdi's broader concerns as a musician. Bacon himself drew upon well-established traditions for his reading of Orpheus as the founder of civilization, going back to Plato, Pausanius, Fulgentius, and Horace. But Bacon draws even more strongly upon classical accounts of the power of rhetoric than upon traditions of mythical exegesis. The founding text for this tradition is Cicero's introduction to *De inventione*, in which a by now familiar story is told of how a man with "wisdom and eloquence" was able to make primitive peoples "gentle and civilized from having been savage and brutal."[51] Cicero's narrative, described by Eric Cheyfitz as "the scene of primal colonization of self and other,"[52] runs throughout the history not only of classical, medieval, and Renaissance rhetoric, but also of political theory and poetics, in which musicians with magical powers such as Arion, Amphion (who musicked the wall of Thebes into being), and Orpheus were regularly adduced as exemplars of the civilizing effects of rhetoric. We might also note that Cheyfitz's suggestion that "colonization of self" goes hand in hand with the colonization of the other accords with the moral that is drawn in *Orfeo* from the fact that Orpheus conquers Hades but fails to conquer himself; a moral that could equally apply to the early modern

---

[48]   Howard Mumford Jones, *O Strange New World: American Culture: The Formative Years* (London: Chatto and Windus, 1965), p. 56.

[49]   *Inferno*, oil on panel, c.1550. Anonymous. Museu de Arte Antiga, Lisbon.

[50]   It has often been noted that the choruses of Greek tragedies usually represented marginalized groups—women, old men, foreigners—groups designated by Helen Foley as "Other": Helen Foley, "Choral Identity in Greek Tragedy," *Classical Philology*, 98/1 (January 2003): p. 5.

[51]   Cicero, *De inventione, De optimo genere oratorum, Topica*, trans. H.M. Hubbell (Cambridge, MA: Harvard University Press, and London: Heinemann, 1949), pp. 5–6.

[52]   Eric Cheyfitz, *The Poetics of Imperialism: Translation and Colonization from The Tempest to Tarzan* (New York and Oxford: Oxford University Press, 1991), p. 113.

bourgeois ethos of rationalism, prudence, and self-denial as to the more esoteric neo-platonic spirituality adduced by scholars such as Tomlinson.

Orphean music and rhetoric took on a particular color when associated with the ideology of colonialism. Writing about music and colonial encounters in the eighteenth century Vanessa Agnew suggests that the Orpheus myth is "a discourse of alterity, a story about music's privileged responsibility vis-a-vis otherness."[53] There is, in fact, some empirical evidence from the sixteenth century for this suggestion. Seafaring expeditions customarily carried musicians for military and ceremonial occasions, as well as "for ornament and delight" (as the purpose of the musicians who were hired in 1577 for Drake's circumnavigation of the globe was described[54]). Musicians were often used to signal friendly intent to native inhabitants when ships put ashore in alien territories, one of the best known instances being an encounter with natives on Columbus's Third Voyage, when we are told that "the Admiral, perceiving that he could nought prevail by signs and tokens, he determined with musical instruments to appease their wildness."[55] Another Italian, Sebastian Cabot, formalized the use of such methods in his 1551 instructions for the Merchant Adventurers on how to deal with natives, recommending the use of such musical instruments as "may allure them to hearkening, to fantasie, or desire to see, and heare your instruments and voyces, but keep you out of danger."[56]

Writing about music and colonialism in the seventeenth century, Olivia Bloechl draws attention to a passage in the Burwell lute tutor of around 1660 in which the conjunction of music and the encounter with native Americans is put into an explicitly Orphean context:

> Orpheus stopped the course of rivers with his playing, caused the trees to daunce tamed the wild beasts made them sociable and kind to one another there is nothing that brings more the wild nature of the Indians to a gentle constitution than musick and especially the lute.[57]

It was through these traditions of interpretation of the Orpheus story that the musical reformers associated with what Monteverdi described as the "Second Practice" found the essential link between the social and political value of rhetoric and a renewed cultural function for music. In my conclusion I can do no more than hint at the wider web of cultural discourses around music, language and power to which the colonial encounter with the New World gave rise. These discourses lie

---

[53] Vanessa Agnew, *Enlightenment Orpheus: The Power of Music in Other Worlds* (Oxford: Oxford University Press, 2008), p. 9.

[54] Ian Woodfield, *English Musicians in the Age of Exploration* (Stuyvesant, NY: Pendragon Press, 1995), p. 5.

[55] Woodfield, *English Musicians*, p. 97.

[56] Woodfield, *English Musicians*, p. 98.

[57] Olivia Bloechl, *Native American Song at the Frontiers of Early Modern Music* (Cambridge: Cambridge University Press, 2008), p.13.

behind the invention of opera itself, and its project to restore to music the powers that late Renaissance scholars found so clearly described in Plato and Aristotle, but which they considered to have been lost in their own day. For the progenitors of opera (Peri and Caccini both wrote operas based on the Orpheus myth before Monteverdi) the Orpheus narrative clearly carried rich connotations. And yet the story also delineates some of the anxieties to which these representations of the power of music gave rise. Historians of early colonialism such as Todorov and Greenblatt have pointed to the extended debates around the efficacy of language raised by the project of what Greenblatt describes as "linguistic colonialism."[58] These included discussion of the infamous *Requerimiento*, the proclamation which, from 1514, Spanish conquistadores were required to read aloud to any natives they encountered before appropriating their land. It informed them (in Spanish) that they had the choice of either voluntary acceptance of the rule of Christ and the kings of Spain, or being violently forced into submission. If the *Requerimiento* demonstrated that limitations of linguistic persuasion could in some circumstances be convenient, the opacity of language proved much more problematic in the vexed problem of converting Native Americans to Christianity—a far more challenging project than that of simply subjugating them.[59] As we have already noted, Orpheus fails to move the slow-witted Charon with his passionate rhetoric, like so many evangelizing Europeans coming up against the obduracy of Native Americans. Instead, dullard that he is, Charon simply falls asleep, leaving it to the aristocratic rulers of the underworld to succumb to the artistry of Orpheus's plea, whilst Orpheus himself grabs Charon's vessel in an act of conquistador-like force.

But what did it mean if music had such power to move (bewitch / enchant / seduce / intoxicate) people? When in 1557 the Genevan Jean de Léry encountered the singing of the Tupinamba Indians in Brazil he was perturbed by the fact that he could be so "transported" by a sound so alien, and could only justify his response by arguing that the natives must be possessed by Satan.[60] In time composers would come to represent their culture's anxiety about the power of music in operatic narratives which revolve obsessively around such bewitchment, enchantment, seduction, and intoxication. But even in its very inception opera recognizes that the power of Orpheus Conquistador carries an ambivalent historical burden.

---

[58]   Stephen Greenblatt, "Learning to Curse: Aspects of Linguistic Colonialism in the Sixteenth Century," in Greenblatt, *Learning to Curse: Essays in Early Modern Culture* (London: Routledge, 1990), pp. 22–51; Tzevetan Todorov, *The Conquest of America: The Question of the Other* (New York: Harper and Row, 1984).

[59]   See Todorov, *The Conquest of America*, chapters 3 and 4.

[60]   Stephen Greenblatt, *Marvellous Possessions*, pp. 14–17.

Chapter 2

Decentering Opera: Early Twenty-First-Century Indigenous Production

Beverley Diamond

While representations of Otherness, and particularly of indigenous people, have been considered in recent opera criticism,[1] this study inverts the gaze. I focus on two operas created by indigenous composers, librettists, and choreographers. A basic question explored in relation to these works is whether the indigenous perspective they each bring to the genre of opera shifts its socio-cultural impact, or succeeds in decolonizing opera audiences. It is clear that some populations were colonized while others were not, and that the most cogent literature on decolonization[2] has outlined decolonizing methodologies for those who have been colonized. I would argue that it is equally clear that "decolonization" is most urgently needed within social groups that were historically the colonizers, not the colonized. I worry, however, about claims of decolonization when actual social impact is hard to ascertain. I tend to prefer considerations of transformative possibilities rather than idealized but unproven assertions of social progress.

The first work is a Sámi opera, *Skuvle Nejla* (2006), on a libretto by playwright and actress Cecilia Persson, composed by Frode Fjellheim, a musician based in Trondheim, Norway. The second is the Aboriginal Dance Opera *BONES* (2001), a Native American creation by composer Sadie Buck (Seneca) and choreographer Alejandro Ronceria (Colombian) in collaboration with musicians David Deleary (Anishnabe) and Russell Wallace (Lillooet), and an international indigenous production team. Both works comment on colonial encounter and use elements of traditional knowledge in both the content and production processes. Implicitly, I explore how they frame cross-cultural encounter in comparison with other (more mainstream) operas.

Timothy Taylor has recently explored how key moments in operatic history have related to colonial expansion, to deal with the "'discovery' of other people at home and abroad" where the representation of a "jumble of different people,

---

[1] Pisani is one of the most thorough, including not only opera criticism but classical repertoire of all genres that contributed, as he argues, to the imagining of Native America in music. Michael Pisani, *Imagining Native America in Music* (New Haven, CT: Yale University Press, 2005).

[2] Particularly Linda Tuhiwai Smith, *Decolonizing Methodologies: Research and Indigenous Peoples* (London: Zed Books Ltd, 1999).

different social groups" served to normalize "the functioning of social power and governance."[3] My aim is to explore indigenous perspectives on cross-cultural encounters such as those Taylor discusses.

Changing Patterns of Indigenous Participation in Opera Worlds

This chapter concerns recent works created by indigenous composers, librettists, and choreographers. Indigenous people, however, have a long and diverse history in opera. Opera has long been a "contact zone"[4] in Mary Louise Pratt's sense of a space where "subjects previously separated by geography or history are co-present."[5] Before the twenty-first century, however, indigenous people have been historically co-present and have had significant agency as both opera audiences and performers.

Indigenous delegates have visited European capitals since the early eighteenth century. Musicologist Olivia Bloechl notes a group of chiefs from the Mississippi valley visiting Paris in 1725, whose itinerary included a trip to the opera. She cites contemporaneous sources that saw the Native American response as a validation of the art form and suggests that, in general, the approval of foreigners was sought "to affirm the naturalness and universality of the principles that organized elite French aesthetic experience."[6]

More sustained was the late nineteenth- and early twentieth-century involvement of indigenous performers in both opera and ballet. By the middle of the twentieth century, for instance, opera groups and choirs in New Zealand such as the Rangatira Maori Opera Group and the Waiata Maori Choir performed a variety of light operatic repertoire, and internationally acclaimed singers were emerging. Inia Te Wiata (1915–1971) sang at Covent Garden, including roles in the premieres of two Britten operas.[7] More recently, sopranos Timua Te Puhi Kai Ariki Brennan-Bryan, Deborah Wai Kapohe and the world-renowned Dame Kiri Te Kanawa are internationally active. For the most part, however, their indigeneity has not been foregrounded, and this sets the Maori scene apart to some extent from the Native American one.

---

[3] Timothy Taylor, Beyond Exoticism: Western Music and the World (Durham, NC: Duke University Press, 2007), pp. 34, 32, 35.

[4] I prefer this concept to Bhabha's "third space," which implies the potential for the emergence of new hybrid creations. In a "contact zone," a resilient insistence that distinctive forms or aesthetics should remain intact is an important possibility.

[5] Mary Louise Pratt, *Imperial Eyes: Travel Writing and Transculturation* (London: Routledge, 2008), p. 8.

[6] Olivia A. Bloechl, *Native American Song at the Frontiers of Early Modern Music* (Cambridge: Cambridge University Press, 2008), p. 217.

[7] Te Wiata played the Blind Ballad Singer in the premiere performance of *Gloriana* in 1953, and Dansker in *Billy Budd* (1951).

By the early twentieth century, a number of Native American classical musicians and ballet dancers were touring continent-wide. The renowned Native American ballerina Maria Tallchief and Iroquois baritone Oskenonton were among them. An institution that provided opportunity and access was the Chautauqua touring circuit (1874–1920), where assemblies gathered in semi-rural locations in both Canada and the United States to hear speakers and performers.[8] Chautauqua combined lectures and variety entertainment, aiming to edify a growing middle class but simultaneously reifying concepts of class and race in North America. Among the Native American opera singers on this circuit was Creek mezzo-soprano Tsianina Redfeather. She included repertoire by the so-called Indianist school[9] in the United States, a group that included Charles Cadman, Arthur Farwell, and Edward MacDowell. Tsianina Redfeather (Blackstone) was the lead soprano in Charles Wakefield Cadman's *Shanewis*,[10] an opera loosely based on her life. Other Native American performers on the circuit included the Indian String Quartet (composed of Fred Cardin, William Palin, William Reddie, and Alex Melovidov). On the Chautauqua circuit, Indian performers appeared part of the time in traditional regalia, not necessarily their own, and part of the time in Western formal attire. Visually, then, the shift is a clear metaphor for assimilation. But, as Philip Deloria has observed, the very presence of Native American performers such as the Indian String Quartet or Tsianina Redfeather asserted, for a period of time, that indigenous people of North America had a place in the cultural centers of their times. As Deloria writes, "the key factor complicating Tsianina's racial position was her talent, for it allowed her to refuse to be seen as either a remnant or an object of assimilation."[11]

These are individuals who exemplify what Philip Deloria has recently called "Indians in unexpected places," and the unexpected, he argues, can "change our sense of the past" and transform cross-cultural relationships in the present.

> I want you to read it as a shorthand for the dense economies of meaning, representation, and act(s) that have inflected both American culture writ large and individuals, both Indian and non-Indian. I would like for you to think

---

[8]   The role of Native American musicians on the Chauttauqua circuit has been studied by Paige Clarke Lush, "The All American Other: Native American Music and Musicians on the Circuit Chautauqua," *Americana: The Journal of American Popular Culture* 7/2 (2008), www.americanpopularculture.com/journal/articles/fall_2008/lush.htm (accessed on October 28, 2010).

[9]   For a critique of this movement, see Tara Browner "'Breathing the Indian Spirit': Thoughts on Musical Borrowing and the 'Indianist' Movement in American Music," *American Music*, 15/3 (Autumn 1997), 265–84, and contributions in the third section of this collection (Volpe in Chapter 8, Browner in Chapter 9, and Smith in Chapter 10).

[10]   Premiered at the Metropolitan Opera in 1918–1919.

[11]   Philip. J. Deloria, *Indians in Unexpected Places* (Lawrence: University Press of Kansas, 2004), p. 213.

34   *Opera Indigene: Re/presenting First Nations and Indigenous Cultures*

> of expectations in terms of the colonial and imperial relations of power and domination existing between Indian people and the United States. You might see in *expectation* the ways in which popular culture works to produce—and sometimes to compromise—racism and misogyny. And I would, finally, like you to distinguish between the anomalous, which reinforces expectations, and the unexpected, which resists categorization and, thereby, questions expectation itself.[12]

I am particularly interested in his distinction between "anomalies," which, like ritual inversions, sometimes provide the exception to the rule that proves the rule, and the "unexpected," which might engender new rules of encounter.

The most immediate forerunners of recent indigenous operas like those explored in this article were mid- to late twentieth-century theater and dance companies, many founded in the 1970s and 80s, two decades that witnessed a burgeoning of indigenous theater and arts in many parts of the world. As Shea Murphy has observed in relation to this emergence in North America, the political activism of the 1960s and 70s—including the 'Red Power' movement—growing interest in identity politics and increased funding for ethnic studies and multicultural programs were influential.[13] The restrictions on Native American dance performance that had been legislated in both Canada and the USA in the 1880s (paradoxically at about the same time as performance was encouraged within the frame of Wild West shows and other entertainments) were gradually lifted between the 1940s and 1960s. Within the two following decades, many ballet and theater companies (e.g., Nakai Theatre, founded 1979, Native Earth Performing Arts, established 1982, and the American Indian Dance Theatre, established 1987, to name only a few prominent organizations) emerged and huge strides were made in establishing indigenous training institutes (e.g., the Native Theater School in Toronto, established 1974). Generically diverse music has been both a theme and a medium in these late twentieth-century theater productions. Harrison (forthcoming) discusses, for instance, the use of the aria concept as a vehicle for monologues by twelve female characters (particularly the "Red Dress singer") in the collaborative production *Rare Earth Arias*.[14] She also references Tina Mason's *Diva Ojibway*,[15] in which the lead character is a young rural Native American girl who loves opera and wants to become an opera singer.

A similar movement, often called the "Sámi renaissance,"[16] blossomed in northern Scandinavia around the same time. This movement, which developed

---

[12]   Ibid., p. 11.

[13]   Jacqueline Shea Murphy, *The People Have Never Stopped Dancing: Native American Modern Dance Histories* (Minneapolis: University of Minnesota Press, 2007), p. 303.

[14]   Produced by Urban Ink in Vancouver in 2009.

[15]   Produced by Native Earth Performing Arts in 1994.

[16]   For a good overview of this period of cultural production, see Veli-Pekka Lehtola, *The Sámi People: Traditions in Transition* (Fairbanks: University of Alaska Press, 2004).

in the wake of protests over the building of a dam on the Alta River (and the consequent flooding of Sámi territory), had an explicit agenda to create a national Sámi "literature" in both print and performing arts.[17] Theater companies in Sweden (Dálvadis), Finland (Rávgoš), and Norway (the Beaivvas Sámi Theater) that emerged in the early 1980s are the forerunners of recent "joik operas." Among Beaivvas's productions is a musical satire *Min duoddarat* (*Our Fells*) about the Alta dam conflict, and adaptations of Sámi mythology and Japanese kabuki, as well as plays by Brecht, Shakespeare, Lorca, and others. Similarly, a multifaceted leader of the cultural renaissance, Nils-Aslak Valkeapää created large-form musical works, sometimes performing with large ensembles or appropriating classical genres (e.g., in his award-winning *Bird Symphony*). The cosmopolitan spirit of experiment and mimicry so crucial to joiking led naturally to works with new sonic and generic elements. By the first decade of the twenty-first century, Sámi composers such as Johan Sara Jr. and Frode Fjellheim—both of whom had classical training but a wide range of experience in film, theater, popular music, and jazz—had enough experience to handle hybrid productions effectively and to bridge orality and literacy in the production process.

The recent body of work[18] that I will now discuss emerges from these late twentieth-century dance and theater initiatives. The move from music-rich plays to fully sung drama composed, choreographed, acted, and produced by indigenous artists[19] was feasible given the strong contingent of highly trained creative individuals in many countries by the 1990s. In some cases these new works turn to the foundational mythology of their people. Among the landmarks is the first Hawaiian "hula opera," *Holo Mai Pele* (1995), a five-act saga of the classic Pele story created and choreographed by sisters Pualani Kanaka'ole Kanahele and Nalani Kanaka'ole. In other cases, the subjects are historical, as is the case with *Trepang*, a 1997 production of the Aboriginal and Torres Strait Island Commission, composed, mostly in the Yolngu language, by Andrish Saint Clare, which relates the contact between Macassan seafarers and the Aboriginal people of Arnhem

---

[17] For a discussion of this movement in relation to popular music production, see Beveley Diamond, "'Allowing the Listener to Fly as they Want to': Sámi Pespectives on Indigenous CD Production in Northern Europe," *Worlds of Music*, 49/1 (2007), pp. 23–49.

[18] Note that I am not considering operas written by non-Indigenous composers about Indigenous themes even though there is a large repertoire of these. Mary Ingraham's list of Canadian "staged dramatic music since 1867" includes more than a dozen Canadian works with Indigenous themes: Mary I. Ingraham, "Something to Sing About: A Preliminary List of Canadian Staged and Dramatic Music Since 1867," *Intersections: Canadian Journal of Music* 28/1 (2007), pp. 14–77.

[19] I acknowledge but do not focus on the many cross-cultural collaborations involving Indigenous playrights and musicians. Among them are the Vancouver Opera's 2007 production of *The Magic Flute*, set in the forest regions of British Columbia in an Aboriginal community; Tomson Highway and Melissa Hui's *The Journey (Pimooteewin)* (both of which are addressed in the last section of this collection), the "concert opera" *Guadalupe* by James DeMars with R. Carlos Nakai, or the Maori production *Waituhi* (1986).

36   *Opera Indigene: Re/presenting First Nations and Indigenous Cultures*

Land; and *Pecan Summer*, composed by Deborah Cheetham (Yorta Yorta), about the 1939 walkoff from the Cummeragunja Mission in New South Wales, and scheduled for production in 2010.[20] The Sámi opera *Skuvle Nejla*, which I consider in this chapter also focuses on revisionist history, while the Native American production *BONES* adapts elements of mythology and history.

The space of these recent indigenous operas differs from earlier operatic (and dance/theater) contact zones—the visits of indigenous dignitaries to European courts, indigenous involvement as performers in non-indigenous creations—in several fundamental ways. Aside from the basic distinction of having indigenous composers, librettists, and choreographers, they have libretti that are often multilingual, partially in indigenous languages or invented languages that draw on aspects of indigenous languages. They straddle orality and literacy by means of innovative production techniques, and they juxtapose traditional idioms with a range of other music or dance styles as an explicit means of embodying and commenting on "encounter."

They also construct the meanings that are mapped onto human bodies differently, challenging mainstream Western gender norms occasionally; furthermore, they implicitly question the very boundaries of species. These distinctive features, I argue, stretch conventional definitions of the genre of opera itself and, in so doing, have greater potential to effect the sort of social transformation that Deloria envisages when audiences happen upon the unexpected. In this chapter I will explore three creative dimensions of the works *Skuvle Nejla* (2006) and *BONES* (2001): language, genre shifts, and embodiment.

Language

Ethnomusicologists increasingly pay attention to language and dialect choices that musicians make in a globalized world.[21] Such choices convey information about the intended audience, and the linguistic sophistication of performers. Dialect may signify ethnicity, class, or region. Opera often crosses language barriers, with surtitles in the local language allowing audiences to understand performance in the original one. The two operas under consideration here, however, are created in multiple languages (including one that is invented), and the way language maps onto character and reveals cultural knowledge is complex and highly nuanced.

Genre Shifts

Both operas draw upon diverse musical genres and traditional as well as operatic and contemporary popular styles. Different performers have skills honed within contrasting artistic worlds, as culture bearers of oral traditions with no music literacy skills, as pop musicians, or as opera singers with no

---

[20]   See Interview with Deborah Cheetham, Chapter 18 of this volume.

[21]   See, for instance, Harris M. Berger and M.T. Carroll, *Global Pop, Local Language* (Jackson: University Press of Mississippi, 2003).

knowledge of or competence in indigenous traditional song. Hence, such productions must bridge orality and literacy.

Embodiment

Both operas have certain aspects that are gendered in heterosexist terms and others that are more alternative. Where bodies are the signifiers, however, gender is not the most pertinent signified in either opera. The fluid boundaries of existence—crossing animal, human, and spirit—are more fundamental and integral. Embodiment also implies the physicality of the production—the central role of dance in *BONES*, but also the process of casting in *Skuvle Nejla*.

Skuvle Nejla

Fjellheim's *Skuvle Nejla* was produced in Ostersund in October 2006.[22] The idea was initiated by the opera department of an academy in the municipality of Jamtland and by the region of Nord Trondelag.[23] It is a worthy successor to several earlier works by Fjellheim in which classical and joik idioms are juxtaposed: His *Arctic Mass*, for instance, involves classical singers, joikers, and popular music performers. His joik-centered music curriculum for Norwegian and Swedish schools is similarly a cross-cultural communication project. His knowledge of both the North Sámi joik tradition (which he learned growing up in Karasjok) and the South Sámi one (more familiar in the context of his family roots and current residence) set him apart from other Sámi musicians.

Librettist Cecilia Persson is a veteran of the Beaivváš Sámi Theater, a skilled joiker, and a playwright. Her historically based plot revolves around a Danish pietist missionary Thomas von Westen, who recruited converts among the South Sámi beginning in 1716.[24] Cecilia Persson[25] explained:

---

[22] Sara's *Skuolfi* (*Snowy Owl*, 2006) was the earliest of the new joik operas. Analogous to the story of Rip Van Winkle, it is a tale about a man who had lived all his life in isolation in the mountains (part of the landscape as the snowy owl is). Never having experienced any part of the colonization process, as an old man he was then forced to leave his area and move to a modern community, where his clear sense of who he was proved inspiring to those around him.

[23] All quotations by the composer Frode Fjellheim are taken from interviews conducted by the author, one in May 2007, and one in October 2008.

[24] Von Weston's writings have been widely used to study pre-Christian religious practices, although he had an obvious bias against such practices.

[25] All quotes by the librettist Cecilia Persson are taken from an interview conducted by the author in October 2008.

38 *Opera Indigene: Re/presenting First Nations and Indigenous Cultures*

He's a person that did both good and bad things for the Sámi. He was called the Sámi apostle. Many Sámis liked him very much because he was the one that wanted the Sámi people to hear their own language in church. But he was very aggressive against the old religion. He scared them into being baptized.[26]

Von Westen's operatic persona is historically faithful. Attracted to the Christian message is the title character, Skuvle Nejla, in spite of the more cautious views of his wife Maria. He leaves her to follow von Westen just before she learns she is pregnant. She gives birth to a daughter, Allaq. The daughter is raised by the spirits of the mountain and becomes a cross-species bear-human. Years later she returns to the community of her parents, but is shot in her bear form by local hunters, among whom is her own father. Her Sámi belt, which her parents gave her, identifies the bear as Allaq. In misery, Skuvle Nejla renounces the church and confronts von Westen, who ceases his manipulative mission. In the final scene, a "dream time" future, Skuvle Nejla is reunited with his daughter.

The set in this 2006 production is minimal: a scaffolding frame at the back of the stage serves multiple purposes. It is von Westen's church, but it also enables the representation of a bifurcated world. For instance, in scenes where von Westen is preaching inside the "church" below, we see Maria atop the scaffolding in the world of the "holy mountain" where she gave birth to Allaq (Figure 2.1). Lighting distinguishes the realms of the quotidian (mostly warmer yellows) and the spaces of nature's spiritual power (the mountain, the bear hunt, the dream world of the final scene) where blue is pervasive.

Language

The bilingual libretto of *Skuvle Nejla*, in Swedish and Sámi—premiered without surtitles—has audience implications. In general, the bilingual Sámi audience members had the very advantage Indigenous populations usually have in colonial contexts. Having been required to learn the oppressor's language, they understand both. The librettist makes shifts, however, to assist the Scandinavian mainstream by repeating text in both languages. At the very beginning of the opera, a flash-forward scene in which Maria explains that she bore a child and hid it in the holy mountain, the words "Holy Mountain" are first spoken in Swedish ("Det heliga fjället") and

---

[26] Her views are corroborated by historians such as Gjessing, who described him as temperamental and ruthless (Gutorm Gjessing, *Changing Lapps: A Study in Culture Relations in Northernmost Norway*, Monographs on Social Anthropology 13 [London: The London School of Economics and Political Science, 1954]), and Håkan Rydving, who writes that "[t]he Sámi were frightened into going to the churches and into following the regulations that had been drawn up—at least when they were in the proximity of the clergyman or someone else who could report them": Håkan Rydving, *The End of Drum-Time: Religious Change among the Lule Saami, 1970s–1740s* (Uppsala: Almquvist & Wiksell International, 1993), p. 59.

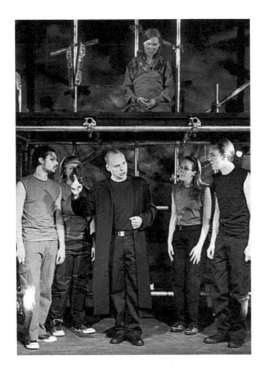

Figure 2.1   *Skuvle Nejla*, Scene 5. Two worlds: the mountain where Maria (Anna Kråik) goes to have her child, on the upper tier, and von Westen (Jan Nilsson) with converts on the lower tier

repeated in Sámi ("Bïssie vaeresne") with echo effects that imply spirituality.[27] In Scenes 5–7 von Westen is preaching in Swedish but the parishioners repeat his words in their own language, nuancing each phrase differently.

The language switches of the Sámi characters are symbolically charged. While von Westen speaks consistently in Swedish until the end of the opera, where he joiks with the chorus, both Skuvle Nejla and Maria vacillate between the two, giving away their emotional allegiance with each language change. Persson describes this as a representation of the process of language erosion that resulted from colonialism:

> It's what happened with the Sámi language ... There has been quite a big process, emotionally and in many other things. I wanted that process to be visible in the play, especially for Skuvle Nejla. When he comes back [to his own beliefs] he's

---

[27] Empirical testing of this and other types of "vocal staging" in audio production has been undertaken by Serge Lacasse, see "'Listen to My Voice': The Evocative Power of Vocal Staging in Recorded Rock Music and Other Forms of Vocal Expression" (PhD thesis, University of Liverpool, 2000).

40   *Opera Indigene: Re/presenting First Nations and Indigenous Cultures*

> speaking Sámi but he's speaking Swedish too and it's easier for him to speak
> Swedish in many situations.[28]

The style of Sámi speech varies, serving as a further means of characterization. The monologues of Allaq, the girl-bear, were very difficult to translate and I asked Cecilia if she had used ancient words or other esoteric language. She explained that indeed Allaq's speech was difficult because it was abstract and entirely in metaphors. "She speaks as if she *is* nature," she said. Then, speaking as Allaq: "I am the stone that you are tumbling over. I am the rain that's coming down on you. I am the ice breaking under your feet. You can never escape me."[29] To enhance the linguistic difference, the composer taught the singer playing Allaq to improvise an individualized "joik-like rap" style of delivery in the Prologue and several other scenes.

Other distinctions in the Sámi text relate to the fact that the actor/singers are from different regions, with identifiable joik styles and dialects: Johan Anders Baer (Skuvle Nejla) from Kautokeino (North Sámi); Anna Kråik (Maria) from Trondheim (South Sámi); Inga-Marit Gaup Juuso (Allaq) from Enontekio (North Sámi in Finland). Their vocables map the geography sonically. South Sámi vocables predominate since, as the composer notes, the story took place in their region. Additionally, Fjellheim regards vocables as "a nice musical element that produces different vocal sounds and musical structures," generating rhythmic ideas, for instance.

Sámi text, furthermore, may have "hidden" meanings that shift the emotional tone of the action. Immediately after the "bear scene" we hear a phrase that occurs nowhere else in the opera: "velle velle." Fjellheim incorporates a joik on these syllables in his joik-based curriculum and live performances. I asked him if this brief reference was significant. He replied: "The joik you are referring to, I used that as an idea. The 'velle velle' joik that I used before is connected to a lyric and a joik [melody] that is intended to calm down the reindeers. I wanted them [the Sámi in this scene] to be calm." Here is a lovely instance of the hidden meanings so prevalent in Sámi language usage. As Gaski has written, Sámi played on the potential of double meanings to communicate secretly in the presence of colonizers.[30] In this opera, then, such subtleties in Sámi usage imply Sámi agency not only in relation to von Westen, but also in relation to the non-Sámi-speaking part of the audience.

In summary, *Skuvle Nejla* makes pragmatic use of Swedish and Sámi languages to attract simultaneously an audience of indigenous insiders and Scandinavian outsiders, but it exploits those language differences for other purposes as well. The slippage when lines are translated from one to the other conveys subtle cultural distinctions best understood by Sámi speakers. The different Sámi dialects and

---

[28]   Interview with author, May 2008.

[29]   She is translating a part of the Prologue.

[30]   Harald Gaski, "The Secretive Text: Yoik Lyrics as Literature and Tradition," in J. Pentikäinen (ed.), *Sámi Folkloristics* (Turku: NFF Publications, 2000), pp. 191–214.

idioms both delineate character and region while nuances of a phrase such as "velle velle" exploit the polyvalent quality of the language.

Genre and the Production Process

The combination of conventional opera performers with Sámi tradition bearers and the composer's respect for oral tradition necessitated a complex bridging of orality and literacy. Fjellheim's score sometimes functioned like a cue sheet, handed out with a rehearsal CD for scenes largely developed orally. *Skuvle Nejla* involved instrumentalists (two keyboard players, flute, guitar, bass, and percussion), and a Swedish opera singer playing the role of von Westen, a singer-joiker (Maria) who has both oral and music literacy skills, a young actor who had some joik skill as well as popular music capacity (Allaq), and a well-known joiker who works only orally (Skuvle Nejla). A quartet, which both librettist and composer liken to a Greek chorus, were classical singers, called upon to sing drone-based counterpoint as the Sámi community, triadic harmony as von Westen's congregation, and more complex polyphony as well as improvised animal joiks as the bear hunters (Example 2.1).

The composer worked differently with each performer, depending on their vocal skills and music literacy. As already mentioned, Fjellheim taught Inga-Marit

Example 2.1 *Skuvle Nejla*, Scene 14: The bear hunt. The church warden and Quartet respond to improvised vocal and keyboard sounds: "A monster rises from the snow. Watch out! Watch out!".

Gaup Juuso (Allaq) the joik-rap style that he uses himself in performances.[31] Anna Kråik (as Maria), who has classical training but also joiks, could shift her vocal timbre and phrasing. At the end of Scene 4, for instance, she expresses her loneliness after Skuvle Nejla's departure, beginning a phrase with a (throatier) joik voice but ending with a clearer classical sound. I read this as a sonic emblem of colonization, but one colleague has suggested that the shift represents her agency, the ability to be (vocally) whatever she wants to be.[32] Johann Anders Baer as Skuvle Nejla, on the other hand, is well known as a joik performer and composer.[33] The composer notes that negotiating which of Johann Anders's joiks to use was the best way to work with him, both to get the most successful performance and to enable the respected tradition-bearer to be part of the creative process. While there was, then, a "surrender of creative control" that Western audiences may associate with collaborative theater,[34] this opera is less about an improvisatory process than Fjellheim's recognition of the diverse vocal abilities and knowledges of each participant. The final kind of joik is one that Fjellheim controlled more directly. As mentioned, he works with a transcription he made of a 1913 recording of a bear joik, predictably associated with Allaq.[35] A pentatonic joik composed by Fjellheim unites all the characters including the priest, whose operatic voice soars with the Sámi in the final scene. Because the bear theme and final pentatonic joik were taught formally, they do not have the subtle timbral and rhythmic inflections of traditional joik (Example 2.2). On the other hand, von Westen (Jan Nilsson), whose part is largely atonal (Example 2.3), worked from the score, as did the quartet and instrumentalists.

Example 2.2 *Skuvle Nejla*, The "bear joik" recorded in 1910 by Karl Tiren, used as a Leitmotif for Allaq

[31] Fjellheim has founded several jazz- and pop-influenced ensembles, most recently the band Transjoik. He also tours extensively with traditional joiker Ulla Pirttijarvi, for whom he is arranger and producer. Of course, rap has migrated far beyond its Bronx roots to become a music that articulates socio-political issues worldwide.

[32] Thanks to Amy Stillman for this interpretation, made in remarks following my presentation of a portion of this paper at the University of Michigan in April, 2009.

[33] He toured previously with the Sámi star Nils-Aslak Valkeapää, and has produced two solo CDs.

[34] Ric Knowles, "The Structures of Authenticity: Collective and Collaborative Creations," in *Collective Creation, Collaboration and Devising*, ed. Bruce Barton (Toronto, ON: Playwrights Canada Press, 2008), pp. 98–113, p. 98.

[35] Performed by Magdalena Jonsson and Bengt Olofsson for Karl Tiren, the notation in Example 2.2 was printed in the program itself. This joik and its association with a bear has been debated by Swedish ethnomusicologists (Olle Edström, personal communication). Fjellheim has arranged this same joik on two other recordings, first on *Sangen vi glemte* (1991) and later for his jazz joik ensemble on *Saajve Dans* (1994).

Example 2.3 *Skuvle Nejla*, Scene 1. Thomas von Westen's prayer: "Lord give me strength to be able to cope with this mission. You Creator who gave me this task to turn the gaze of heathens from darkness."

44 *Opera Indigene: Re/presenting First Nations and Indigenous Cultures*

Finally, in addition to the complex and individualized production process, there is a further joik connotation. The librettist emphasized that the whole opera was "like a joik," expressing the dramatic capacity of the tradition for capturing the essence of people and things, in the process of communicating and disagreeing. The composer and performers had the hard task of realizing that artistic vision.

Embodiment

In *Skuvle Nejla* the nuclear family (parents Maria and Skuvle Nejla, and their child Allaq) as the central unit of the plot is conventional. The male and female domains of Maria and Skuvle Nejla are stereotypic in that he is drawn to the world of public action and "modern" commitment, she to the traditional world of the "holy mountain," a domain that is sometimes associated with the sound of the flute. There is, however, a certain irony here since Baer, who plays Skuvle Nejla, is the most skilled as a "traditional" joiker.

The patriarchal von Westen, who embodies rigid and authoritarian power, represents a stereotypical masculine identity construct, one that maps onto the real protagonist, colonialism. Unlike many opera plots, however, where the fatal flaw of a character leads to their tragic demise, *Skuvle Nejla* offers the promise of redemption as von Westen recants and sings with the community in their own language by the final scene.

It is Allaq who embodies the greatest alterity, challenging the boundaries of both gender and species categories. Her physicality—her appearance and style of movement—were key factors in casting Inga-Marit Gaup Juuso in this role. The composer noted that this slight, blond teenager "looked fantastic on stage." He clarified what he meant when I asked if he was trying for an "animal-like" portrayal. Fjellheim replied: "The term animal-like is of course irrelevant because she looked like an animal ... It was natural for her to look this way and also to sound this way."[36] He doesn't mention her blond hair, but it is perhaps not a coincidence that blondness is associated with special power in Sámi narratives, and not with the stereotypes of facile beauty invented by the Euroamerican world.[37] To invest the crucial turning point of the plot in the role of a child (played by a teenager) was arguably a risky and somewhat unusual choice. Here, however, her resemblance to the bear in movement and sound over-rides the importance of extensive experience (Figure 2.2).

In sum, the ironies and fluidities of characters in this opera reinforce the heterogeneity of language use and musical style. These characteristics of this particular Sámi approach to opera contrast with the Native American one described below. In his introduction to *Aboriginal Drama and Theatre*, Rob Appleford

---

[36] Frode Fjellheim, interview with author, October 10, 2008.

[37] Most notably in the story *The Frost Haired and the Dream Seer*, the only play by the late Nils-Aslak Valkeapää. Certain artistic figures of note in contemporary Sámi history (including Valkeapää himself) are or were blond, unlike the majority of Sámi.

Figure 2.2   *Skuvle Nejla*, Prologue. Inga-Marit Gaup Juuso as Allaq, at one with nature

writes that Native American Aboriginal theater has been characterized by a "fear of heterogeneity," and has "typically placed undue pressure on Aboriginal playwrights and performers to adopt a voice which can be judged as inherently unified, homogeneous, and political."[38] Persson and Fjellheim exhibit no such fear. In addition to the transformative potential of revisionist history, the power relations implicit in privileging Sámi languages generally and regional dialects specifically, this heterogeneity is an element that arguably upsets mainstream expectations.

BONES

Billed as an "Aboriginal Dance Opera," *BONES* was premiered at the Banff Arts Festival in Alberta in 2001. It emerged from two programs in Aboriginal Arts that the Banff Centre pioneered in the late 1990s, the Chinook Winds Aboriginal Dance program and Aboriginal Women's Voices. The directors of those two programs, Colombian-born choreographer Alejandro Ronceria and Seneca composer and singer Sadie Buck, conceived and created the work, involving David Deleary and Russell Wallace in the music production, and other singers/actors/dancers from eight First Nations, as well as Métis, Maori, Hawaiian, and Mixteco people.

---

[38]   Rob Appleford, *Aboriginal Drama and Theatre* (Toronto, ON: Playwrights Canada Press, 2005), p. ix.

46 *Opera Indigene: Re/presenting First Nations and Indigenous Cultures*

The Directors' Statement in the program conveys their intent. "The story of BONES is the life of a people," they write. "We love the land we were placed in. We work to keep our lands safe and healthy. We are sovereign in our hearts and our minds. We try our best to work in harmony with the earth, the sustainer of our life. Our memory. BONES is about our life. BONES is about our love, our peace, our existence. Take this journey with us ... " The "we" of the *BONES* directors—unlike the creators of *Skuvle Nejla*, who emphasize historical specificity and regional distinctiveness—seems initially to present indigenous people as homogeneous, in keeping with Appleford's aforementioned assertion.

There is little plot or action; the narrative—abstract, cyclical—is one of the un-operatic and hence unexpected features. Act I, Earth: People revel in the bounty of the earth, a couple gives birth to a baby; they learn to live in harmony with the cycles of life. Act II, Body: The people celebrate in a game, the grandmother dies, but the community carries on, building a big house, coping with the fracturing of knowledge as the colonial period unfolds. Act III, Spirit: Seven boys whose knowledge is ignored by the adults become the seven stars of the Pleiades. The people are lost. But a lullaby begins to reawaken the adult child. Finally, they achieve spirit, merging their bones with the earth as the cycle begins anew.

The staging is minimal. A single rock is the set for many scenes; in others, giant bones become seats, houses, or suspended skeletons. A sheet is the ocean. The lighting shifts from blackness to warm golds in the community scenes. A series of "watermarks" are projected onto the rear of the stage or the stage wings. Some of these are abstractions such as a spiral. Others, such as the giant shadow figures that frame the gambling game, are figurative.

Like *Skuvle Nejla*, the set for *BONES* has two tiers, but here the "ground" of the upper one is black and invisible. The spirit figures (who are also the primary musicians) occupy the upper tier, where they seem to be suspended in air. Humans move on the lower tier, sometimes joined by the spirits, who can roam in either world (Figure 2.3). The movement of the human and spirit realms is often parallel or mirror-like.

Language

BONES uses multiple language references. There is very little English and most of it is uttered by Spirit Woman,[39] particularly in the initial scene—a practical decision, to give the audience some basic information. In this first evocative scene where Earth Singer calls to the people, Spirit Woman translates: "Her voice carries life." The next scene is the only one where a song is actually translated into English orally (the program has translations for all the songs): "We will take care / we love her gifts / we hear her song / Earth she is our bone." Particularly at the beginning of the opera, then, audiences are helped to comprehend the basic scenario.

---

[39] Played by the noted Aboriginal actress and founder of Spiderwoman Theater in New York, Muriel Miguel.

Figure 2.3   *BONES*: The tiered worlds of humans below (first family played by Carlos Rivera, Cherith Mark, and Santee Smith) and spirits above (Kalani Queypo as Fire Man, Jani Lauzon as Wind Woman, and Faron Johns as Rattle Man)

English is again used in Act II where the pressures of colonial encounter become more intense and the people are unsettled by new values. A scene called "The Game," for instance, could be read visually as an enactment of an Eastern Woodlands dice game or a gambling game of Native Americans elsewhere. We hear in English: "You have to play to win. Just like life."

Most of the libretto, however, is in an invented language. Virtually every press release, review, or other mode of discourse about *BONES* mentions the unique "language of the world" created primarily by Sadie Buck. The program and a Banff Centre media release tell us that "the concept is borrowed from the Cansa people of South America".[40] Colombian-born choreographer Ronceria explains further: "The Cansa people of South America maintain a ceremony to this day that ensures the earth's rotation. In this ceremony, they speak a language that is essential to the maintenance of the ceremony and thus the continued rotation of the earth. They refer to this language as the 'Language of the World.' For BONES, we

---

[40] *BONES* program, p. 9.

48   *Opera Indigene: Re/presenting First Nations and Indigenous Cultures*

have borrowed this concept, this idea for the opera; each of the songs is translated into this language."[41]

Because so many different indigenous groups were involved, the concept of a libretto in an Esperanto-like "Language of the World" seemed apt. Buck and Ronceria studied different languages over the four-year preparation for the production. Sadie Buck, however, describes how, at an earlier stage, she found vocables that had rhythms and emotional moods to suit some of the key scenes: "Oma bema" for "earth baby," for instance. Only later did she assign meaning to vocables and compile a dictionary of the invented words. Her description resonates partially with musicologist Gary Tomlinson's interpretation of vocables as "surplus over speech." Vocables, he posits, "which seem always destined to be chanted or sung, seek out a liminal position between non-linguistic cry and semi-semantic word. The very fact that the most specifically meaningful capacity of language is sidestepped at the moment of their irruption adds to their impact, granting them power to encapsulate and deepen a song's most general import."[42] On the other hand, her creation of a dictionary and careful assigning of meanings that conveyed indigenous constructs of relationship are more like Fjellheim's use of deeply embedded cultural reference points (hidden to outsiders), not "liminal" but definitive of the differences between knowledge systems.

The conceptual relationships *between* sounds convey Buck's Seneca-shaped philosophy. She explained to me: "It is the sound of what I hear on earth. ... Aboriginal people understood it at a core level. The [non-Indigenous] audience had it too but had no vocabulary for it."[43] She emphasizes the texture and feeling rather than the semantics of individual words. Nonetheless, there is logic in their meaning and relationships. A couple of examples are indicative. "Oma" relates the oneness of humans, bones and earth; the morpheme "se," which signals "spirit," is embedded in words for "love" and "gift."

> *Oma* – earth
> *Omanipa* – humans
> *Oman* – bones
> *Seoma* – spirit land
> *Omase* – love
> *Omasespa* – gift

---

[41]   Media release, July 27, 2001. The Cansa reference is obscure, however. In other sources the language is said to have been influenced by indigenous languages worldwide. Furthermore, Sadie Buck's description is divergent in that she describes her preliminary search for vocables that had suitable rhythms and emotional connotations for key scenes.

[42]   Gary Tomlinson, *The Singing of the New World: Indigenous Voice in the Era of European Contact* (Cambridge: Cambridge University Press, 2007), p. 85.

[43]   All quotations are from an interview with the author in March 2006 unless otherwise indicated.

Kinship is communicated by combining the sound of existence ("ema") with morphemes for family roles. Buck's vocabulary for "words" combines the spirit morpheme "se" with "existence" ("ema").

> *Bema* – baby
> *Nema* – mother
> *Manema* – grandmother
> *Machiema* – grandchildren
> *Ema* – exist
> *Sema* – words

Other languages are drawn upon fleetingly. There are words that resemble English (*kap* – keep; *melod* – melody; *sev bres* – seven brothers), and German (*wasen* – water).[44]

Genre Shifts and the Production Process

As in *Skuvle Nejla*, different musical styles and genres symbolize distinct cultural worlds in *BONES*. The music draws to some extent on traditional repertoires: during the chanted telling of the traditionally based Pleiades story, a traditional Haudenosaunee stomp dance is sung in the background; in a hunt episode, a deer dance is performed; and powwow steps animate the joyous community scenes. Throughout, the skillful choreography of Ronceria effects a fusion between the predominantly modernist aesthetic and what he describes as an Indigenous sensibility.

Although there are such traditional references, the music is original: Buck's compositions with arrangements by David Deleary and Russell Wallace. One significant musical theme of the work is "Oma Bema" (Earth Baby), a song that is introduced in Act I, Scene 3 and repeated in Act III, Scenes 3 and 5. Like virtually all of the twenty songs that Buck composed, "Oma Bema" is pentatonic, a scale that marks nowhere and everywhere in some interpretations, but also a scale that, as Michael Pisani has observed, has become a stereotype in representations of Native America.[45] The song, a three-measure phrase repeated (Example 2.4), is easily remembered; its return in Act III consolidates its importance as the aural "ground" of the opera. Significant, however, are the stylistic nuances of the repetitions, each shifting the ground, especially in the final scene where the phrase is sung in turn by each performer, individualized by each, often with blues inflections. Contemporary pop styles now transform the tune, aurally symbolizing the impact of encounter in the vocal delivery while also intensifying and individualizing the lullaby.

---

[44]   Interviewer Elma Miller says there is Michif and Maori (and Sadie did not deny this in the interview), but I was unable to spot Michif or Maori words.

[45]   Pisani, *Imagining Native America.*

Example 2.4 *BONES*, the lullaby "Oma Bema" used in several scenes: "Earth Baby / With me exist / in love."

Another memorable pentatonic song accompanies the movement of the grandmother[46] from life to death (Act 2, Scene 1). Accompanied by solo cello, string sounds, and a gentle rattle, she repeats her song in her distinctive timbre, many times. Giant bones are carried onto the stage for the first time, but the humans seem uncertain of what to do with them. Finally they lift them in the air and the bones re-form into a skeleton, a spirit welcoming grandmother into their realm. This is the longest sonically unchanging section in the opera. Such repetition has been interpreted variously. Native Americanist scholars sometimes articulate repetitions as a strengthening process, with each circuit in the dance circle, for instance, or a symbolic structure where certain numbers of repetitions are called for. Tom Turino has recently described repetition in relation to (Zimbabwean) participatory performance: "Long performances and extended repetition offer the opportunity to connect with a number of people in this direct, unspoken way that seems to exclude any possibility of duplicity—for those moments, at least, people are truthfully intimately connected."[47] This same directness and connectedness is arguably achieved here, implying a cross-over between the realms of participatory and presentational performance.[48] For me, the most unexpected and transformative element of *BONES* was this new sense of embodied engagement. As Buck explains, "you are not going to be sitting back as a comfortable audience person watching this show. You are going to be involved in it."[49]

The same bones reappear in the next scene, "Build the Big House," in which the community carries on with the guiding assistance of the spirits who are now in their midst: the imposing figure of "Rattle Spirit" in the center of the arch, the white-clad wind spirit on stage left with the women, the ever present Spirit Woman directing things. Musically, the shifts in metric subdivision from two to

---

[46] Grandmother was played by Soni Moreno from the well-known trio Ulali.

[47] Thomas Turino, *Music as Social Life: The Politics of Participation* (Chicago, IL: University of Chicago Press, 2008), p. 136. The theorization of repetition can undoubtedly be nuanced further. A minimalist instrumental piece, for instance, may shift bodly awareness but lack the intense communicative power of either participatory performance or dramatic presentational performance.

[48] The boundary between participatory and presentational is often challenged in other Native American contexts, powwow for example.

[49] Interview by Elma Miller, online at www.native-dance.ca/index.php/Scholars/Sadie_Buck?tp=z&bg=6&ln=e&gfx=l&wd= (accessed October 27, 2010).

Example 2.5 *BONES*, Act II, Scene 4: Excerpt from the antiphonal choral singing during the building of the "big house": "Carry, carry the words / raise, raise the words…"

three create a hemiola effect that marks this as a lively Mexican-flavored dialogue in which the women and men answer each other antiphonally (Example 2.5).

Two subsequent scenes, labeled "Fracture" and "Duality," shift the mood. In duality, the stage becomes a vivid red as Wind Spirit, played by Jani Lauzon, sings a blues called "This Old Road." Spirit Woman reminds the people at the outset that their minds should be "as one"—recalling a line familiar to Haudenosaunee, a line that closes each portion of their Thanksgiving Address. The dancers, however, are not "as one." Individuals are frequently walking opposite to their fellows. Buck described an audience member who told her afterwards that she had to "lose the nasty pop music" because it didn't fit the overall aesthetic. "That's what was happening to our people at that point in time," she replied. "You got it. You were supposed to feel uncomfortable." The "garish guitar scene" as she called it served as a metonym for colonial contact—a long road indeed.

The cool dark colors return in Act III, Spirit. The sky is now lit by stars, seven of them for the seven brothers of the Pleiades, now augmented by other souls. We hear the lullaby "Oma Bema" throughout, now with the aforementioned changes of voice and individualized style inflections. The humans move closer and closer to the earth, lying on/in it. They become the bones—the earth itself.

Style juxtapositions, the diverse cast from different countries and cultures, as well as different learning modes, necessitated a thoughtful and innovative process of production, as with the Sámi opera. In an interview with Elma Miller, Buck describes some aspects of this process:

> For aboriginal people it is the process that is important … Your end product is going to be as strong as the process so you take care of the process … I felt we had to show it [i.e., the idea of process in creation] to get the point across about how it was and is different in its creation.[50]

---

[50] Ibid.

52   *Opera Indigene: Re/presenting First Nations and Indigenous Cultures*

Unlike *Skuvle Nejla*, however, members of the cast had worked together previously in the Banff programs and in pre-production workshops. Buck emphasizes the significance of a "thread of continuity" from one year of the Banff programs to the next: "You always have something from the first group that comes into the second, and on to the third and so on."[51] When the Banff Centre undertook a series of workshops in preparation for the production of *BONES*, Buck was again looking for "threads" of similarity in the process of each workshop leader and participant. She describes herself as a "story weaver," crafting a whole from the pieces that each participant offers. She also emphasizes trust and respect within the group: "I think that the performers I work with also trust me and know that I will not put them into a position that goes counter to their culture or against their aesthetic ideals. I am always very respectful of all the cultures that I work with … . I try to honour all that they believe in. … I would rather leave something out completely or change it rather than dishonour somebody's culture."[52] Like *Skuvle Nejla*, the process of creating *BONES* is collaborative but firmly shaped by one composer's vision, an individual whose deep respect for community values earned the trust of the participants.

Embodiment

Like *Skuvle Nejla*, *BONES* includes a nuclear family with parents and child but extending the generations from the newborn Earth Baby to the Grandmother at the point of death. However, again like the Sámi opera, *BONES* challenges an adult- and human-centered frame in radical ways. Cross-species boundary crossing includes the virtuosic performance of a deer dance mentioned earlier. The most important boundary crossing, however, is between human and spirit worlds, staged on different levels. The spirits who reside on the upper level may roam among the humans, or change realm in the case of the grandmother. Three spirits are played by male actors and one by a female, but gender is hardly obvious here. The female spirit, Wind Spirit, played by Jani Lauzon, wears buckskin pants that resemble the outfits of the male actors (except that she is clad in white). Her movements in the scene "This Old Road," where she sings a blues number, include guitar gestures that suggest an exaggerated masculinity. Spirit Woman and Rattle Man both wear outfits with many accessories; this feature and their dominating physical presence (although Spirit Woman is almost always busy while Rattle Man is often stationary) give them a kind of embodied relatedness. These descriptions of the spirit roles suggest androgyny, and the same quality is frequently evident in the rest of the cast. They often move in a block, emphasizing the power of the collective and down-playing individuality, except in the blues scene where, in the wake of colonialism, we see individuals moving counter to the group. Where

---

[51]   Ibid.

[52]   Ibid.

smaller sub-groups are engaged in different activities as in the "big house" scene, they are sonically one, singing the same music antiphonally.

Central to the cyclical unfolding of the work is the merging of humans with the natural environment itself. The children in the Pleiades myth[53] become stars, joining the souls of the departed. The title, however, points to the central boundary crossing element: our bones are the earth. Our sustenance comes from the earth and we become one with it when we die. The earth is a character in this opera, a living force that determines all that occurs. Both composer and choreographer have spoken about the aural and physical qualities implicit in this. Ronceria describes the Indigenous sensibility of the dance thus: "We don't interpret music on the upbeat [like Western music]; we interpret it on the downbeat. The beat is down, your heels are going into the ground, you pound it; we want to be as close as possible to the earth."[54] Buck similarly described a quality of "listening toward the earth." Conceptually, then, sound emanates from the earth.

Dance scholar Jacqueline Shea Murphy also emphasizes the physicality of the opera:

> Instead of foregrounding the events themselves, what emerges most viscerally in this "Aboriginal Dance Opera" is a sense of grounding in physicality—in the earth, bones, bodies—that continues over time even as its particularities shift and change. The recognition of this physicality, in and through a dance piece, swelled by the physical presence and rhythms and movements of dancers and musicians, imparted a vision in which both the present and the ever-present exist together.[55]

Some reviewers responded positively to this form of embodiment and some did not. In a review for *Wind Speaker* magazine, Debora Lockyer Steel writes:

> Alejandro promised if I surrendered myself, I would be touched ... I had come a long way, two hours out of my way, in fact, and was well behind schedule. Time only to wolf down something. I was not in a fair mood to be reviewing a theatrical production that I understood from others was, well, different. Surrender yourself, Alejandro reminded. Without that surrender, you have conflict. But it turned out

---

[53]   The use of traditional narrative here is reminiscent of the reference to narratives about children and bears in *Skuvle Nejla*. Arguably, storytelling opens audiences to new conceptual possibilities.

[54]   Hollis Walker, "Contemporary Dance," *Native Peoples*, 11/1 (2005), online at www.nativepeoples.com/article/articles/149/1/Contemporary-Dance/Page1.html/print/149 (accessed May 16, 2007).

[55]   Murphy, *The People Have Never Stopped Dancing*, p. 248.

54   *Opera Indigene: Re/presenting First Nations and Indigenous Cultures*

there was no need. From the opening minutes of Bones: An Aboriginal Dance Opera, I was vanquished.[56]

On the other hand, another reviewer found the lack of a protagonist, and the absence of crisis and resolution problematic[57]:

> Although some of the 17 scenes were so richly conceived and well performed that the problematic dramatic structure of *Bones* was momentarily forgotten, the overall lack of unifying narrative line, dramatic tension and development of any of the characters ultimately prevailed to make *Bones* more a dance cycle than an opera. The songs themselves, with their limited range, had mostly the appeal of a catchy, repetitive melody danced with similarly simple and repetitive movements.[58]

In my view, the unexpected impact that this work offers, the intent to engage us in a different physical way, is an important part of the potential that Deloria mentions, a mechanism for changing the structures of feeling, preparing listeners as well as actors to be part of the community building, but nonetheless part of the more disturbing histories of encounter as well. I'm inclined to think it is the way in which *BONES* shifts our sense of embodiment that, to a large extent, takes it beyond Deloria's "anomaly" category to the more socially transformative realm of the "unexpected."

Some Comparisons

As a number of indigenous writers have argued with reference to theater, I suggest that opera is a natural outgrowth of storytelling in aboriginal cultures. As anthropologist Julie Cruickshank and others have demonstrated, both songs

---

[56] Debora Lockyer Steel, "Bones: An Aboriginal Dance Opera. Eric Harvie Theatre. Banff," *Windspeaker*, 19/5 (2001), p. 14.

[57] The wide-ranging reviews illustrate what Alan Filewood has indicated about recent aboriginal playwriting and performance, that such works "challenge critical strategies by which mainly white scholars synthesize cultural histories": Alan Filewood, "Receiving Aboriginality: Tomson Highway and the Crisis of Cultural Authenticity," in Rob Appleford (ed.), *Aboriginal Drama and Theatre* (Toronto, ON: Playwrights Canada Press, 2005), pp. 37–48, p. 37). In the same anthology, Aboriginal playwright Drew Hayden Taylor observes that "lack of conflict seems to be one of the fundamental differences between European and Native drama": "Alive and Well: Native Theatre in Canada," in Rob Appleford (ed.), *Aboriginal Drama and Theatre* (Toronto, ON: Playwrights Canada Press, 2005), pp. 61–68, p. 65.

[58] Bob Clark, "Opera in Review: Canada—Banff," *Opera Canada*, 42/4 (2001), p. 21.

and stories are constantly being recast to be relevant in new contexts.[59] The two operas considered in this chapter are different in their contexts and contact zones. Both explore history, but the Sámi work is rooted in a specific time and place while *BONES* suggests a timeless cycle. The creative teams had, in both instances, the very challenging but rewarding task of working with very skilled performers but ones trained in different genre worlds. They respected the oral traditions, knowledges, and creative processes of each participant. While Fjellheim has developed ways of working across oral and written traditions, Buck and Ronceria saw their Aboriginal dance opera as the culmination of a long process of work with singers and dancers in their respective Banff programs of the late 1990s. At the same time, both works differ from much collective creative work in theater by respecting the creative vision of a composer/librettist.

Both works challenge several conventions of opera. The use of diverse languages and music styles is fundamental, reflecting, as both Sámi librettist Cecilia Persson and composer Sadie Buck described, the actual duality that their communities had endured in the colonization process. In both cases the linguistic nuances are not easily grasped by audiences, particularly non-Indigenous audiences. The slippage in translation between languages and the connotations that are directed to cultural insiders become forms of critique and agency. Language becomes a mechanism to resist the homogenization of indigenous people. The regional distinctions in vocables and joik idioms in *Skuvle Nejla* are overt in this respect. The many languages embedded in the "language of the world" simultaneously references plurality but also fundamental relatedness in *BONES*. The range of music and dance idioms distinguish character and historical circumstance.

The different forms of embodiment in each case are potentially transformative, particularly in *BONES*. Dance is not featured in *Skuvle Nejla*, but the physicality and movement styles of Allaq in particular defined who would play this part. While gender alterity has been part of opera for centuries, the blurring of other physical boundaries—with animals, with spirits, with the earth itself—is a much more radical alterity, one that reflects a fundamental tenet of traditional teaching in many Indigenous communities and societies. Repetition shifted the embodied experience of audiences, blurring the distinction between participatory and presentational performance. Not sitting back comfortably, as Buck put it, but engaged.

The fact that these works were *not* cross-cultural (Indigenous/non-Indigenous) productions is significant. The theaters where these operas were premiered were contact zones in which culturally diverse audiences arrived with pre-formed expectations about "opera," but where each production team established its own terms. Expectations were redefined for those open to the indigenous visions of these creative teams.

---

[59] Julie Cruikshank, "'Pete's Song': Establishing Meanings through Story and Song," in *The Social Life of Stories: Narrative and Knowledge in the Yukon Territory* (Lincoln: University of Nebraska Press, 1998).

While neither opera has been remounted as yet, both have had considerable spin-off effects. Fjellheim's ability to work simultaneously with traditional and classical musicians has led to unique choral and orchestral projects that make use of ability to cross oral and print knowledges. He continues to teach respect for the oral traditions of his people. *BONES* has often been cited as a success story, by scholars, journalists, and government officials. It has had an impact on the dancers, several of whom have created subsequent companies and large-scale theater works which continue the decolonizing work that the creators intended. Both works, then, have continued the process of transforming intercultural relationships well beyond the final curtain.

Do these operas "decolonize" the imagination? We might first ask whose imagination we are talking about. Privileging indigenous languages and thought structures, respecting the knowledge and learning processes of oral culture bearers, and revisionist history might all be considered projects that affirm the agency and strength of indigenous cultures. But, as mentioned earlier, decolonization is arguably needed more among populations who were historically the privileged, the colonizers. Here, I suggest that the new concepts of embodiment might be the most transformative. It is audiences whom the indigenous creators of these recent works are inviting into a new relationship.

Chapter 3

"Singing from The Margins":
Postcolonial Themes in *Voss* and
Waiting for the Barbarians

Michael Halliwell

The presence or absence of writing is possibly the most important element in the colonial situation.[1]

Opera has a long history of addressing postcolonial themes, either directly or obliquely, and this chapter investigates two recent operas that build on this tradition. Postcolonial literature is distinguished by the dialectic between center and margins, metropole and colony, and a concern with the "development or recovery of an effective identifying relationship between self and place."[2] The range of subject-matter in postcolonial fiction is vast, but recurring themes include "exile, the problem of finding and defining 'home', physical and emotional confrontations with the 'new' land and its ancient and established meanings."[3] The limits of the "old" language of the center to reflect the "new" reality is central to the understanding of the relationship between the Indigenous people and the settlers.

This chapter investigates connections between two apparently dissimilar postcolonial novels through their operatic adaptations: the Richard Meale/David Malouf opera *Voss* (1986), and the Philip Glass/Christopher Hampton opera *Waiting for the Barbarians* (2005). Strong thematic parallels link both operas which, although separated by less than twenty years, are fundamentally different in musical conception and idiom and are revealing as a reflection of their particular *Zeitgeist*.

The operas are based on important novels by Nobel laureates: *Voss* (1957) by Patrick White, and *Waiting for the Barbarians* (1980) by J.M. Coetzee, and each engages with the relationship between the colonizers and the Indigenous peoples but in strikingly different ways. Both have vividly drawn mythic elements dealing critically with the notion of "the heroic Quest," eminently suitable for operatic amplification. The central figures in each novel have much in common and, in

---

[1]   William Ashcroft, Gareth Griffiths, and Helen Tiffin, *The Empire Writes Back: Theory and Practice in Post-Colonial Literatures* (London: Routledge, 1989), p. 82.

[2]   Ibid., pp. 8–9.

[3]   Ibid., p. 27.

particular, are seen as isolated and in conflict with their respective societies: the German-speaking Voss is "doubly" foreign in the context of early English-speaking colonial Australia, while the central character of the magistrate in *Barbarians* has deliberately isolated—indeed, "exiled"—himself to the fringes of the nameless empire.

Voss is significant in its interrogation of national identity and Indigenous rights, from both the novel's perspective of the 1950s and the opera's 1980s view. Meale and Malouf engage critically with White's view of immediate postwar Australia and adumbrate issues that are perhaps tangential to the novel but become central to its adaptation. *Barbarians* obliquely, yet recognizably, deals with the situation current in the late 1970s in South Africa at the height of the apartheid era, but its operatic reworking situates it as a veiled critique of the conduct of the Iraq war, particularly the issue of torture, as well as in more universal terms as a portrait of the post-9/11 world. However, the opera retains many of the novel's larger thematic concerns dealing with the relationship between the colonizer and the colonized.

The journey of exploration in *Voss* is essentially a metaphysical one although the actual expedition to cross Australia in the 1840s upon which it is based is depicted in great physical detail, something which the opera can only do in limited, abstract terms.[4] Similarly, the journey undertaken by the magistrate in *Barbarians* is described in graphic detail, and, while this journey occupies only a fraction of the time compared with that in *Voss*, it is the culmination of the curious relationship between the magistrate and the girl and encapsulates many of the postcolonial themes of the novel.

The limitations of language and writing and the possibilities of their transcendence are vital thematic concerns of both novels and their respective operas. In their groundbreaking work on postcoloniality, *The Empire Writes Back*, Ashcroft, Griffith, and Tiffin offer some important theoretical observations on language and writing in the colonial situation. They argue that language does not "merely introduce a communicative instrument, but also involves an entirely different and intrusive (invasive) orientation to knowledge and interpretation."[5] In many ways both novels reflect a "model" for the beginnings of postcolonial discourse: "the invasion of the ordered, cyclic, and 'paradigmatic' oral world by the unpredictable and 'syntagmatic' world of the written word."[6] In novels of this kind, the "gap which opens between the experience of a place and the language available to describe it forms a classic and all-pervasive feature of post-colonial texts."[7] It is with this issue

---

[4] Rodney Edgecombe describes the expedition as "a painstakingly realistic documentation" which "coexists somewhat uneasily with half-defined, transcendental concerns that finally defy any diagrammatic exposition." Rodney Edgecombe, *Vision and Style in Patrick White: A Study of Five Novels* (Tuscaloosa: The University of Alabama Press, 1989), p. 26.

[5] Ashcroft et al., *The Empire Writes Back*, p. 82.

[6] Ibid.

[7] Ibid., p. 9.

"Singing from The Margins" 59

of language and its transcendence, as well as writing in various forms, that I wish to investigate the operatic response to the respective novels.

The situation in the opera *Voss*, where the two Aboriginal characters, Dugald and Jackie, are "mute"—as opposed to the novel, where they are given "voice"— is significantly symbolic of the "silencing and marginalizing of the post-colonial voice by the imperial centre."[8] The Indigenous Australians are marginalized by the colonists, who are themselves isolated from the metropole. In *Barbarians*, the voices of the characters are mediated through the consciousness of the first-person narration of the magistrate, and we are never allowed access to their thoughts or emotions. In its operatic reworking they are given "equal" voice but, as we shall see, it is problematic whether Glass's musical style allows access to these characters in the same way as Meale's.

The issue of writing in its various forms emerges early in *Voss*. In the colonial context, maps are a fundamental form of inscription. In the opera, when questioned about the lack of knowledge of the interior of Australia, to which Voss is about to journey, his reply is revealing: "I do not need a map. The map is in my head ... I have imagined it. Now it must be found."[9] The merchant, Mr. Bonner, who is funding the expedition, attempts to impress upon Voss the fact that there are places that have already been named on a map, but Voss's response is significant: "Names are nothing. We do not possess things by giving them a name. We must become them."[10] He goes on to illustrate the futility of attempting to "name" this land: "If I fail, Mister Bonner I will write your name and your wife's name on a paper, seal it in a bottle, and bury it beside me. So that your name will be perpetuated in Australian soil."[11]

Voss's gesture also looks forward to the fate of his letter to Laura, which is torn up by Dugald, as well as the fate of Laura's prayers for him, which Voss describes in the novel as "little pieces of white paper ... fluttering."[12] Laura in the opera says of him: "you scatter words like torn up bits of paper—but they blow away in the vastness of you."[13] It is the ironic scrutiny to which writing is subjected in both novel and opera which locate them, as well as *Waiting for the Barbarians*, within postcolonialism.

Early in the first act of the opera, Voss sings a song in German. Laura's reaction to the song, and the subsequent exchange, is ambiguous: "That was very—German, sir," she says. Voss counters with the remark: "There is no translation," to which Laura replies: "I know ... We lose the words but catch the music," representing the opera's concern with the power of the non-verbal as embodied in music compared

---

8   Ibid., p. 83.

9   Richard Meale, *Voss* (Sydney: Sounds Australian, 1987), pp. 39–41.

10   Ibid., p. 43.

11   Ibid., p. 49.

12   Patrick White, *Voss* (Harmondsworth: Penguin, 1960), p. 90.

13   Meale, *Voss*, pp. 91–2.

60   *Opera Indigene: Re/presenting First Nations and Indigenous Cultures*

with the unreliability and inefficiency of words.[14] This is underlined by Voss's remark "I try to catch your music," and is an indication that the real communication between them occurs on some level beyond the purely verbal, even when face to face.[15] In fact, the exchanges in their brief encounters are characterized by extreme awkwardness on both a verbal and physical level, although one is aware of the beginning of a deeper psychic communion. Of course, music in itself is not a discrete "language," but the fusion of words and music into operatic discourse is a metalanguage that transcends both the purely verbal and musical, more connotative than denotative. This is revealed in the highly charged first act, "Garden Scene," where their feelings for each other are first made apparent, the stage direction indicating: "They stand absorbed in one another, abstracted. The music holds them."[16]

It is with the appearance of the two Aboriginal characters, Jackie and Dugald, that the opera explicitly addresses the notion of non-verbal communication. Voss, in the novel, shows that he is receptive to this:

> Voss would have liked to talk to these creatures. Alone, he and the blacks would have communicated with one another by skin and silence, just as dust is not impenetrable and the message of sticks can be interpreted after hours of intimacy.[17]

This "translates" in the opera to Voss's comment: "Men can speak without the use of tongues."[18] The opera has the advantage over the novel in that Jackie and Dugald now perform a dance; its visual "meaning" is part of the whole choreographic structure of the opera, which is made up of the various kinds of social dances of colonial Sydney which occurred in the opening scenes and which are now contrasted with the Aboriginal dances, as well as with Le Mesurier's 'primitive' dance just prior to his death. This choreographic narrative structure is completed in the Sydney epilogue of the opera, where the children dance round Judd, the only survivor of the expedition, singing "blind-man's-buff," with its symbolic overtones. Sydney society is subjected to critical and ironic scrutiny throughout the opera—made musically apparent in the banal period dance-tunes, usually played by stage piano, which form the musical backdrop to these scenes. Voss, in the opera, remarks that men can speak "by skin and silence. Wörter haben keine Bedeutung. Nonsense. Irrsinn."[19] Transcendence of ordinary speech acts is the essence of opera: the words on their own in opera are probably the weakest link in this communication chain, and thus the mode of performance of this adaptation is

---

[14]   Ibid., pp. 86–7.
[15]   Ibid., p. 87.
[16]   Ibid., p. 102.
[17]   White, *Voss*, p. 170.
[18]   Meale, *Voss*, p. 194.
[19]   Ibid., p. 195.

in itself a telling commentary on the ironic scrutiny to which language is subjected in the novel.

The fact that the expedition members and the two Aboriginal characters do not have a "verbal" language in common does not limit their ability to communicate. There is great irony in Voss addressing Dugald in German in that it is a language which is, as it were, "twice removed" from his comprehension. Translated, Voss says, "words have no meaning," they are "irrsinn"—"madness"; this is a word that Voss utters frequently in the opera when under physical or psychological stress, suggestive of his own, frequently precarious, mental state. His path to sanity is not through verbal communication but through his supra-verbal psychic exchanges with Laura. As if to emphasize this, Laura, in her scene with a heavily pregnant Rose, has an extended wordless musical vocalise as she thinks about Voss. It is the plangency and visceral impact of the sound of the human voice, not its verbal signification, that is the means of communication.[20]

In Act II, the "Sydney" musical discourse and that of the "outback" merge to create a kind of metalanguage capable of giving meaning to the relationship between Voss and Laura and, indirectly, to the "new" country that must be created. The Sydney music is characterized by dance-tunes accompanied by piano and strings based on actual contemporary music that Meale has skillfully incorporated into the larger sonic world of his opera. However, when the outback discourse intrudes, the full range of orchestral color frequently overwhelms this "thin" discourse. This is emblematic of a postcolonial desire to establish indigeneity in musical terms.[21]

A duet between Voss and Laura, during which Voss writes a letter to her, is interrupted by Voss calling Dugald: "Dugald, hör wohl zu. Tomorrow you will leave for Jildra. Verstanden? I write paper. I give letter. Verstanden?"[22] Voss persists in speaking to Dugald and Jackie in pidgin German, making verbal communication almost farcical in this situation. What now occurs, in a mime sequence, is described in the stage directions: "During the following duet [Dugald] begins to dance as if in a trance. He casts off his frock coat, he opens the bag he carries and takes out the letters. Slowly he tears them up and scatters them."[23] His actions reflect Laura's words during this duet: "You scatter words like torn up bits of paper and they blow away in the vastness of you."[24] Dugald's gesture is probably the most powerful reference in the opera to the futility, particularly in regard to written language, of achieving true communication. Rather, it is through gesture that Jackie and Dugald

---

[20] Michelle Duncan remarks of the capacity of the voice to participate in the "creation, disruption or dissolution of registers of meaning independent of linguistic signification." Michelle Duncan, "The Operatic Scandal of the Singing Body: Voice, Presence, Performativity," *Cambridge Opera Journal*, 16/3 (2004), p. 284.

[21] See Ashcroft et al., *The Empire Writes Back*, p. 135.

[22] Meale, *Voss*, p. 221.

[23] Ibid., p. 222.

[24] Ibid., pp. 220–21.

communicate, and their dances assume a portentous ritualistic quality which can be seen in relation to the larger structural pattern of ceremonial movement. Dugald's dance is part of the metalanguage of the opera and can perhaps be interpreted in terms of the Aboriginal's "unique conception of textuality" wherein the "land itself is constituted as a text of the Dreaming."[25] In essence, what Meale and Malouf achieve is the acknowledgment of the silencing of the Indigenous peoples, both politically and, in this case, musically.

The Epilogue sees the drawing together of many of these themes. A group of children is playing "blind man's buff"—the game is part of the larger ritual pattern of dances—and then the familiar stage piano is heard playing its recurring melody which evolves from the children's game. It is as if the intrusion once more of the "Sydney" discourse suggests that nothing has really changed in this society: its values are still the same even though it is twenty years later. Echoing the children, this society is still "blind" to the country in which they live—they have not yet awakened to its possibilities and remain huddled on the periphery— "fringe-dwellers."

Laura intimates that she would rather be alone: "I shall sit here. I have never learned the language."[26] Laura has not bothered to learn the superficial language of society, which is epitomized by the humdrum rhythm and melody of the waltz in the piano as well as by the fact that Laura's words do not seem to fit comfortably into the 3/4 rhythms of the dancers. Laura remarks that Voss "has entered the history books. They will speak of his place in history. He is safe, now he is dead." He has been "hung with garlands of newspaper prose."[27] Laura's brief confrontation with Judd is significant in terms of the theme of inscription. Judd, who appears confused and possibly even mad, falsely claims that he witnessed Voss's death: "He left his mark on the country. He was cutting his initials on the trees. He is still there in the heart of the country and always will be."[28] This is a false claim in terms of fact but contains an essential truth.

The statue of Voss dominates this final picture, and this seems to realign the focus on Voss and Laura, but Laura's words direct the attention away from Voss toward Australia.[29] She observes that the response of future generations to the land will vary; some will "make music of it."[30] Meale and Malouf here make a final

---

[25]   Ibid., p. 144.

[26]   Ibid., p. 332.

[27]   Ibid., pp. 343–4.

[28]   Ibid., pp. 346–7.

[29]   The mythification of Voss in the novel is explained by William Walsh, who considers that "Voss, and a central truth about, or experience of, Australia itself have become one. Australia is almost another character in the novel, certainly an impressive and influential force ... . Australia is the sole opponent worthy of Voss's will. The will to know Australia is the initiating impulse of the novel." William Walsh, *Patrick White: Voss* (London: Edward Arnold, 1976), p. 38.

[30]   Meale, *Voss*, p. 353.

gesture to the power of music as a means of "true" communication. Laura sings that Voss's legend "will be written in the air, in the sand, in thorns, in stones," and as the music fades (to a "simple" open E♭ chord after much complex chromaticism) she indicates that "what we do not know, the air will tell us."[31] The ending of the opera points beyond the concerns of Laura and Voss and attempts to offer insights into what the term "Australia" actually means. The main insight is perhaps that there is no single meaning, and that the term signifies hybridity. The ending reasserts the primary focus of the opera on the psychological investigation of the relationship between Voss and Laura as well as their relationship with "Australia". This, as Laura suggests, is written in the air: a hybrid combination of language, writing and music.

To someone cognizant with the political and social conditions in South Africa in the 1970s, much of J.M. Coetzee's novel *Waiting for the Barbarians* will have an uncomfortably familiar feel to it. Many of the enigmatic Colonel Joll's comments on the necessities of "protecting" the state could have come from the official mouthpieces of the media apparatus of the National Party government of the time. The torture that was never officially admitted but that all knew was taking place is reflected in the novel, and the death of the barbarian girl's father has parallels with the deaths of Steve Biko and many lesser-known political activists. The ominous threat that the barbarians pose had its parallels with the all-pervasive "communist threat" that was often advanced for the gradual dismantling of the legal system as well as increasingly restrictive media and other laws.

It is not surprising that this novel attracted Philip Glass, particularly after September 11, 2001, and the United States of America's controversial response to the threat of terrorism. However, Glass has stated on several occasions that he contacted Coetzee to see whether he was willing for an adaptation to occur in 1991, and actually began preliminary work at that time. The power of the novel has continued to garner critical acclaim (including a film currently in production), and it is clear that Glass did not feel the need for a particular political situation to be current in order to adapt the novel into an opera.[32]

The opera premiered in Erfurt, Germany, in September 2005, and most critics and audiences immediately recognized the opera's thematic links with the USA's role in Iraq, and in the prominent theme of torture, which is present in both novel and opera, connections with the notorious Iraqi prison Abu Ghraib were inevitably made. It can be argued that both novel and opera can be "read" in this way without

---

[31]   Ibid., p. 358.

[32]   Glass, in a brief foreword to the recording of the opera, states: "I'd begun to do this kind of social/political opera in 1979 with *Satyagraha* ... . To reduce the opera to a single historical circumstance or a particular political regime misses the point. That the opera can become an occasion for dialogue about political crisis illustrates the power of art to turn our attention toward the human dimension of history." Philip Glass, "Note from the Composer," *Waiting for the Barbarians* (New York: Orange Mountain Music, 2008), p. 4.

64 *Opera Indigene: Re/presenting First Nations and Indigenous Cultures*

diminishing their power. However, it is also possible to draw from both novel and opera strong thematic elements in which broader postcolonial themes can be discerned.

The first-person narrative mode of the novel—"homodiegetic simultaneous present"—is significant for its operatic transformation.[33] This narrative mode, with its sense of immediacy and open-endedness, does not allow the barbarian peoples their own "voice," but only allows them a form of heavily mediated "communication." Of course, the novel is concerned with "interpretation" of the "other" as well as the self—an exploration of alterity—and this is bound up with the whole notion of language and writing.[34] Naturally, this narrative mode has implications for any dramatization of the text as the task of adaptation is seemingly made "easier," with the narrative mode suggesting the immediacy of drama.

This lack of giving voice to the "other," in the form of either speech or writing, is countered somewhat in the opera where an old man and the girl are given sung speech which essentially is no "different" from the other characters. This is the most striking form of undercutting of the novel's narrative mode where the immediacy of the human voice—and, indeed, the trained operatic voice—has a visceral impact far in excess of the mediated "voices" in the novel. This reflects the whole nature of musical adaptation, where much more than the speech of a particular character can be represented. Definition of character can be achieved by the shape of the vocal line itself, and emotional states can be conveyed by rhythmic and pitch variations as well as the actual timbre and color of the voice.

However, this is problematic in Glass's music, where by its very nature musical characterization takes a very different form when compared to Meale's work. Here we have music where repetitive musical figures underscore what seems at time an almost "detached" vocal line, which invariably does not appear to have

---

[33] This is a narrative strategy, James Phelan argues, which places the reader in "a very different relationship to the magistrate and to the events of the narrative than would any kind of retrospective account. The strategy takes teleology away from the magistrate's narrative acts: since he does not know how events will turn out, he cannot be shaping the narrative according to his knowledge of the end. Consequently, we cannot read with our usual tacit assumptions that the narrator, however unselfconscious, has some direction in mind for his tale." James Phelan, "Present Tense Narration, Mimesis, the Narrative Norm, and the Positioning of the Reader in *Waiting for the Barbarians*," in *Understanding Narrative*, ed. James Phelan and Peter J. Rabinowitz (Columbus: Ohio State University Press, 1994), p. 223.

[34] Michael Valdez Moses observes that "In general, the Empire's interrogation of barbarian prisoners—whether fisherfolk or nomad—requires the skills of interpreters whose command of the barbarian tongue is suspect at best. While limited linguistic exchange does take place across the borders of Empire, and although individual acts of imperfect translation occur, the Empire directs its efforts first and foremost towards writing and reading its *own* script. Accordingly, the barbarian *Other* generally appears in the novel as a blank slip onto which the Empire engraves itself; that is, the Empire gives itself form by writing on its subjects." Michael Valdez Moses, "The Mark of Empire: Writing, History, and Torture in Coetzee's *Waiting for the Barbarians*," *The Kenyon Review*, 15/1 (Winter, 1993), p. 120.

much connection to the harmonic or rhythmic orchestral palette that supports it. It does, however, at times reveal an angularity and rhythmic shape that reflects the emotional and physical "action." What Glass achieves in his work is a broad sense of character in a particular context rather than a particular musical distinctiveness of character. This effects a stylized performance mode while emphasizing the continual tension between the "realistic" situations being portrayed and the attempt at idiomatic and "natural" cadences in the vocal line.

Obviously, the question arises whether the minimalist idiom can convey the range of psychological subjectivity that more "mainstream" opera sees as its raison d'être.[35]

Arved Ashby notes that Glass's music alters the listener's

> chronological sense by engineering an entirely new relationship between foreground event and background ... Glass' minimalism effects a new, disproportionate distance between quickened foreground activity and slower background motion: the fast (the figuration prolonging the harmony) becomes faster, the slow (the harmonic rhythm itself, the rate of change) slower.[36]

It has been observed that as Glass moved from the non-linear, often circular structures of his early stage works to more literary-based ones, his focus on the words has become more acute. Glass's operatic structures have shown an increasing tendency to narrative linearity in his more recent works, particularly as he has used fiction as the basis for many of his new operas even as he moved toward "mainstream" opera production techniques and, indeed, into traditional opera theaters. However, understanding character through the music that surrounds them is not the primary focus as it is, for example, in Meale's opera, which reveals the diegetic use of the orchestration for characters' events and inner lives. Of course, Meale emerges directly out of the modernist aesthetic even though there is much use of tonality in his opera. Carolyn Abbate has memorably described minimalism as music with "no past tense," and the devices of harmonic development and transformation—as well as leitmotivic techniques common in opera since the early part of the nineteenth century—have little place in these operas.[37] Glass has observed that "it is surely no coincidence that it was at the moment that I was

---

[35] Arved Ashby describes it as "distinguished by repetition, and repetition is innately poetic in that it disrupts signification and literal meaning; it moves music from a system of signs to a world of symbols. For what is each individual statement of a repeated musical figure: an authentic expression of the moment or a simple replication of that which was just heard, hiding behind the fact of repetition?" Arved Ashby, "Minimalist Opera," *Cambridge Companion to Twentieth-Century Opera*, ed. Mervyn Cooke (Cambridge: Cambridge University Press, 2005), pp. 244–66, pp. 246–7.

[36] Ibid., p. 249.

[37] Carolyn Abbate, *Unsung Voices: Opera and Musical Narrative in the Nineteenth Century* (Princeton, NJ: Princeton University Press, 1991), p. 52. However, critics have

66   *Opera Indigene: Re/presenting First Nations and Indigenous Cultures*

embarking upon a major shift in my music to large-scale theater works that I began to develop a new, more expressive language for myself."[38]

Another way of approaching Glass's operas is through viewing them as employing a quasi-Brechtian approach to theatrical representation. Glass is quoted as saying that from his early work in the theater he was "encouraged to leave what I call a 'space' between the image and the music. In fact, it is precisely that space which is required so that members of the audience have the necessary perspective or distance to create their own individual meanings."[39]

Glass's music theater works have a "tension" between the abstract nature of the music, which is in constant conflict with the visual, and the visceral aspects of the performers' voices and bodies. There is a sense of abstraction regarding what is occurring on stage, while at the same time there is a striving for empathy with the characters: it combines a distancing allegorical element with the immediacy of dramatic representation. Glass regarded realism as "a matter of faithfulness towards dreams as the true, perhaps post-Freudian reality."[40] Music's essential capacity to enhance character also lends itself to the move away from the allegorical mode into something more immediate and direct.

As with White and Meale's *Voss*, the nature of language and writing assumes a great prominence in both Coetzee's novel and Glass's adaptation. The first-person narrator of the novel, the magistrate, meditates on the link between writing and civilization explicitly at one point:

> Do I really look forward to the triumph of the barbarian way: intellectual torpor, slovenliness, tolerance of disease and death? If we were to disappear would the barbarians spend their afternoons excavating our ruins? Would they preserve our census rolls and our grain-merchants' ledgers in glass cases, or devote themselves to deciphering the script of our love letters? Is my indignation at the course that the Empire takes anything more than the peevishness of an old man who does not want the ease of his last years on the frontier to be disturbed?[41]

It is a Hegelian notion that the distinction between civilization and barbarism lies in writing, and this is given thematic prominence in the novel as exemplified in the attitude of the magistrate.[42] It is not only writing that is examined, but also the

---

argued that these later works have shown a composer attempting to speak through his characters, very much in the standard operatic tradition.

[38]   Quoted in Ashby, "Minimalist Opera," p. 256.

[39]   Quoted in Ashby, "Minimalist Opera," p. 254.

[40]   Ibid.

[41]   J.M. Coetzee, *Waiting for the Barbarians* (Johannesburg: Ravan Press, 1981), p. 52.

[42]   What Moses argues is that the novel suggests "that writing—and we may include legal codes and historical narratives under this rubric—is necessarily implicated in and complicit with the worst excesses of Empire. Most distressingly, Coetzee renders writing

"Singing from The Margins"

concept of language's capacity to articulate thought. At one point in the opera, the magistrate meditates:

> I've often thought
> What few ideas we put into words
> Are never clearly expressed
> And what we cannot clearly express
> We are condemned to live through.[43]

In the novel, the magistrate has excavated some ruins close to the town, where he has found "a cache of wooden slips on which are painted characters in a script I have not seen the like of."[44] These slips are central to several confrontations between the magistrate and Colonel Joll in the novel, which are dramatized in two extended scenes in the opera.

The main confrontation concerning these wooden slips occurs after the magistrate's journey to return the girl to her people. He has been imprisoned and has been further humiliated after his attempted intervention to prevent the public torture of prisoners in the town square. He is summoned to Joll and is requested to explain the meaning of the script on the slips. Joll describes them as being coded messages passed between the barbarians, while the magistrate counters by seemingly interpreting them:

> In this one he sends greetings to his daughter
> He hopes the lambing season has been good
> He hopes to see her soon and sends his love.
> *(He looks at another slip; Mandel has his pencil poised over a notebook, not quite sure whether to take note)*
> Here he tells her his son has been arrested
> Taken away by the soldiers
> He searched for days and found him in a barracks
> Wrapped in a winding-sheet
> His ankles broken and his eyes torn out.
> *(Mandel puts down his pencil and half-rises to his feet; but Joll gestures for him to sit down again; meanwhile, the Magistrate has reached for a third slip)*
> This one is interesting
> A single symbol
> The barbarian word for "war"
> But if you hold it on its side...

(inscription and interpretation) as a form of torture." Moses, "The Mark of Empire," p. 120.

[43] Philip Glass, *Waiting for the Barbarians* (New York: Dunvagen Music Publishing, 2005), p. 150.

[44] Coetzee, *Barbarians*, p. 15.

(He does so)
It means justice.
(He puts the slip down and stares truculently at Joll)[45]

What he has done is to deliberately taunt Joll with his knowledge of the events that had previously occurred. The insult is compounded by the fact that he is suggesting that he is actually "reading" the slips when he had previously informed Joll that no one has been able to decipher the script. This causes a furious reaction from Joll and leads to the accusation that the magistrate is aiding the enemy, to which he violently retorts: "You are the enemy … . History will not forgive you!" Joll's reply is chilling in its implications both for the magistrate and for everyone else: "There is no history / Not out here on the dusty fringe of Empire."[46] Without a written record, in the view from the metropole, there can be no history.

The theme of language again emerges prominently in the scene of the magistrate's public torture, where he is made to "bellow" and "roar."[47] In the opera the chorus is prominent in this scene, and language as a trope is implicit in their singing as they fragment the word "barbarians" into a single syllabic chant, which then becomes transformed into the word "enemy." As the magistrate is tortured, and to the syllabic chanting of the chorus, an officer comments: "That's the barbarian language! He's calling his barbarian friends!"[48]

Actual inscription such as that on the wooden slips and the letter written by the magistrate is not the only form of "writing" that is subjected to critical scrutiny in the novel and the opera. One of the most horrific instances occurs when the prisoners brought back by Joll's expedition are paraded and tortured in front of the townsfolk. The stage directions describe it as follows:

> As [the guard] leads the Magistrate across the courtyard and through the barracks gate into the main square, the first four Prisoners have been moved into the center of the square. As they turn, it becomes clear that the word "Enemy" has somehow been etched on their backs. They are made to kneel in front of a kind of low hitching post, to which they are secured by a rope which passes in and out of the loops of wire through their cheeks and hands.[49]

---

[45] Glass, *Barbarians*, pp. 221–3.

[46] Ibid., pp. 230–31.

[47] Moses observes that it is this "language that connects the civilized magistrate with the barbarian victims of the Third bureau [which] proves indistinguishable from the subhuman roar of a tortured animal body. The unmediated language and prehistorical language of men and beasts naturally contains no discrete or articulate words; in such a tongue the name of justice cannot be spoken." Moses, "The Mark of Empire," p. 127.

[48] Glass, *Barbarians*, pp. 248–9.

[49] Ibid., p. 208.

"Singing from The Margins" 69

These prisoners are beaten until the word "Enemy" becomes illegible. Here one sees bodily mutilation and torture overtly presented as a form of inscription as part of the trope of erasure.[50]

However, perhaps the most interesting and subtle use of writing as a trope is found in the relationship between the magistrate and the barbarian girl. Coetzee refuses to "name" her—indeed, he does not name the magistrate either—thus highlighting the alterity of the character: she remains an object rather than becoming any depiction of a subjective consciousness. The Magistrate's ritualized washing of her feet and body is first made plain in the novel in his comment as he looks at the results of torture to her eyes: "It has been growing more and more clear to me that until the marks on this girl's body are deciphered and understood I cannot let go of her."[51]

These marks have evident thematic links to the wooden slips and hold the same mixture of fascination and frustration for the magistrate. A prominent trope in the novel and opera is the erasure of features as one would erase writing. In the novel, he muses: "So I begin to face the truth of what I am trying to do: to obliterate the girl. I realize that if I took a pencil to sketch her face I would not know where to start. Is she truly so featureless?"[52] In the dreams of the magistrate, the girl often appears to him with a blank, featureless face. This is expanded in the opera in the series of "Dreamscapes." Dreams are as central to this opera as they are in *Voss*: another strong link between these two works. Dreams, in both operas, are seen as the manifestation of a form of communication which "erases" both the need for writing and, indeed, language itself. The magistrate makes no effort to learn the girl's language, and comments in the novel that "in the makeshift language we share there are no nuances."[53] This has echoes of Voss's almost comic attempts to communicate with the Indigenous characters in that novel.

Earlier, during their journey in the novel, the magistrate reflected on his obsession with the marks on her body:

> [I]t has not escaped me that in bed in the dark the marks her torturers have left upon her, the twisted feet, the half-blind eyes, are easily forgotten. Is it then the case that it is the whole woman I want, that my pleasure in her is spoiled until these marks on her are erased and she is restored to herself; or is it the case (I am not stupid, let me say these things) that it is the marks on her which drew me to her but which, to my disappointment, I find do not go deep enough? Too much or too little: is it she I want or the traces of a history her body bears?[54]

---

[50]   Moses describes it as "a culminating instance" of a "disturbing congruence of writing, torture, and the execution of the law." Moses, "The Mark of Empire," p. 121.

[51]   Coetzee, *Barbarians*, p. 31.

[52]   Ibid., p. 47.

[53]   Ibid., p. 40.

[54]   Ibid., p. 54.

70 *Opera Indigene: Re/presenting First Nations and Indigenous Cultures*

Is this a reflection of his guilt as a sense of complicity in her torture? These marks exert a powerful fascination for the magistrate as they seem emblematic of a hidden story which he cannot penetrate, just as he cannot penetrate the mysteries of the text on the wooden slips. His actual lack of penetration during their "sexual" encounters suggests his lack of desire for possession: in a sense he would like to restore wholeness to what has been damaged.[55] Writing and sexual activity are directly linked in the novel where the magistrate, before leaving on the journey, contemplates writing some kind of "testament" or "history" of his time in the town. After three days of fruitless attempts to compose it, he meditates: "It seems appropriate that a man who does not know what to do with the woman in his bed should not know what to write."[56] The intense physical, though sexless, relationship between the magistrate and the girl is vividly depicted in the opera and conveyed in sometimes very striking music. However, the ambiguities of the magistrate's changing attitudes to the girl, which form such a crucial part of the novel, are not depicted to nearly the same extent in the opera. We are not offered anything near the same kind of access to his "tortured" psyche. It could be argued that this is not Glass's intention, but the musical idiom by its very nature does not allow this to anywhere near the same extent as is evident in *Voss*.[57]

Both the magistrate and Joll are complicit in the damage that the girl has suffered; in a sense they have both left the "writing" of the colonizers on her body. Her whole body has become a history, a map, of empire. Just as White's novel does in a very different context so too does this novel emphasize alterity through the magistrate's fetishization of her body rather than through any attempt to learn her language. However, when the magistrate himself is subjected to extreme physical torture, he reaches a sense of common ground with the barbarians through the discovery of a common humanity when, in his agony, he is described as speaking the language of the barbarians as he is tortured.

Much as in *Voss*, where the image rather than any ambiguous written history of Voss dominates the final scene of the opera, in the novel the magistrate meditates

---

[55] Brian W. Shaffer suggests that "the girl is ultimately indecipherable to the magistrate—that she remains stubbornly unreadable and obscure, 'opaque' and 'impermeable', 'blank' and 'incomplete'—is beyond question. Just as the 'sand drifts back', frustrating his attempts at excavation, just as the wooden slips of script from the former civilization remain stubbornly unreadable, so the girl yields little of her foreign meaning to him." Brian W. Shaffer, *Reading the Novel in English: 1950–2000* (Oxford: Blackwell Publishing, 2006), pp. 136–7. Rosemary Jolly remarks that both Joll and the magistrate "turn the girl into a text from which they believe the truth will originate." Rosemary Jane Jolly, *Colonization, Violence, and Narration in White South African Writing: André Brink, Breytenbach, and J.M. Coetzee* (Athens: Ohio University Press, 1996), pp. 127–8.

[56] Coetzee, *Barbarians*, p. 58.

[57] The kind of access to the psyche of the main characters in *Tristan und Isolde* which we gain through the complexity of Wagner's music, for example, is not possible in Glass's aesthetic.

"Singing from The Margins" 71

on the futility of attempting a written account of what has happened during the previous year. He has "wanted to live outside the history that Empire imposes on its subjects," but although having lived through "an eventful year" he understands "no more of it than a babe in arms. Of all the people of the town he is the one 'least fitted to write a memorial'."[58]

Similar to *Voss*, the ending of this opera is equivocal. The soldiers and bureaucrats from the Third Bureau have gone and the town returns to a sense of normality. When the magistrate had instructed Joll on the importance of how to find evidence of previous civilizations, he commented that it is best to "simply dig at random," but qualified this with the observation that "the air is full of sighs and cries."[59] In a strong echo of Laura's comments at the end of *Voss*, he remarked: "if you listen carefully, with a sympathetic ear, you can hear them echoing forever."[60] Like Voss, the magistrate's journey is never finished. He sings: "I am a man travelling down a road which may lead nowhere. A man lost in a cruel and stupid dream. But still I keep walking ... walking ..."[61] The ending of the opera is the combination of dream and reality, and the open-endedness of the music complements the dramatic situation.

In answer to the question "What is opera?," Hans Keller replied: "It all depends on the next one, not the last one."[62] Both these operas point the way toward possible future directions for the art form. Particularly through their exploration of alterity embodied in the tropes of language and writing, both works contribute in no small way to the interesting operatic sub-genre that is postcolonial opera.

---

[58] Coetzee, *Barbarians*, pp. 154–5.
[59] Ibid., p. 112.
[60] Ibid.
[61] Glass, *Barbarians*, pp. 307–308.
[62] Quoted in Ashby, "Minimalist Opera," p. 264.

Chapter 4
Performativity, Mimesis, and Indigenous Opera

Pamela Karantonis

This is so operatic.
(Louis Nowra, *Radiance*)

Introduction

This chapter begins with the possibility that opera scholars and anthropologists have become collaborators. Those drawn to view, hear, compose, perform in, and study opera often do so for all its powers of imagination and expression—musically, mythically, linguistically, theatrically—while the study of the functions, customs, and belief systems of diverse peoples have entered into something of a crisis in recent decades. As this collection appears within a series devoted to interdisciplinary explorations of opera, I hope here to disclose my own misgivings about the relationship of my discipline of performance studies to opera analysis. To account very briefly for the discipline's history, in the latter half of the twentieth century a branch of the discipline of anthropology was renamed "cultural studies," but not before two eminent North American scholars—Richard Schechner and Victor Turner—decided that there was a productive category to emerge from their dialogue between theater and anthropology (to paraphrase one of Schechner's works).[1] The 1980s offspring of that dialogue is now called "performance studies." As the name suggests, the remit in discussing any aspect of "performance" is broad, but the methodology still belongs to the ethnographic fieldwork designed to analyze ritual, and can borrow from associated disciplines such as sociology and psychology. Terms such as "performativity" and "agency" began to relate both to the ceremonial and symbolic qualities of ritual and to the socio-political and psychological transformation possible for individuals and communities through a wide range of performing arts. So when this approach is added to the harsh social inequalities to emerge from colonial histories, in the form of postcolonialism, theater scholars and musicologists alike have a complexity of choice in their

---

[1] See Victor Turner, *Drama, Fields and Metaphors: Symbolic Action in Human Society* (Ithaca, NY: Cornell University Press, 1976) and Richard Schechner, *Between Theater and Anthropology* (Philadelphia: University of Pennsylvania Press, 1985).

74 *Opera Indigene: Re/presenting First Nations and Indigenous Cultures*

methods for discussing this very specific topic of opera and Indigenous cultures. I want you, the reader, to be guided through the material in this chapter by a fan of the Western operatic canon, but also by an Australian whose voice is from a Greek-speaking background. I am sympathetic to the postcolonial condition of having origins that are off-center in relation to the Anglophone empire along the burdensome "Greekness" of the concept of mimesis—which, in Platonic terms, means both to "imitate" and to "represent"—something at the very heart of musical and dramatic characterization in opera.

Only recently have audiences and scholars appreciated how much Indigenous cultures can theorize mimesis in terms that recognize the postcolonial condition, in terms that break down an "us and them" ethnographic version of cultural difference. This is most evident in the work of Michael Taussig in the USA and Marcia Langton in Australia (whose scholarship on Australian Aboriginal mimesis in contemporary media is most relevant to this chapter).[2] So while the content of this chapter will survey some key operas composed by Australians and New Zealanders since the early twentieth century, it will argue in relation to these works that the staging of "character" could no longer ignore the reality of being Aboriginal or Māori in these societies. While there will be the inevitable theoretical tangents, as "acting" in opera begins to unravel, by the end of this chapter I hope you might conclude, along with me, that as Indigenous communities engage with and develop cultural practice through opera (even as Western definitions of opera are destabilized in the process), these moments both transform opera as a genre and extend cultural expression for those cultures.

Theoretical Frames

In looking at the theories of dramatic representation of Indigenous peoples in opera, I am advocating for a revised history of mimesis. Michael Taussig, in his work *Mimesis and Alterity: A Particular History of the Senses*, describes it as a human "faculty" that is historically contingent: "if it is a faculty, it is also a history and just as histories enter into the functioning of the mimetic faculty, so the mimetic faculty enters into those histories."[3] That history, for Taussig, is the Western colonial enterprise. He points to the "othering" of the parodic and subversive mimetic forms used by Indigenous cultures, particularly Australia's Aboriginal nations, which historically has led to the discursive "primitivization of mimesis." This includes Charles Darwin's 1896 account of a Western Australian "corrobery or native dance." Taussig places this firmly within the colonial project:

---

[2]   Marcia Langton, *Well I Heard it on the Radio and I Saw it on the Television: An Essay for the Australian Film Commission on the Politics and Aesthetics of Filmmaking by and about Aboriginal People and Things* (Sydney: Australian Film Commission, 1993).

[3]   Michael Taussig, *Mimesis and Alterity: A Particular History of the Senses* (New York: Routledge, 1993), pp. xiii–xiv.

"mimesis is an essential component of socialization and discipline, and in our era of world history, in which colonialism has played a role, mimesis is a piece of primitivism."[4]

Although Taussig is at pains to discern the "controlled" mimesis of imperial aesthetic forms (which always speak from the superiority of empire), from the politically resistant reverse ethnography of the colonized, he makes a strong case for mimesis as one of the instruments of empire. This bind of representation still persists in postcolonial discourses, as Indigenous scholar Marcia Langton argued in relation to late twentieth-century film aesthetics: "Increasingly, non-Aboriginal people want to make personal rehabilitative statements about the Aboriginal 'problem' and to consume and reconsume the 'primitive'."[5]

So I would advocate returning to a model of mimesis that recognizes both aspects of the word—*imitation* and *representation*—with a recognition that an *imitation* of Indigenous peoples by non-indigenous performers is in no longer an acceptable *representation* of people from those cultures. Rather, they reveal the power operating within the colonial culture. The examples I show in this chapter suggest a shift from colonial imitation to a more empowered model of Indigenous performers re/presenting their own stories, through the material fact of their presence on the operatic stage. I would finally like to link the word *representation* to a cogent term borrowed from socio-linguistics via performance studies: *performativity*. I mean this in the sense coined by J.L. Austin, who saw "speech-acts" as immanently powerful and transformative because of their necessary association with status-changing actions.[6] This would mean by the very act of singing, speaking, and participating in opera, an Aboriginal person's presence is performative, in the broadest cultural sense. To paraphrase Austin, we have the possibility to *do something* with opera—it is not just singing something.

Another significant term is *authenticity*. What makes a performance authentic in its expression of Indigenous identity and experience? This is argued by the postcolonial musicologists in relation to the works in this chapter, where judgments are made about the optimum combination of Indigenous participation, truth in storytelling, and artistic integrity in the musical and dramatic languages.

---

[4]   Ibid., p. 216.

[5]   Langton, *Well I Heard it on the Radio*, p. 10.

[6]   According to J.L. Austin's 1955 Harvard University lecture *How to Do Things with Words*, "The name is derived, of course, from 'perform', the usual verb with the noun 'action': it indicates that the issuing of the utterance is the performing of an action – it is not normally thought of just saying something." Many of these categories of actions are either "contractual," "declaratory" or "operative" in a juridico-political sense. J.L. Austin, *How to Do Things with Words: The William James Lectures delivered at Harvard University in 1955* (Oxford: Clarendon Press, 1972), pp. 5–6.

76   *Opera Indigene: Re/presenting First Nations and Indigenous Cultures*

From Melodrama to the Method

For the purposes of looking at relevant works in the twentieth century, the starting point for the postcolonial legacy is not the escapist European repertoire that was mounted on the colonial stages of Melbourne and Wellington or in gold-rush towns of Ballarat or Otago, but in the late nineteenth-century stereotype of the "stage-black" on the British stage. While history may judge these characterizations as politically oppressive and being in bad taste, they raise some interesting issues as to why and how Aboriginality could be represented at the center of Empire, but not on "home ground." Ian Henderson's groundbreaking study of an 1865 re-adaptation of Charles Reade's stage melodrama *It's Never too Late to Mend* (1865), which was performed throughout the United Kingdom, features an extended discussion of "the Aboriginal Australian" character Jacky-Kalingaloonga.[7] The scholarship reveals that Reade defended his invention of the Aboriginal character as partly "realistic" for its connection to non-fiction accounts and news reports from the gold-rush fields of southern Australia. The rest, Henderson argues, capitulates to Victorian melodrama's political ideology of empire's "civilizing project," which would be unacceptable in stagings of Aboriginal identities today. His remaining scholarship on the staged productions of Reade's work from the period 1853–1865 reveals a veritable wasp's nest of mimetic violence that mirrored real colonial massacres of history. Aboriginal characters, both in Reade's *Gold!* (1853) and *It's Never too Late to Mend*, are rendered as both comic and savage, without the psychological complexity of earlier staged "subalterns," such as Shakespeare's Caliban; instead collapsing into the demonized "other" or "commedia" *buffo* of Mozart's Monostatos, among enchanted and comical animals, which are subdued by colonial power.[8] The character is thus unable "to mend," as suggested by Reade's characterization because of his Aboriginal identity and natural resistance to self-mastery: "Jacky-Kalingaloonga's slippage in and out of blood-lust demonstrates a subjection to, rather than a mastery of, an 'other' self … . The author [Reade] suggests we jot down Jacky-Kalingaloonga's whole race as suicidal. Aboriginality will die at its own (lack of) hand."[9] Such displays are arguably an aesthetic and ideological form of mitigating the culpability of the British involvement in the colonial massacres that took place, to reassure white Victorian audiences of the irreconcilable differences between the two cultures.[10] Significantly, the casting of

---

[7]   Ian Henderson, "Jacky-Kalingaloonga: Aboriginality, Audience Reception and Charles Reade's *It Is Never Too Late to Mend* (1865)," *Theatre Research International*, 29/2 (July 2004), p. 97.

[8]   The kangaroo "battle scene" in Reade's *Gold!* is an unrealistically scripted pantomime in which flying kangaroos add light relief to a battle scene that is "dangerously reminiscent of an historic massacre." Ibid., p. 102.

[9]   Ibid., p. 104.

[10]   Bruce Elder, *Blood on the Wattle*. By the year of Reade's stage success, 1865, and since the British invasion of 1788, the massacring of Aboriginal peoples throughout

Performativity, Mimesis, and Indigenous Opera 77

a white actor Stanislaus Calhaem in black-face is the colonial prerogative—that real political power is sublimated through this imaginary, tragic-comic stereotype, with which actual Indigenous people have no real collaboration. It is due to the shallow nature of the stereotype that this model of imitation and representation has failed to endure. This touches upon our theoretical issue of the *representation* of Indigenous peoples in opera where "blackness" in this specific instance is a make-up color, irrelevant to socio-political realities and colonial histories.[11]

So let us return to that point in history and place in empire when these issues began to grow in relevance in Australia—from the 1930s onwards. Due to the influence of theatrical and cinematic characterization, "authenticity" became a desirable feature of characterization in music theater at this time. While it is some leap from musicals to opera (a debate larger than the remit of this discussion), there is a relevance in the theatrical approaches of "progressive" popular forms which later was mirrored in high art genres. For instance, in 1933 Melbourne, Frank Thring's Efftee Productions staged the musicals *Collitt's Inn* and *The Highwayman*. The first appropriated an Aboriginal song from the Illawarra region and the second featured an Indigenous man from the Yarra River "who was to play a black tracker in the show" and was cast by auditioning with a song his mother taught him. Neither the musical material nor the live performer was credited or acknowledged in either piece.[12] Clearly the participation of the Indigenous performer was an early attempt at "authenticity" on the part of producers, although the unnamed man remains uncredited.

Then there was the shift from authenticity (via tokenistic efforts to consult Indigenous people and practices) to essentialism (an attempt to abstract and contain certain sounds and images) in art music that influenced new operatic writing in Australia. From 1940 to 1960, there was a musical experiment that mirrored an earlier literary movement, known as *Jindyworobakism*, which was, according to a 1938 manifesto: "to free Australian art from whatever alien influences trammel

---

Australia by colonials through indiscriminate shootings alone (as opposed to the poisoning of food supplies) numbered close to a conservative figure of 3,000 documented deaths. By the early twentieth century, estimates suggest, that figure was more likely to have reached into the tens of thousands. Bruce Elder, *Blood on the Wattle: Massacres and Maltreatment of Aboriginal Australians Since 1788* (Sydney: New Holland, 1998), p. vi.

[11] The meaning of "agency" here is in the Gramscian political sense, where the opportunity to represent one's own culture allows the participant social and cultural power. To this effect, the black British tenor Lloyd Newtown, founder of the Pegasus Opera Company, is concerned that an end to "blacking up," paradoxically, will mean less diversity on stage, in case black singers are subject to the same rule: "There are two sides to the coin … I don't want someone to tell me I can't play Siegfried because I don't have blue eyes. We can't sing *Show Boat* and *Porgy and Bess* all the time." David Smith, "So Long Mammy: Opera Says Farewell to Blacking Up," *The Observer*, (November 20, 2005), p. 3.

[12] Peter Wyllie Johnston, "Australian-ness in Musical Theatre: A Bran Nue Dae for Australia?" *Australasian Drama Studies*, 45 (October 2004), p. 158.

78   *Opera Indigene: Re/presenting First Nations and Indigenous Cultures*

it."[13] This ideology, Symons argues, was not in order to express an actual indigenous voice but to manufacture something that was appropriated as quasi-indigenous.[14] In relation to opera, this would be most applicable to Clive Douglas (1903–1977). His dramatic work *Kaditcha: A Bush Legend* was said to synthesize concepts of "Australianism" via the appropriation of Aboriginal music influences.[15] In 1938, Clive Douglas completed *Kaditcha*, a one-act operatic "fantasy drama" based on traditional folklore, presented in three scenes with a ballet. It was scored for a dramatic soprano in the title role and an orchestra of wind instruments. It was revised in 1958, but there is no record of its live performance to an audience. Over a decade after the completion of *Kaditcha*, James Pemberthy's operas dealt with Indigenous Australians as characters, rather than music motifs, although there are no records of these works ever being performed publicly: "the operas *Larry* (1955), *The Earth Mother* (1957–1958) and *Dalgerie* (1958) are all concerned with the uneasy relationship between the Aboriginal and European races."[16] The significant exception is in a 1973 revival of *Dalgerie* in the opening year of the Sydney Opera House, which featured a new segment: "a sequence of actual Aboriginal dances, which were performed by a group of dancers from Arnhem Land and the Kimberleys."[17] It is clear that the "participation" model demonstrated by the *Dalgerie* revival is one which mainstream Australian audiences have come to appreciate for its faithful citation of traditional, Indigenous performance. This is a popular model of "folkoric" citation that has a similarly iconic currency as the Māori *haka*.

However, Indigenous peoples needed to tell their contemporary stories in ways that appeared more diverse to general audiences than a celebration of their traditions. As we start to arrive at the 1960s, Australian Indigenous stories were developing an expressive urgency, both creatively and politically. There were traumas that were unique to Indigenous Australians that were not shared in the colonial experiences of their trans-Tasman neighbors in New Zealand. It was a time of activism, popular music, and political theater for Aboriginal Australians— a fertile basis for the dance-theater and music-theater produced by the next generation of artists in the 1990s. One such artist was the pioneering Method actor, director, and teacher Brian Syron. Theater scholar Liza-Mare Syron accounts for her uncle's Method actor training with Stella Adler in the 1960s in New York:

> One day Brian was standing in front of a mirror in his New York City apartment when he caught a glimpse of a spirit; it was an old Aboriginal man dressed in a traditional ceremonial outfit. Brian took this as a visitation and quickly packed

---

[13]   David Symons, "The Jindyworobak Connection in Australian Music, c.1940–1960," *Context*, 23 (Autumn 2002), p. 33.

[14]   Ibid., p. 34.

[15]   Ibid., p. 36.

[16]   Ibid., p. 40.

[17]   Ibid., p. 43.

his bags to return to Australia. On his arrival, Brian began a long engagement with the Redfern Aboriginal community in Sydney, utilizing his creative abilities by establishing acting classes and joining the fledgling Black theatre.[18]

The shift during Syron's engagement with Aboriginal Australians is of participating in aesthetic and theatrical forms of mimesis, which creates its own challenges in a postcolonial environment. Lisa-Mare Syron suggests that the "Method" could be seen as problematic to some Indigenous beliefs about the appropriate "methods" of public performance and storytelling. The Method, for its emphasis on the individual actor's imagination in creating a role, is predicated upon the actor's ability to elicit "affect" from the audience due to his or her believable "inner" state; whereas performance studies suggests that there are many more systems of performance and theatrical languages through which audiences can experience a connection to a story. Furthermore, theatrical space, song and dance space, ritual space, and spaces of the everyday in Aboriginal communities are governed in ways which observe beliefs arising from the natural environment and the immanent spirituality of these spaces. These are also materials that are indispensable to Western ideas of theater and opera. In a study of the songs and dances of the Yirrkal language group of Northern Australia, Fiona Magowan describes the performance of a creation story as an engagement with the *essence* of the place or "country" that can only be approximated in Western discourses by psychoanalytic theory of sensory experience and belonging:

> Performance renders country spiritually, physically and sensually vibrant and dramatic. Sensing place is the socialization of sound and movement via body memories as an affirmation of "living" experience ... Western conceptions of landscape as object, scenery and vista and enclosed areas are problematic as the land is brought to life by performing country ... Indeed, olefactory, tactile and taste senses are equally implicated in an acoustemology of flow that conjoins people, places and ancestors.[19]

---

[18] Liza-Mare Syron, "'The Bennelong Complex': Critical Perspectives on Contemporary Indigenous Theatre and Performance Practice and the Cross-Cultural Experience in Australia," *Australasian Drama Studies*, 53 (October 2008), p. 76.

[19] Fiona Magowan, "Dancing into Film: Exploring Yolngu Motion, Ritual and Cosmology in the Yirrkala Film Project," in *Landscapes of Indigenous Performance: Music, Song and Dance of the Torres Strait and Arnhem Land*, ed. Fiona Magowan and Karl Neuenfeldt (Canberra: Aboriginal Studies Press, 2005). This principle is also emphasized in an interview I conducted with community arts worker, Mahona Maia Kiely, on July 30, 2008 following the workshop "Conversing with Community: Creative Collaborations and Social Landscapes" at the *International Conference of the Arts in Society*, Birmingham Institute of Art and Design, July 28–31, 2008. Kiely worked with Indigenous and farming communities, whose view of the land were at odds, to produce staged stories, which she calls "fire operas"—works that are visual, sonic, and kinaesthetic. This embraces an indigenous model of spectatorship where listening must be done with everything except

80 *Opera Indigene: Re/presenting First Nations and Indigenous Cultures*

This model of mimesis is in line with the concept of the multisensory "site-specific" performance—or "open-air" performance (which opera achieves through amplification and microphones).[20] However, there is a difference between Western composers, librettists, and artists appropriating these traditional rituals or concepts and contemporary Indigenous artists "performing" their identity by creating new works that must negotiate that legacy. Liza-Mare Syron sees traditional and urban Aboriginal cultures as sharing an overlap of performance practices but she is at pains to point out that it is only a limited sub-set, which is equally engaged with contemporary performance practice from Western influences: "Post-colonial discussions are … limited by exploring cultural representation through the use of European theatrical devices … From within this premise, contemporary Indigenous theatre practice has been validated on the basis of how it differs from Euro-Australian theatre practices …"[21]

This suggests that Indigenous artists need the opportunity not only to participate in canonical works, but to author and negotiate a body of works (including adaptation/redress of the canon) on their own terms, given the diversity of contemporary Indigenous experiences. This chapter will now address some works from the Pacific, including Aotearoa.

---

the ears. One female Aboriginal actor said that she didn't want to tell her story because "they [non-Indigenous audiences] don't listen to us." It curbed her desire to perform in the contemporary sense. She felt adrift from the audience, and her relationship to them needed healing and adjustment. In the end, the white farmers came up with the metaphor of torches and the burning of wheat, which the Indigenous women wanted to convey in their criticism of agriculture on their lands. "The land will tell you something, only if you listen with everything but your ears." Kiely's workshop abstract rationalizes her approaches to social lore and aesthetics: "Working with Aboriginal people in Central Australia, I was told that when someone needs to fully comprehend story or Jukurrpa (social lore) they must receive it visually, aurally and kinaesthetically (thus Dreamtime stories are sung, danced and painted) … Performing outdoors and working with uncontrollable elements such as weather, means artists operate differently and the incidence of the 'happy accident' is increased. The audience responds instinctively to the primal elements of fire sculpture, live music and physical performance and is also engaged in an intuitive rather than cerebral process. It seems ensuring the show reflects each point in the content visually, aurally and kinaesthetically (never at the same moment), can create shows that are transformative for participants and communities and can become catalysts for local social change."

[20] In exceptional cases, opera performances can enjoy open-air, natural acoustics, as is the case in Dalhalla, Sweden—a performance space that was fashioned in a meteor crater and filled with an artificial lake.

[21] Syron, "The Bennelong Complex," p. 79.

The Pacific Islands and Aotearoa/New Zealand

In New Zealand/Aotearoa, the Treaty of Waitangi, signed in 1840, declares the nation bi-cultural—of both Māori and Pākeha groups. In surveying the Indigenous theater scene throughout the North and South Islands, Lisa Warrington finds allegiances to Japanese theatrical conventions, as well as expressions of the hybrid identities of artists with backgrounds from Polynesia, India, China, and Malaysia.[22]

However, the Anglophone minority still maintained a construction of cultural "mainstream versus indigenous" minorities, when it came to opera. In 1965, the New Zealand Opera Company looked to stage Gershwin's *Porgy and Bess*:

> This was intended as a showcase for Maori vocal talent, particularly the superb artistry of Inia Te Wiata (1915–1971), who was delighted to forego more lucrative overseas contracts to play the arduous role of Porgy in his own country. The Gershwin family had never allowed the opera to be performed by a non Afro-American cast before ... Kiri te Kanawa was approached to sing Clara and the popular entertainer Howard Morrision, Sportin' Life but neither was available for the projected eighty-eight-performance tour and the roles instead became triumphs for Isobel Cowan and pop singer Toni Williams.[23]

The tour resulted in a great commercial success and was a turning point in the professionalization of the opera company within New Zealand. But it was not until 1984 that New Zealand audiences saw a professional company present Indigenous opera. Significantly, this was a decade before such a collaboration was to emerge in Australia (the latter being in 1993, with *Black River*). The New Zealand works marked musico-dramatic and cultural history:

> Perhaps the most significant premieres have been Ross Harris's *Waituhi* and Christopher Blake's *Bitter Calm*—both landmarks in the emergence of indigenous opera. Witi Ihimaera's libretto for *Waituhi* dealt with ethnic tensions between Māori and Pākeha New Zealanders and the bitterness of family strife; Harris's music mixed conventional arias and ensembles with Māori musical elements. The work was premiered in Wellington on 8 September 1984 ... Blake's *Bitter Calm*, with an historically based libretto by Stuart Hoar, centered on conflicting values and lack of understanding between Māori and Pākeha in colonial New Zealand. First performed on 11 March 1994 ... [and] Iosefa Enari

---

[22]   Lisa Warrington, "Brave 'New World': Asian Voices in the Theatre of Aotearoa," *Australasian Drama Studies*, 46 (April 2005), p. 98.

[23]   Adrienne Simpson, *A History of Professional Opera in New Zealand* (Auckland: Reed, 1996), p. 213.

82   *Opera Indigene: Re/presenting First Nations and Indigenous Cultures*

in the central role of Matiu, the young Māori torn between two cultures, gave a telling performance.[24]

In 1998, Gillian Whitehead's opera *Outrageous Fortune* had its premiere in Dunedin, New Zealand. It is based on the nineteenth-century gold-rush in Otago and the successful challenge made by Māori miners to a colonial dispossession of their discovery of gold. The dancing of the *haka* is the act of aggression that wins the colonizers over. The composer, who has part Māori heritage, expresses the divergence between European operatic languages and the song traditions in New Zealand:

> In Europe in 1862 when *Outrageous Fortune* is set, Chopin, Mendelssohn and Schumann had recently died, and Liszt, Brahms and Wagner, whose Tristan dates from 1859, were in the ascendant ... Few echoes of that European culture would have reached Otago ... By contrast, Māori music would still have mapped the country; the variety of chants crucial to the carrying of knowledge in an oral culture ...[25]

The composer describes the traditional instruments used in her work: "Fifteen taonga pūoru are used in this piece: instruments which are blown in the manner of flutes ... instruments made of bone, of shell ... of New Zealand jade, of wood, of gourd."[26] The work synthesizes a number of musical languages, drawing upon the traditional Māori elements, as well as nineteenth-century ballad forms.

Despite being perceived as an ethnic minority within New Zealand, Pacific Islanders have enjoyed international success in creating their own, distinctive work.[27] The New Zealand-based Pacific Islander theater company The Conch toured their devised work *Vula* to the London stage in 2008, after its full-budget Australasian debut at the Sydney Opera House (SOH) studio on June 7–25, 2006. The piece is the product of collaboration between a Fijian performance-maker, Nina Nawalowalo, and a non-Indigenous New Zealand composer, Gareth Farr. According to the media release in 2006:

> "*Vula*" is the Fijian word for moon, a particularly important force when your life revolves around the sea. *Vula* explores the practical, sensual and spiritual

---

    [24]   Ibid., p. 228.

    [25]   Gillian Whitehead, *Outrageous Fortune* CD cover insert (Sounz Wellington, 1998), p. 4.

    [26]   Ibid., p. 5.

    [27]   While the Pacific Islanders are regarded as a cultural minority in New Zealand, the term "Indigenous" is a misnomer for them, as they are immigrants. They share, perhaps, in this case, with many of the other cultures discussed in this volume, a "First Nations" status because they were subject to British and French domination on their lands, while not being indigenous to Aotearoa.

relationships between Pacific Island women and water ... Nawalowalo formed The Conch after returning from Europe where she spent many years creating visually arresting work using a blend of magic, mask and clowning. With *Vula*, Nawalowalo wanted to explore a uniquely theatrical language dedicated to combining European theatre traditions with the profound depth of her Pacific Island heritage.[28]

It can be argued that the political status of the Māori peoples and the historical treaty would never have permitted the colonizing Pākeha to represent Māori culture on colonial terms, as was done in Australia. The Australian history of European invasion and denial of citizenship and suffrage until the late twentieth century was reflected, at the very least, in the power of empire to fashion mimesis on the musical stage.

Australia: *Black River* and Beyond

In his study of opera by Australian composers in the 1980s and 1990s in the previous chapter, Michael Halliwell looks at the nostalgia for the period of the 1950s as being a preoccupation for librettists, the effect of which made opera a billboard for sanitized, suburban, white Australia, and excluded Indigenous artists or stories; this absence was out of step with Aboriginal artists appearing on theater stages, television, and cinemas screens. Any work that gave voice to Aboriginal Australia was literally at the margins.[29]

The opera *Black River* by Andrew Schultz was premiered as a staged work by the Sydney Metropolitan Opera in 1989 and made Australian operatic history, firstly, by narrating an unwelcome truth about the treatment of Aboriginal Australians and, secondly, with the its notable Indigenous cast, led by the Songwoman Maroochy Barambah, who possesses social and artistic recognition among the Turrbal people. It is no coincidence that after the success of *Black River* Maroochy Barambah, who plays the central role of Miriam, was asked to sing for the United Nations, in 1993. By 1993, the opera was on film and had won the Grand Prize for Opera on Screen at the Internationales Musikzentrum Wien (IMZ) "for its depth of creativity, visual power and courage."[30] The following year, it appeared in a television broadcast on Australia's Special Broadcasting Service (SBS-TV), which claims itself as dedicated to the arts and multiculturalism. This example demonstrates a model of performativity through the power of the speech/song action, where words can

---

[28] Sydney Opera House in Partnership with the Biennale of Sydney Presents The Conch *Vula* February 7, 2006, www.sydneyoperahouse.com/About/2006_MRE_Conch. aspx (accessed January 6, 2009).

[29] Michael Halliwell, "'A Comfortable Society': The 1950s and Opera in Australia," *Australasian Drama Studies*, 45 (October 2004), pp. 11–12.

[30] IMZ Opera Screen Jury, Paris, 1993.

84   *Opera Indigene: Re/presenting First Nations and Indigenous Cultures*

transform a person's (and a culture's) status and recognition. The fact that this is done through song demonstrates the political power of opera, which may be unprecedented historically—at least in this region of the world. The other sung roles in the film are played by opera singers, and the non-singing roles showcase Indigenous talent, with the Bangarra Dance Theatre appearing as the spirits of the land and the award-winning Aboriginal singer/songwriter Jimmy Little as Miriam's father.[31]

The reason for the existence of this work is the crisis leading to the Royal Commission into Aboriginal Deaths in Custody 1987–1991. According to the National Archives of Australia, the purpose of the Commission was to: "examine all deaths in custody in each State and Territory which occurred between January 1, 1980 and May 31, 1989, and the actions taken in respect of each death."[32] While the opera did not represent any individual story, the libretto reflects the circumstances of the Commission's report—Miriam's son is imprisoned, then commits suicide, and her father dies from grief after identifying the body.

In the opera-on-film, the visual score sees the Bangarra dancers emerging as cinematic spirits, overlaying concrete images of the trees and landscape. They achieve a remarkable technical practice in the opera-film that is consistent with the traditional beliefs that song, dance, geographical location, and Ancestral Law are inseparable: "singing over objects is a way of conversing with the land and emplacing identities within it, just as singing about the white clay on dancers' faces and bodies is a means of emplacing the signature of the country on their bodies."[33] To this effect, at various points in the film the Bangarra dancers appear to emerge from the landscape, their bodies covered in clay. The dancers could be imitative of spirits or could be seen as re-writing Miriam's tragic events into a healed outcome in what is known as somatographia, or the body-writing of cultural memory.[34] The "ancestral" presence of the dancers aids Miriam's traumatic facing-up to her tragic circumstances and her re-integration with her sense of place, with the wide lens image of a flooded river and extra-diegetic birdsong completing the film. In its cinematic form, this opera suggests the creative overlap between new technologies and indigenous creative practice. To reprise the epigram at the beginning of this chapter—"this is so operatic," from the 1997 screenplay (based on the 1993 play)

---

[31]   With the exception of Cindy Pan, who mimes to the singing of Akiko Nakajima in the role of Anna: an employee from the fictitious "Department of Race Relations." Other principal characters are Judge Gray (John Pringle), Les the complacent police officer (Clive Birch), and Reg the "racist" (James Bonnefin).

[32]   National Archives of Australia, *Fact Sheet 112: Royal Commission into Aboriginal Deaths in Custody* (Canberra, 2004).

[33]   Magowan, "Dancing into Film," p. 61.

[34]   In her example of Australia's northern Tiwi Islands, Lesley Delmenico argues this practice rewrites events in postcolonial history through Indigenous discourses. Lesley Delmenico, "Official Amnesias and Embodiments of Memory in Australia"s Top End," *Australasian Drama Studies*, 46 (April 2005), pp. 117–23.

of Louis Nowra's *Radiance*—there is a narrative in which three Aboriginal sisters, one of them an opera singer, confront their traumatic past and the death of their mother by ritualistically burning down their childhood home. This is done in a culturally self-reflexive mode, as the sisters revel in the act, to the recorded strains of Puccini's "Un bel dì vedremo" from *Madama Butterfly*. Once again, the opera-on-film hybrid genre is so significant to this field of creative practice.

In the time between *Black River* in 1993 and the anticipated premiere of *Pecan Summer* in 2010 (see the interview in Chapter 18), the participation and representation of Indigenous Australians in opera has been patchy, to say the least. What has been significant, though, is an emerging body of creative work featuring Indigenous composers, choreographers, and singers in areas of music theater genres that are closely related to opera—and to which contemporary opera (and postoperatic practice) may draw inspiration. These genres include the musical, public ceremony, and music video.

Firstly, the musical. To develop a point that was raised earlier in this chapter, there is a productive relationship between certain "progressive" popular forms of music theater and their eventual translation into so-called "high art" genres. In relation to Aboriginal composition, the influence of pop, country and western, gospel, and reggae music, among other styles, has been the subject of study by Peter Dunbar-Hall and Chris Gibson.[35] This is most relevant to the compositions of Jimmy Chi and his band Kuckles, who cite a number of popular musical influences in his musicals. Attendant to this is the inventiveness of naming new genres, such as a "rock-opera." In her work on Australian Aboriginal theater, Helen Gilbert raises a useful point on this appropriation of popular song—as a form of meta-theater.[36] Jimmy Chi's musicals hold to an episodic structure where popular songs may feature and the choices reflect his cultural background of both Chinese and Aboriginal heritage. The first and most successful[37] of these works is *Bran Nue Dae* (1993), which narrates a young man's rite-of-passage in the 1960s. Following this was *Corrugation Road* (1996), an autobiographical piece, which deals with mental illness and Indigenous identity, and *The Sunshine Club* (1999), the libretto of which deals with Indigenous war veterans and black-white relations in the postwar period.[38]

---

[35]   Peter Dunbar-Hall and Chris Gibson, *Deadly Sounds, Deadly Places: Contemporary Aboriginal Music in Australia* (Sydney: University of New South Wales Press, 2004).

[36]   Helen Gilbert, *Sightlines: Race, Gender and Nation in Contemporary Australian Theatre* (Ann Arbor: University of Michigan Press, 1998), p. 77.

[37]   The film version of the musical was released in Australian cinemas in January 2010 (*Bran Nue Dae*, dir. Rachel Perkins, Screen Australia, Melbourne, 2009, DVD R-109813-9), starring the Oscar-winning actor Geoffrey Rush and acclaimed Indigenous artists Deborah Mailman and Jessica Mauboy, who have established nationally prominent careers in film, television, and popular music.

[38]   It is significant to note that while Aboriginal Australians were able to fight alongside other Commonwealth soldiers in World Wars One and Two, they were not granted full rights of citizenship until 1967.

86   *Opera Indigene: Re/presenting First Nations and Indigenous Cultures*

Secondly, there is the public ceremony. From 1998, anticipating the lead up to the Sydney Olympics opening ceremony, the Bangarra Dance Theatre choreographer and director Stephen Page worked with traditional songman-dancer-didjeriduist Djakapurra Munyarryun from the Munyarryun clan of northeast Arnhem Land. This collaboration was significant in bringing cultural integrity to representations of Indigenous Australians at such a nation-building event as an Olympics opening ceremony. In terms of its operatic content, the ceremony featured Indigenous opera singer Deborah Cheetham, who performed the Australian national anthem, and the gold medallist and indigenous athlete Cathy Freeman, who lit the Olympic cauldron, with operatic overtones, as Berlioz's *Te Deum* was played through the sound system: "in the climactic, Wagnerian-scale lighting of the cauldron, Freeman virtually metamorphosed into a black female Parsifal."[39] These operatic metaphysics were deployed quite deliberately by the ceremony's organizers, implicating Indigenous ritual in the mass spectacle that signifies Olympic ceremonial symbolism. The segment Page co-ordinated was called "Awakening" and featured close to one thousand performers from diverse regions of Australia. Robin Ryan argues that the Indigenous participation was performative in that song and dance were working to reconcile cultural tensions—though the lack of specificity of multiple clan identities was regrettable: "internal differences between language groups were downplayed as music and dance furnished a standardized referent for ethnicity."[40]

Lastly, there is the music video. In 2001, Rachel Perkins's *One Night the Moon* brought a new genre of Indigenous music theater to audiences, as it was a television film that was not anticipated for cinematic release.[41] The production team was Music Drama Television, which followed in the tradition of the television broadcasting of the opera-on-film *Black River* (with the same producer and cinematographer, Kevin Lucas and Kim Batterham). It was given financial support by Opera Australia's outreach body, OzOpera. The score was written by Indigenous songwriter Kev Carmody (who is part of Australia's surviving Stolen Generation) as well as Mairead Hannan and popular folk and rock singer Paul Kelly. It starred Indigenous actor Kelton Pell as the "Aboriginal tracker" and Indigenous singer Ruby Hunter as his wife in a 1930s tragedy about a missing white farm girl who wanders into the wilderness. Her parents organize a search, which is thwarted by her racist father, played by Paul Kelly, who refuses to allow "blacks on my land," excluding Aboriginal assistance in the search. Her dead body is eventually found when the Aboriginal tracker intervenes.

---

[39]   Robin Ryan, "Awakening 'The Fire Within': Symbols, Rituals and Reconciliation," *Australasian Music Research*, 7 (2002), p. 92.

[40]   Ibid., p. 90.

[41]   The film's director, Rachel Perkins, is the daughter of the late Aboriginal activist Charles Perkins. See Kathryn Millard, "*One Night the Moon:* Interview with Rachel Perkins," in *Senses of Cinema*, www.sensesofcinema.com/contents/01/17/moon_interview_perkins.html (accessed December 11, 2007), p. 2.

The score deploys a range of folk musical styles, with the soundscape of white Australia being expressed through the historically marginalized sound of Irish folk music. Arguably the Irish-Australian composers were suggesting a revised Australian history of the early twentieth century, by building upon a mythology of an unspoken alliance between Irish and Aboriginal Australia, as both had suffered under British rule for over a century together (but of course in very different ways). Given the funding source of the film (a subsidiary of the national opera company) and the multicultural team of composers, there is a strong argument for the film's operatic structure and influence, with recitative conveying some of the storytelling.[42]

In terms of its musical language, the tenor and baritone duet "This Land is Mine" provides a recitative-style narrative ballad in which the cinematic composite of actor Kelton Pell and vocalist Kev Carmody can deliver the performative statements of Indigenous claims to land rights: "This land is me, rock, water, animal, tree, they won't take it away from me," as against Paul Kelly's claim "This land is mine." This duet also features a didjeridu, which is an aural signifier for Aboriginality even though musicological research reveals that the instrument was only associated with a specific region in Australia's north.[43] There is a crucial mimetic issue to consider here—whether it is the place of contemporary music drama to restage specific musical traditions of the Indigenous people who belong to the named geographical places in the drama: "The music in the film is heavily embedded within western modes of musical practice with the style and instrumentation of predominantly Anglo-Celtic origin."[44] It therefore invites the question of authenticity in terms of the representation of any specific Aboriginal language group in the narrative. The question could even be expressed as simply as "to didj or not to didj?" (see Chapter 5 in this volume by Anne Boyd) when the didjeridu becomes an aural marker of Australian Aboriginality, indispensable to any narrative, regardless of the fact that the instrument has very specific cultural and geographical functions.

The issue of performativity becomes a challenge in the face of making opera, where creators must negotiate dramatic and musical languages that are authentic and have cultural integrity. Marcia Langton is uncompromising in her resistance to any paternalistic or tokenistic models of cultural production for Aboriginal people: "There is a naive belief that Aboriginal people will make 'better' representation of us, simply because being Aboriginal gives 'greater' understanding. This belief is based on an ancient and universal feature of racism: the assumption of the undifferentiated *Other*."[45] The assumption here is that there are some better

---

[42]   Kate Winchester, "Moon Music: Musical Meaning in *One Night the Moon*," in *Reel Tracks: Australian Feature Film Music and Cultural Identities* (Southampton: John Libbey, 2005), p. 177.

[43]   Ibid., p. 182.

[44]   Ibid., p. 186.

[45]   Langton, *Well I Heard it on the Radio*, p. 27.

forms of representation than others, and that those better forms nurture the *quality* of creative processes: the avoidance of stereotypes and diversity of identities portrayed. Langton, crucially, conveys the complexity of being an Aboriginal in a postcolonial world: "'Aboriginality', therefore, is a field of intersubjectivity in that it is remade over and over again in the process of dialogue, of imagination, of representation and interpretation."[46]

Transforming the Future

In the twenty-first century, regardless of whether their work features Indigenous artists, there is a greater sense of mainstream composers, librettists and directors responding to issues of Indigeneity which their work may touch upon. Gale Edwards and John Senczuk's libretto for *Eureka*, which premiered in Melbourne's Princess Theatre on September 28, 2004 (with music by Michael Maurice Harvey) was careful to frame its narrative about the Australian gold-rush as predicated upon the violation of Aboriginal people and their land.[47] This was unusual, given that the piece was a commercially produced musical, but Peter Wyllie Johnston suggests that after *Bran Nue Dae*, *Corrugation Road* and *The Sunshine Club* the omission of Indigenous voices from the Australian music theater stage would have been unacceptable. It is clear that audiences in the twenty-first century expect to hear the Indigenous voice within historical nation-building narratives:

> The impact of these events became even clearer when, in September 2004, an Aboriginal Australian character called Kardinia [played by Pauline Whyman] appeared from a swirl of mist in the opening moments of *Eureka* ... . In a few well-chosen words, Kardinia told the story of how her people had lived on the land for thousands of years and suffered as a result of European invasion ... . Edwards' direction ensured that Kardinia's presence and her message underlay all of the action.[48]

It could be argued that this falls into what Langton calls the "rehabilitative" statement for non-Indigenous Australians, rather than being an authentic moment of Aboriginal self-expression. But such mimesis is historically contingent, if we believe Taussig's model, and will ideally be replaced by a more equal share in the aesthetic stakes.

---

[46] Ibid., p. 33.

[47] These librettists and composer work in both opera and commercial music theater.

[48] Johnston, "Australian-ness in Musical Theatre," p. 174.

Conclusion

The scholarship on Australian Aboriginal, Māori and Pacific Islander musical and dramatic performance since the early 1990s has been concerned with "decolonizing" the discourse by challenging the durability of Eurocentric operatic languages: performance space, linear time, narrative, character, audience, and the object of performance itself. According to E. Ann Kaplan, it is a matter of apprehending the Western gaze: "we can only enter from where we stand, unless we want to mimic those we aim to know about. Mimicry ... is not knowledge," to which Marcia Langton responds that the aim is not to abandon "our" framework in the face of the other.[49] This has interesting implications for overcoming the colonial legacy. This area of scholarship is new in relation to opera and has been enriched by the voices of emerging Indigenous scholars, who merge traditional knowledge, perspectives from urban Aboriginal artists, contemporary performance theory, and the added perspective of intercultural dialogue between Indigenous communities across the globe. By providing the multiple case studies of Australia, New Zealand and the Pacific Islands, it is hoped that the reader sees the relationship between different kinds of cultural and political upheaval and the resulting mimetic forms in storytelling through opera.

---

[49] Langton, *Well I Heard it on the Radio*, pp. 24–5.

PART II
Australian Perspectives

Chapter 5

"To Didj or Not to Didj":
Exploring Indigenous Representation in Australian Music Theater Works by Margaret Sutherland and Andrew Schultz

Anne Boyd

On February 13, 2008, Australian Prime Minister Kevin Rudd made an "Apology to Australia's Indigenous Peoples," foreshadowing the possibility of a new era in the nation's reconciliation with its Indigenous inhabitants. He spoke of a future "based on mutual respect, mutual resolve and mutual responsibility," in which "all Australians, whatever their origins," were to be "equal partners, with equal opportunities and an equal stake in shaping the next chapter in the history of this great country, Australia."[1] In the context of the previous Howard government's persistent refusal to apologize,[2] Rudd's long-awaited remarks highlighted the lack of social justice afforded Indigenous Australians in the country's colonial and postcolonial history, as well as an appreciation of the significance of Aboriginal worldviews, long recognized among Australian artists and intellectuals—if not among politicians.[3] This event signaled the possibility of re-setting the start button in Australia's troubled relations with its Indigenous population.

Listening to the Prime Minister's speech broadcast directly from Canberra into a lecture theater packed with staff at the University of Sydney, I was struck by the powerful response of weeping—engendered in both Indigenous and non-Indigenous listeners alike. Was this the kind of "weeping that moves men [and women] to song"?[4] The question had a special relevance as I was at that time

---

[1]   The full text of this speech is available as a pdf at www.aph.gov.au/house/Rudd_ Speech.pdf (accessed July 17, 2009).

[2]   "PM again rejects calls to say sorry," October 12, 2007, AAP, www.thewest.com. au/default.aspx?MenuID=145&ContentID=43307 (accessed July 17, 2009).

[3]   In 1948 The Commonwealth Citizen and Nationality Act for the first time gave a category of "Australian Citizenship" to all Australians, including all Aborigines, but it was not until 1962 that the Commonwealth Electoral Act was amended to give the vote to all Aboriginal people. www.dreamtime.net.au/indigenous/timeline3.cmf (accessed August 22, 2008).

[4]   Steven Feld, *Sound and Sentiment: Birds, Weeping, Poetics and Song in Kaluli Expression* (Philadelphia: University of Pennsylvania Press, 1990).

considering material for a paper to be delivered to an international conference in London on Indigenous representation in opera.[5]

As a cultural form, opera, in its special bonding of text and music, presents a canvas broad enough to capture the social mores of the time of its creation. It is particularly suited both to the creation and presentation of myth in a contemporary social context. In an Aboriginal setting a similar ontological and emotional impetus results in ceremony, both sacred and secular, combining singing and dancing through which the close spiritual and physical connection to country is enacted and renewed—in its more extended form such ceremony is better known by the term "corroboree."[6] What might be the result when two such cultural forms are brought together? How can artists in an ever changing postcolonial setting, both Indigenous and non-Indigenous, deal with the sensitive problems of re/presentation of the cultural "other"?

With such questions in mind, I set about investigating works by two Australian composers—Margaret Sutherland's *The Young Kabbarli* (1965) and Andrew Schultz's *Journey to Horseshoe Bend* (2003)—as offering special perspectives upon Indigenous representation in music reflected across three generations of Australians. Remarkably, in both works I found embedded "Two Ways" thinking, a philosophy underpinning many contemporary Indigenous communities in Australia.[7] In order to more fully understand the significance of this, it quickly became clear that it was necessary to establish a counterpoint with the thinking of the Jindyworobaks, an influential literary movement established in Australia in the 1930s, whose ideas on the establishment of Australian cultural identity by assimilating Indigenous language and landscape features are carried forward in music by important composers such as John Antill (1904–1986) and the iconic and canonical Peter Sculthorpe (b.1929). The incorporation of Indigenous materials in music by non-Indigenous composers is today further complicated by the new thinking regarding the sanctity of Aboriginal cultural property arising from broadened intellectual debate and by the most welcome developments in political legislation supporting property and land-rights of Australia's indigenous inhabitants since the early 1990s. It is in this context that "Two Ways" thinking becomes especially significant in assessing the negotiation of cultural property in works such as the symphonic cantata *Journey to Horseshoe Bend*.

---

[5]   Opera Indigene Conference, London, September 28, 2008.

[6]   The word "corroboree" was first used by early European invaders to describe Aboriginal ceremonies that involved singing and dancing. *Corroboree* was the English version of the Aboriginal word *caribberie*. www.indigenousaustralia.info/culture/corroborees-a-ceremonies.html (accessed July 16, 2009).

[7]   "Two Ways" can be understood as the promotion and use of local cultural forms, including Indigenous languages, alongside and as equal partners with Western knowledge and educative practice, particularly in schooling new generations of Indigenous children.

Mission History and "Two Ways" Thinking

There are striking similarities in the two works by Australian composers/librettists: Sutherland/Casey's *The Young Kabbarli* and Schultz/Williams's *Journey to Horseshoe Bend*. Separated by three generations, as well as the significant gender differences of their creators, the works have important common features: both tell an Australian story drawn from a similar period, the first two decades of the twentieth century; both are situated in the context of the work of Christian missionaries in remote outback Indigenous communities; and both are based upon autobiographical accounts of their experiences, written by the work's "observer" protagonists, Daisy Bates and T.G.H. Strehlow.

The heroine of the Sutherland/Casey work is the astonishing Irish woman and self-styled anthropologist Daisy Bates (1859–1951), who arrived in Australia in 1884. Known as *Kabbarli* ("wise woman," "grandmother"),[8] Bates lived most of her adult life among Australia's Indigenous population, firstly in the West and then in South Australia, recording her experience in her autobiographical *The Passing of the Aborigines* (1938).[9] It was from this source that Maie Casey (1892–1983) and composer Margaret Sutherland (1897–1984) drew the material for their chamber opera *The Young Kabbarli*. The incident upon which this opera is based occurred during the young Bates's visit to the Trappist Mission at Beagle Bay north of Broome in 1899, traveling from Perth in the company of a Catholic Bishop Gibney and Dean Martelli.[10] During his visit the Bishop determined that all the natives surrounding the mission be presented for confirmation into the Catholic faith. Bates records the incident of a young Aboriginal man, Goonderwell, who, upon observing the confirmation ceremony, parodies it. He dresses himself in an old red blanket, places a red billy-can on his head and coerces the newly confirmed Aboriginal girls to join his angry dance of protest at the coming of the white man. His actions are observed with an unusual understanding and respect for cultural difference by the young Daisy Bates, who sympathetically ruminates that "all creatures have their own understanding but for their own kind alone."

Daisy Bates has emerged, today, as a much more complex character than her previous almost saintly status would suggest. Her decades of dedication to the cause of protecting Aboriginal people—enduring a life among them in the harshest of outback conditions, observing and recording (perhaps not always completely accurately) their languages, customs and beliefs—is an heroic achievement,

---

[8]   *AUSTLIT The Australian Literature* Resource, www.austlit.edu.au/run?ex+ShowAgent&agentId=A%23FT (accessed August 23, 2008).

[9]   First published in Great Britain by John Murray in 1938, Daisy Bates's *The Passing of the Aborigines* was reprinted four times and was issued in a second edition with a foreword by Alan Moorhead in 1966. My references here are to the publication issued by Panther Books (London) in 1972.

[10]   Daisy Bates, *The Passing of the Aborigines* (London: Panther Books, 1972), pp. 35–7.

96   *Opera Indigene: Re/presenting First Nations and Indigenous Cultures*

qualifying her for the iconic title of "Grand Dame of the Desert,"[11] and *Kabbarli* to her Aboriginal friends. Her story proved a fitting subject for an opera by a composer who might similarly be thought the "grandmother" of Australian music, Margaret Sutherland.

Working nearly four decades later, Gordon Kalton Williams (b.1956) and composer Andrew Schultz (b.1960) turned to another autobiographical literary source, T.G.H. Strehlow's novel *Journey to Horseshoe Bend* (1969),[12] an account of a tragic twelve-day journey made in 1922, by the author as a fourteen-year-old boy traveling with his parents to seek medical assistance for his seriously ill father, Carl Strehlow, a German Lutheran missionary who had been based at Hermannsburg in Central Australia for the previous twenty-eight years. Carl died at Horseshoe Bend, well short of their destination. After burying his father in the rocky ground behind the isolated travelers' inn at Horseshoe Bend, Theo Strehlow (1908–1978) continued on with his mother to Adelaide, where he completed his secondary and university education. As an adult, he returned to a lifetime's work among the Aranda people, collecting and publishing a massive amount of ethnographical material including his monumental *Songs of Central Australia.*[13] It was only after suffering his own life-threatening illness that Theo was able to write about his father's final fateful journey. The rich blend of Christian and Aranda ethnography placed side by side in this novel makes it a fertile source for the creation of Williams's and Schultz's epic "symphonic cantata"—a work which includes the participation of Aboriginal performers alongside their non-Indigenous peers, on an equal footing.

The Young Kabbarli and *Journey to Horseshoe Bend* are situated in the context of the problematic missionization of Australia's Aboriginal populations and highlight something of the spiritual issues embedded in these stories, as well as illuminating the process by which a new society constructs the mythology needed to sustain it. Most interesting of all are the differences and similarities apparent in the individual writer's productive approaches to the problems of representing indigenous materials within their musical works. Despite their generational and gendered difference, both works promote the "Two Ways" philosophy now practiced in many Aboriginal communities. I will say more about this in the context of the discussion of each work.

---

[11]   Bob Reece, *Daisy Bates: Grand Dame of the Desert* (Canberra: National Library of Australia, 2007).

[12]   T.G.H. Strehlow's *Journey to Horseshoe Bend* was first published by Angus and Robertson in 1969. The references in this chapter, however, are to the Rigby edition published in 1978.

[13]   T.G.H. Strehlow, *Songs of Central Australia* (Sydney: Angus and Robertson, 1971).

Didj-ing Australia and Jindyworobak Thinking in Music

Indigenous representation in music by Australian composers is likely to include, or at least refer to, the sound of the didj,[14] with little regard to the appropriative problems that may arise from such cross-cultural borrowing for the purpose of establishing a distinctively *Australian* sound.[15] While *The Young Kabbarli* and *Journey to Horseshoe Bend* both include parts for Aboriginal performers, Sutherland's work, in response to Daisy Bates's own references in *The Passing of the Aborigines* to the didjeridu sound, includes a significant part for this instrument. Further, in the first ever commercial recording of any opera by an Australian composer, made in 1973, Sutherland not only uses a didjeridu, played by an aboriginal performer, at key moments in her work, but even appends a traditional Aboriginal song,[16] accompanied by didjeridu and clapping sticks, at the work's conclusion.[17] The inclusion of Aboriginal performers presenting their own material in a musical work by a non-Indigenous artist on Aboriginal subject material may well constitute a first in Australian musical history. Although the practice of involving Aboriginal performers is continued in Williams's and Schultz's *Journey to Horseshoe Bend*, Schultz elected NOT to use the didj in his work. The instrument is not found in the ceremonial music of Central Australia,[18] nor is it played at the Hermannsburg (*Ntaria*) mission. Its inclusion would have been neither authentic nor appropriate.

In contextualizing the work of Sutherland and Schultz in terms of their use of Indigenous material in their compositions, music by two further composers—John Antill and Australia's best-known composer, Peter Sculthorpe—becomes significant. John Antill's ballet score *Corroboree* (1936/46) provides a particularly important historical example of Aboriginal representation in Australian music of the mid-twentieth century. This is a landmark composition particularly because of its connection to the "Jindyworobak" movement in Australian literature.

---

[14]   Didj is an abbreviation of didjeridu, the famous wooden trumpet, or drone-pipe, used in Aboriginal music-making.

[15]   "To Didj or not to Didj?" is my encrypting of a title of an informal talk given to students at the University of Sydney by Australian composer Andrew Schultz on his work involving indigenous representation. His actual title was "To Use the Didj or Not to Use the Didj."

[16]   The singer is David Gumpilil (Gurlpiril is linguistically correct though the spelling most commonly used today is Gulpilil), who was to become a particularly famous Aboriginal singer, dancer, and actor on stage and screen.

[17]   Dick Bundilil is listed as the didjeridu player on the original recording reproduced in the Anthology of Australian Music on Disc CSM:32 (1999).

[18]   Steven Knopoff, "Didjeridu," *Oxford Music Online* www.oxfordmusiconline. com.ezproxy1.library.usyd.edu.au/subscriber/article/grove/music/ 07750?q=Didjeridu&search=quick&source=omo_gmo&pos=1&_start=1#firsthit(accessed August 7, 2009).

98   *Opera Indigene: Re/presenting First Nations and Indigenous Cultures*

"Jindyworobak" is an Aboriginal word meaning "to annexe" or "to join." The term was adopted by a group of writers in the 1930s to mid-40s, led by the Adelaide poet Rex Ingamells (1913–1955), who resisted European influence "bought on ships from across the seas" and sought a distinctively Australian voice. The Jindyworobaks based their texts around words and images appropriated directly from Australian Aboriginal culture, as well as Australian flora and fauna, as a means to guarantee an authentic Australian national identity.[19]

Somewhat in the Jindyworobak spirit, Antill's ballet is based on a childhood memory from 1913 of an Aboriginal corroboree performed on the outskirts of Sydney,[20] the form of which he describes as follows:

> A feature of Australian Aboriginal life is the dance ceremony known as the Corroboree. The Aborigine is the master of mimicry and burlesque, and the Corroboree generally takes the form of realistic imitations of humans or animals. Any current event may furnish the theme from which the "tribal" poets, musicians and actors produce the ceremony, which is usually of very elaborate proportions. Everyone in the camp, men, women and children take part, but, as a general rule, the dancing is confined to men.
>
> The performances take place after sundown, in the glow of campfires, creating a most impressive atmosphere and causing great excitement.[21]

This experience inspired in him a lifelong fascination with Aboriginal culture, especially music, examples of which he recorded onto wax cylinders for later study.

Corroboree is scored for symphony orchestra and features a large percussion section including Aboriginal *thora* sticks (clapping sticks) and bullroarer (a cigar-shaped wooden flat, attached to a cord and twirled about the head rapidly). The

---

[19]   The movement was swelled by several circumstances: the economic depression focused attention on comparable hardships of an earlier era (the early 1890s); the influx of "alien" culture threatened to overwhelm the young literature then in the making; and travellers described with wonder the little-known Australian Outback. Among the discoveries of the period was a romantic notion of the spirit of place and the literary importance of what could still be discerned of Aboriginal culture. Xavier Herbert's *Capricornia* (1938) typifies the goals of the Jindyworobak movement. The poet and novelist James Devaney (1890–1976) took the name Jindyworobak from a nineteenth-century vocabulary of Wuywurung (an Aboriginal language formerly spoken in the Melbourne region), in which *jindi woraback* is said to mean "to annex." *Encyclopaedia Britannica Online*, www.britannica.com/EBchecked/topic/303975/Jindyworobak-movement (accessed June 26, 2009).

[20]   R. Covell, *Australia's Music: Themes of a New Society* (Melbourne: Sun Books, 1967), p. 70.

[21]   John Antill's *Corroboree*, annotation by the composer in the CD liner notes compiled by Vincent Plush (1977), Sydney Symphony Orchestra, conducted by John Lanchberry (CDOASD 793060).

inclusion of the latter is problematic as this is likely to give offence to central Australian Aboriginal groups for whom the sound of the bullroarer is thought to be the voice of the Rainbow Serpent and associated with "secret men's business." It is therefore taboo for women, children, uninitiated men, and outsiders to even listen to. Antill would have been unaware of a taboo unlikely to have been observed in the corroboree he had witnessed as a child on the outskirts of Sydney. Apparently, this event was put on as a weekly entertainment for Sydney's weekend picnickers by the displaced and marginalized Aboriginal community then living at La Perouse on Botany Bay.

Aside from the problems associated with the large-scale appropriation of the corroboree into a Western ballet, in which all the dancers would have been non-Aboriginal performers, Antill's work also suffers from inevitable comparisons with Stravinsky's much earlier and much more successful ballet *The Rite of Spring* (1912). Given its first early reading by members of the Sydney Symphony Orchestra conducted by the composer in 1944, *Corroboree* was found "strange yet powerful."[22] A concert version of the work for symphony orchestra was conducted by Sir Eugene Goosens,[23] who described it as "the most significant work from the pen of a contemporary Australian composer that it has been my privilege to examine."[24] He was later to make a recording with the London Symphony Orchestra,[25] thus providing an unusual instance of international success afforded a work by an Australian composer.

Listening to *Corroboree* today, one is aware of the not entirely convincing stylistic collisions in the music as the composer attempts to habituate an Aboriginal sound world to a Western symphonic tradition. The influences of contemporary European composers such as Ravel, Arnold Bax, Stravinsky, and Bartók all rub shoulders somewhat unconvincingly in the context of the sometimes overloud and dominating sound of Aboriginal percussion, especially of clapping sticks. Low-register bassoon is used to invoke an atmosphere of mystery, as well as representing the sound of the didjeridu. Despite its stylistic and technical flaws, as a cultural artifact John Antill's *Corroboree* remains a monument in Australian musical history as one of the most original and striking works created by any Australian composer.

---

[22] Plush, CD liner notes compiled for John Antill's *Corroboree*.

[23] http://nla.gov.au/nla.ms-ms437 states that *Corroboree* was composed between 1936 and 1944, based on the rhythms that had impressed Antill during a trip to the La Perouse Aboriginal settlement in about 1912. The music for *Corroboree* was first performed in 1946 by the Sydney Symphony Orchestra, conducted by Eugene Goosens at the Sydney Town Hall. Goosens later toured the work to London and Cincinatti. The Berlin Philharmonic performed it at the 1949 Edinburgh Festival.

[24] Eugene Goosens in *ABC Weekly*, September 21, 1946, quoted by Vincent Plush in the CD liner notes compiled for John Antill's *Corroboree*. Sydney Symphony Orchestra conducted by John Lanchberry (CDOASD 793060).

[25] Everest Recording (SDBR-3003).

100   *Opera Indigene: Re/presenting First Nations and Indigenous Cultures*

Corroboree sets the stage for a consideration of what constitutes the deep fibers of the Australian musical voice and how this seems to grow most significantly from a respectful contact with Indigenous Australia. If this seems to imply a cultural attitude similar to that of the Jindyworobaks, then the spirit of this movement is carried forward most persuasively in the music of Peter Sculthorpe. In the mid-1960s he claimed that "Australia and Asia are the present and the future; Europe, the dead and the past," thus aligning himself and Australian music with the Jindyworobak view of Europe as "conditional culture."[26] Sculthorpe has taken a keen interest in the fate of Tasmania's Indigenous inhabitants and, like Antill before him, from an early age he compiled an extensive personal archive of Aboriginal materials. Some of Sculthorpe's earliest compositions draw upon Aboriginal mythology (*The Loneliness of Bunjil*, the Piano Sonatina and the *Irkanda* series) and, in his most recent work, he frequently collaborates with the Aboriginal didjeridu virtuoso William Barton.[27] One of Sculthorpe's most significant recent works, his choral Requiem (2004), is based upon a postcolonial appropriation of a haunting Aboriginal melody, the "Maranoa Lullaby". This work was premiered to great acclaim in England's Lichfield Cathedral and includes a significant part for didjeridu written for and performed by William Barton.

From the early 1970s, Sculthorpe adopted a practice of incorporating Aboriginal melodies directly into his music, the most famous, and to some the most problematic, being his extensive use of the North Arnhem Land melody *Djilile* (Whistling Duck). These melodies are used over and over again in his music, forming distinct "song-lines." He complicates this issue of incorporation by claiming he only chooses melodies which he might have fashioned himself, drawing as evidence a tune he had crafted in his early Fourth String Quartet (1950) as being nearly identical to *Djilile*, which he had first used in the 1976 soundtrack for a documentary film on the failed settlement at the remote Port Essington in the far north of Australia.[28]

In response to an invitation to compose a work to open the Sydney Opera House in 1973, Sculthorpe created his own text for his little-known opera *Rites of Passage* drawing upon the language and ritual of the Aranda culture of central Australia,[29] mixed with Latin texts from Boethius' *Consolation of Philosophy* concerning the universality of love.[30] Performed in 1974, *Rites of Passage* became the first occasion upon which the Aranda language was heard upon the stage of the

---

[26]   Peter Sculthorpe, *Sun Music: Journey's and Reflections from a Composer's Life* (Sydney: ABC Books, 1999), p. 213.

[27]   See p. 346 for a further reference to William Barton by Daniel Browning.

[28]   Sculthorpe, *Sun Music*, p. 213.

[29]   Sculthorpe draws upon Strehlow's monumental *Songs of Central Australia* as a primary source for the text of the "Rites" sections of his opera.

[30]   Michael Hannan provides an account of the genesis of *Rites of Passage* as well as a detailed analysis in Chapters 7 and 8 of *Peter Sculthorpe: His Music and Ideas 1929–1979* (Brisbane: University of Queensland Press, 1982).

Sydney Opera House, paving the way for the use of the same language found thirty years later in Williams and Schultz's *Journey to Horseshoe Bend.*

The Young Kabbarli

At first glance, the Jindyworobak spirit might similarly be thought to inform Margaret Sutherland's music for *The Young Kabbarli*, which uses instrumental techniques to create the sounds of insects and birds, evoking the outback landscape setting of the drama. It also includes a part for didjeridu, creates didjeridu drones in bassoons, and references the tumbling strain typical of Aboriginal melody.[31] Yet this work seems at some distance both from *Corroboree* and the music composed at a similar time, in the early 1960s, by Peter Sculthorpe. In his study of Margaret Sutherland's music, David Symons objects to the Jindyworobak tag, rejecting the possible accusations of such cultural borrowing and assimilation. He points out that even though her opera incorporates Aboriginal elements its purpose is not overtly nationalistic, but rather it seeks to explore the complex relationships between Indigenous and European Australians—thus creating a distinction between Sutherland's compositional intentions and the nationalist aspirations of her male contemporaries John Antill and Clive Douglas (1903–1977).[32]

Margaret Sutherland, like the heroine of her opera, did not advocate assimilation, a policy popular with the Australian government at the time, contributing directly to the iniquity of the "stolen generation," but emerges as an early proponent of the "Two Ways" philosophy now embraced within contemporary Australian Indigenous communities, including at Beagle Bay where her opera is set.[33]

---

[31] Curt Sachs in his iconic *The Well Springs of Music* (The Hague: M. Nijhoff, 1962) explains: "The most fascinating of the oldest melody patterns may be described as a 'tumbling strain'. Its character is wild and violent: after a leap up to the highest available note in screaming fortissimo, the voice rattles down by jumps or steps or glides to a pianissimo respite on a couple of the lowest, almost inaudible notes; then, in a mighty leap, it resumes the highest note to repeat this cascade as often as necessary. In their most emotional and least 'melodious' form, such strains recall nearly inhuman, savage shouts of joy or wails of rage and may derive from such unbridled outbursts. The crudest style of this kind of melody seems to be preserved in Australia" (p. 51). www.archive.org/stream/wellspringsofmus027137mbp/ wellspringsofmus027137mbp_djvu.txt (accessed on July 20, 2009).

[32] David Symons, *The Music of Margaret Sutherland* (Sydney: Currency Press, 1997), pp. 119–20.

[33] The Sacred Heart School, founded at Beagle Bay in 1892 by the Trappist monks referred to by Daisy Bates in her *Passing of the Aborigines*, has established a tradition of caring for stolen children. Today, its adoption of Two Ways promotes the study of traditional Indigenous culture in the language of the local area alongside a modern Australian curriculum taught in English.

102   *Opera Indigene: Re/presenting First Nations and Indigenous Cultures*

The Young Kabbarli received its first performance in the 1965 Hobart composers' conference entitled "A Festival of Contemporary Opera and Music."[34] The part of the didjeridu called for in the score was most likely pre-recorded for this performance—if it was used at all. In 1965 even this would have been immensely difficult to achieve. Furthermore, the notion of Aboriginal parts played by Europeans would have been considered completely normal.[35]

Sutherland's *The Young Kabbarli* is a one-act chamber opera comprising a number of set pieces structured as seven main sections. It calls for seven characters, four of whom are singing roles and three Aboriginal girls who are assigned non-singing roles, accompanied by a small instrumental ensemble of two flutes (one doubling piccolo), two clarinets (one doubling bass clarinet), bassoon doubling contrabassoon, horn in F, percussion, piano, viola, and double-bass. The absence of upper strings and strident oboe from this ensemble gives its timbre a mellow, darkly hued character well suited to the representation of the ochre colors of Australian landscape of this area. The upper winds are called upon to represent the landscape sounds of insects and birds, in which task they are assisted by a percussion section of all non-pitched instruments—castanets, wood block, sticks, flints, and wooden shaker. At one point we are reminded of the coastal proximity of the mission setting by the sound of blowing through a conch shell. This replaces the function of a monastery bell tolling canonical hours and calling the congregation to worship.[36] The flute represents spiritual purity when accompanying suggestions of Catholic liturgical chant. The instrumental ensemble plays an important role in scene setting, providing musical material identified with each character, imitating the sound of the didjeridu and providing vigorous ostinati to accompany the extended dances which lie at the heart of the drama.

Daisy, the young "Kabbarli" (described as a Protestant Irish woman—though she is now known to have been born a Catholic), is sung by a mezzo-soprano. Her music ranges from the modally lyrical Irish folk melody, supported by clarinet and underpinned by a didj-like drone in contrabassoon (Example 5.1), to impassioned unaccompanied declamation. Declaring the central theme of the work referring to the Aboriginal people, she cries out: "How can they hold their ancient knowledge and beliefs ... Their structure, their taboos; And yet move forward to our faith. What twilight zone divides their lives from ours?" To which the Trappist Brother, a bass,

---

[34]   A student composer myself at the time, I had the good fortune to be in the audience at its premiere. I cannot remember clearly if there were any Indigenous cast members taking the Aboriginal roles, but I think it unlikely in an era when any available actors were unlikely to admit to their Aboriginal descent.

[35]   Margaret Sutherland's personal regard for Aboriginal people is not in doubt; she had already shown special support for the Indigenous Australian tenor Harold Blair (1924–1976), whom she had known since 1945. It is possible that she had Blair in mind when she assigned the tenor voice to Goonderwell, the young Aboriginal protestor in her opera. See also Daniel Browning's citation on the topic of Harold Blair on p. 346

[36]   Bates, *Passing of the Aborigines*, p. 31.

Example 5.1 *The Young Kabbarli*, Daisy, the young Kabbarli, singing an Irish folk melody

104   *Opera Indigene: Re/presenting First Nations and Indigenous Cultures*

replies: "They must be bought to God *our* God." The young Kabbarli continues: "All creatures have their own understanding but for their own kind alone .... "

The aforementioned central male character, the young Aboriginal Goonderwell, is assigned a tenor role and his music veers between parody and an angry song protesting the coming of the "white fella." His young wife Yooliban, a soprano, lies ill in the shade of a bush for much of the opera, refusing the food he brings to her, her life-force returning only in the climactic ceremonial dance, triggered by the sound of the didjeridu, near the work's ending. It is this penultimate section, which is the longest in the opera, framed by Goonderwell's increasingly despairing cries of "No good, no good, What for? What for? White fella kill us quick time; Don't want white fella here, Chase 'em white fella longa way, longa, longa, longa way, longa way." His singing, like that of the Kabbarli, is similarly cast in a tumbling strain, spanning an octave, characteristic of much Aboriginal singing. The isorhythmic treatment of his "pidgin" word patterns resembles that of text treatment in traditional Aboriginal ceremonial singing. The melody is pitched over an ostinato, with woodblock and pizzicato strings filling the space that in Aboriginal ceremony would be occupied by a clapping stick pattern. This leads to an outraged parody of the recently conducted confirmation service. The climax of the work comes as the music, awakened by the sound of the return of the didjeridu, transforms through a passage in the unusual meter of 10/8 into a vigorous ceremonial dance in which all the Aboriginal characters participate. The ailing Yooliban revives during its performance and the group exits to the sound of the didjeridu, which forms a bridge into the final scene.

The structure and musical idioms of the opera are shaped by the neo-classical influences to which Margaret Sutherland would have been exposed in her overseas studies in Vienna and London in the early 1920s. The bitonality and octatonic sound world of much of the musical material used in *The Young Kabbarli* is projected across rhythmic ostinati presented in episodic and repetitive blocks of material, which would not have seemed out of place in a work by Stravinsky at this time. The folk-like modality of the Irish music, representing the young Daisy Bates, reminds us of the importance of the English folksong revival that was well under way when the young Sutherland arrived in London, where her principal mentor was the English composer Sir Arnold Bax. What is particularly interesting is the musical representation of Indigenous ceremonial performance, which gives such prominence to dance accompanied by the rhythmic pulsations of the didjeridu, and the isorhythmic treatment of text within a repetitive verse structure. The "Two Ways" philosophy is anticipated in the clear separation of European and Aboriginal identity throughout this work. Though connected through cultural ties to the European world of the Christian missionaries, the young Kabbarli remains faithful to her role as observer; she participates neither in the confirmation service, nor the Aboriginal dance that follows: she understands and sympathizes with the spiritual qualities of both. There is little sense of the projection of a dominant cultural paradigm in the narrative structure of this work, rather its drama is underpinned by a sense that it is possible to exist in two worlds with understanding, the very essence of contemporary "Two Ways" thinking.

Sutherland's opera emerges as a moving and culturally significant work through its gentle sorrowing and the visionary quality of its advocacy of non-assimilation, as well as its clear sense of recognition of the all-important connection to country as the basis of Aboriginal spiritual life. It is worth noting that, in the Introductory Note for her earlier orchestral work *Haunted Hills* (1950), she writes: "This work attempts to define, in the language of music, two cultures so long at variance— those of the dark-skinned and the light. In it the gulf between them emerges, yet the fine qualities of each are never in doubt."[37]

Appropriation in its Political Context

To composers of the generation of Sutherland and Antill, the use of indigenous materials would not have been considered problematic. Similarly, Sculthorpe, working in the early 1970s, had unrestricted access to Aboriginal materials lodged in the University of Sydney Library. A growing awareness of the secret nature of some of this material, coupled with the growth of Aboriginal activism in the 1980s and 1990s, has led to much of it being withdrawn to closed archives accessible only with the special permission of the rightful owners.

In Australia, the development of the indigenous political agenda, leading to the Rudd Apology, provides an especially significant background for considerations of artistic practice involving indigenous representation. The 1990s saw the enactment of important legislation recognizing Aboriginal Land Rights and Native Title. This significant legislation re-enfranchised the indigenous population who, in the Constitution instituted at Federation in 1901, were not counted as members of the Australian population.[38] By such means the Aboriginal people had been not only marginalized, but rendered invisible, deemed not even to exist. How easy then to ignore their human rights—including their ownership of cultural property. It was against this political background that Gordon Kalton Williams and Andrew Schultz set out to create their collaborative symphonic cantata *Journey to Horseshoe Bend*.

---

[37] M. Sutherland, program notes for the "Prom" March 1971 as supplied to the ABC. ABC Library, Ultimo, Sydney quoted by Chérie Watters-Cowan, *Reconstructing the Creative Life of Australian Composer Margaret Sutherland: The Evidence of Primary Source Documents* (University of New South Wales: PhD thesis, 2006), p. 424.

[38] The Commonwealth Constitution states "in reckoning the numbers of people ... Aboriginal natives shall not be counted." It also states that the Commonwealth would legislate for any race except Aborigines and that the States would therefore retain their power over Aboriginal Affairs.

106　　*Opera Indigene: Re/presenting First Nations and Indigenous Cultures*

Journey to Horseshoe Bend

In cross-cultural collaboration, the achievement of a proper balance of power in representation of indigenous culture, as in the case of Williams and Schultz's *Journey to Horseshoe Bend*, is a complex undertaking compounded by Aboriginal ceremonial forms being swallowed by an invading culture intent on establishing its own system of spiritual beliefs. However well intentioned, this outcome would seem to be the inevitable consequence of the establishment of Christian missions— the mission, established in 1877 by the Lutheran Church at Hermannsburg, in central Australia, being no exception.

As artists, both Williams and Schultz had previous experience of collaboration with Aboriginal peers: Williams, as actor and director, worked with the Darwin Theatre Group (1987–1988) as well as co-producing and presenting the ABC Classic FM programs *Black Meets White* and *Bridging the Gulf*, exploring indigenous music in the concert hall; Schultz, in his prize-winning music theater work *Black River* (1988), explores Aboriginal deaths in custody and draws upon Indigenous and non-Indigenous characters. Both men were acutely aware of the complex negotiations required to appropriately represent Indigenous issues in a contemporary musical setting.

The germ of an idea for a musical work to be based upon T.G.H. Strehlow's *Journey to Horseshoe Bend* occurred to Gordon Kalton Williams when he was exploring a possible screenplay based upon the life of its author. He came across a passage describing the emotive Aboriginal singing of *Karrerrai worlamparinyai*, the Lutheran chorale "Wachet Auf" ("Sleepers Awake"), used most famously by J.S. Bach in his Cantata 140 (see Example 5.2). The novel recalls that as Strehlow's seriously ill father leaves the Lutheran mission station at Hermannsburg (*Ntaria* – also spelt 'Ntarea'), where he had been its seemingly indestructible Pastor for some twenty-eight years, the people whom he loved and to whom he had dedicated his life break into the singing of the chorale, translated by him into their own language, as a deeply moving gesture of farewell.[39] This incident, translated across several generations, was to provide the inspiration for a re-enactment of this scene by some of this group's descendants on the stage of the Sydney Opera House on May 28 and 29, 2003.

In 1922, Theo Strehlow had known little of life other than that of the mission where he had been home-schooled by his parents. As a consequence, he had become fluent in German, Aranda, and English; all three languages which are carried forward in the cantata. On the journey Theo traveled behind his parents in another van with his Aboriginal guardian, Njitiaka. The party had decided to head for the railhead at Oodnadatta some 380 miles south across rugged terrain following the course of the dry Finke River bed. Pastor Carl's health deteriorated quickly and twelve days later he died at Horseshoe Bend, some hundreds of miles short of their destination. The novel, Theo (Ted) Strehlow's autobiographical account of this

---

[39]　　Strehlow, *Journey to Horseshoe Bend*, pp. 22–4.

Example 5.2 *Karrerrai worlamparinyai*, "Wachet Auf" ("Sleepers Awake"), from J.S. Bach, Cantata 140

108   *Opera Indigene: Re/presenting First Nations and Indigenous Cultures*

journey, was written when he was in his early 60s. The translation of the novel into a symphonic cantata—thought of as a large-scale travel song, or even a symphonic opera—provides an opportunity to explore the significant rites of passage of its principal characters, father and son, in the context of their journey along the Finke, a landscape shot through with Aboriginal spiritual significance, explained along the way to the young Strehlow by the third principal character Njitiaka.

The musical symbolism in the work is described as "polysemous— many meaning" and therefore "like the words of an Aboriginal language."[40] Biblical imagery is mapped upon landscape features along the route, which are also explained in the context of the Aboriginal stories attached to this area—a sentient landscape captured in a beautiful documentary film on the cantata by Hart Cohen.[41] Cohen has also written on the impact of the landscape upon the physical layout of Schultz's orchestra. It was a helicopter ride along the Finke which enabled the composer to conceive a bird's-eye view; so when Schultz looks out the window of the helicopter, he not only sees but *hears* the landscape below.[42] This experience affected Schultz's reading/sounding of the Strehlow narrative at many levels, which he explains as the orchestra physically reflecting the course of the Finke River bed, with its towering cliffs and ridges on either side, amongst which are situated more distant sites:

> You have a middle group of the orchestra which is largely warm sounds—strings, electronic organ, marimba, vibraphone, two horns, solo trumpet, bass clarinet—they're like a central warm body of sound and they are playing most of the time. They're often very quiet, they're very much background sounds, but they are there as the core of things.
>
> On either side of them, we've positioned the wind and brass … . They're like a ridge; they're raised physically off the level of the other players, and behind them, further, we have four percussion players—who I sort of perceived as being rather like things in the ridges, sights [sites] if you will, having a symbolic role in the piece … you can look at this and say, this whole orchestral landscape is just like a map, you know?[43]

In this way the orchestra becomes a character in its own right, fusing the sound and structure of the landscape of the journey, bringing it vividly to life and projecting

---

[40]   Ibid.

[41]   Hart Cohen, director and producer, *Cantata Journey: A Documentary* (Sydney: Research Decisions, 2006).

[42]   Hart Cohen, "Repertoire, Landscape and Memory: Williams' and Schultz's Journey to Horseshoe Bend Cantata," in *Intercultural Music: Creation and Interpretation*, ed. Sally Marcarthur, Bruce Crossman, and Ronaldo Morelos (Sydney: Australian Music Centre, 2006), p. 118.

[43]   Ibid.

it into the present moment through the ear of the listener. This is a unique way of representing landscape in music. Arguably, this process is somewhat analogous to an indigenous perception of country as a resonant outdoor cathedral whose various topographical features may be specific sites of totemic significance celebrated in song and ceremony. What is especially interesting here, too, is the way in which the physical layout of the orchestra influences the architecture of this composition: the principal characters track their way from back stage right (Hermannsburg) to front stage left (Horseshoe Bend), snaking along the course of the Finke River bed in the center of the stage.[44]

Lasting nearly an hour, in eight scenes distributed across three movements which mark the main stages of the journey, *Journey to Horseshoe Bend* draws upon the resources of actors, singers, choruses, and orchestra. There are spoken roles for a "European"/Australian narrator (the adult T.G.H. Strehlow, whose role parallels that of the Evangelist in a Bach Passion) and the Aboriginal Njitiaka, guardian and guide to the young Strehlow, a boy soprano, who both sings and speaks. The work's most distinctive feature, however, is its use of the Hermannsburg *Ntaria* Ladies' Choir. The Aboriginal women sing the music of Bach using chest rather than head voices, appropriating the chorale melody to their own sense of tuning and timbre, and spinning it into their complex and sophisticated knowledge systems. Their distinctive singing style uses a focused nasal sound rich in harmonics, heard several times throughout the work, separately and together with the European-styled singing voices of the Sydney Philharmonic Choir, presenting the possibility of the co-existence of both cultural difference and a coming-together of Indigenous and non-Indigenous Australia.[45]

In a communication with Gordon Williams, I queried the composer's use of chorales rather than indigenous song. His response is given below:

> Why have chorales, but not traditional chant? Partly because there are issues with using traditional chant, or touching on anything secret-sacred. So this was a way of providing a real Aranda flavor; the Central Australian choirs' vocal production is instantly aboriginal.[46]

Despite its communicative power, the work has attracted some criticism, especially among anthropologists, for its use of an Indigenous choir singing Bach chorales, for it is indeed this vocal production that instantly brands the work as

---

[44] Fascinating sketches of these "maps" developed from an aerial photo of the Finke River Valley can be found in the 2002 Strehlow Conference proceedings and reproduced (without attribution) in the Music Resource Kit prepared by Kim Waldock and published by the Australian Music Centre (2007), p. 32.

[45] Fortunately this sound quality is excellently reproduced in the CD recording of *Journey to Horseshoe Bend* conducted by David Porcelijn issued by the Australian Broadcasting Corporation, 2004 (ABC 476 2266).

[46] Williams, e-mail communication with author, September 10, 2008.

110   *Opera Indigene: Re/presenting First Nations and Indigenous Cultures*

"Aboriginal." This is thought by critics to reinforce the iniquity of indigenous traditions being swallowed up in the dominant culture. In constructions of Western musical imperialism there is none more powerful than the universalizing of J.S. Bach. The referencing therefore of his most famous church cantata in telling an Australian story in which Aboriginality is re/presented through the singing of one of his most famous chorale melodies can certainly be viewed as problematical. To its critics this is demeaning to the Aboriginal women engaged in this performance and therefore ethically and culturally inappropriate.

According to Professor Diane Austin-Broos, an eminent anthropologist, whose fieldwork has been based at Hermannsburg for a number of decades and who has close friends singing in the *Ntaria* Ladies Choir, these Aboriginal women would have been very surprised to be told that it was inappropriate for them to sing Bach chorales, for they had been doing so for nearly a century. Using texts translated into Aranda by Carl Strehlow, sung by their parents, grandparents and great-grandparents, these Aboriginal women felt a distinct sense of ownership of this material.[47] Their traditions had been extinguished more by the coming of the pastoralists, whose dissemination of grass seeds, as fodder for their cattle, devastated the sensitive plant ecology of the area bringing near starvation to local tribes. That Aranda culture has survived at all was partly a consequence of the coming of the missionaries whose teaching was in the local language(s), which itself became a vehicle for the survival and later revival of indigenous knowledge. Both Strehlows, father and son, were engaged in translation: Carl took a serious interest in Aranda spiritual beliefs and respected their traditions—although his strict Christianity prevented him from attending ceremonies, he nevertheless documented much of the information he received from elders concerning their customs and beliefs, sending his papers back to his native Germany for publication, where they were received with great interest by European scholars.[48] In discussing the Aranda response to Christianity, Diane Austin-Broos explained how the concept of *Altjira* (referred to in the cantata as meaning Eternity) might also be interpreted as meaning God. Jesus is his *Ingkata.* Thus Aranda cultural beliefs are permitted to overlay Christian concepts.

Librettist Gordon Kalton Williams explains the participation of the *Ntaria* Ladies Choir in this way:

---

[47]   A lunch-time meeting on August 15, 2008, in which Professor Austin-Broos explained to me some of the ways in which the Hermnnannsburg community had absorbed Christianity into their own worldviews. She had in her possession the original Lutheran Prayer Book translated by Carl Strehlow into Arrernte and still in use at Hermannsburg.

[48]   Strehlow's findings on totemism were accepted by many contemporary European scholars, among them Durkheim, Malinowski, Freud, and Roheim; more recently, Worms, Lommel, and Petri have used his work; Lévi-Strauss's *Les Structures élémentaires de la parenté* (Paris, 1949) and Eliade's *Australian Religions* (Cornell, 1973) also drew substantially on his research. *Australian Dictionary of Biography On-Line Edition* www. adb.online.anu.edu.au/biogs/A120138b.htm (accessed on February 7, 2009).

I wanted to involve the Hermannsburg Choir right from the start ... I didn't see this as a collision; I was more amazed that they were singing Bach; regard it as their tradition; and in the old days sang it in four-part harmony. (There are 78 recordings from the 1950/60s of the Hermannsburg Chorus, then including tenors and basses, singing Bach conducted by T.G.H. Strehlow.) I provided Andrew [Schultz] with a tape not only of the Hermannsburg Choir, but of the Ernabella Choir (comprising Pitjantjatjara people) singing what they call "Kata miilmiilpan nyara" (Oh sacred Head, sore wounded) from the *St. Matthew Passion*. Some people see the Aranda singing of Bach as "being swallowed by the dominant culture," but I think those people would now have a job convincing the Ntaria people that this is not part of their tradition.[49] Andrew too has said that he is interested in the deepest joins between apparently irreconcilable cultures.[50]

The choice of the form of cantata (rather than opera) for the *Journey to Horseshoe Bend* narrative is especially appropriate, representing as it does a connection to the Lutheran church. Especially associated with J.S. Bach, the cantata offers a vehicle for the dramatization of Christian biblical stories performed in a sacred context—this is the closest the church has come to sanctioning what might be thought of as opera. Bach's Cantata No. 140 is referenced throughout *Journey to Horseshoe Bend*, not only in the statement of the three verses of the chorale melody sung in Aranda at key points, but in the replication of its religious theme, and, in some respects, its structure. Based upon Christ's parable of the ten wise and foolish virgins, its main theme is the preparation of the soul (represented as a Bride) for union with Christ (represented as a Bridegroom) in readiness to enter Zion (Eternity/Heaven). This parallels the testing of Carl Strehlow's faith and spiritual preparedness as he draws closer to his own agonizing death, supported only by the prayers of his pious wife, whom, with his final words, he silences with the despairing command: "Don't pray that prayer Frieda, God doesn't help."

At a structural level, too, there are many parallels to the Bach cantata, which similarly sets the three verses of the original chorale melody as separate movements (First, Fourth, and Seventh). Bach's statement of the chorale melody in the first movement of Cantata 140 is as a *cantus firmus* overlaying a complex choral fantasia depicting the excitement of townsfolk awoken by the watchmen's bugle calls announcing the coming of the Bridegroom. In *Journey to Horseshoe Bend*, the excitement of Bach's townsfolk is replaced by the sorrowing of the Aboriginal *Ntaria* community, as their seriously ill Pastor leaves them, for the final time. The bugle call of the Biblical watchmen, signified in the triadic melodic shape of the chorale melody, is referenced in Schultz's music by a solo trumpet, often associated with Carl's utterances, almost as a *Doppelgänger*, forecasting death or coming disaster. The Bach tonality of E♭ major is also reproduced in *Journey* in the

---

49   Williams, e-mail communication with the author, September 10, 2008.

50   Williams continues, giving a link to an interview partly touching on this issue: www.abc.net.au/rn/relig/spirit/stories/s870551.htm (accessed September 10, 2008).

first statement of the chorale melody (shown in Example 5.2) placed upon a low B♭ pedal. In Bach's music, Christian certainty is conveyed in that the chorale always remains in the same key, which, with its signature of three flats, symbolizes the Holy Trinity—Father, Son, and Holy Ghost. How appropriate that Schultz would replicate this symbolism in a narrative concerned with a father-son relationship, in this case mediated by the presence of the Aboriginal guide *Nkitiaka* standing in the place of the Holy Spirit. Unlike Bach, however, Schultz's music changes the key for each statement of the chorale's verses: the second, in Scene 2, is in D♭ and the final statement, in Scene 8, is in the white light key of C major—used in Peter Sculthorpe's music to signify the warmth of God's love.

In addressing the question originally posed by Schultz "to didj or not to didj?" in musical re/presentation of indigenous Australia, considerations of his use of harmony and of tonality in *Journey to Horseshoe Bend* become particularly significant. The droned characteristics of the didjeridu are referenced in his use of long pedals underpinning each of the scenes of his work. His harmonic language is drawn from a recycling of chords based upon the natural harmonic series, in which diatonic clusters appear in the higher registers. An important starting place for the musical material for *Journey* is found in an earlier work, a piano trio, *Tonic Continent* (2000), the title of which already suggests a preoccupation with sounding/tonicizing Australian landscape. The opening motifs and B♭ pedal sonority are carried directly from one work into the next (not unlike Bach's recycling of his materials from one work to another). The fusion of Schultz's harmonic language with the representation of landscape through slowly moving pedals *suggests* the droned presence of didjeridus even though this instrument is not physically present: as previously mentioned the didj is not found in the traditional indigenous music of Central Australia.

The Lutheran lineage of *Journey to Horseshoe Bend* is continued into the present: Andrew Schultz is himself the son of Lutheran pastor and thus deeply familiar with Lutheran music. In addition to Bach's, he adds two further chorales of his own composition, "But God Cannot Be Known" and, significantly, as the work's closing statement, "This Land is from Altjira."

The Aboriginalization of Lutheran liturgy is perhaps the most significant factor in considering indigenous re/presentation in *Journey to Horseshoe Bend*, where Aranda spiritual beliefs are placed over those of Christianity. This is emphasized by Gordon Williams and Di Austin-Broos, both of whom have been so helpful in assisting me negotiate issues involved in this investigation. Theirs is the final say on "Two Ways" at Hermannsburg, carried forward in *Journey to Horseshoe Bend*:

> I'm glad to see that you contacted Di Austin-Broos. I think she has most interesting things to say about the unique culture that is Ntaria and about Two Ways. ... I love the concept of Two Ways. I think it's exciting that that the Aranda use Altjira (which Spencer and Gillen translated—reduced in meaning?—as Dreamtime) for God, and Wenton Rubuntja in his autobiography (*The Town*

Grew Up Dancing) says God is ingkata (ceremonial chief), and Jesus is his kutungula, placing Arrernte ceremonial categories over Christianity.[51]

An Ending or a Beginning?

Each of the works discussed in this chapter warrants more detailed study, as stages in the making of Australian culture—for these are valuable repositories of knowledge that help with understanding the process of becoming a nation, a process determined most significantly in the care and treatment of Australia's Indigenous community—the oldest living human culture on earth. It is dispiriting that the language policy, so important to the enactment of "Two Ways" in schools in Aboriginal communities, is under threat because of the lack of the availability of suitably qualified teachers. A ray of hope lies in the continuing successful implementation of this policy in the Aboriginal communities referred to in this investigation of Australian music: Beagle Bay—the backdrop to Maie Casey and Margaret Sutherland's *The Young Kabbarli* and Hermannsburg (*Ntaria*)—the central site in Gordon Kalton Williams and Andrew Schultz's *Journey to Horseshoe Bend*. Further hope resides in the increasing awareness of the preciousness of Australian indigenous cultural heritage—in the postmodern world obsessed with the appearance of things, the Australian "brand" is decidedly influenced by the cultural forms of Australia's First Nations. The music investigated here shows a way forward in the rejection of policies of assimilation in favor of the "Two Ways" of placing indigenous and non-indigenous material on an equal footing, permitting the kind of healthy cross-cultural influence and fusion which will continue to yield new music of significance and difference, enriching the stockpile of human artistic expression.

---

[51] Ibid.

Chapter 6
Giving Voice to the Un-voiced "Witch" and the "Heart of Nothingness": Moya Henderson's *Lindy*

Linda Kouvaras

Introduction

The tragic saga surrounding the disappearance of ten-week-old baby Azaria Chamberlain at Australia's Uluru[1] in 1980 and the subsequent legal proceedings against her parents—in particular, her mother, Lindy—resulted in a most appalling miscarriage of justice.[2] The case led to two wrongful convictions, including one for murder (Lindy), and one for accessory after the fact (Michael, Azaria's father, who received a suspended sentence). How was this possible? What stories did the media, law enforcement agencies, and the legal professionals involved tell themselves (and the general public)[3] that could have resulted in an innocent person

---

This project was funded by the Australian Research Council. My deep thanks to Richard Ward and Judith Hemschemeyer for proof-reading and to Moya Henderson for her generosity in granting me interviews and access to her own marked copy of the score.

[1] Or Ayers Rock, as it was called before 1985.

[2] For details of the events, see, for example, Adrian Howe, "Introduction: Trial by Sex," in *Lindy Chamberlain Revisited: A 25th Anniversary Retrospective*, ed. Adrian Howe (Canada Bay, NSW: Lhr Press, 2005). Howe notes: "In November 1989, *The Sunday Age* included the Azaria case in its list of the biggest media events of the 1980s, along with John Lennon's murder, the Challenger space shuttle disaster, the Tian'anmen Square massacre and Gorbachev's glasnost and perestroika policies," p. 3. And at time of writing, a piece in *The Australian*, Australia's prominent national daily newspaper, likened the divisiveness in community reaction to the "Matthew Johns / Cronulla Sex Scandal" affair to that which occurred in relation to Lindy Chamberlain. David Penberthy, "Budget Has Interest but Sex Is Current," *The Australian*, 16 May 2009. This demonstrates the enduring currency that the Chamberlain case holds.

[3] Some members of the public were Lindy supporters and sent thousands of letters to her. Adrian Howe, "Marginalised Voices: The Silent Majority," in *Lindy Chamberlain*

116   *Opera Indigene: Re/presenting First Nations and Indigenous Cultures*

being convicted of murder and imprisoned for several years? Why were those who held vital evidence—Indigenous expert witnesses, eyewitness testimony including that of Lindy herself—not believed?

The events have since been intensely scrutinized from a number of feminist perspectives, from journalism through to anthropology; there is also a high-profile 1988 film, *Evil Angels* (also known as *A Cry in the Dark* in the northern hemisphere) based on the saga, starring Meryl Streep as Lindy (dir. Fred Schepisi). The opera *Lindy*, by composer Moya Henderson and co-librettists Judith Rodriguez and Moya Henderson (completed in 1997 and staged in 2002),[4] offers its own insights into this episode. It illuminates the connectedness of Indigenous with non-Indigenous Australia, and also restores "voice" to those silenced or ignored. The reasons for this silencing contain paradoxes and gross inequities and are inextricably linked with gender issues and mythologizing—particularly regarding non-Indigenous Australia's sense of nationalism. In this chapter I examine the ways in which the opera shows the myth-making about Lindy herself, as well as that of indigenous Australia. In particular, I synthesize relevant theoretical responses to the events and position the opera in accord with these texts.

My analysis explores how *Lindy* addresses the sets of binary oppositions that emanate from the Chamberlain case and are located within the so-called "heart of nothingness" commonly drawn by non-Indigenous people as Australia's core. Couched in terms of Norm and Other, these oppostions include:

- *race* (white/black);
- *religion* (normative Christianity/"suspect" sub-group Christian denominations and Indigenous legends);
- *pack mentality* (dingo/the press);
- *nationalism* (Western civilization/the outback);
- *systems of knowledge* ("acceptable" scientific/"unacceptable" layperson observations, plus Indigenous wisdom); and
- *gender* ("correct"/"unnatural" performance of motherhood, and male/female).

Revisited: A 25th Anniversary Retrospective, ed. Adrian Howe (Canada Bay, NSW: Lhr Press, 2005).

[4]   The CD recording of the work is a realization of the opera's premiere. It contains a vast number of cuts from the original score (John Carmody refers to these cuts as "artistically inexplicable": John Carmody, "Moya Henderson's Passionately Polychrome Take on the Lindy Saga," *Opera-Opera* 298 (October 2002), p. 12). As I imagine more people will have access to the CD than the score, and as I engage with reviews of the performance, I confine my discussion to the CD's truncated version. See Moya Henderson, Judith Rodriguez and Opera Australia, *Lindy*, sound recording, ABC Classics, [Australia], 2005. Capture session: Recorded live 31 October, 2 November 2002 in the Opera Theatre of the Sydney Opera House. Performers: Joanna Cole (Lindy); David Hobson (Michael); Opera Australia; Australian Opera and Ballet Orchestra; Richard Gill (conductor). Act I, Darwin Prison Dreaming, 64'11"; Act II, Awakening, 30'14". Also see Moya Henderson and Judith Rodriguez, *Lindy [Music]: An Opera in Three Acts* (Church Point, NSW: Henderson Editions, 1997).

Tracing *Lindy*'s cross-fertilization of these categories with one another, this chapter suggests *Lindy* promotes rightful respect toward indigenous knowledge and toward Lindy Chamberlain in her own account of, and position within, the events and her own belief system.[5]

The "Witch-hunt"

My first consideration is a highly charged aspect of gender in the Lindy Chamberlain case. Diane Johnson's compelling scholarship reveals what "essentially underlies the Azaria Chamberlain case: the making of Lindy the witch,"[6] where "[t]he imagery which informed the public discourse was peppered with potent allusions to creatures and moods of other times and other places long past."[7] While Lindy was never actually called a witch, the implication was nevertheless discernible; she *was* referred to indirectly as a witch when newspaper articles termed her scape-goating a "witch-hunt."[8]

Johnson comments, "As a symbol of female freedom, power and sexuality, the witch also represents and reminds women of potential brutal retribution which the exercise of this freedom, power and sexuality can bring."[9] The way Lindy dressed became a media preoccupation. Like the witch of medieval times, who made her own cloak, Lindy, a qualified tailor, made her own clothes. Just as the witches triggered masculine alarm at the threat of feminine sexuality, Lindy's sexuality

---

[5] It is important to note that Henderson and Rodriguez consulted with Lindy (now Lindy Chamberlain-Creighton) and with the Mutitjulu Aboriginal people in Uluru, asking their permission to use the names of their trackers, Nuwe Minyintirri and Barbara Tjikadu. The creators of the work underline that "this is not *Lindy: the authorised opera*." At Lindy Chamberlain's insistence, the line "A dingo's taken my baby" was included. "Initially, it was not to be, partly as a way of separating the opera from the film," says the opera's director, Stuart Maunder. "We wanted to get away from Meryl Streep-land. But Lindy asked for it to go in as it was what she had said." Joyce Morgan, "Rock Opera," *The Age* (2002), www. theage.com.au/articles/2002/10/26/1035504923144.html (accessed June 2, 2009); Judith Rodriguez, "Writing Lindy (CD Liner Notes)," *Lindy* (ABC Classics: 476 7489, 2005), pp. 9–10. Sally Macarthur has briefly contextualized *Lindy* within a broader discussion of Henderson's exploration of aspects of spirituality and the Australian psyche. See Sally Macarthur, "Women, Spirituality, Landscape: The Music of Anne Boyd, Sarah Hopkins and Moya Henderson," in *The Soundscapes of Australia: Music, Place and Spirituality*, ed. Fiona Richards (Burlington, VT: Ashgate, 2006).

[6] Diane Johnson, "From Fairy to Witch: Imagery and Myth in the Azaria Case," in *Lindy Chamberlain Revisited: A 25th Anniversary Retrospective*, ed. Adrian Howe (Canada Bay, NSW: Lhr Press, 2005; 1984), p. 131.

[7] Johnson, "From Fairy to Witch," p. 132.

[8] See, for example, Morgan, "Rock Opera." Rodriguez also refers to the "witch-hunt" that was the "media-stimulated public opinion." Rodriguez, "Writing Lindy," p. 9.

[9] Johnson, "From Fairy to Witch," p. 132.

became a discussion point among male journalists: "The pert brunette had worn a different outfit to court each day so far ... and always managed to look striking."[10] And her affect, plus the way she disported herself, rankled with the public/press: she did not dissolve into tears "appropriately," and laughed "inappropriately," resulting in her reception as an "unnatural" woman and, worse, an unnatural mother.[11]

The consideration of gender is further complicated, even by some of those who would champion her. In *Evil Angels*, film director John Bryson is very supportive of Lindy.[12] But he states: "All the messy complications of motherhood were beyond explanation," and for him Lindy Chamberlain was an exemplar of motherhood. Kerryn Goldsworthy's view is to identify "a declaration of male ignorance of female culture; of a desire to maintain that ignorance, as somehow admirable; and finally of a conviction that female culture cannot be accounted for in language—that it has no place in language."[13]

Composer and co-librettist Moya Henderson believes Chamberlain's tale can tell us much about Australians' deep-seated attitudes to strong women, treatment of "outsiders," and fear of the interior landscape. Part of the hostility Chamberlain provoked came about from a backlash against 1970s feminism, she argues, even though some of her most trenchant critics were women. "The times were mean, the going was tough and men were looking for an adjusted position in the world because of feminism and here was this uppity person who answered back."[14]

The opera's visual artist, Neville Dawson, emphasizes the spatial concept of the outback as de-naturing of women and deepening the gender divide:

> The Great Dividing Range is aptly named in many ways because we cling rather precariously to the coastline where it's comfortable. But over there, towards the centre, we often in our literature refer to it as the dead centre or the dead heart.

---

[10] Quoted in ibid., p. 145.

[11] Adrian Howe, "Chamberlain Revisited: The Case against the Media," in *Lindy Chamberlain Revisited: A 25th Anniversary Retrospective*, ed. Adrian Howe (Canada Bay, NSW: Lhr Press, 2005), pp. 234; 236ff. Also see Kerryn Goldsworthy, "Martyr to Her Sex," in *Lindy Chamberlain Revisited: A 25th Anniversary Retrospective*, ed. Adrian Howe (Canada Bay, NSW: Lhr Press, 2005; 1986). Howe reports that Lindy explained, after her exoneration, that her lawyers had told her to stay expressionless. Howe, "Chamberlain Revisited," p. 256.

[12] *Evil Angels*, dir. John Bryson, Penguin, 1986.

[13] Goldsworthy, "Martyr," p. 161. She quotes *Evil Angels*. Her point about the "ineffableness" of female culture is a recurring theme in Western music history and is also critiqued by many feminist musicologists. See, for example, Leslie C. Dunn and Nancy A. Jones (eds.), *Embodied Voices: Representing Female Vocality in Western Culture* (Cambridge and New York: Cambridge University Press, 1994).

[14] Quoted in Morgan, "Rock Opera."

To some extent the land, which we refer to as a mother, is a hostile mother ...
Lindy became a substitute for the way we vent our hostilities on the mother.[15]

Lindy calls all these attitudes into question when the opera depicts Lindy as a loving, "normal" mother, innocently on holiday with her family. Before Azaria's disappearance, she sings, "I am here with my children, / here with my new baby, Azaria, / my darling Azaria."[16] Sally Lowe, camping too at the site with her family, recounts: "Lindy shone with the glow of a new mother."[17] When Lindy realizes the dingo has taken the baby, she is distraught, grief-stricken: "(*screaming*) Azaria's gone! The dingo has taken Azaria! Azaria, Azaria, my baby, Azaria."[18] The opera also presents her considered reflections and logical thinking in the direct transcripts from her court cases and other quotations from the press. Lindy demonstrates an acute awareness of her situation regarding the public, media, and legal opinions: "What difference does it make, / Whether I laugh or cry wrong? / Whatever I wear wrong! / So I can't be worried what anyone thinks."[19] But Lindy's predicament was very much a product of "what people think."

Feminine Transgressions of "the (Australian) Wild"

During a flashback to the night when Azaria's disappearance is about to be discovered, a seemingly inconsequential comment is made by Greg Lowe, one of the sympathetic fellow-campers at the site: "That's the mysterious bush for you / it comes to life at night time." This remark follows Michael Chamberlain's comment that the butcherbird usually only sings when there is a moon, and this night, there was none, yet the bird sang.[20] This deeply held attitude—on the unknowableness of the Australian outback—is wrought cleverly and subtly. It is a complex notion, and one that has highly significant ramifications for Lindy Chamberlain.

The mythologizing that sealed Lindy Chamberlain's unjust fate in the years immediately following her baby's disappearance is informed by aspects of a nationalism conflated with gender considerations. Anthropologist Julie Marcus has investigated this "contest" between the two potential suspects in Azaria's disappearance—namely, the dingo, the "*wild dog*," and the Chamberlains,

---

[15] Quoted in ibid. I have discussed this trope in relation to another two Australian contemporary compositions. See Linda Kouvaras, "From Port Essington to the Himalayas: Music, Place and Spirituality in Two Recent Australian Works," in *The Soundscapes of Australia: Music, Place and Spirituality*, ed. Fiona Richards (Burlington, VT: Ashgate, 2007).

[16] Act I, Scene 1, "Dingo," CD 1, Track 2.

[17] Act I, Scene 5, "Trial," CD 1, Track 17.

[18] Act I, Scene 3, "Kill," CD 1, Track 10.

[19] Act I, Scene 5, "Trial," CD 1, Track 16.

[20] Act I, Scene 3, "Kill," CD 1, Track 10.

120   *Opera Indigene: Re/presenting First Nations and Indigenous Cultures*

especially Lindy, the "*bad woman*": "Mrs. Chamberlain was punished not simply for killing her baby (a crime which is in much of Australia treated with considerable sympathy), but because she had charged the dingo with what came to be seen as her own 'wickedness'."[21] Lindy's accusation of the dingo touched upon "a nationalistic discourse on the wild ... in which women are subordinated to men through the male conquest of the wild Australian outback, and in which the wild female land is appropriated by men."[22] Accordingly, when Lindy Chamberlain accused a dingo of stealing her baby and eating it she also challenged a male iconic symbol that represented both the wild and the male defeat of it. "In the gendered world of Australian frontier nationalism, the land and its wildness is female and it is through the conquest of this feminized wild that men realize both their masculinity and civilization."[23] The crux of the matter, according to Marcus, is that Lindy

> reactivated the great fear of Australians, one developed at length and in detail within aesthetics and literary criticism, that at the heart of their being is nothingness. ... Hence, Mrs Chamberlain was sacrificed upon the Rock of the gods of Australian frontier nationalism, and she was truly captured and imprisoned within the discourse of *the nation*.[24]

This is reflected in composer/co-librettist Henderson's statement that, when she was writing the opera, novelist David Malouf's idea of "trespass" became very important to her.[25] The most obvious aspect of "trespass" in this situation is white people encroaching upon Indigenous people's sacred ground. In the opera Michael Chamberlain articulates this view when he sings, "We were ordinary people, unsuspecting tourists / We didn't mean to step outside our Church and family / or out beyond our everyday lives. / We never meant to trespass."[26] But Lindy enacted a further trespass—against masculinist nationalism:

> Mrs Chamberlain was a woman at the heart of Australia's centre, at the centre of the wild "outback." Women have no place in the Australian wild. They have, of course, always been there, but they are marginalized and contained and their presence is ignored or minimized. The outback, the bush, is a male domain, a male space of mateship from which women are ideally absent. Ayers Rock, the very centre of this white domain, is becoming a place of pilgrimage for

---

[21]   Julie Marcus, "Prisoner of Discourse: The Dingo, the Dog and the Baby," *Anthropology Today*, 5/3 (1989), p. 15.

[22]   Marcus, "Prisoner of Discourse," p. 17.

[23]   Ibid., p. 18.

[24]   Ibid., p. 19. Italics in original.

[25]   Moya Henderson, "Forum: 'Relationships-in-Progress'," *Sounds Australian*, 15/49 (1997), pp. 16–19.

[26]   Act I, Scene 2, "Mother," CD 1, Track 7.

Moya Henderson's Lindy   121

settler Australians. To visit the sacred site is to reinforce the authenticity of the elements of a national cult of masculinity in which a gender hierarchy and the conquest of the land's wildness are essential elements. In this context, the charge against the male dingo in male space where woman had no right to be at all, let alone a woman with *her* baby [Australian babies belong to women, despite their patrilineal heritage], either converted the dingo into an avenger, as in the minority New Age view of the curse of Ayers Rock, or in the majority view of the nation, it brought into play the reversal of the totem to produce the dog.[27]

Diane Johnson quotes a letter from *The Sun*, November 11, 1982: "I know a dingo took your baby, a two-legged dingo like you."[28] As Johnson notes, "Whether Azaria was killed by the 'Devil-Dog' (*The Sun*, July 21, 1983) or by her mother, Lindy was blamed. ... [W]hen a child misbehaves, gets lost or dies, the mother is, covertly at least, held responsible."[29] One of many appellations Lindy was called by the press was "Dingo Baby Mother" (*The Sun*, February 5, 1981), which conflated her story with the supernatural.[30] Even her defense counsel referred to her account as "the dingo story."[31] Johnson notes that, in medieval times, "every woman was a potential witch," and such illogical cultural fears were to sway legal proceedings to a scandalous extent in the Chamberlain case. Lindy's reappropriation of the dingo signifier from supernatural to archetypal is aimed squarely at her accusers: "So you maul me to get even with the Coroner!," drawing attention to the dingo-like qualities of her accusers in the court. She remarks, when the media turns and is on their side, "We must be the underdogs at last!"[32] Lindy adopts a canine quality herself to mirror the Prosecutor when she sings, "Yes!," repeatedly, at very high pitch, sounding like a yapping dog.[33] Regarding the hate-mail the family is receiving, Lindy sings, "They scratch and gouge at our lives. / Lock away that rubbish from their eyes. / Save the children from reading such venom,"[34] thus both showing herself to be a responsible mother and pointing out the dingo-like behavior of the press. Immediately, the Dingo music follows. As Marcus comments, "when used as an adjective, the meaning [of 'dingo press'] is strongly pejorative."[35] This connectedness between animal and human behavior, between cultures, that the opera shows so starkly is one that we ignore at our peril.

---

[27]   Marcus, "Prisoner of Discourse," p. 18.

[28]   Johnson, "From Fairy to Witch," p. 142.

[29]   Ibid.

[30]   Ibid., p. 143.

[31]   Howe, "Chamberlain Revisited," pp. 241–2.

[32]   Act I, Scene 4, "Blood," CD 1, Track 14.

[33]   Act I, Scene 5, "Trial," CD 1, Tracks 21 and 22.

[34]   Act I, Scene 4, "Blood," CD 1, Track 15.

[35]   Marcus, "Prisoner of Discourse," n. 5, p. 15. Italics in original.

The Dichotomy between Faith and Knowledge

Co-librettist Rodriguez writes: "Everywhere in this story, there was *belief*: Mrs Chamberlain's supposedly outlandish religious faith which sustained her, Aboriginal knowledge of the land, as well as volatile public opinion ..."[36]

> The dingo's legendary significance as a devil was introduced at the first inquest when the Coroner asked a local Aboriginal tracker, Mr. Nipper Winmatti, to tell the court about Aboriginal legends relating to dingoes and children. If twins were born, he said, the stronger one was kept and the other was left out in the bush "for the dingo spirit, which was classed as a devil."[37]

And whites are not exempt from mythologizing Uluru:

> One report described the prevailing atmosphere as spooky and creepy; ... and one person in the same report thought there was "something eerie about the atmosphere that night. And her dog, he was unusually quiet;" when the search was abandoned about midnight, the searchers "closed their door on the evil blackness of the night."[38]

Composer and co-librettist Moya Henderson, a former nun, is aware that the Chamberlains being Seventh Day Adventists also aroused suspicion.[39] "Some talked of sorcery. Others told of fearful rites carried out in the desert. And countless people were firmly and wrongly convinced that Azaria meant 'sacrifice in the wilderness'."[40]

Lindy, however, is presented as someone who is also well informed about Indigenous culture. On the fateful day events are about to unfold, she reflects on the cave the family is visiting near the Rock, acknowledging, respectfully, "This place, this place is sacred." She points out that because of "too many hands touching the walls" of the cave, she "finds it hard to make out the lines of / ancient paintings ... the ochre has faded," demonstrating her awareness of the intrusion of tourism and its deleterious effects on the environment. She admonishes her children, "Don't disturb the paintings," when they boast that they can touch the roof. She contrasts here even with Michael, who says he needs more light to take photos.[41] The opera's

---

[36] Judith Rodriguez, "Forum: 'Relationships-in-Progress'," *Sounds Australian*, 15/49 (1997), pp. 16–19, p. 16.

[37] Johnson, "From Fairy to Witch," p. 148. She quotes *The Age*, 19 December, 1980.

[38] Ibid., p. 136. She quotes from Richard Shears, *Azaria* (Melbourne: Nelson, 1982).

[39] Morgan, "Rock Opera."

[40] *Daily Mirror*, April 29, 1983, cited in Johnson, "From Fairy to Witch," p. 151.

[41] Act I, Scene 1, "Dingo," CD 1, Track 2. Michael does show that he has some knowledge of indigenous culture by his comments on the butcherbird. See n. 20 (Act I, Scene 3, "Kill," CD 1, Track 10).

creators demonstrate their sensitivity to Indigenous culture through the Defense QC statement that women are not allowed to utter the name of the "devil dingo of the Dreamtime," Kurrpanggu. Lindy herself is depicted as being aware of this legend and its gender sensitivities: when she warns her children, "Don't disturb the spirits of the Dreaming," Henderson has her purposefully trailing off at, "Least of all that one they call..." and an offstage chorus utters the dingo's name.[42]

Yet the opera presents a balanced, realistic picture of cultural difference: the Chamberlain family and fellow campers, the Lowes, "Westernize" the stars by quoting the words of "Twinkle, Twinkle, Little Star." This occurs straight after they hear the butcherbird's song.[43] The alienness of the bird is delineated by Sally Lowe: "How can a bird that sounds like that / be called a butcherbird?," and the Man replying, "They swoop on their prey, / But if it's too big to swallow at a gulp, / they hook it up in the fork of a tree, / or on a barbed-wire fence; / and they dismember the creature"; Sally responds, "Agh, the laws of nature! / But the song of the butcherbird is glorious."[44] Aidan Chamberlain comments, "Great minds think alike,"[45] in response to learning that one of the Lowe children has the same name as Azaria's middle name. This shows that mindset is all-important (the Lowes are on the Chamberlain's side in the legal battle).

Dangerous Knowledge

When a news story is repeated enough, it can transmute in the collective consciousness into "knowledge." The "scientific" evidence—proved later to be completely erroneous—was "frequently obtained from the police and then reported in the media as scientifically determined facts which were shortened into headlines such as 'Azaria's Injuries "Caused by Scissors"' (*The Sun*, October 20, 1981)."[46] During the second inquest, similar headlines were repeated across the nation, resulting in many readers convinced of Lindy Chamberlain's guilt before her trial began.[47] *Lindy* neatly encapsulates the situation when the Prosecuting Council sings, "The woman's a killer. / It says so in the Sunday papers."[48]

In the opera, the Defense Counsel refutes the fallacious demonstration offered by the "Teeth Expert," who tries to "prove" that a baby's skull cannot fit into a dingo's jaw, by demonstrating that it actually *can*. The Teeth Expert counters, "That evidence looks contrived." Lindy points out, "Was there ever any of *their*

---

[42]   Act I, Scene 1, "Dingo," CD 1, Track 2.

[43]   Act I, Scene 3, "Kill," CD 1, Track 10.

[44]   Act I, Scene 3, "Kill," CD 1, Track 9.

[45]   Act I, Scene 3, "Kill," CD 1, Track 10.

[46]   Howe, "Chamberlain Revisited," p. 246.

[47]   Ibid., pp. 246–7.

[48]   Act I, Scene 1, "Dingo," CD 1, Track 4.

124   *Opera Indigene: Re/presenting First Nations and Indigenous Cultures*

evidence / that didn't look contrived?"[49] Howe comments on the irony that it was Lindy, the "central non-expert witness, who seemed to most clearly understand why there was a legal rule against opinion evidence being given outside of one's expertise" and refused to offer a reason for the spray pattern (submitted as blood and later proved as sound deadener) under the dashboard, acknowledging that "I'm not convinced in my mind how that got there; ... it would only be pure speculation."[50] In the opera, Henderson and Rodriguez retain Lindy's conduct here when under cross-examination: "Look, the truth is, I wasn't there. / I can only go on the evidence of my own eyes."[51]

But "'the aura of scientific certainty which created a shield of accurate objectivity' around it and which accorded status to 'expert opinion evidence' in the Chamberlain case"[52] was created. In this instance, a double move was enacted which privileged the Crown's opinion evidence:

> First, a polarisation of "expert" opinion/eyewitness testimony fixed the superiority of the former. But the superiority of the Crown's opinion evidence had to be secured against that of the defence by bringing into play a second crucially significant binary opposition—that between forensic science and academic science. Here, the "field of expertise" evidentiary rules that are intended to determine whether proposed witnesses are qualified in a particular field were manipulated by the prosecution in order to discredit academic scientists [... which were merely] theoretical, supine and naïve, [as opposed to] forensic science [which] was professional, "real," "practical" or hands-on and therefore truly "expert."[53]

Thus the strategy was to create and then use a "binary opposition between 'hard' or practical forensic science and 'soft' or theoretical academic science" and "it worked perfectly at both the trial and the appeals."[54] A further string to the prosecution's bow was to set up imported expert versus local expert opinion (the London forensic scientist versus the Geelong academic). The notion that the

---

[49]   Act I, Scene 5, "Trial," CD 1, Track 18.

[50]   Adrian Howe, "Imagining Evidence, Fictioning Truth: Expert Evidence in the Chamberlain Case," in *Lindy Chamberlain Revisited: A 25th Anniversary Retrospective*, ed. Adrian Howe (Canada Bay, NSW: Lhr Press, 2005), pp. 289–90.

[51]   Act I, Scene 5, "Trial," CD 1, Track 22.

[52]   Howe, "Imagining Evidence," pp. 276–7. Through the prism of Foucault's theories Howe presents a compelling analysis of the way expert knowledges were privileged over local, subjugated knowledges here: Howe, "Imagining Evidence," p. 274. She quotes Michel Foucault, Mauro Bertani, Alessandro Fontana, François Ewald, and David Macey, *Society Must Be Defended: Lectures at the Collège De France, 1975–76* (New York: Picador, 2003), pp. 7–11.

[53]   Howe, "Imagining Evidence," pp. 277–8.

[54]   Ibid., p. 278.

expertise must come from London is an acute example of a colonial discourse at play, one that sets up what postcolonial insights illuminate as a center/margins dichotomy, according rightness and privilege to the perceived center:[55]

> The reported scientific "discoveries" overwhelmed the knowledge of the trackers ... Not until 1986 was Barbara Tjikadu, wife of the head tracker, Nipper Winmarti, given the opportunity to give evidence that she had identified tracks of a dingo carrying a baby and the places where it had put the child down on the sand. Justice Morling described her as an impressive witness, with the reputation of being an excellent tracker.[56]

Theater director Robyn Nevin's preoccupation with the Aboriginal Australians in the opera—shared by Henderson and Rodriguez—was to highlight that "their testimony has still not been acknowledged in the final coroner's inquest ... It was good to have those ideas reinforced."[57] The trackers' evidence is fully represented in the opera.[58]

While the previous examples demonstrate how the libretto carefully disentangles the binary oppositions embedded within the media and court's treatment of Lindy, the opera also addresses these oppositions through Henderson's compositional techniques.

Operatic Workings: Crossing the Black/White Divide

Operatic convention frequently has characters sing and converse while other events play out simultaneously; characters who are dead often sing from beyond the grave. In *Lindy*, Lindy sings with and to Azaria throughout the opera. The first instance of this aligns Lindy with the "world" of "real truth," and, by extension in the context of the Chamberlain case, with the world of Indigenous "real knowledge." It occurs very early on in the work, in the midst of the court-case scene where the jacket is unearthed[59]—five years after the disappearance of the child, three years of which Lindy has spent in a Darwin jail. The jacket has been discovered by chance at the site where a man has fallen from the Rock. Detailing the specifics of the place, "Where butcherbirds sing, / and grevilleas grow at the rock," Lindy aligns herself with the Indigenous world; the Prosecuting Counsel and Scribbler (court stenographer) can only refer to the area in a general way, at best—Prosecuting Council: "Confound it! A man falls / from the top of Uluru"—or, at worst, in a

---

[55]   Ibid.

[56]   Howe, "Chamberlain Revisited," p. 249. She quotes Lindy Chamberlain in K. Houghton, "Trackers Say Blood, Dingo Near Tent," *Daily Sun*, June 12, 1986.

[57]   Henderson, "Forum," p. 17.

[58]   Act II, Scene 2, "Inquiry," CD 2, Track 6.

[59]   Act I, Scene 1, "Dingo," CD 1, Track 5.

numbingly ignorant way: Scribbler: "Out of nowhere. / Out of the blue!" Lindy follows with, "Right at the outset I told ev'ryone that / my little baby was wearing a knitted jacket," to drive the point home that she had the necessary knowledge of what the investigators should be looking for.[60] And in amongst the true, hard evidence of the jacket, the Prosecuting Council is still trying to cling to the earlier prejudice: "Stop all that crap! / Remember the car *awash* with blood! / And bugger the jacket! / Bugger the jacket!," while the Dingo/Journalist pack sing: "Remember it was 'Sacrifice in the Wilderness' / Azaria means 'Sacrifice in the Wilderness,'" which Lindy counters with "Remember that Azaria means 'Blessed of God.'" In the middle of the first vilifying court case, Azaria sings, "Mother," pointing out that this is a mother who has lost her baby, not some unnatural female child-killer.[61]

There are third-person shifts where Lindy sings, "pity the Mother" (often echoed by Azaria) occurring throughout. This estranging effect steps outside the confines of the event/medium, with the purpose of reminding listeners that they are witnessing a contrived artwork, disallowing them to "lose themselves" in the sweep of the unfolding narrative. It thereby acts as the prevailing moral voice and maintains focus on the issue, exhorting us to empathize with the mother who has lost her child to a dingo.

One of the most striking musical tropes in the work is the Dingo music. Jazz-like, with its swung rhythm, melodic contour outlining a minor 7th chord (with "groovy" major 6th added) and simple, I–V accompaniment texture, raucous in tone, its truncated nature—lasting a mere two measures—is cleverly sarcastic: the composer is *commenting* at the same time as *presenting*. The prominent instrument is the saxophone, roughly hewn (Example 6.1, see pp. 128–9).

Henderson relates: "we progress to a lascivious blood scene where we have the sax coming out of the orchestra to everybody's surprise, the sexy sax."[62] "Surprise" in the orchestral setting is conjured through both this instrumentation and the musical style that conflicts with the primary, neo-Romantic/early twentieth-century, unmistakably art-music symphonic texture. "Surprise" here mirrors the "surprise" factor in the case: that it was (as Lindy, Sally Lowe, and the trackers had maintained all along) the dingo who had taken the baby. This music recurs throughout the opera to signal the dingo-like behavior of the prosecution and the media, reinforced by double-casting the dingo pack as the media mongrels.

---

[60]   Henderson informs me that "some of my favourite text is taken from the transcript of the trial. ... On CD 1, Tracks 19–22, I try to make Lindy's music 'fly.' Ian Barker, the prosecution counsel, was wily and rehearsed and menacing. Lindy was flying by the seat of her pants, so to speak: the learned barrister against the feisty woman. In my opinion Lindy won hands down. She reveals herself here as a very gutsy dame and admirable in every sense. She thinks on her feet and nimble she is. She takes it right up to Barker every single time." Moya Henderson, e-mail correspondence with the author, 2009.

[61]   Act I, Scene 1, "Dingo," CD 1, Track 4.

[62]   "Interview with Moya Henderson," *The Music Show* October 26, 2002, Radio National, www.abc.net.au/rn/music/mshow/s726689.htm (accessed May 29, 2009).

As Howe states: "To the extent that the media failed to report or played down the testimony of Aboriginal trackers, their construction of the criminality of Lindy Chamberlain could be said to have been at least implicitly racist."[63] What the opera achieves most distinctly is the allying of Lindy herself with the object of the racism.

But the opera also ameliorates much of the black/white divide. It focuses on Azaria becoming "red sand," part of the Australian ground where she died:

> She now becomes an indissoluble bond between the two worlds of the opera—the ancient landscape of the Rock and the modern world of western civilization. ... A victim as innocent as Lindy now becomes a symbol of reconciliation, of resignation, and of peace of mind. Lindy is able to declare that her spirit is unbroken and her faith intact.[64]

When Lindy positions herself as a new mother at the cave, she also notes that she is not the first: "Ancient mothers from the Dreaming / are ranged around the low cave, / in the womb of the red rock. / We know this is where from ancient times / the mothers came. / One with the red land, owned by this red land. / They say that even today / young mothers come here to give birth," and "here in these caves it's so safe and still, secret places where women came to give birth."[65] The space that is conjured here is a female space, one that is aligned with Aboriginal culture. When she says later, during the court proceedings, to Michael, "Too many hands ... / touching, clawing, scraping" and then "(doubles up in pain),"[66] she echoes her earlier remarks on the hands obliterating the indigenous cave paintings,[67] drawing an association between herself and the misunderstood and mistreated indigenous culture.

The work effects an "antidote" to another contentious issue with relation to women's position. Catherine Clément's critique of traditional (particularly nineteenth-century) operas argues that the beauty of the arias can distract the listener from the inordinately high incidence of heroine murder.[68] Significantly, *Lindy* focuses on facts and the complex unfolding of events, rather than succumbing to what could well be a temptation for a composer dealing with this chronicle to devote musical space to essaying the attendant emotions or personal reactions in extended arias. Judith Rodriguez confides that all of the extraordinary

---

[63] Howe, "Chamberlain Revisited," p. 249.

[64] Janet Healy, "Cry 'Havoc!' and Let Slip the Dogs of War: The Genesis of Moya Henderson's Opera, *Lindy*," *Encounters: Meetings in Australian Music: Essays, Images, Interviews* (Brisbane: Queensland Conservatorium Research Centre, 2005), p. 58.

[65] Act I, Scene 1, "Dingo," CD 1, Tracks 1 and 2.

[66] Act I, Scene 4, "Blood," CD 1, Track 15.

[67] See n. 41.

[68] Catherine Clément, *Opera, or The Undoing of Women*, trans. Betsy Wing (Minneapolis: University of Minnesota Press, 1988).

128 Opera Indigene: Re/presenting First Nations and Indigenous Cultures

Example 6.1 *Lindy*, Dingo music

Example 6.1 *concluded*

130   *Opera Indigene: Re/presenting First Nations and Indigenous Cultures*

circumstances "forebade us to concentrate on mere personal heartbreak."[69] Yet Lindy's music stands out: it is the most passionate yet also the most stably tonal. This is in contradistinction to Susan McClary's charge, similar to that of Clément, that traditional operatic heroines' music is the least tonally stable, thus according the audience the greatest sense of narrative "pleasure" when she is killed off and tonal resolution ensues.[70] Choosing Lindy's music as that which is most stable in effect "de-witches" her.

A vivid example of this obverse treatment occurs where Lindy sings, "What end? What end? / For us in the end the Law will be too late! / Too late, too late, too late, too late!," after Michael has reassured her that "in the end the Law *will* save us."[71] Both characters are accorded very powerful, passionate, tonal music, but again it is short-lived, so that the listener does not have a chance to be swept away by this very affecting music other than for a moment. The music fails to cadence, after building confidently to what feels like a resting point of G♯ minor, only to slip down a tone to F♯ minor, and then to fall further, "crumbling" down to D minor (the music does not modulate "smoothly"). The resultant effect is to question Michael's positive-seeming words as belying the true sense of doubt that underpins them. Further, Lindy's music "trumps" Michael's in terms of power, passion, and affect, thus calling his assertion into question. Michael's music's affective qualities lie in the use of mixture and the brass harmonizations; for Lindy's music, in the use of sequences. For Lindy, the more protracted treatment overall, the higher register, the alto voice on the trombone that harmonizes with her on "too many hands" and the brass section on "too late" in strong perfect fifths below her line, all work with the canonic treatment of her melody in the strings (Example 6.2).

Goldsworthy and Howe respectively make two vital points that render all the more powerful Henderson's and Rodriguez's contribution: "Male observers from the legal profession, including her own defense counsel, have said that Lindy Chamberlain talked her way into jail, and that if only she had kept her mouth shut she would have been acquitted."[72] Rather than presenting motherhood as "unable to be accounted for in language,"[73] *Lindy* affords its mother-figure full voice: operatically and verbally. Howe decries

> the casual, unthinking gender-skewed opinions of the male journalists covering the case [that] went largely unchallenged. This curious silence highlights one

---

[69]   Rodriguez, "Forum," p. 16.

[70]   Susan McClary, *Georges Bizet, Carmen*, Cambridge Opera Handbooks (Cambridge and New York: Cambridge University Press, 1992).

[71]   Act I, Scene 4, "Blood," CD 1, Track 15. Here the opera suggests a gendered divide in attitude between Michael and Lindy, as he has faith in the law "Saving" them, while she argues that "For us in the end the Law will be too late!" It is also noteworthy that, while he is sympathetically drawn, Michael's music is never as powerfully affecting as Lindy's.

[72]   Goldsworthy, "Martyr," p. 164.

[73]   See n. 13.

Example 6.2 *Lindy*, "What end? What end?", CD 1, Track 15

continued

132 Opera Indigene: Re/presenting First Nations and Indigenous Cultures

Example 6.2 continued

Example 6.2 *concluded*

134 *Opera Indigene: Re/presenting First Nations and Indigenous Cultures*

of the most remarkable features of the Lindy Chamberlain case—the dearth of critical commentary in the very places one might expect to find it: cultural studies, legal scholarship, criminology or, indeed, in any field of critical social inquiry. It is as if the saga so overwhelmed the national psyche that it defied feminists and other intellectuals working inside or outside the academy, left-wing activists and most trained thinkers of any ilk to make any sense of it. Even more remarkably, there are few signs that their curiosity has been aroused over time.[74]

Lindy fills this silence.

"Missed Opportunities?"—or, the Cathartic Filling of the "Heart of Nothingness"

By the time Australia has caught up with what actually transpired, Lindy and Michael have already moved on in their own minds; they sing "ethereally," "Ah, the jacket is stiff with red earth / and aged to orange / and black, black with dry blood."[75] Concentrating on the colors and equating them with the surrounds, they recapitulate Lindy's opening remarks about the cave paintings, colored ochre.[76] Anne Power makes an astute point: "After the evidence of Aboriginal trackers is admitted, the judge finds that a conviction cannot be supported. Catharsis comes from Lindy's belief that the land has become a paradise, that Azaria and the land have become one."[77] Lindy (and Azaria's spirit) sing, in rich harmonies, "Where butcherbirds sing, and grevilleas grow at the rock." The music is permitted to reach a rare cadence, and is followed by one of the few slight pauses in the work, which is mostly continuous (Example 6.3, see pp. 136–7). The rhetorical pause and sense of musical closure from the plagal cadence allows the import of the words to sink in. Lindy and Azaria's short duet cuts across the Ensemble's account of the man who fell from the top of the Rock and landed near the all-important matinée jacket worn by Azaria (and disbelieved by the Prosecutor). Henderson shows Lindy's deeper understanding of her surrounds compared with the white

---

[74] Adrian Howe, "Marginalised Voices: Feminist Responses," in *Lindy Chamberlain Revisited: A 25th Anniversary Retrospective*, ed. Adrian Howe (Canada Bay, NSW: Lhr Press, 2005), pp. 112–13. Howe does acknowledge Kerry Goldsworthy's "Martyr to Her Sex," the only feminist analysis of the Chamberlain case to appear in the mainstream media (and reproduced in Howe's collection). See Goldsworthy, "Martyr."

[75] Act I, Scene 2, "Mother," CD 1, Track 6.

[76] The composer/co-librettist tells me she intended an endorsement here of the Aboriginal flag through the reference to its colors, albeit slightly altered—yellow becoming ochre. Moya Henderson, e-mail correspondence with the author, 2009..

[77] Anne Power, "Voiced Identity: A Study of Central Characters in Seven Operas from Australia 1988–1998," (PhD dissertation, University of Wollongong, 1999), p. 78. See also Anne Power, Chapter 7 in this volume, pp. 141–55.

Moya Henderson's Lindy

men, who focus on its direct threat to them: "P.C.: Confound that *bloody* jacket! What idiot dug it up!"[78] Lindy's description of the jacket, by contrast, is as though describing the colors of the Rock as in the opening scene, the separate music for them both contrasting appropriately.

In this opera, the Indigenous content is subtly rendered; there are no direct quotations from Aboriginal culture, for example. Rather, a sensibility of respect toward the Indigenous people runs through the work, as a theme of equal importance and significance as that afforded to the wronged heroine. Sonic Indigenous reference comes in the form of the butcherbird transcription. The trackers are included as scored characters. The setting comes to life in the descriptions of the colors of the Rock and the sand, and mention of the cave paintings and of sacred legends. In this way, the work avoids insensitive didacticism and the potential pitfalls inherent in cross-cultural enterprises. It shows as blatantly as is imaginable the heinousness of a situation where Aboriginal knowledge should have been one of the first avenues called upon and what transpired when it was derided and ignored. It also presents a highly original "example" of an "injured" reconciliation through the figure of the dead baby, reclaimed by the land, and through the wisdom of her mother, a white woman who knew that the black trackers could tell the representatives of the white legal system the truth of what occurred that night in 1980 and who had a level, realistic apprehension of the history of the land she and her family visited. The opera thus sets up a complex, elided space of gender and race. It allows Lindy to operate outside a stereotype of a white person subscribing to an "alternative" Christian belief system to simultaneously respect and be informed about Indigenous beliefs.

What of the *effect* for the listener of this work? It is worth quoting from two reviews of the opera at the time of its premiere:

> On opening night, I was painfully aware of too many missed opportunities. The music rushes through a nice evocation of something called a butcherbird, which lives around Uluru. I wanted to hear more, but the composer didn't trust her music to carry a scene for long...[79]

> *Lindy* took the Chamberlain case so literally that it failed to engage as musical theatre. The subject would appear to be rich with possibility: the witch-hunt of an innocent woman and the uncertain relationship European Australians have with the continent's interior are just two themes that could have been given greater dramatic power. Yet the opera had its characters singing from a court transcript for a libretto. ... The closer a dramatic work comes to documentary realism, the more limited its potential for theatre. It's the same with opera, but

---

[78]   Act I, Scene 2, "Mother," CD 1, Track 5.

[79]   Harvey Steiman, "Lindy," *International Opera Review* (2002), www.musicweb-international.com/sandh/2002/Aug02/lindy.htm (accessed November 23, 2008).

Example 6.3 *Lindy*, "Where Butcherbirds Sing", CD 1, Track 5

here the gap between life and art is even greater, by virtue of the fact that opera demands people sing.[80]

As a pleasure-seeking audience member, I could concur readily with these sentiments: there is a wealth of beautiful musical passages in *Lindy*, and the most

---

[80] Matthew Westwood, "Here Lies Love," *The Weekend Australian* (March 25, 2006), www.davidbyrne.com/here_lies_love/press/03_25_06_The_Weekend_Australian.php (accessed December 18, 2008).

Example 6.3 *concluded*

138   *Opera Indigene: Re/presenting First Nations and Indigenous Cultures*

gorgeous of these do flit by quickly and are replaced by vastly contrasting ones that are either similarly tantalizingly attractive in their own right or purposefully repellent. I find myself wishing aesthetically for more development, repetition, or lingering on the seductive moments, as occurs in traditional approaches to opera. It is significant that Westwood describes the "missed opportunities" as "painful": it is indeed a kind of pain when aesthetic expectations are set up only to remain unfulfilled. But I am grateful in this instance that my desires are *not* gratified. Steiman does suggest that the composer "perhaps just wanted to get on with the story."[81] The thwarting of my aesthetic desires indeed forces me to remain focused on the storyline, the plot, and to remember that this is not a made-up fancy to suit the operatic medium but a real-life happening, one that has had tragic, irreparable consequences for a family, and, in the utterly incredible miscarriages of justice and the majority of community sentiment for most of the time, is a blight on Australia's postcolonial history as a whole.

The ramifications of this are not confined to the legal dimension. Henderson states: "I think this opera demonstrates that there's a little bit of dingo in all of us."[82] Sinisterly, with its jaunty, jazzy rhythm and strong melodic riff, the "Dingo music" is the most "catchy" music in the opera. This reminds us that ideas—no matter how crass, maybe especially—can "catch on" all too readily, if they are presented in such bite-sized, easily consumed packages; they can become part of our belief system, no matter how erroneous. *Lindy* demonstrates how very ill advised and scurrilous it is to ignore a knowledge base that is entirely "scientifically" suited to finding the truth of such a situation. The truth of Azaria's disappearance could have been solved by a knowledge base offered firstly from white, female eyewitnesses, one of whom, the mother of the missing child, was constructed into a voiceless witch-like figure. The other source of knowledge was provided by Indigenous people and was relegated to the "heart of nothingness" that forms traditional white perception of the red center, which this masculinist attitude has sought to own and contain.

Westwood also criticizes the work for its "documentary realism," asserting that this "limit[s] its potential for theater."[83] Contrary to such criticism, I would instead suggest that, by sticking to a realist portrayal of events, through the use of transcripts from the court and from newspaper reportage, the opera allows the story of the true eyewitness, Lindy, and that of the Aboriginal trackers, to be set

---

[81]   Steiman, "Lindy."

[82]   Moya Henderson, "The Composer 'on the Spot' (CD Liner Notes)," *Lindy* (ABC Classics: 476 7489, 2005), pp. 8–9.

[83]   In a television program, the interviewer asks Henderson, "Doesn't opera, though, risk turning the Chamberlain's tragedy into farce?" Henderson replies, "How could it? No. The music is not that kind of music. The farce is the way the country behaved." Rebecca Baillie, "Azaria Chamberlain Story Provides Inspiration for New Opera," *ABC TV: The 7.30 Report* (2002), television program, www.abc.net.au/7.30/content/2002/s708262.htm (accessed May 31, 2008).

in sonic stone. It also delivers the necessary reminder of a legal system that needs constant monitoring, and that public opinion can be firstly spuriously formed—with grave legal consequences—and then flip in a heartbeat.[84]

There is no plaque to commemorate Azaria Chamberlain's death at Uluru, no monument, and no mention of the momentous events in tourist brochures or maps, nor in the tourist mementoes or local history books; the otherwise readily available paperbacks on the subject are also absent from the site.[85] *Lindy* makes its operatic contribution to the other well-meaning accounts of the saga in books such as *Lindy Chamberlain Revisited* and the film *Evil Angels*. The opera achieves the considerable feat of keeping all these attendant issues to the forefront and provides a subtle, non-didactic "example" of how ill-informed, prejudiced attitudes conflated the issue of gender and race to act out one of the most shaming incidents in recent colonized Australian history.

The year 1997 was when Henderson completed writing *Lindy*; it was also the year of the *Bringing them Home* report on Australia's Stolen Generations, which—like the opera in its own, non-didactic way—highlighted the need for major rethinking on Indigenous issues.[86] Some twelve years later, Flora MacDonald, from the ACT Branch of Australians for Reconciliation, stated in 2009:

> we need to include Aboriginal people and Torres Strait Islanders in our communities so that we can all learn from one another and develop a real awareness, understanding, appreciation and respect for the culture and history of Indigenous Australia ... Its basis is the inclusion of the Indigenous peoples of Australia, not their exclusion. And that is healing for all of us.[87]

---

[84] The work is also consistent with new theatrical practices of verbatim theater (as practised by Australia's acclaimed Version 1.0 political theater-director: David Williams) and reflects the approach to subject matter of much postmodern opera along the lines of, for instance, Philip Glass's *Einstein on the Beach*, and John Adams's *Death of Klinghoffer* and *Nixon in China*. For a discussion on this topic regarding Australian chamber operas produced at around the time of *Lindy*, see Caroline Baum, "Forget Fantasy, Opera Gets Real," *Australian, Weekend Review* (May 23–24, 1992), p. 12.

[85] Johnson, "From Fairy to Witch," p. 154. "At the mention of the Chamberlain case, an otherwise rather garrulous, verbose and friendly Uluru park ranger froze and became mute at a further enticement into discussion. The silence which followed was huge and unforgiving, and there was a clear feeling of trespass." Johnson, "From Fairy to Witch," p. 155.

[86] See, for example, Australian Human Rights Commission, *Bringing Them Home: The 'Stolen Children' Report (1997)*, n.d., www.hreoc.gov.au/social_justice/bth_report/index.html (accessed July 9, 2009).

[87] Australian Government Culture Portal, "Reconciliation" (2009), www.cultureandrecreation.gov.au/articles/indigenous/reconciliation (accessed June 23, 2009).

140   *Opera Indigene: Re/presenting First Nations and Indigenous Cultures*

Of course, inclusion does not *equal* reconciliation; there is much more that can be said on the legacy of multiculturalism and reconciliation.[88] But *Lindy* shows that recently arrived and first Australians *are*, in fact, connected in myriad ways, surely a vital step in the continuing process of decolonization. As Lillian Holt, for example, declares,

> what has diminished me, as an Aboriginal woman, has also diminished white people. For our journeys are the same; our stories are the same; our histories are the same. And race politics and practices for the past 200-plus years have informed our views of each other. If we can understand that connectedness, we are well on the way to healing and reconciliation.[89]

Lindy gives full voice to the wrongfully convicted, silenced mother of the dead child and portrays its protagonist (along with the defense counsel) as providing the "healing" example of taking due note of, and paying due respect toward, Indigenous knowledge. *Lindy* thus belies the false notion of the "nothingness" of the heart of the country and its people.

---

[88]   See, for example, Tess Lea, Emma Kowal, Gillian Cowlishaw, and Charles Darwin University (eds.), *Moving Anthropology: Critical Indigenous Studies* (Darwin, NT: Charles Darwin University Press, 2006).

[89]   Lillian Holt, "Reflections on Race and Reconciliation," *Reconciliation: Essays on Australian Reconciliation*, ed. Michelle Grattan (Melbourne: Bookman Press, 2000), p. 146.

Chapter 7

The Eighth Wonder:
Explorations of Place and Voice

Anne Power

Introduction

The idea of place as an organizing principle and framework of research has a noteworthy pedigree among both Indigenous and non-Indigenous Australian scholars.[1] In this chapter about *The Eighth Wonder* by Alan John, with its evocation of social memories about the period of the construction of the Sydney Opera House, place shares significance with voice. The place is Bennelong Point; from a sociologist's perspective, Mike Featherstone states that a nation provides a sense of belonging when the landscape and people hold collective memories with the emotional power to generate a sense of community.[2] Yet world-wide migration patterns have meant that the notion that ties a culture to a fixed terrain has become increasingly problematic. Such a way of thinking has only *seemed* natural and permanent and needs to accommodate hybrid memories[3] where people's identities draw on multiple sources.

However, Featherstone has captured part of the picture. It is when people share individual memories that they enter the realm of social or collective memory.[4] As people share memories that they perceive to be relevant to their identity, they can incorporate a memory of events outside of their lived experiences. The opera at

---

[1]   See Stephen Muecke, "Introduction," in *Reading the Country: An Introduction to Nomadology*, ed. Krim Benterrak, Stephen Muecke, and Paddy Roe (Fremantle: Fremantle Arts Centre Press, 1984); Deborah Bird Rose, *Dingo Makes Us Human: Life and Land in an Aboriginal Culture* (Melbourne: Cambridge University Press, 2000); and Margaret Somerville, "Life History Writing: The Relationship between Talk and Text," *Australian Feminist Studies*, 12 (1991), pp. 29–42.

[2]   See Mike Featherstone, *Undoing Culture: Globalization, Postmodernism and Identity* (London: Sage, 1995).

[3]   In Anzaldua's model, hybrid identity fractures into multiple subjectivities as the results of tensions "between unequal cultures and forces, in which the stronger culture struggles to remake the subordinate": Smadar Lavie and Ted Swedenburg, *Displacement, Diaspora and Geographies of Identity* (London: Duke University Press, 1996), p. 9.

[4]   Kate Darian-Smith and Paula Hamilton (eds.), *Memory and History in Twentieth-Century Australia* (Melbourne: Oxford University Press, 1994).

142   *Opera Indigene: Re/presenting First Nations and Indigenous Cultures*

the center of this paper explores communication by "codes."[5] These codes, such as vernacular language and familiar story, define the experience of being on the "inside" and incorporate recognizable Australian images and idioms.

Place Literacies

Place provides a lens through which to read *The Eighth Wonder* via a framework that comes from the writings of educator Margaret Somerville. The evolving conceptual framework she defines has three key elements: our relationship to place is constituted in stories, the body is at the center of our experience of place, and place "learning" involves a contact zone of contested place stories.[6] Somerville's framework offers connections with David Gruenewald's work on "decolonization" and "reinhabitation." Decolonization involves developing an ability to recognize ways of thinking that "injure and exploit other people and place," and reinhabitation involves "identifying, affirming and creating those forms of cultural knowledge that nurture and protect people."[7]

Relationship to Place Constituted in Stories

The Eighth Wonder is a layering of stories. Completed in 1994 and premiered by the Australian Opera in Sydney in 1995, *The Eighth Wonder* intertwines stories of the building of the Sydney Opera House and a young singer's path to success. Composer Alan John and librettist Dennis Watkins describe the opera

---

[5]   Edward Said says of Palestinian culture: "the experience of being inside is presented as a series of codes which, though incomprehensible to outsiders, are instantly communicated by Palestinians when they meet one another": Said in S. Rushdie, *Imaginary Homelands* (London: Granta, 1991), p. 169.

[6]   The lens of place is not to be confused with site specificity that has been wonderfully explored by contemporary Australian opera composers in such works as *The Sinking of the Rainbow Warrior* by Colin Bright (first performed outside the Maritime Museum in Sydney, with singers making entrances via motor boats) and *Quito* by Martin Wesley-Smith, with its story of schizophrenia as a metaphor for invasion (first performed at a Sydney psychiatric facility at Gladesville). Place in *The Eighth Wonder* is not simply the setting of the story but the story itself. See Patsy Cohen and Margaret Somerville, *Ingelba and the Five Black Matriarchs* (Sydney: Allen and Unwin, 1990); Margaret Somerville, *Body/Landscape Journals* (Melbourne: Spinifex Press, 1999); and Margaret Somerville, *Wildflowering: The Life and Places of Kathleen McArthur* (Brisbane: University of Queensland Press, 2005).

[7]   David Gruenewald, "Foundations of Place: A Multidisciplinary Framework for Place-Conscious Education," *American Educational Research Journal*, 40/3 (2003), pp. 619–54.

The Eighth Wonder: *Explorations of Place and Voice*   143

as about "Australia's cultural coming-of-age" in the 1970s.[8] The year 1973 saw the completion of the Sydney Opera House after a period of construction which spanned almost twenty years. The Opera House design competition was held in 1957, in a period of postwar enthusiasm, and won by the Danish architect Jørn Utzon. However the mood of the 1960s and 1970s was more politically and economically pragmatic. When Utzon left the project in 1966, the interior of the building was incomplete. Compromises to interior plans were affected because of budgetary considerations. The controversy over the circumstances of the completion suggests that Australians "were aware that something crucial in terms of identity was at stake in the building of the Opera House."[9] The opera celebrates creativity by reconstructing memories of building the Opera House link allegorized through the story of the young singer.

With the "flat" or "archetypal" character called the Architect, John's concern is to convey or narrate an artistic vision. By contrast, a "whole" or "round" characterization is found in the young singer, Alexandra—called "Alex" in the libretto.[10] Indeed, her wholeness completes the fragment, which is the Architect.[11] In discussion after the premiere season of the opera, John confirmed that it was his intention for music associated with Alex's vocal art to evolve from music about the shape of the building.[12] It is through this connection that she becomes an embodiment of memories about the period of construction. Her story explains the building. She exemplifies its purpose.

The untold story here, looking through the lens of "place," concerns the original owners of the land the Opera House is built upon, Bennelong Point, where

---

[8]   Dennis Watkins, "The Score on the Opera House. Interview with Janet Hawley," *Good Weekend* (July 29, 1995), p. 34.

[9]   James Waites, "The Sydney Opera House: A Cultural Complex or Sacred Site," program to premiere season of *The Eighth Wonder* (1995), p. 43.

[10]   The terms "flat" and "round" are discussed in H. Porter Abbott (ed.), *The Cambridge Introduction to Narrative*. The terms come from E.M. Forster. "Flat" refers to characters whose presentation is limited to a narrow range of predictable behaviors. Their existence in the story is represented without complexity. Hence the Architect is represented only in his construction of the building. "Round" refers to characters having varying degrees of complexity and therefore not conducive to being "summed up in a single phrase": E.M. Forster, *Aspects of the Novel* (New York: Harcourt Brace, 1927) p. 69. Hence Alex is seen as singing student, wife, expectant mother, and mature singer.

[11]   Trinh writes that "each story is at once a fragment and a whole" and that "you may also be me while remaining what you are and what I am not": T. Minh-ha Trinh, *Woman, Native, Other* (Bloomington: Indiana University Press, 1989) pp. 123, 90. This is an expression of Trinh's understanding of the theory of multiple identities. She explores the premise that personal identity involves both the "other" and the "person"; or, to put it another way, that a person's story is theirs, but not theirs alone.

[12]   Alan John, personal interview (October 18, 1997).

144   *Opera Indigene: Re/presenting First Nations and Indigenous Cultures*

Bennelong, an Aboriginal man of the Camaraigal people of the Eora nation,[13] lived after he had been abducted from the area around Manly by Governor Arthur Phillip in 1788. The Eora occupied land from the Hawkesbury River to Botany Bay and the Georges River.[14] The Aboriginal peoples all regarded the people and the land as inseparably linked, created together by Father Sky and Mother Earth. When Arthur Phillip arrived, Australia was regarded as *terra nullius*, a view that did not recognize Aboriginal rights as a conquered people, nor did it allow the Indigenous population rights to negotiate treaties and be treated as people defending their own country.[15] Relations between Aboriginal peoples and the British settlers quickly deteriorated and punitive military expeditions were led against Eora leaders (such as Pemulwuy and, later, Tedbury, his son). Over a period of little more than ten years the Eora were severely reduced in numbers by shootings and disease. Pushed from fertile land to more barren tracts or persuaded reluctantly to new "homelands," displaced Aboriginal peoples were left with loss of cultural property, language dislocation, and broken links with the land, their "place."

While there is no reference in the opera to this history from two centuries ago, there is reference to Earth and Sky at the opening of the opera. Aboriginal people were Australia's first astronomers, and an exhibition in the Sydney Observatory in 2009 explains how constellations in the southern skies were created from an Aboriginal perspective. It highlights how Indigenous Australians used the stars for navigation, land and water management and ceremonial use. The Dreaming stories associated with the constellations are used to explain Aboriginal laws and teach children about the morals associated with these stories.[16] In Aboriginal Dreaming,[17] Father Sky and Mother Earth created the world and all the plants and animals that inhabit it. Place is also linked with questions of identity in the sense that "my connection with this place of my birth makes me the person that I am."

The importance that is given to Earth and Sky in the opera brings the natural world into prominence. There is also a portrayal of the Aztec story of Quetzlcoatl that invokes an Indigenous element and is integrally connected with the architectural vision that translated into the platform base of the Opera House. This story is not included for its exoticism but for its power as a structural influence on the architectural design (through its connection with Utzon's study of Mayan

---

[13]   "Eora" means "from this place": City of Sydney Barani Indigenous history of Sydney, available online at www.cityofsydney.nsw.gov.au/barani/main.html (accessed on November 9, 2010).

[14]   Eric Willmott, *Pemulwuy: Rainbow Warrior* (Sydney: Weldons, 1987).

[15]   Kevin Butler, Kate Cameron, and Bob Percival, *The Myth of Terra Nullius* (Sydney: Board of Studies NSW, 1995).

[16]   Sydney Observatory website, www.check-in.com.au/Sydney/Sydney_Observatory. htm (accessed March 11, 2009).

[17]   Aboriginal Dreaming is concerned with "creation histories," as referred to in the *Aboriginal and Torres Strait Islander Thesaurus*, compiled by Heather Moorcroft and Alana Galwood (Canberra: National Library of Australia, 1997).

The Eighth Wonder: *Explorations of Place and Voice*   145

temples) and for its suggestion of the sacrifice of a part of the self that is embedded in artistic endeavor.

Design of the Opera

The opera is designed in two acts, subdivided into fifteen scenes. The chronology of the scenes is shown in Table 7.1.

Table 7.1   Chronology of scenes

Act I
Prologue: Earth and Sky
Scene 1: Parliament House, 1955
Scene 2: Mexico, 1456 and 1956
Scene 3: The Sydney Conservatorium, 1957
Scene 4: The Art Gallery of New South Wales, 1957
Scene 5: Denmark
Scene 6: Construction Site of the Sydney Opera House
Scene 7: Sydney Backyard, 1962
Scene 8: Construction Site of the Sydney Opera House
Act II
Scene 1: The Royal Yacht in Sydney Harbour, 1963
Scene 2: Parliament House, 1965
Scene 3: Sydney Home of Stephen and Alexandra, 1965
Scene 4: Flag Raising at the Sydney Opera House, 1965
Scene 5: The Politician's Office, 1966
Scene 6: Opening Night, 1973
Scene 7: *The Feathered Serpent*

The Prologue is concerned with a vision, in which Earth and Sky personified proclaim that the spirit of man is torn between them, searching for a space to inhabit. Earth and Sky return as commentators on the action in subsequent scenes and lead the chorus in the finale. The first scene, set in 1955, shows the political leader of the State of New South Wales, the Premier of the day, instigating the design competition for the Opera House. This scene also establishes that many participants in the story will be known by archetypal names.

While the majority of scenes follow chronologically, contained in an urban naturalism, the second scene breaks that convention. An Aztec ceremony, happening five hundred years earlier in Mexico, opens the scene, with a sacrificial victim giving his strength to the gods. In the scene, the continuation of the ceremony merges with the year 1956 and introduces the Architect. As he studies Aztec structures, he is powerfully affected by the image of the Aztec people ascending

146 *Opera Indigene: Re/presenting First Nations and Indigenous Cultures*

to the clouds, journeying to their gods on the stepped sides of the temple. When the Aztec victim is sacrificed, there is also a symbolic release for the Architect. He envisions a stage rising out of the sea and surmounted by sails, a wonder of the modern world.

In the third scene, a young soprano, Alex, works with her voice teacher, Magda. While Alex hopes to study in Europe, she is also in love with Stephen, a young aspiring conductor. At the unveiling of the winning design, Alex interprets the sketch as a dream[18] come true and she foresees her song, floating as an offering to the Sky.

Gradually, the stories of the Architect and Alex begin to connect. In Denmark, the Architect learns that he has won the competition. Meanwhile, Alex defers her plans to study away from Australia and Stephen. Work progresses on the Opera House but there are ongoing problems of construction to be solved. Some six years later, Alex and Stephen are married and expecting a child. At a family backyard party, Alex's father reflects on the hopes they had held for her career and Alex, too, is uncertain about the future, symbolized by the incomplete Opera House. When the Architect finds the solution to the problem of the roof-construction sails in the curves of a sphere, Act I concludes with a splendid vision of the exterior of the building.

Act II opens in 1963 on the Royal Yacht in Sydney Harbour. At this event, Alex sings in a recital for the Queen. Mingling with the guests, she learns of the Architect's ideas for the interior of the building and her ambitions for an operatic career rekindle. The next scenes reveal pressures, domestically for Alex and politically for the Architect. When they meet again, each is making an important decision. For the Architect, trying to realize his designs for the interiors, the decision is to re-negotiate government approval. For Alex, it is to study in Europe to further her career. The final confrontation with the Politician results in the Architect leaving the project. His legacy is the final scene: the opening of the Opera House is celebrated by a performance, with Alex in the leading role of an opera-within-an-opera, and opera about a ritual which both echoes and completes the Aztec inspiration of the vision in Act I.

The Story of the Opera House

In the opening of the opera, the immediate focus is on conflict in the human spirit, between realization of the creative vision and destruction of it in compromises and deferred plans. The Prologue presents the theme of Earth and Sky, which returns at significant moments in the opera (Example 7.1).

The composer acknowledges that his approach to pivoting between chords sometimes produces slightly odd harmonic spelling.[19] The opening two major chords (D and E) and the melodic line are ostensibly unrelated, producing an idea

---

[18] Alex connects the idea of dream and creativity throughout the opera.

[19] John sometimes uses sharps where more traditional harmonic spelling would use flats, and the reverse is also true. Alan John, personal interview (August 1, 1998).

Example 7.1 *The Eighth Wonder*, the Prologue – Earth and Sky

of sounds moving in and out of harmonic resolution, as a metaphor of conflict expressed in the libretto of the Prologue.

The Aztec scene is a pivotal one in the opera, providing the framework for the Architect's design and for Alex's vocal expression. John describes it as the richest source of musical themes for the whole work.[20] The staggered entries and curving phrases musically parallel architectural features. In particular, the rising motif: B–C–D–E♭, parallels the visual image of steps (Example 7.2). This motif, with its inherent tensions, appears frequently in the opera at critical moments.

Example 7.2 *The Eighth Wonder*, the rising step motif

The Architect's solo, "In Elsinor," provides musical metaphors of creative stages: preliminary imaginings and later realization of a specific design. In the solo, these stages are related to different inspirational places, to Denmark and the Aztec "ancient avenue" in Mexico. Melodic lines and accompaniment styles are different for these stages of the creative journey. In the preliminary stage, the melodic range is contained and a sense of incompleteness is conveyed by unresolved harmonies. For design inspiration, the melodic range is expansive and "freedom from the

---

[20] Alan John, interview with David Marr, television broadcast, October 20, 1995. ABC Television.

148   *Opera Indigene: Re/presenting First Nations and Indigenous Cultures*

commonplace" is accompanied by rhapsodic arpeggiated figures which have a more complete realization in music for Alex later in the opera.

The idea of "ascending to the clouds" takes musical shape in rising dotted triadic figures.[21] The ascent becomes a metaphor of the Architect's future, as the High Priest proclaims the Aztec belief that the spirit flies out toward the sky as an offering to the visitor god, Quetzlcoatl. Attention to the act of singing prepares the audience for the introduction of Alex's character, as the chorus state the purpose of the sacrifice is so that "dreamers on earth can sing one more song."

When the Architect reveals his vision of a stage rising out of the sea, the static harmonies in the triplet patterns of the accompaniment and the high, glittering tones are a musical parallel of dazzling light. Phrases in the vocal line define the shape of the sails, and, in turn, they provide the changed direction in the curves of Alex's vocal line in later scenes. The ecstatic outburst culminates in a description of the Opera House as a "wonder of the world." Symbolically, the Sydney Opera House, whose shapes were unlike anything previously envisioned, epitomized a breaking with the past and a new energy. In its way, the Opera House articulates a creative resistance to residual colonial issues (countering negative ideas of inferiority to Great Britain, its society and culture). Its postmodernism sits alongside the modernity of the Harbour Bridge and the colonial architecture of buildings such as Government House. Consequently, the architectural shapes of the Opera House intersect with postcolonial and identity theory, and, to a large extent, explain the mythology that has grown up around the building.

Alex's story is framed by the idea of the relationship between creativity and sacrifice, for the end of the opera returns to the Aztec scene as the opera-within-an-opera. The Architect's vision blurs into the scenes which follow it, as musical memories of it continually reappear. The ceremony of Scene 2 also establishes the idea of ritual re-enactment as a metaphor for the pain that may accompany the creative process. At the end of the scene, Earth and Sky recall the theme of the Prologue while, in the orchestra, arpeggiated accompaniment figures continue. A new textural complexity is reached when the Aztec chorus is added, providing a platform of chordal harmony over which rises the expression of the Architect's excitement at the inspiration of these images.

---

[21]   Connerton argues that, through the essentially embodied nature of our social existence, oppositional terms (high and low, superior and inferior) provide us with metaphors by which we think and live: Paul Connerton, *How Societies Remember* (Cambridge: Cambridge University Press, 1989), p. 74.

The Eighth Wonder: *Explorations of Place and Voice*

The Body is at the Center of our Experience of Place: Alex's Story

The body at the center of the experience of *The Eighth Wonder* is Alex. Her moment of becoming[22] potentially represents this for the audience who discover the story of the creation of the building through her embodied connection to the place.

The most evocative writing in this opera is for the character of Alex; she represents performing energy, and, through her character, memories of the period of construction of the Opera House are colored with positive qualities of enthusiasm, humor, and pride, mixed with some regret. From a historian's perspective, Paul Connerton writes that, in a person's experience of the present, there is a two-way distortion effect at work; when present factors influence recollections of the past, and past factors influence experience of the present. This is true of Alex, whose music generates motifs which emerge in the music of other characters. This is not mere coloratura decoration; the music of Alex is expressive of curves and soaring natural shapes, the musical equivalents of the design.[23]

This use of natural shapes, of arcs and curves, defines the design approach of the building: functional strength and power transformed in the beauty of the shelled roof. Feminist philosopher Luce Irigaray writes that "everything should be rethought in terms of volute, helix, spiral, curl, turn, revolution" and that the properties of such shapes disconcert attempts to view them as static.[24] The character of Alex, without written text and from the music alone, can be read as having properties of these shapes mapped on to her identity. These properties include a resistance to being seen as "static" and a capacity for transformative power and strength. It is also noteworthy that motifs which are introduced by other characters, and which are shaped in curves, are often developed in Alex's music. From her first appearance in Act I, Scene 3, many of the musical motifs that are developed in her part take to completion motifs established in the Aztec scene.

The first scenes of Alex musically establish some of her attributes: her determination, her fear of being submerged, her awareness of her special gift, her dream of success, and her confidence released by the design image. The first impression of Alex, in her music and her gestures, is of a young singer on a journey

---

[22] Lacan discusses the transformation that takes place in a child watching his own image in a mirror, still trapped in "motor impotence and nurseling dependence" and aspiring to free movement. Jacques Lacan, *Ecrits: A Selection* (London: Tavistock, 1977), pp. 4–5. He then relates this stage to dreams and the moment of becoming that projects the individual's formation into the event they make happen.

[23] Architect Philip Nobis describes the Opera House as a continuation of nature: Nobis in M. Waldren, "Utzon's Lost Interiors," *Sydney Morning Herald, Good Weekend* (October 22, 1994), p. 30. Utzon himself says that the buildings that inspire him lie in place as "part of nature's splendour" (Utzon interview in *Clouds*, a film by Pi Michael, DRTV Fakta, 1994).

[24] Luce Irigaray, *This Sex Which Is Not One*, trans. Catherine Porter (New York: Cornell University Press, 1991), p. 64.

of discovery.[25] Light tone colors of vibraphone and violin, before she begins singing, surround her with sound that has a quality of enchantment. Her teacher Madga's comments offer rhythmic counterpoint to the musical expression. Alex is aware of the quality of her voice, and her fear is of being "buried alive" (Example 7.3) before she can "climb the steps" and set her will free.

Example 7.3 *The Eighth Wonder*, buried alive motif

This "buried alive" motif (Example 7.3) recurs at significant moments, such as when Alex chooses marriage and family over her career plans, and when the Premier fears that his project will be ambushed if it is delayed; it is also a frequently used accompaniment figure, giving the composer an opportunity to comment on the action. The tonality links with the "In Elsinor" aria of the Architect in the Aztec scene. The key of G is used for the realization that Alex's time is coming to make her name as a singer, in a similar way to the Architect realizing his time had come to design an extraordinary building.

In Act I, Scene 4, Alex internalizes the visionary quality in the winning design. It is the catalyst for her, and her spontaneous response "There's a change in the air" signals the release of her will, and the beginning of her future. As a soliloquy, she sings "The dream awakens," which develops in rhapsodic lines.[26] It explores rising curves which derive from the style of melodies in Act I, Scene 2 at the Architect's moment of inspiration; but Alex's aria also extends them vivaciously, for example at the melisma on "glory" (Example 7.4). Over the top of the "buried alive" motif (see Example 7.3), she claims the road as "mine to follow." Dotted rhythms retranslate the Architect's idea of the climbing Aztec people (see Example 7.2), into the energy of bringing "alive the dream within me" as soaring lines of the final bars project the image of the voice reaching to the stars.

Specific patterns in this music relate Alex's dream to the design of the building; they provide musical memories by which she is connected to its creation. The phrase Alex sings, "my future," and the phrase sung by the Architect in Act I, Scene 2, "a wonder of the world," both use the descending tetrachord, placed

---

[25] Roger Covell's comments on the integration of music and action in his review of Alan John's musical *Jonah Jones* are formative to this observation. Roger Covell, "Review of Alan John's *Jonah Jones*," *Sydney Morning Herald* (October 28, 1985), p. 14.

[26] In Aboriginal contexts, awakening from a dream brings control. Artist Tracey Moffatt is on record as saying that she dreams her images before she paints them: www.abc.net.au/rn/arts/atoday/stories/s229128.htm (accessed on November 9, 2010).

Example 7.4 *The Eighth Wonder*, Alex's aria in Act I, Scene 4: "The dream awakens"

in a high tessitura. Alex's use of the pattern extends it. This motif consolidates its significance in this aria, as the same pattern returns in "what's possible with dreaming," and again in "floating free." In its descending contour and its text associations, it expresses calm certainty. It also resonates with Irigaray's idea of arcs and curves having properties of transformative power and strength.

The next scenes in which Alex appears alternate public and personal events. On the one hand, there are stages in completion of the Opera House; on the other, there are Stephen's career plans, which conflict with Alex's. As Alex promises to stay in Australia and marry Stephen, the "buried alive" motif (see Example 7.3) emerges in orchestral accompaniment figures.

At a family barbecue with her father, Alex reveals something of her aspiration, the realization of which has been delayed by marriage and family. The two singers who portray Earth and Sky reappear in this scene as Alex's aunts.[27] When her father sings "you could 'a been a star," his music echoes the motif of the rising steps (see Example 7.2) and, in the orchestral accompaniment, the motif of the awakening dream is heard (see Example 7.4). He expresses regrets that Alex has not put into words. As they duet, Alex sings of her "other child," her voice (Example 7.5).

Example 7.5 *The Eighth Wonder*, Act I, Scene 7, Alex and Ken, "Why must it wait?"

---

[27] Significantly, in Aboriginal culture, the aunties are wise women who are guardians of respect and rules of behavior. Boni Robertson, Catherine Demosthenous, and Hellene Demosthenous, *Stories from the Aboriginal Women of the Yarning Circle: When Cultures Collide* (Brisbane: Hecate Press, 2005).

152   *Opera Indigene: Re/presenting First Nations and Indigenous Cultures*

The scenes at the construction site present a different range of conflicts: of political expediency and engineering logic. The focus of the final scene of Act I is the construction problem of the roof. Left alone, the Architect finds the solution with "another logic." The end of the act joins the voices of Earth and Sky, creator energies in the Dreaming, with the Architect in a celebration of the creative spirit.

While the end of Act I celebrates a stage in the completion of the artistic vision in the external realization of the building, the second act follows the successful arc of Alex's artistic ambitions and the decline of those of the Architect. Alex's aria in the opening of Act II describes Sydney Cove as a "port of dreams." This aria focuses attention on place and its importance to the initial "framings" of dispossession of the Sydney tribes. Their essence and their place change Sydney's history and the historical sign of Bennelong Point, the "place" that has become the Sydney Opera House. While the aria draws attention to Alex as a singer, it allows the composer to focus upon the act of singing, through phrasing, exploration of register, and opportunities for expressive contrasts. It functions as the entertainment on the royal yacht and, at the same time, it reveals the development of the singer, the journey that has been traveled since the singing lesson in Act I. It looks back to previous moments in the opera where the act of singing is represented and looks forward to the opera-within-an-opera in the final scene.

The aria also represents the composer's acknowledgment of other musical styles in Euro-Australian composition.[28] Its opening bars are a conscious tribute to the style of Malcolm Williamson, with echoes of his studies and work in England. With relevance to Australian music of the 1960s, the second part of Alex's aria then evokes Peter Sculthorpe's engagement with Indonesian gamelan music by using a Balinese scale that removes the tonal center and creates a moment of stasis, while the text reflects on the timelessness of the harbor.[29]

In its entirety, the aria musically establishes that Alex's identity as an opera singer is dormant. The text has the harbor "watch[ing] a city grow and tread[ing] time" (Example 7.6). Marking time was also a focus of the Architect's first solo. When the aria closes, celebrating the harbor's waking, it signals a second catalyst for Alex deriving from the Architect's encouragement.[30]

Before the resolution of the final scene, there are a series of arguments and crises. In the argument between Alex and Stephen, his taunt, that she is a true *prima donna*, only strengthens her determination to claim that status. While Alex tries to decide on her future direction, orchestral commentary is made through the return of motifs of the awakening dream (see Example 7.4), "buried alive" (see Example 7.3), and "another logic"; the last motif, associated with the design of

---

[28]   Alan John, personal interview (October 18, 1997).

[29]   Ibid.

[30]   The conversation between the Architect and Alex recalls Utzon's plans for the interior, skillfully shown in an Exhibition mounted in October 1994 at the Mitchell Library, Sydney, which included video simulation of the interiors (Philip Nobis, architect, and John Murphy, senior manuscript librarian at the Mitchell Library, 1994: Exhibition, *The Unseen Utzon*).

Example 7.6 *The Eighth Wonder*, Act 2, Scene 1, Alex, "It watched a city grow and treaded time"

the building, leads to the final meeting of the Architect and Alex. Both stand on the platform—metaphorically close to the gods—and Alex acknowledges that the vision of the building has possessed her and promised fulfillment and purpose. Similarities in their dilemmas are shared, and their duet celebrates the achievement and potential of the artist in the phrase "we're halfway there."

Place is a Contact Zone of Contested Place Stories

In 1949, some seven years after he graduated from the Academy of Fine Arts, Jørn Utzon traveled to Mexico. In particular, he learned from the temples that:

> The Maya people used to live in this jungle in villages surrounded by small cultivated clearings. On all sides, and also above, there was the hot, humid, green jungle. But by building up the platform on a level with the roof of the jungle, these people had suddenly conquered a new dimension that was a worthy place for the worship of their gods. From here, they had the sky, the clouds and the breeze, and suddenly the roof of the jungle was transformed into a great, open plain, and a grandeur that corresponded to the grandeur of their gods.[31]

---

[31] Jørn Utzon, interview with Pi Michael, in *Clouds*, a film by Pi Michael (DRTV Fakta, 1994). English version copyright SBS 1995.

154   *Opera Indigene: Re/presenting First Nations and Indigenous Cultures*

In *The Eighth Wonder*, the overt invocation of Indigenous peoples recurs in the Aztec ceremony with its metaphors of power including people who wield power, such as the Aztec High Priest, and structures, such as steps rising to a platform. While it is not site specific for the original owners of the land, it is connected with the Utzon story. There is also the dimension of sacrifice that is first indicated in the Aztec ritual and then borne out in the loss of the Architect's completed vision for the sake of economic rationalism, and the temporary denial of Alex's ambition for the demands of family and her husband's career.

Alex's role in the projection of reconstructed memories begins at the design competition, when the experience of her reaction to the winning design is shared with the audience in her aria. It is given importance by being directly expressed to the audience, as a soliloquy. She, rather than the chorus, is the representative of a positive response expressed on behalf of an intended future audience, "I've seen what's possible with dreaming." The narrative of her life is part of an interconnecting set of narratives; it is embedded in the story of those groups (family, teacher, inspirational concept), from which her character derives its identity.

Social memory, Connerton suggests, may find expression in commemorative ceremonies.[32] In the opera, it is a re-enacting of historical events, even the re-enactment of an Aztec ritual, with the purpose of establishing a spiritual vision. Behind the spiritual animation of Earth and Sky, there are echoes of ancient beliefs.[33] The music, too, evokes styles of composition contemporary to period of construction.

Alex's embodied connection to place is demonstrated in links between her performing art and the shape created by the Architect for the performing site. Her final verdict on the building, in the penultimate scene, sees it as "a wonder it was ever finished, a wonder [they] couldn't see what it would have been if [they'd] trusted the Architect." The final scene is a revelation of the identity of Alex as acclaimed singer and an intensification of the Aztec scene, celebrating an inspiration becoming reality. Into this scene, prominence is given once more to Earth and Sky.

---

[32]   Connerton, *How Societies Remember*.

[33]   In Aboriginal Dreaming, the children of Sky and Earth are Sun, Moon, Sea, and Rock. Trees, birds, animals, reptiles, and insects lived in balance with one another. Noonuccal Oodgeroo, *Father Sky and Mother Earth* (Sydney: John Wiley & Sons, 2008, pp. 2, 16. In Greek mythology, the Triple Muse at Helicon, or White Goddess, encompassed three characters: the Goddess of the Sky, Earth, and Underworld. As Goddess of the Earth, she ruled the seasons, trees and plants, and all living creatures. As Goddess of the Sky, the Moon, she directed the passions and creative energies. As Goddess of the Underworld and Harvest Maiden, Persephone, she represented death and rebirth. The sowing of the seed was expressed as her descent into the Underworld, and her reappearance in spring signified the sprouting of the young crop. Robert Graves *The White Goddess* (London: Faber & Faber, 1948), p. 386.

The Eighth Wonder: *Explorations of Place and Voice* 155

In this context, Tacey's notion of colonization-in-reverse grips the imagination.[34] In the finale, the recall of the Aztec ceremony connects with the recall of Earth and Sky bringing the natural world into focus once more. Tacey writes of the deep world of the psyche, which is "nature" inside us, as being directly influenced by the forces of "nature" outside us; and he argues that, in Australia, "where land and aboriginality are fused, white Australians are slowly aboriginalized in their unconscious."[35] This has connections with Gruenewald's ideas of reinhabitation, rendered by poet Judith Wright in the reminder that the word "landscape" is inadequate to describe the "earth-sky-water-tree-spirit-human continuum which is the cosmological and existential ground of Aboriginal Dreaming."[36] Sociologist George Morgan suggests that the global environmental crisis has prompted people from "developed" nations to question their belief systems. He further maintains that Indigenous culture and spirituality have been swept up in a search by non-Indigenous Australians, whom he calls "Indigenous wannabes," for "something primordial, something not tainted by modernity."[37] This serves to reinterpret Featherstone's theory that a sense of belonging can grow when the landscape and people hold collective memories with the emotional power to generate a sense of community. While this opera does not overtly refer to the immediacy of local Aboriginal history or to Aboriginal spirituality, it implicates Aboriginality in creative expressions of wonder. It does this within a different Indigenous setting—that of Aztec myth—and a strong emphasis on the cosmology of Earth and Sky.

Alex's presence in the final scene signifies a continuum with the energy to be "freed from the commonplace" that was the catalyst for the Architect's design in which she performs. The story of the young singer, by its success, is a foil to the story of the Architect, and her music is the completion of the motifs and phrase shapes that begin in the scene of his inspiration. The contested place stories conclude in a positive realization that can be termed a 'D'ream.[38]

---

[34]   David Tacey, *Edge of the Sacred* (Melbourne: Harper Collins, 1995).

[35]   Ibid., p. 135. This is further supported by the processes of the Reconciliation movement.

[36]   Judith Wright, "Landscape and Dreaming," in *Australia: The Daedalus symposium*, ed. S.R. Grabaud (Sydney: Angus & Robertson 1985), p. 32.

[37]   George Morgan, "Indigenous Wannabes," *Meanjin*, 60:1 (2001), p. 87.

[38]   In this, the Dreaming and the dream combine.

PART III
Indianism in the Americas

Chapter 8
Indianismo in Brazilian Romantic Opera: Shifting Ideologies of National Foundation

Maria Alice Volpe

Introduction

Indianismo has been considered merely a literary element in Brazilian opera with no major consequences as to its musical expression and socio-cultural meaning. The contribution of *Indianismo* to the nationalization process of Brazilian music needs to be reframed, not only because its literary subjects were central to the operatic genre, but because *Indianismo* conveyed major ideological issues concerning the construction of national identity. Although *Indianismo* did not imply the use of authentic Indian music (it could not do so since no systematic research on the music of the Indigenous cultures had been undertaken at the time), its ideological turn was key to the nationalization of Brazilian music during the Romantic period.

This study proposes a comparative analysis between Indianist literary works and their operatic adaptation with specific regard to the myth of national foundation. The ideological discourse (conceived as a social discourse expressed through literature) is built upon the myth of national foundation and touches on issues of inter-ethnic contact and miscegenation. This study analyzes *Indianismo*'s changing ideologies reflected in the operas *Il Guarany* (1870) by Carlos Gomes, *Moema* (1895) by Delgado de Carvalho, and *Jupyra* (1900) by Francisco Braga. It shows how nineteenth-century Indianist operas corroborated or denied the narratives of national foundation as conveyed by these literary works. Underscoring all this is the historical fact that these narratives were largely disseminated by, and among, the Brazilian elite.

The construction of a historical discourse that could forge a national identity for Brazil had been taking place since the 1830s. Indianismo's literature had been the frame of reference for national identity, since the nineteenth-century Brazilian intelligentsia's revival of eighteenth-century epic poems, and the writing of new literary works in the genres of both epic poems and historical novels from the 1840s to the 1870s. The ideology embedded in Indianismo's literature converged with the cultural policies fostered by the Brazilian Emperor D. Pedro II. However, this official discourse on national identity was subject to increasing criticism by Brazilian intellectuals, particularly from the 1870s onwards.

160   *Opera Indigene: Re/presenting First Nations and Indigenous Cultures*

The international success of Gomes' opera *Il Guarany* epitomized D. Pedro II's continuous support for the arts and sciences in Brazil. When the opera was composed, Brazil was going through political and economical crises. The victorious war against its neighboring country Paraguay had cost the nation dearly, and the monarchy was beginning to falter in the face of the Abolitionist and Republican movements. After the Abolition of Slavery in 1888 and the Proclamation of the Republic in 1889, the new regime continued to face political and economic instability, which was only partially relieved after 1894. Composed during Brazil's early Republican regime, Carvalho's opera *Moema* and Braga's opera *Jupyra* were still the result of D. Pedro II's patronage, and their ideological issues reflected the critical thinking of this transitional period.

The adaptation of literary works into libretti was more than a matter of turning literary into operatic conventions; rather, it affected the ideology conveyed by these works. Based on literary critical studies, *Indianismo*'s narratives of national foundation may be regarded as a system of myths. In each case, this new operatic setting is viewed in its response to these Indianist myths, and whether they are maintained, denied, deflated, or omitted in comparison to the literary work upon which the opera is based. Ultimately, this chapter aims to evaluate how this new setting of mythical relations reconfigures the ideological message conveyed by the opera.

Indianismo and Myth Studies

Indianist literature and its precursory works have been studied as a mode of discourse closely related to myth. Such epic poems and historical novels frequently attempted to locate primordial events in Brazilian history to explain national origins. As mythical narratives, they were "quintessential stories" that offered "matrices for the creation of collective conscience,"[1] and "framing stories" that "provide[d] a mode of ordering significant events."[2] Like myth, Indianist literature was largely constructed upon foundational materials. The border between literature and reality, and national history and fiction overlapped.[3]

The scholarly approaches arising from the literary criticism of myth have been applied to the study of *Indianismo*. The so-called "myth-lit-crit" interpretations have allowed us to build a theoretical framework that recognizes the myth of national foundation as a system of (sub-)myths, as shown in Table 8.1.

---

[1]   Clifford Geertz, *The Interpretation of Cultures* (New York: Basic Books, 1973), p. 220.

[2]   William G. Doty, *Mythography: The Study of Myths and Rituals* (Tuscaloosa, AL: University of Alabama Press, 1986), p. 17.

[3]   Lilia Moritz Schwarcz, *As Barbas do Imperador: D. Pedro II, um monarca nos trópicos* (São Paulo: Companhia das Letras, 1999), p. 136.

Indianismo *in Brazilian Romantic Opera*   161

Table 8.1   The myth of national foundation: system of (sub-)myths[4]

(Sub-)myth	Description
frontier myth	encounter/warfare Portuguese x Indian in a mythical time and locale
myth of conquest	exaltation of the role of the Portuguese: epic of conquest
myth of national origins	union Portuguese + Indian
primordial couple	Portuguese noble character + noble savage
Edenic myth	natural environment = paradise; "heaven on earth"
noble savage	good Indian: natural man and virtue
Indian = nature	the identification of Indian with nature
primitive savagery	bad Indian
captivity myth	rite of passage: physical, sentimental, or sexual
diluvian myth	rite of passage: destruction of old order brings a new order
sacrificial myth	rite of passage: physical or symbolic death
outcast myth	miscegenation; displacement

The *frontier myth* narrates the encounter of the Portuguese with "the Indian" in a mythical time and locale. This encounter is usually marked by warfare between

---

[4]   Studies that have adopted some brand of myth literary criticism for the study of *Indianismo* include: Norwood H. Andrews, Jr., "Some Notes on the Mythology of Bernardo Guimarães," *Hispania*, 56/2 (1973), pp. 371–8; Regina Zilberman, *Do mito ao romance: tipologia da ficção brasileira contemporânea* (Porto Alegre: Escola Superior de Teologia São Lourenco de Brindes, 1977); Afonso Romano Sant'Anna, *Análise estrutural de romances brasileiros* (Petrópolis: Editora Vozes, 1973); David Treece, "Caramuru the Myth: Conquest and Conciliation," *Ibero-americanisches Archiv*, 10/2 (1984), pp. 139–73; David Brookshaw, *Paradise Betrayed: Brazilian Literature of the Indian*, Latin American Studies 47 (Amsterdam: Centrum voor Studie en Documentatie van Latijns Amerika, CEDLA, 1988); Renato Ortiz, "O Guarani: um mito de fundação da brasilidade," *Ciência e Cultura*, 40/3 (1988), pp. 261–9, reprint in Renato Ortiz, *Românticos e Folcloristas: cultura popular* (São Paulo: Olho D'água, 1992); Maria Eunice Moreira, *Nacionalismo literário e crítica romântica* (Porto Alegre: IEL, 1991); Alfredo Bosi, "Um mito sacrificial: o Indianismo de Alencar" and "Sob o signo de Cam," in *Dialética da Colonização* (São Paulo: Companhia das Letras, 1992); and Ramon Magrans, *El indio brasileño en la obra de Alencar y Guimarães* (Madrid: Editorial Pliegos, 1995). Other studies that have contributed to 'myth-lit-crit' interpretations, although they are not directly affiliated to this particular approach, are Afonso Arinos de Mello Franco, *Arinos de Mello. O índio brasileiro e a Revolução Francesa* (Rio de Janeiro: Livraria José Olympio Editora / Instituto Nacional do Livro / Ministério da Educação e Cultura, 1976); Sérgio Buarque de Hollanda, *A visão do paraíso: os motivos edênicos no descobrimento e colonização do Brasil* (São Paulo: Companhia Editora Nacional / Editora da Universidade de São Paulo, 1969); Antonio Candido, *Formação da*

162   *Opera Indigene: Re/presenting First Nations and Indigenous Cultures*

the two parties. The frontier is the place for warfare, and also for everything that is necessary for engendering the new nation. *Mythical time* is realized by its remoteness and conveys the "state of original purity" of a "history that had not begun yet."[5] It constitutes the "prototypical time of origins," "the foundational period" when "new patterns are established and old ones reformulated."[6] The *mythical locale* is realized by the remoteness of place, a place untouched by civilization, symbolizing Brazil in its "original chastity," "when the land had not yet been profaned."[7] The frontier myth merges mythical time and place by "locating the events at the margins of civilization, at the frontier line of the land to be conquered, a mythical locale that stands so isolated from the metropolis that it can to some extent operate outside historical time and colonial rule."[8]

The mythical locale merges with the *Edenic myth*, by associating nature's abundance and mysteries with the Christian hope of a piece of "heaven on

---

Literatura Brasileira, 2 vols. (Belo Horizonte: Itatiaia, 1980); Antonio Candido, *Literatura e sociedade; estudos de teoria e história literária* (São Paulo: Companhia Editora Nacional, 1965), English translation: *On Literature and Society*, trans. and ed. Howard S. Becker (Princeton, NJ: Princeton University Press, 1995); Afrânio Coutinho, *A literatura no Brasil*, 6 vols. (Rio de Janeiro: Editora Sul-Americana, 1969–1972); Afrânio Coutinho, *A tradição afortunada; o espírito de nacionalidade na crítica brasileira* (Rio de Janeiro: Jose Olympio and Editora da Universidade de São Paulo, 1968); Roque Spencer Maciel Barros, *A função educativa do Romantismo Brasileiro* (São Paulo: Editora da Universidade de São Paulo and Grijalbo, 1973); Alfredo Bosi, *História Concisa da Literatura Brasileira* (São Paulo: Cultrix, 1981); and Benedito Nunes, "Historiografia literária do Brasil," in *Crivo de papel* (São Paulo: Editora Ática, 1998). Also, it is worth mentioning studies on the Indian in Brazilian literature, including David M. Driver, *The Indian in Brazilian Literature* (New York: Cambridge University Press, 1942); and David Treece, "The Indian in Brazilian Literature and Thought: 1500–1945" (doctoral thesis, University of Liverpool, 1987); and on the issue of race in Brazilian literature by David T. Haberly, *Three Sad Races: Racial Identity and National Consciousness in Brazilian Literature* (Cambridge and New York: Cambridge University Press, 1983); and David Brookshaw, *Race and Color in Brazilian Literature* (Metuchen, NJ, and London: Scarecrow Press, 1986). Ortiz ("O Guarani") was the first author to discuss Brazilian *Indianismo* literature from the perspective of the myth of national foundation. Brookshaw (*Paradise Betrayed*) is still the most updated study on the Indian in Brazilian literature, comprehensively covering from Colonial times until the present. Brookshaw's framework draws heavily on Slotkin's study of the Myth of the Frontier in the USA, which defines it as a complex system of myths, symbols, patterns, and archetypes that conveys ideologies: Richard Slotkin, *The Fatal Environment: The Myth of the Frontier in the Age of Industrialization, 1800–1890* (New York: Atheneum, 1985). Brookshaw has offered a myth-lit-crit framework by defining a number of Indianist myths, to which the myths proposed by Andrews, Ortiz, and Bosi can be added.

[5]   Moreira, *Nacionalismo literário*, pp. 128, 138; Ortiz, "O Guarani," p. 81.

[6]   Doty, *Mythography*, pp. 8–9, 27.

[7]   Ortiz, "O Guarani," p. 80.

[8]   Brookshaw, *Paradise Betrayed*, p. 4.

earth."[9] Additionally, the *myth of conquest* gives meaning to the encounter of the Portuguese with the Indian by exalting the role of the Portuguese as they conquer a new land and people. Similarly, the *myth of national origins* was created out of the experience of discovery and conquest, and involved the union of the Portuguese with the Indian as a necessary condition for the birth of the Brazilian nation.

The *mythical* or *primordial couple* "engendered the nation and offers an account of the nation's genesis."[10] In this mythical union between a Portuguese noble character and an Indian noble savage, the Portuguese "goes native" by living in the tropics with Indigenous people, and the Indian "goes Western" by converting to Catholicism. Ultimately, the mythical couple consummates the conciliation between culture and nature, legitimating the basis of the nation's genesis. Furthermore, the *noble savage* or the "myth of the good Indian" arose from the Rousseaunian view of the "natural man." The Indian that *Indianismo* recognizes as the ancestor of the Brazilian nation lives in perfect communion with nature, and is invested with "natural virtue," the values of which are in close affinity with Christianity.[11] This idealized construction of the noble savage entitled him to the fulfillment of his historical and mythical destiny. The archetypal good Indian was also in close communion with the colonizer,[12] bound as an individual by the *captivity myth* and as a mythical race by the *sacrificial myth.* Captivity can be physical (such as being held hostage or captivity through sexual contact) or of the heart.[13] The sacrificial myth is a narrative in which the Indian sacrifices his or her identity or life by dying—either symbolically or actually—so that "civilization" can prevail.[14] The *primitive savagery* myth, however, is the binary opposition to the noble savage. It vilifies the Indigenous person, creating the figure of the bad Indian, frequently dehumanizing Indians by portraying them as a collective "primitive."

The *identification of the Indian with nature* is a literary convention of *Indianismo* that portrays the Indian in perfect communion with nature. This could be in a variety of ways: from establishing similarities in physical or psychological qualities between the Indian and surrounding fauna and flora to scenes showing the Indian struggling with (and winning over) nature. The Indian is to some extent considered part of the natural world, more than part of humankind. Eventually nature manifests itself through the Indian. This is in direct contrast to the *diluvian myth*, which is a rite of passage by which nature's "might" triggers a catastrophe that destroys the old order and brings a new one without the necessary collusion of the Indian.

---

9   Hollanda, *A visão do paraíso.*

10   Moreira, *Nacionalismo literário*, p. 139.

11   Candido, *Formação da Literatura Brasileira,*, p. 82.

12   Bosi, *Dialética da Colonização*, p. 177.

13   Brookshaw, *Paradise Betrayed.*

14   Bosi, *Dialética da Colonização.*

164   *Opera Indigene: Re/presenting First Nations and Indigenous Cultures*

Finally, the *outcast myth* expresses a pessimistic view of inter-ethnic contact by dooming Indian female lovers of the Portuguese, whose union was not blessed by Catholic faith, and their miscegenated offspring to social displacement.

This system of (sub-)myths is embedded in the narrative structure of a rite of passage that operates within the mythical-historical principle that enacts the birth of Brazil as a nation. Rendered by a tripartite structure (Table 8.2), the narrative begins with the withdraw of the colonizer from Portuguese civilization into the American Eden (pre-liminal phase), followed by some sort of drastic conflict resulting in the symbolic destruction of the old order (liminal phase), and culminates with the union of the mythical couple (symbolizing the two mythical races), which brings the new order (post-liminal phase).

Table 8.2   The myth of national foundation: mythical structure: rite of passage (tripartite)

Pre-liminal phase	Liminal phase	Post-liminal phase
Retreat from Portuguese civilization into the American Eden	Drastic conflict followed by the symbolical destruction of the old order	The reunion of the mythical couple symbolizing the beginning of the new order

Myth Study of *Indianismo* in Literature and Opera: *Il Guarany*, *Moema*, and *Jupyra*

As demonstrated in Table 8.3, in a comparative analysis between the literary sources and the three operas, only *Il Guarany* confirmed, even in a modified form, nearly all of the (sub-)myths pertaining to the myth of national foundation. *Moema* denied some important (sub-)myths of its literary source, undoing the myth of national foundation. And *Jupyra* was already based on a literary source that undermined the myth of national foundation by undermining the system of (sub-)myths, and placing the emphasis on the outcast.

The historical or fictional events narrated in the literary sources upon which the operas were based can be placed in chronological order. These events of the sixteenth and seventeenth centuries are represented in *Indianismo* literature as the beginning of Brazil as a nation – rather than the apogee of Portuguese colonial expansion as it would be from the perspective of Portuguese identity. Later *Indianismo* literature also poses questions as to the defectiveness of Brazil's historical destiny.

A relevant eighteenth-century source is Santa Rita Durão's epic poem *Caramuru, poema épico do descobrimento da Bahia* (1781), which can be considered an allegory of the opening episode of Brazilian colonial history. It recounts a founding episode of the Portuguese conquest of Brazilian lands and native people, and invented the primordial couple that engendered the nation. The

Table 8.3   Comparative analysis of the myth of national foundation in Indianist operas

	Il Guarany		Moema		Jupyra	
	Lit. source	Opera	Lit. source	Opera	Lit. source	Opera
frontier myth	●	●	●	●	■	■
myth of conquest	●	●	●	■	■	■
myth of national origin	●	●	●	■	■	■
primordial couple	●	●	●	■	■	■
Edenic myth	●	●	●	■	■	■
noble savage	●	●	●	●	■	■
primitive savagery	●	●	●	●	*	*
captivity myth	●	*	●	●	—	—
diluvian myth	●	■	—	—	—	—
sacrificial myth	●	*	●	●	*	*
Indian = nature	●	*	—	—	*	*
outcast	●	—	●	●	●	*

Note: ● = confirmed; ■ = denied; * = modified

poem is rooted in some historical basis: the episode happened at the beginning of the sixteenth century, and is reported to be among the earliest contacts of the Portuguese with the new land and native people. Durão's *Caramuru* conveyed, from the Portuguese perspective, the myth of conquest, and, from the Brazilian perspective, the myth of national foundation. Durão's *Caramuru* and Varnhagen's historical and literary writings are the sources of Carvalho's opera *Moema*.

José de Alencar's novel *O Guarany* (1857) is among the major works that empowered the myth of national foundation in the Brazilian nineteenth-century imagination. The plot is set at the beginning of the seventeenth century. This is in the context of the Portuguese struggle to consolidate its primacy within the territory. In this Indianist novel, many of the precepts of the Romantic historical novel merge with the structure of mythical narratives; including its time and place, portrayal of characters and their destinies with the unfolding of events. It constitutes "a foundational novel that, by searching the origins of Brazilian society, [re]invents the primordial couple that engendered the nation and offers an account of the nation's genesis."[15]

---

[15]   Moreira, *Nacionalismo literário*, p. 139.

166   *Opera Indigene: Re/presenting First Nations and Indigenous Cultures*

Both the epic poem and the novel have a narrative structure that enacts the nation's rite of passage. In addition, both set up the frontier myth merged with mythical time and place, creating a "mythical center" that can operate outside colonial rule. Moreover, both literary works present the union of the noble Portuguese with the noble Indian, symbolizing the creation of the new nation. Both the protagonists go through a rite of passage that prepares them to fulfill their historical destiny when they are finally united as a mythical couple. These rites ultimately legitimize the origins of Brazil as a nation: the "naturalization of culture" is again represented by the Portuguese living in the tropics with Indigenous people, and the "taming of nature" is represented by the conversion of the Indian to Catholicism.

Bernardo Guimarães' short novel *Jupyra* (1872) can be considered a successor to Alencar's *O Guarany* in chronological terms.[16] As Alencar's novel concludes, promisingly, with the union of the mythical couple in the emergence of the Brazilian nation, Guimarães' short novel narrates the destiny of the following generations represented by the *mestiço*[17] offspring Jupyra. Guimarães promotes an inversion of the Alencarian myth of national foundation by eliminating the noble origins of the Portuguese and Indian progenitors and by putting emphasis on the social displacement of their *mestiço* offspring.[18] The outcast's life story stands for Brazilian historical destiny. Jupyra embodies the failure of the historical contact between the Portuguese and the Indian, constructing a view of Brazil as the land of outcasts. It is important to note that the narrative structure of this short novel does not enact the rite of passage of the nation.

The Myth of National Foundation: *Il Guarany*

Gomes' opera *Il Guarany* maintains most of the myth system of Alencar's novel. The opera maintains some archetypal characters of Alencar's novel, and the binary oppositions between them: namely, the myth of the good Indian is emphasized by its opposition to the myth of primitive savagery, and there is a similar opposition between the "good white" as the archetypal Portuguese colonizer and the "vile white." The archetypal characters have a mythical destiny; more than living out

---

[16]   Guimarães' *Indianismo* continues the social approach to the theme of integration in literary form that Alencar had begun; in other words, the integration of the Indian and the *mestiço* in Brazil's nineteenth-century socio-political and economic system. Magrans, *El indio brasileño*, pp. 59–60; author's translation.

[17]   The Portuguese term "mestiço" refers to people of miscegenated ethnic origins, and in Brazil it can involve any mixing of the European, particularly the Portuguese, the native Indian, and/or the Blacks from Africa.

[18]   The idea of Guimarães' inversion of Alencar's values was proposed by Magrans, in *El indio brasileño*. While Magrans discusses inversion in relation to the integration of the Indian into Brazilian society, I also focus on its relationship to the myth of national foundation.

Indianismo *in Brazilian Romantic Opera* 167

their individual life courses, they represent social roles and fulfill the necessities of the mythical narrative.

The opera, however, deflates the multidimensional characterization of the protagonist. The opera does not feature the *Indianismo* convention of the Indian struggling with and winning over nature, since it omits two major episodes: namely, the scene that introduces the Pery character by portraying the brave Indian imperturbably and skillfully confronting the jaguar, and the final scene in which Pery mightily unearths the palm tree in the middle of the deluge. These omissions are among the libretto's most frequently criticized oversimplifications. More than downplaying the "picturesque" and "local color" of the novel, the omission of these episodes in the opera cuts off the *Indianismo* convention of portraying the Indian in perfect communion with nature. This mythical dimension of the Indian character ultimately ensured the survival of Pery and Cecília from a natural catastrophe: a crucial accomplishment of the rite of passage that brought the couple to the mythical beginning of the Brazilian nation. In another concession to operatic clichés through the apparently unimportant change in the captive motif, the libretto adaptation impaired the sacrificial myth. Pery carries out the sacrificial myth in many episodes of the novel. The opera maintains Pery's symbolic self-sacrifice carried out by his conversion to Catholicism, but suppresses one of his major gestures of bodily self-sacrifice. Whereas, in the novel, Pery lets himself become a prisoner of the Aimorés so Cecília and her father can be saved, in the opera Cecília is abducted and held prisoner by the Aimorés. The sacrificial myth is turned into a conventional motif of the rescue opera in which the female waits to be saved by the hero. By curtailing the complexity of the sacrificial myth, the opera does not reproduce the magnitude of Pery's character as it appears in the mythical narrative of national foundation.

The narrative structure of the novel operates within the mythical-historical principle according to which the birth of Brazil as a nation comes out of a rite of passage. This can be charted as the retreat of the Portuguese civilization into the American Eden (pre-liminal phase), the fatal attack of the Aimorés followed by the deluge that destroys the old order (liminal phase), to the renewing union of the surviving couple Pery and Cecília symbolizing the two mythical races (post-liminal phase).[19] The libretto adaptation maintains this tripartite narrative structure in its great lines, but promotes some changes in the liminal phase that affects the mythical structures of the narrative. First, while the novel places agency in the Aimorés to burn D. Antonio Mariz's castle (implying that the American wilderness unleashed a primitive savagery in order to preclude the corruption of the American Eden by European civilization), the opera places the agency in D. Antonio Mariz. This implies that it is a Portuguese consciousness that recognizes the impossibility of establishing European order in the American Eden. Secondly, the enactment of the liminal phase that had started with the destruction of D. Antonio Mariz's

---

[19] The rite of passage concept is based on the analysis of Alencar's *O Guarany* by Ortiz, "O Guarani," p. 81. A similar idea is defended by Moreira, *Nacionalismo literário*, p. 138.

168   *Opera Indigene: Re/presenting First Nations and Indigenous Cultures*

castle is not consummated by the deluge, which withdraws the cosmic power of the rite of passage that brought the mythical couple to the mythical beginning of the Brazilian nation.

Although these libretto adaptations do not change the ideology of the novel substantially, they disrupt the symbolic relationships that empowered the novel as a mythical narrative of national foundation. As the opera maintains Brazil's Second Empire's official ideology, uncritically it also enacts the breaking-down of its discourse.

The Undoing of the Myth of National Foundation: *Moema*

Like Gomes' *Il Guarany*, Carvalho's opera *Moema* is based on a literary subject that conveys the myth of national foundation—but, unlike Gomes' *Il Guarany*, Carvalho's *Moema* does not sustain the same ideology. By denying four myths of the system— conquest, national origins, the primordial couple, and the Edenic myth—and placing the emphasis on the myth of the outcast, the opera subverts the ideology of Durão's epic poem. The opera undoes the myth of national foundation by degrading the Portuguese archetype of the conqueror, by dooming the love between the Portuguese and the Indian, by depriving the Portuguese and the Indian of any rite of passage that could symbolize the "naturalization of culture" and the "civilizing of nature," by shifting the emphasis to the Indian female, whose contact with a white male will transform her into an outcast, and, ultimately, by expressing a pessimistic view of interethnic contact during a foundational period.

The opera's plot is a loose adaptation of the Caramuru myth. It maintains the mythical time and locale established by Durão's epic, but reflects "the trend towards diminishing the traditional status of Diogo Álvares as repository of all that was best in colonial values". This followed the reception of Varnhagen's historical and literary writings challenging the traditional view of the historicity and role of this Portuguese sailor shipwrecked on the coast of Bahia at the beginning of the sixteenth century.[20] The opera does not reflect any attempt to depict him as the archetypal colonist: it makes no reference to his supposedly aristocratic ancestry, it shifts his Iberian name Diogo to the Italian name Paolo, it omits his famous feat with the musket, which earns him the name of Caramuru, and turns the Portuguese sailor into an ordinary "white" hunter from an undetermined European country. Like Varnhagen's historical romance, the opera deflates the traditional heroism of Diogo Álvares in his role of pioneer and colonizer by defining his alter ego Paolo as a character who lacks determination and courage, and who flees to save himself, letting his Indian beloved fall into dishonor among her tribe. Also, by not contextualizing Paolo's appearance among the Indians within the Portuguese overseas expansions, the opera eliminates much of the conquest and foundational material of the Caramuru myth.

---

[20]   Treece, "Caramuru the Myth," pp. 140–41, 164.

A major difference between Durão's epic poem and the opera is the shift of the title, and therefore of the heroic role, from the masculine to the feminine protagonist. Also, the opera merges the role of the two female Indians, Paraguaçu and Moema, under the name of the latter. The opera does not put the white man and the Indian woman through the reciprocal rite of passage of the "naturalizing of culture" and the "taming of nature" that would legitimize their union, making their sexual contact an illicit love. The couple does not fulfill the mythical conditions that would allow them to engender the Brazilian nation. The ill-fated love between the white male and the Indian female symbolizes the inevitability of the fusion and friction of the Portuguese and the Indian, and, therefore, implies the undoing of the myth of national origins.

The dissolution of the epic nature of the work by the operatic version is demonstrated by the lessening importance of the myth of conquest and national foundation, and in the increasing importance of the romantic love encapsulated by the conventional pairing of the two lovers separated by two different worlds. Carvalho's *Moema*, with its "de-hero-izing" of the European man and the "hero-izing" of the Indian female, along with the shift of emphasis from the Indian male to the Indian female, points to an increasing tendency in *Indianismo* toward musical representation and focus upon the outcast. The undoing of the myth of national foundation shifts from the optimistic to the pessimistic view of the inter-ethnic contact, which brings the outcast to the foreground.

This opera reflects the critical thinking put forward by Brazilian intellectuals, since the 1840s with Varnhagen, and more emphatically since the 1870s with Silvio Romero: the denial of the Second Empire's official ideology, the search for historical and anthropological authenticity, and the revision of all knowledge and understanding involved in the construction of national identity, including the role of the various ethnic groups and the issue of miscegenation.

The Land of Outcasts: *Jupyra*

Braga's opera *Jupyra* follows Guimarães' novel in the subversion of the myth system. It clearly oversimplifies the novel by omitting all the episodes in Jupyra's early and later life that contextualize her actions, transforming the narrative of her social displacement into a Romantic chain of love, betrayal, vengeance, remorse, and suicide. The tragic destiny of interethnic contact is dismissed in the opera as caused by flawed human nature rather than resulting from a historical process. *Naturalismo*'s view of the "genetic determinism of race," and the pessimistic view of miscegenation based on (pseudo-)"scientific" theories of the late nineteenth-century that must have informed Guimarães's novel, is missing in the opera. The novel constructs the determinism of its protagonist Jupyra over the first part of the book. The opera cuts this part off, reducing this theme to the conventions of the earlier Romantic literature. The novel and the opera depict the Indian-Portuguese offspring as an outcast, and in both accounts Jupyra resolves her social displacement through self-destruction by committing suicide.

Guimarães' novel destroys the myth of the noble savage by describing Jupyra as a low-born *mestiço* woman and her Indian community as weak, vulnerable, and unable to protect itself—even from other Indian communities. As a *mestiço* woman who lived partly with the Indians and partly with the white, Jupyra cannot reconcile the duality of her social, cultural, and ethnic identity.[21] *Jupyra*'s operatic version eliminates the protagonist's progenitors, which results in two consequences: firstly, it does not contextualize the protagonist socially; and, secondly, it omits the novel's undoing of the noble origins of the Brazilian nation. The opera maintains the *Indianismo* convention of identifying the Indian with nature by using the *cliché* "the daughter of the forest," leading to the conclusion that Jupyra's communion with nature makes her unsuitable to live within the white world. Her association with the wilderness ultimately leads her to kill the man who undermined her integration into the white world. The operatic adaptation selects some characters and situations from the novel that emphasize the love plot rather than the outcast's life story allegorizing Brazilian historical destiny. The opera cuts the first two-thirds of the novel that promote a cumulative effect in Jupyra's characterization, failing to depict Jupyra's multidimensional character tormented by social displacement, and recasting her as a mono-dimensional character who kills simply out of jealousy.

Alternately, the novel does not justify Jupyra's passionate love, revenge, and murder solely on the basis of European Romantic love conventions but through the biological determinism of Naturalism: her *mestiço* "condition" and social displacement are the roots of her behavior, which is a crucial ideological difference.

The theme of religious and cultural conversion, which fulfills the necessary rite of passage of national foundation narratives, is not present in the novel. At no point does the novel or the opera legitimize the Portuguese and Indian love through any rite of passage. On the contrary, the rite of passage that both of them go through (death) is in fact their punishment.

The difference between the way Jupyra dies in the novel and in the opera is also impregnated with symbolic meaning. The novel provides the image of Jupyra wandering in the depths of the forest, until she finds death outside the eyes of the white and the Indian community, and it is the climax of her tormented life in a continuous search for identity. A woman's skeleton is eventually found hanging in a tree in the depths of the forest, from which it is presumed that Jupyra committed suicide. The opera condenses this image by depicting Jupyra's death with a brief action of her jumping into the depths of the water, witnessed by white characters, implying a value judgment not present in the novel. Through that desperate event, Jupyra is condemned and punished not only by herself but also by the colonial

---

[21]   Magrans, *El indio brasileño*, p. 61.

society that bears witness. Although the opera deflates the novel's mythic system, it corroborates its pessimist view of the nation as the land of the outcasts.

Conclusion

A comparative analysis between the literary sources and the operas of *Il Guarany*, *Moema*, and *Jupyra* shows that only the first opera confirms, even in a modified form, the myth system of national foundation. The second opera denies some important myths of its literary source, undoing the myth of national foundation. The third opera was already based on a literary source that denied the myth of national foundation by flawing the myth system, and placing the emphasis on the outcast. The characterization of the Indian protagonists of these three operas shows changing ideologies of national identity: *Il Guarany* illustrates the myth of the noble savage who converted to Catholicism as symbolic of the birth of a nation. *Moema*'s sacrificial myth is justified by the Indian female's heroic stature as the symbol of a nation to be immolated, while *Jupyra*'s sacrificial myth is explained by the Indian female as the symbol of a nation in decay. The feature of social displacement becomes increasingly central, with a paradigmatic shift from the male noble savage as the genuine progenitor of Brazilian ethnic origins in the opera *Il Guarany* to the representation of the Indian female with Carvalho's opera *Moema*, and then to the Indian-*mestiço* female with Braga's *Jupyra*. While foundational narratives sanction interethnic relations, making them a necessary element of the myth of national origins, Carvalho's and Braga's operas express a pessimistic view of the outcome of this historical interethnic contact. These three operas reflect changing ideologies of national identity through which the myth of national foundation is gradually changed until its mythic system becomes completely flawed and turns itself into its ideological opposite. From Carlos Gomes' *Il Guarany* (1870), to Delgado de Carvalho's *Moema* (1894), and Francisco Braga's *Jupyra* (1900), the construction of national identity evolved from the ratification to the undoing of the myth of national foundation, from the positive to the negative view of interethnic contact and miscegenation, up to the representation of Brazil as the land of outcasts.

Chapter 9
Native Songs, Indianist Styles, and the Processes of Music Idealization

Tara Browner

Although a great deal has been written about American and European composers who used Indigenous American songs in their piano works, orchestral compositions, and operas, very little of that discussion has centered upon the initial stage of the process—that is, the moment when Native singers first met ethnographers and performed for either pen and paper or cylinder recorder. The complexities of those relationships, and the impact of tribal singer's decisions to render their sacred songs in a way that both revealed them to outsiders and fixed them permanently in written form, has repercussions to this day in Native North American communities, where in recent years access to the internet has also given access to finding resources that are only now revealing the full extent of ethnographic recording undertaken in tribal communities. Although singers and tribal ceremonial specialists of more than a century ago certainly understood that recording technology could preserve their songs, most of them probably did not comprehend how technology would also make sacred and restricted intellectual property available to composers, who would in turn give those songs new meaning in works intended for public, non-Indian consumption. But, even then, some Native singers, consultants, and performers acted in ways that shielded their communities' songs and cultural practices from the greater public's view.

The course of a song's transition from a personal or tribal knowledge base to American stages and parlors was multistaged, beginning with contact between the ethnographer—usually accompanied by an acculturated Native collaborator— and tribal singers, almost always middle aged or older (the exception to this was Theodore Baker, who collected songs from students at Indian boarding schools). Singers were often given keynotes from pitch pipes to make transcription easier, nevertheless the scales of songs rarely fit into the Western tempered system, making initial transcriptions approximate to begin with. Then, when these songs were "idealized" and set for piano (usually the first step), they were even further altered to fit the Western harmonic system. Therefore, by the time a song setting was performed publicly, it often bore relatively little resemblance to its original incarnation other than the general shape of the melody, and had often picked up a series of generic "Indian"-sounding musical traits along the journey.

My intentions in this chapter are threefold: first, to examine the relationships between composers and field ethnographers; second, to study the actual process of

174   *Opera Indigene: Re/presenting First Nations and Indigenous Cultures*

"idealization" from field ethnography to finished product; and, third, to discuss the repercussions of these choices on the American Indians who served as consultants and collaborators in this chain of events. My primary focus is the opera *The Robin Woman* (*Shanewis*) by Charles Wakefield Cadman (1881–1946), which I intend to use as a case study to illustrate how some late nineteenth- and early twentieth-century composers collaborated with ethnographers in choosing songs for their scores. The genesis of *Shanewis* is especially appropriate to this discussion given the complexity of a pair of relationships: that between Saucy Calf (Osage), the original ceremonial specialist and singer whose performances provided a song central to the opera, and Francis La Flesche (Omaha), the ethnographer who took down and made available Saucy Calf's songs in Western staff notation; and that involving Tsianina Redfeather (Creek) and Charles Cadman, whose long-term musical collaborations ultimately formed the basis for *Shanewis*.[1] But before the narrative begins, a short diversion is in order, to the brief partnership of ethnologists La Flesche and Alice Cunningham Fletcher with composer John Comfort Fillmore (1843–1898), whose configurations of Native songs with piano accompaniments set the stage not only for *Shanewis*, but also the works of a number of American composers commonly referred to as "Indianists," a grouping which includes not only Cadman, but also Arthur Farwell (1872–1952), Carlos Troyer (1837–1920), and Thurlow Lieurance (1878–1963).[2]

Transposing Musical Languages

Alice Fletcher began her career as an ethnographer in 1881, having studied archeology with Frederic Ward Putnam of Harvard's Peabody Museum. After deciding that live Indians were of greater interest than inert artifacts, she moved to Nebraska in 1881 to live with and study the Omaha tribe, and there met Francis La Flesche, a chief's son who became her collaborator and eventually her adopted son. La Flesche's cultural knowledge and linguistic skills were invaluable to Fletcher's projects, and Fletcher did her initial work of musical transcription before the advent of the Edison cylinder recorders that would become commonplace in fieldwork after 1890; her basic transcriptions did not include the drum parts, and were at this time not directly taken down from cylinder recordings but instead sketched out during live performances and later refined.[3] She acted quickly to

---

[1]   Saucy Calf's name is more accurately translated as "Playful Calf."

[2]   For a longer listing and definition of "Indianists," see Tara Browner, "'Breathing the Indian Spirit': Musical Borrowing and the 'Indianist' Movement in American Music," *American Music*, 13/3 (1997), p. 266.

[3]   For an example of an early handwritten transcription by Fletcher, see Victoria Lindsey Levine, *Writing American Indian Music: Historic Transcriptions, Notations, and Arrangements*, Vol. 11 of *Music in the United States of America* (Middleton, WI: Published for the American Musicological Society by A-R Editions, 2002), p. 45. Because of the nature

obtain a graphophone (an Edison cylinder-type recorder) once they became available, and by the summer of 1895, in collaboration with La Flesche, she was recording Omaha songs. But for her earliest ethnographic volume, published in 1893, all transcriptions were done entirely by ear. It is impossible to know whether or not the use of a graphophone had a serious impact on what songs Fletcher chose to record, but she and La Flesche both stayed within the music-cultural boundaries of the greater Omaha prairie culture, which included the Osage, Kaw, and Ponca peoples, and a song repertory made up almost exclusively of strophic songs structured in an A–B–B form.

In 1888 Fletcher enlisted academic and composer John Comfort Fillmore (1843–1898) in a project to transform Native songs into pieces for piano and voice, to be titled *A Study of Omaha Indian Music* (1893). Fillmore's basic technique was to locate the vocal melody in the right-hand part, and use the rhythmic pattern of the drum as a left-hand ostinato. But because Fletcher had considered the drum parts not important enough to transcribe in her initial sketches, she, La Flesche, and Fillmore created those drum parts from memory, something that would not seem much of a problem considering that the drums parts were simply repetitive patterns—except that the drum accents as Fillmore wrote into his piano score are backwards (they should be on the second eighth-note of each grouping). Moreover, in order to keep the vocal line from being overwhelmed by the piano accompaniment, Fillmore transposed the melody upward, often as much as an octave. While this vocal register might work for Northern Plains tribes such as the Cree or Blackfeet, in the Southern "Prairie" style common to the Omaha, Ponca, and Osage peoples, this was the female vocal register, not the male one.[4]

Although Fillmore's rhythmic strategy for writing Indian polyrhythmic music never went further than a single group of pieces, according to Philip Deloria, his "successes and failures helped produce the sound of Indian that would call up imagery and expectation for most of the twentieth century."[5] Fillmore's compositions fed two primary Indian musical stereotypes: Those of *all* men singing in a high, often falsetto range, and a stressed downbeat, signifying a kind of musical marching in place that gives the music a static affect, both of which eventually entered the larger American musical vocabulary as an "Indian" sound through film scores. Before Fillmore's death in 1898, Fletcher expanded her range of tribal musical cultures and persuaded him to arrange a number of songs from the Dakota, Pawnee, and Pueblo peoples for her planned new volume, *Indian Story*

---

of the graphophone's "microphone," drum parts were difficult to hear on the recordings, and most often sound like a slapping sound in the background.

[4] See Tara Browner, "An Acoustic Geography of Intertribal Pow-wow Songs," in *Music of the First Nations: Tradition and Innovation in Native North America*, ed. Tara Browner (Urbana and Chicago: University of Illinois Press, 2009), pp. 131–40, for a discussion of vocal range and singing style in intertribal powwow singing.

[5] Philip Deloria, *Indians in Unexpected Places* (Lawrence: University Press of Kansas, 2004), pp. 191–2.

176   *Opera Indigene: Re/presenting First Nations and Indigenous Cultures*

and Song From North America (1900). This volume is aimed primarily at children (and their teachers) of grammar-school age, matching songs with various stories drawn from Native oral texts, and the musical settings are quite basic.

Anthropologist Steven Feld, who places this Fillmore/Fletcher collaboration in what he calls the "prehistory" of the contemporary genre of "World Music," has this to say about Fillmore's endeavor:

> Consider then John Comfort Fillmore, a pianist and pioneer field recordist of Native North America active at that time. In 1895 and 1899 he wrote articles in the *Journal of American Folklore* and *American Anthropologist* to argue that natural and universal acoustic laws underlie the latent harmonic logic of Native American vocal melodies. Accordingly, he produced transcriptions of early wax cylinder field recordings in the form of harmonized piano arrangements, and presented them as revelations of what American Indians really meant to sing, but couldn't realize. This work initially suckered the most prominent ethnomusicologist (Frances Densmore) and anthropologist (Franz Boas) of the day, although both later repudiated Fillmore's methods, recognizing them as reflective more of the romantic nationalism of his compositions (for example, *Indian Fantasia Number One for Full Orchestra*, 1890) than a scholarly inquiry into acoustic universalism.[6]

After publishing *A Study Of Omaha Indian Music*, Fletcher returned to more purely ethnographic projects and ceased directly collaborating with composers. Her Native collaborator La Flesche, however, began a strange and often frustrating partnership with composer Charles Wakefield Cadman. The relationship between Cadman and La Flesche began in about 1907, when Cadman approached La Flesche about looking for Native musical resources for his compositions, and ended up being drafted as a transcriber of cylinder recordings.[7] Their rocky partnership would ultimately provide musical raw material for two operas, one stillborn, but the other surprisingly successful.

Shanewis

By the late 1890s, Indianist music had begun to rise in popularity, although much of what was written was in the realm of sheet music masquerading as art songs, marketed to be played at home in the parlor. As a potential material for "national" music, transcribed Indian songs started to interest composers of art music as well, and the melodies transcribed by ethnologists became the basis for piano solos,

---

[6]   Steven Feld, "A Sweet Lullaby For World Music," *Public Culture*, 12 (2000), pp. 165–6.

[7]   Victoria Lindsay Levine, however, comments on Cadman's occasional ineptness in this regard. See Lindsay Levine, *Writing American Indian Music*, p. 181.

pieces for piano and voice, and a surprising number of operas. What all three of these genres had in common was the potential for mass-market appeal, and composers such as Cadman and Farwell set about building their audiences by means of the traveling lecture-recital, where they gave programs on Indian music that included information on the cultural contexts of each song, and its potential for further musical development. In addition, a number of Indianist composers had either developed relationships with ethnologists or visited tribal communities in order to make their own transcriptions, and Cadman even toured extensively with the Creek singer/activist Tsianina Redfeather (1882–1985). By the early years of the twentieth century, Indians were being touted as representing the earliest epochs of a shared *American* history, and with their music now recognized as an American folk music the moment was set for a brief but intense Indianist appearance on the North American musical stage. It is noteworthy that while the descendants of European settlers were willing to incorporate Indigenous peoples into an "American" history, rather than a continental pre-history, this was usually not the case when it came to African-descended peoples living within the boundaries of the Nation, and native-born composers of the time were no different than the general public in their exclusion of blacks from the American historical narrative.[8]

Opera was a genre that seemingly presented unlimited possibilities for Indianist composers, offering a combination of colorful staged drama that could potentially be combined with a more humanizing portrayal of Indians (for composers such as Cadman who had this aim). During the time period of 1880–1900, Helen Hunt Jackson's novel *Ramona* (1884) was swaying public opinion of citizens in the Eastern states in a direction more favorable toward Natives, and Wild West shows were piquing America's curiosity about their now vanquished enemies.[9] This fertile turf offered a large potential audience for composers wanting to capitalize upon the public's newly born curiosity about Indians. Catherine Parsons Smith has created a taxonomy categorizing Indianist operas produced between 1907 and 1918 (their heyday) as "Eastern" and "Western" depending upon the geographic location of their premiere.[10] Notably there were five "Eastern" opera premieres but only two "Western" ones during this period, even though all except for one were set in the West (the lone exception was *Azora, Daughter of Montezuma*,

---

[8] A ballet by Henry Gilbert (1868–1928), *Dance in Place Congo* (Op. 15), was a rare exception to this rule, and received its premiere as part of a double bill: the same Metropolitan Opera performances as *Shanewis*. A parallel and somewhat similar movement to Indianist styles of composition, known as "indigenismo" happened in Mexico during the 1920s and 1930s. Although the movement was centered more in literature and the visual arts, such prominent composers as Carlos Chavez (1899–1978) and Silvestre *Revueltas (1899–1940) wrote works in this style.*

[9] Helen Hunt Jackson, *Ramona* (Boston: Roberts Bros., 1884).

[10] Catherine Parsons Smith, "Composing Wild Indians: Reflections on Race and Place in a Western Opera," unpublished paper presented at the Annual Meeting of the Society for American Music, Eugene, Oregon, February 17, 2005.

178   *Opera Indigene: Re/presenting First Nations and Indigenous Cultures*

set in Mexico), suggesting that the audience for these productions was more in the Eastern states. Two of these Indianist operas had active Native participants, namely Zitkala-Sa (Getrude Bonnin, Yankton Dakota, [1876–1938]) working with William Hanson on *The Sun-Dance Opera* (1912–1913) in Utah, and Tsianina Redfeather's collaboration with Cadman and Nelle Eberhart (1894–1943) on *The Robin Woman* (*Shanewis*) in 1918. Francis La Flesche had consulted with Cadman concerning some of the music for *Shanewis*, but he was far more involved with an earlier venture, *Da-O-Ma* (1911), based upon a story of two Sioux men in love with the same woman. Why would La Flesche be involved in such an undertaking? Sherry Smith suggests that,

> Although La Flesche wanted an opera that would be true to Indians, one that would present "authentic" aspects of (in this case) Sioux culture, and one based on an Indian story, it was inevitable that using the opera as a vehicle would alter the effect. Opera derives from European, not Indian, culture. The costumes might be accurate, but the melodies, the words, and the lion's share of the production values would be non-Indian. So why attempt it? Presumably La Flesche hoped to reach a different audience from those who read either his anthropological or his autobiographical works.[11]

Da-O-Ma would never reach the stage, but *Shanewis* did, premiering at the Metropolitan Opera in 1918. During the time between the two projects, La Flesche and Cadman had somewhat of a falling out, in large part because of La Flesche's perception that Cadman had not given him credit for the work he had done on *Da-O-Ma*.[12] But Cadman was able to find a new Indian collaborator, his old touring partner Creek singer Tsianina Redfeather, to assist him with concocting an Indian opera with a twist: this plot would occur in the present day, not the mythologized past.

From Redfeather's outline, Cadman and Eberhart created a libretto based loosely upon Redfeather's life. Set in Southern California and Oklahoma in the years prior to World War One, the story revolves around Shanewis, a young Creek woman, and the turmoil she experiences coming to terms with living between two cultures. Dramatic devices include interracial love and poisoned arrows, and in the end Shanewis vows to throw away her white ways and return to the traditions of her people, a behavior commonly known at that time as "going back to the blanket." The outline written by Redfeather (and Cadman), although emotive and overly dramatic, encompassed many of the important issues then confronting Indian people, yet still contained the traditional literary themes regarding the fate of Indians romantically involved with Euro-Americans—but with a twist. Usually, the Indian woman dies and the Indian man lives on in melancholy despair, but this time the Native woman's white male romantic interest loses his life instead.

---

[11]   Sherry Smith, "Francis La Flesche and the World of Letters," *The American Indian Quarterly*, 25 (2001), p. 595.

[12]   Ibid., p. 596.

Native Songs, Indianist Styles, and the Processes of Music Idealization   179

Cadman, however, did everything he could to fit *Shanewis* into the larger American historical framework, writing in the staging instructions: "For added spectacular effect, the musicale in Part One may be given in costume, the characters representing the various phases of America in the making. The following are suggestions: Mrs. Everton – Queen Isabella of Spain, Amy Everton – Evangeline, Lionel Rhodes – John Alden; Shanewis – Pocahontas."[13] He goes even further for the chorus, including Sir Francis Drake, Hernando de Cortez, George Washington, Betsy Ross, Salem Witches, Norsemen, Cow Boys, and Creoles in his lineup.[14]

Cadman sent a rough draft of *Shanewis: The Robin Woman* to La Flesche for comments and approval. But then, in an unexpected turn of events, Metropolitan Opera director Giulio Gatti-Casazza—who was under pressure to program an American opera— telegraphed Cadman accepting the opera for the 1917–1918 season, in spite of having never seen it. Ecstatic, Cadman and Eberhart moved to New York to supervise the production of their opera. Gatti-Casazza wanted Redfeather to sing the title role of *Shanewis*, but she declined, citing stage fright. Redfeather did, however, stay on as an advisor for the production. *Shanewis: The Robin Woman*, had its premiere on March 23, 1918, and was performed four more times that season: March 28, and April 5, 10, and 15. It was successful enough to be renewed for a second season, and played three more times. After that, *Shanewis* was dropped from the Metropolitan's repertoire. Other performances followed, including at the Hollywood Bowl with Redfeather in the title role. But, as Cadman's career slowed, *Shanewis* faded, eventually disappearing almost completely from the American scene except for a few scattered performances, including a brief revival at a 1958 opera workshop by Constance Eberhart (librettist Nelle Eberhart's daughter) at Eureka Springs, Arkansas.

Shanewis was unusual for the time for two reasons: its contemporary setting and its use of an Indian song that was essentially unchanged from its transcribed version, a feature that it shared only with the earlier (1913) production *The Sun-Dance Opera*. In order to accommodate a traditional song in as unchanged a form as possible, Cadman needed a traditional setting, and chose an Oklahoma reservation powwow for the scene in which the song was performed. Below are his staging instructions:

> Approaching sunset. The closing scenes of a modern summer encampment or pow wow of an Oklahoma tribe of Indians is in progress … . The pow wow is held in an enclosure of canvas fence stretched on tall, slender poles beyond which are visible teepee tops and improvised shelters for the campers. The ceremonial dancers in full regalia stand against this fence waiting their turns.

---

[13]   Charles Wakefield Cadman, *Shanewis: The Robin Woman* (Boston: White Smith Publishing Co., 1918), p. 5.

[14]   Ibid.

180   *Opera Indigene: Re/presenting First Nations and Indigenous Cultures*

> The crowd consists of full-blood Indians and half-breeds in ceremonial, mongrel, or modern dress and white spectators in holiday attire … . Ice-cream and lemonade vendors are crying their wares. Balloon sellers add noise and color. Shanewis, in red beaded buckskin, and Lionel in an immaculate and correctly cut white summer suit, stand right front and watch the scene with interest.[15]

While the location seems quite contemporary (for circa 1916), it is more modern than even Cadman could have imagined, because powwows of this type, commonly known as "fairs," did not take place in Oklahoma until the early 1920s.[16] The first true intertribal Osage powwow—which is the presumed location of the powwow in *Shanewis*, because it was the only remaining reservation at that time—did not occur until 1926. Moreover, powwows did not come about in Creek country (east-central Oklahoma) until the 1950s, so it is safe to assume that, just as he used an Osage song as a source, Cadman was placing his powwow on the Osage Reservation.

Into this backdrop enter four "old Indians," who "range themselves in the center of the stage." Playing rattles (the rattle part is separate from the other percussion, so it was probably performed by the singers), they launch into an "Osage Indian Ceremonial song," sparsely accompanied by only timpani and lower strings masquerading as a drum. And just as in the earlier Fletcher/Fillmore collaborations, the male vocal part is in treble clef—in this case with clear instructions for the singers to use falsetto—and the "drum" accents are on beats two and four of each 4/4 measure, giving the beat a sluggishness that directly conflicted with its Osage cultural meaning as music for dancing. Adding insult to poor realization, at the bottom of the page is the notation "This is an Osage Indian ceremonial song and is used by permission of the U.S. Bureau of American Ethnology," with no mention of Saucy Calf (Tsezhi^{n}ga Wadai^{n}ga) who sang it for the recorded version, or its origins in the Osage *we'-ga-xe* ceremonial repertoire (see Example 9.1).[17]

Cadman had taken the original song verbatim—both melody and Native language text—from La Flesche's volume *The Osage Tribe: Rite of the Chiefs, Sayings of the Ancient Men*, and should have known its inappropriateness for a social or war dance setting, but choose to use it anyway, perhaps because of his

---

[15]   Ibid., p. 95.

[16]   The exception to this was a brief period in Western Oklahoma, where the Cheyenne and Arapaho in 1912 organized a fair that included traditional Indian dances and vendors of various kinds, and invited their white neighbors to the event. It was extremely successful, so much so that the Bureau of Indian Affairs closed it down after that year. See Gloria Young, "Powwow Power: Perspectives on Historic and Contemporary Intertribalism," (1981) for a history of Oklahoma powwows.

[17]   Cadman, *Shanewis*, p. 99. This ceremony was documented by Francis La Flesche in "The Osage Tribe: Rite of the Chiefs, Sayings of the Ancient Men," in *36th Annual Report of the Bureau of American Ethnology, 1914–15*, pp. 35–604 (Washington DC: US Government Printing Office, 1921).

Example 9.1 Excerpt from Charles Wakefield Cadman, *The Robin Woman (Shanewis)* (Boston: White Smith Publishing Co., 1918), p. 95.

participation in the transcription of songs sung by Saucy Calf and recorded by La Flesche at Cahokia, Illinois, in 1910.[18] The personal relationship between Saucy Calf and La Flesche had been close, with Saucy Calf adopting La Flesche as his "ceremonial son," although he does not seem to have done the same with Cadman.[19] During their four-day-long recording session, Saucy Calf performed ceremonial rites consisting of ninety songs, six long ritual prayers, and seven symbolic ritual acts of the *we'-ga-xe*, using a notched tally stick on which each notch represented a song—a finger holding his place as a memory aid. As La Flesche recorded Saucy Calf, he noticed that the priest would at times pass over notches without singing a song, and asked why he did so. According to Garrick Bailey, "Saucy Calf replied that he should not concern himself about those songs, for the ones he had forgotten were of no particular importance."[20] An alternative explanation is that Saucy Calf, understanding the power and permanence of recording technology, knew that once La Flesche walked away with the recordings, those songs could never again be taken back or "put away," a common term on the Southern Plains for a song that for various reasons is no longer performed. In many Native cultures, the power of a song manifests in its literal sound, and this power would not be present if the song was represented on paper. Strangely enough, the processes of musical idealization

---

[18] There was a history of problems between La Flesche and Cadman over this set of songs, with La Flesche at one point accusing Cadman of taking credit for his work with Saucy Calf. See Smith, "Francis La Flesche," p. 596.

[19] Margot Liberty, *American Indian Intellectuals of the Nineteenth and Early Twentieth Centuries* (Norman: University of Oklahoma Press, 2002), p. 54.

[20] Garrick Bailey, "Continuity and Change in Mississipian Civilization," in *Hero, Hawk, and Open Hand: Indian Art of the Ancient Midwest and South*, ed. Richard Townsend (New Haven, CT: Yale University Press), p. 83.

employed by Cadman, Farwell, and a host of other composers, which involves a series of musical filters (fitting into the Western scales system, adjusting notes for better harmonization, etc.) would also most likely remove the elements of spiritual and cultural power from a song that was recontextualized in the form of an opera aria or piano work, although the singing of a song's text might still compromise it. This means that, from a Native perspective, Cadman's most "authentic" rendering of an Indian song in *Shanewis* (the powwow song), which was arguably done as a homage to Saucy Calf, was also the most threatening to traditional cultural concepts of song function and spiritual power.

Interestingly enough, Tsianina Redfeather probably played a role in Cadman's setting of the powwow in the second scene, because, as a Creek, she would have known that Creeks at that time did not participate in powwow-like dances, but instead held Stomp Dances as part of their Green Corn Ceremony at sacred ceremonial grounds (Philip Harjo, the step-brother of *Shanewis*, was also Creek, but appears in the opera at the powwow in Plains Indian garb). If Redfeather chose to steer Cadman away from her own people's music and cultural lives, it was not the first time a Native woman had done so with a composer: Zitkala-Sa (Gertrude Bonnin) had recommended the Lakota song "Ink-pa-ta" as a theme to William Hanson for *The Sun Dance Opera*, labeling it as a "love song," when in fact it was (and is) the rather risqué version of the vocal song that pairs with and old-style flute melody.[21] In both cases, each woman seems to have used her role in the project to direct the composers away from certain musical repertoires and ceremonial events, in effect hiding what they deemed inappropriate from outsiders by deflection to other musical sources, just as Saucy Calf had chosen to avoid the recording of specific songs by La Flesche through the passive device of stating that they were unimportant.

The Final Curtain

After his glory days at the Metropolitan Opera, Charles Cadman was not yet finished with idealized Indian melodies and *Shanewis*. Following years of touring, in 1920 he settled down in Southern California and began work on a West Coast premier of *Shanewis* in the newly constructed Hollywood Bowl (which he helped found), an outdoor amphitheater in the Hollywood Hills of Los Angeles, while at the same

---

[21] The song, from a genre called *Wioste Olowan* (flute songs) and properly known as "Inkpataya Toki-ya," is included in Natalie Curtis's *The Indians' Book* (1907) with a sanitized English translation. The lyrics actually translate as "I am standing where the water begins, I wave a blanket, Come back over here" (translation by Calvin Jumping Bull for the author). Colloquially, the song is known as "The whore next to the river" because the woman was waving at men as an overture for sexual relations. For a more detailed overview of this opera, see Catherine Parsons Smith, "An Operatic Skeleton on the Western Frontier: Zitkala-Sa, William F. Hanson, and The Sun Dance Opera," *Women & Music*, 5 (2001), pp. 1–31.

time continuing to write Indianist works, publishing an "Operatic Cantata" titled *The Sunset Trail* in 1925, which was subtitled "Depicting the Struggles of the American Indians Against the Edict of the United States Government Restricting them to Prescribed Reservations," but which had an ending similar to Longfellow's *Hiawatha*, where the Indians vanish into the sunset.

For the West Coast premiere of *Shanewis*, Cadman was able to persuade Tsianina Redfeather to sing the lead role (she had performed it in Denver in 1924), and Mohawk baritone Oskenonton to sing the part of Philip Harjo. In concert with opera impresario Gaetano Merola and the "Clubs and Civic Organizations of the Southwest" (a consortium of women's clubs), the opera premiered at the Hollywood Bowl on June 24, 1926, on a double bill with Nikolai Rimsky-Korsakov's (1844–1908) "Oriental Ballet" *Scheherazade* (as adapted by Michel Fokine for the Ballets Russes production). Cadman had special stationery printed up for the occasion, with an odd juxtaposition of a bare-chested Woodlands Indian in full Plains headdress standing next to a canoe on the left side, and a homoerotic representation of the Golden Slave, taken directly from Vaslav Nijinsky's Ballet Russes costuming, on the right (see Figure 9.1). The contrast of the manly "American" with the degenerate "Oriental" is obvious, but it is also possible that Cadman was simply trying to create publicity for the performance with imagery that was racy and possibly scandalous for the time period.[22]

Figure 9.1   Artwork from Charles Cadman's personal *Shanewis* stationery, 1926

Although the Hollywood Bowl performance (and a second one two days later) sold out, drawing an estimated 47,000 attendees over the two nights, this event

---

[22] None of the publicity materials from the opera seem to have survived, so it is impossible to say whether or not the image on the stationery was also on playbills and programs, but it is highly likely that it was.

184   *Opera Indigene: Re/presenting First Nations and Indigenous Cultures*

marked the last time *Shanewis* would be seen on a major public stage until 1954. Soon after his Hollywood Bowl triumph, Cadman moved to San Diego with his mother in tow, and set about writing music for films, a career in which he was moderately successful. And although Cadman's works faded into obscurity after his death in 1946, his method of scoring "authentic" Indian singing—so heavily influenced by Fillmore—lived on in countless film scores and Broadway depictions of Indians, where the exaggerated elements such as incredibly high vocal styles, sung in falsetto, mixed with Fillmore's rhythmic mistakes, Fletcher's omission of correct drum notations, and just a hint of Minstrel show to give us the "Indian" sound heard today in American Westerns and chanting crowds at football stadiums.

As for Indianist music, the movement ran out of steam in the early 1920s, and its fall from favor dovetailed with the rise of jazz. For the most part, Natives had not been particularly supportive, in large part because the concept of music as something listened to for pleasure, offered to an audience purely for its own sake, was almost completely foreign to Indians in tribal communities, who subscribed to (and often still believe) that songs were instruments of spiritual power, existing as personal, community, or collective tribal property. As conflicts arose between these two ideologies—one primarily of aesthetic pleasure and other of tribal-specific meaning and supernatural power—Indians became less and less cooperative with ethnologists aiming to record their musical expressions, as singers and other tribal members began to question just what was happening to their songs once the ethnologists departed with their collections of cylinders. Fundamentally, most Indians did not care whether or not non-Indians found their music appealing, and with the exception of unique individuals such as Francis La Flesche and Zitkala-Sa, there was no real basis of tribal support for converting Indian songs into piano sonatas and tone poems. But exclusive of Christian religious music and popular/ social styles (early versions of country/hillbilly and, in some cases, jazz), Natives continued to sing their songs just as they had for generations on end, without concern that the songs' survival might hinge upon whether or not they could be translated into a Western musical language.

Had Native American communities been more involved in promoting Indianist works perhaps they might have enjoyed a longer life span, because in the rare cases where tribal communities were behind the projects the musical style has endured, in the uniquely American stepchild of opera known as the "pageant." Part amateur theatrical, part (often mythic) local or regional history, and part community enterprise, pageants emerged on to the American musical landscape as a form roughly in the early 1880s, about the same time as Wild West shows began touring. Unlike Buffalo Bill and his Wild West, however, pageants survived the onslaught of radio and film following World War One, and the burgeoning popularity of jazz. Michael McNally has documented in rich detail the survival of composer Frederick R. Burton's opera (in actuality an early pageant) *Hiawatha* through the 1960s in Michigan, performed for tourists by members of the Ottawa and Ojibwe communities in the area around Little Traverse Bay.[23] Although the support of these peoples should not be interpreted as an endorsement of the authenticity of Longfellow's poem, the performances—often in the Ojibwe language—did provide needed income, and in general were considered positive portrayals of Great Lakes Indian culture. While Burton's version of *Hiawatha* is no longer performed in Michigan, there are no fewer than twelve "outdoor dramas" featuring Indian themes currently in rotation in a variety of venues across the United States, with at least three—*Strike at the Wind!*, *Trail of Tears*, and *Unto These Hills*—being produced by Indian tribes, and including Native musical numbers.[24] Today, few of these productions refer to themselves as "pageants" (with the exception of California's venerable Ramona Pageant, inspired by the Helen Hunt Jackson novel), but, in retrospect, there is little difference between them and Indianist operas (and operettas), except that most the of the pageant productions are semi-professional, draw participants from the surrounding communities, and, unlike operas, do not aspire to be considered high art—all attributes that tribal communities view with approval.[25]

---

[23]   Michael D. McNally, "The Indian Passion Play: Contesting the Real Indian in Song of Hiawatha Pageants, 1901–1965," *American Quarterly*, 58 (2006), pp. 105–136. Also see Frederick Russell Burton, *Hiawatha* (Boston, New York, and Philadelphia: Oliver Ditson Company, 1889).

[24]   Outdoor dramas with significant Native characters currently in production include: *The Hiawatha Pageant* (Pipestone, Minnesota), *The Aracoma Story, Blue Jacket, The Legend of Jenny Wiley, Salado Legends, The Ramona Pageant, Star of the Hills, Tecumseh!, Trumpet in the Land,* and *The Lost Colony*. Native-produced dramas are: *Unto these Hills* (Cherokees of North Carolina), *Trail of Tears* (Cherokee Nation of Oklahoma, Tahlequah, Oklahoma), and *Strike at the Wind!* (Lumbee Nation of North Carolina). *Unto These Hills* was recently reworked by Kiowa playwright Hanay Geiogamah and includes a substantial element of traditional Cherokee music, incuding Booger Dance and Stomp Dance scenes, with Geiogamah referring to the style as "Tribal Drama."

[25]   The Ramona Pageant has a long history of having local Native people as extras in the production (Luiseño, Serrano, and Cahuilla) and currently features a Lakota actor, Vincent Whipple, in the role of Alessandro.

Chapter 10
Composed and Produced in the American West, 1912–1913: Two Operatic Portrayals of First Nations Cultures

Catherine Parsons Smith

Cultural production in the United States has catered to and encouraged a longstanding interest in exoticized representations of native persons and their cultures. In the nineteenth century, such production ranged from the novels of James Fenimore Cooper and the poetry of Henry Wadsworth Longfellow to Wild West shows and the sensationalized frontier tales popularized in dime novels. In the early twentieth century, community-based pageants routinely featured scenes of local Indians happily signing away their land to the white settlers who displaced them. Cowboy-and-Indian movies were an early and lasting staple of the film industry, and Tin Pan Alley riffs on ersatz "Indian" melodies have abounded. These representations resonated with composers who wished to develop a self-consciously "American" operatic tradition.[1] The so-called "Indianist" operas of the early twentieth-century drew from these manifestations to become, despite claims of authenticity to their Indigenous subjects, a sub-set of an even longer European tradition of operatic exoticism.

Theatricals of all types, whether amateur or professional, formal or informal, public or private, were just as important an American practice. These ranged from burlesque shows and vaudeville through opera and spoken drama, all of them

---

[1] Cooper (1789–1851), especially *Last of the Mohicans*, 1826; Longfellow (1807–1882), especially *The Song of Hiawatha*, 1855. For secondary accounts, see Eugene H. Jones, *Native Americans as Shown on the Stage, 1753–1916* (Metuchen, NJ: Scarecrow, 1988); L.G. Moses, *Wild West Shows and the Images of American Indians, 1883–1933* (Albuquerque: University of New Mexico Press, 1996); David Glassberg, *American Historical Pageantry: The Uses of Tradition in the early Twentieth Century* (Chapel Hill: University of North Carolina Press, 1990); Michael Pisani, *Imagining Native America in Music* (New Haven, CT: Yale University Press, 2005). Scholarly interest in American indigenous music began with Theodore Baker, *Über die Musik der nordamerikanischer Wilden* (PhD, University of Leipzig, 1882), translated as *On the Music of North American Indians* by Ann Buckley (Buren and New York: Frits Knuf and W.S. Heinman, 1976). Regarding subsequent ethnological collectors, Frances Densmore collected Ute songs on the Uintah-Ouray Reservation in Utah within a year following the first production of *The Sun Dance Opera*.

188   *Opera Indigene: Re/presenting First Nations and Indigenous Cultures*

supported by music as well as scenery and, occasionally, dance. Not limited to Indigenous subjects, these forms of entertainment were fundamental elements of popular culture in the USA right up to the time of World War One and even beyond. Although opera generally occupied the higher end of this array of genres, its popularity crossed class lines, making it surprisingly ubiquitous.[2] That was as true in recently settled, sparsely populated corners of the Far West as in the more populous East and Midwest. An "opera house," however modest and ill-suited to large stage productions, became a feature of almost any new town in the Far West that lasted more than a very few years. To be sure, the "operatic" fare in many such houses was decidedly flexible. It might include occasional high spots from popular European operas—excerpts from English-language versions of *Der Freischütz* and *La sonnambula*, say, along with the best-known scenes from *Il trovatore*—sung by local talent or small traveling companies. It is not surprising, then, that the medium of opera, sometimes quite loosely defined, was adapted by various Western Americans to tell stories about the Indigenous cultures they observed, and, not incidentally, about themselves and their environment.

The two operas discussed here may thus be considered part of an extensive tradition of representations of Native Americans across classes and genres, and as part of an equally long tradition of creative expression through theatricals. It almost goes without saying that they, like all of the "Indianist" operas, and like most other representations of Native Americans, are invariably, unavoidably, and sometimes intolerably colonialist, racist, and/or sexist when viewed from a twenty-first-century perspective. Although the information in Table 10.1, a list of Indianist operas produced in the USA between 1907 and 1918, is only suggestive of this principle, we may safely take it for granted. The questions become how those colonialist, racist, and/or sexist positions are constructed, and what those constructions can tell us about the operas' creators, their audiences, and contemporary views of American history and culture.

The fact that the two operas discussed here were based on local cultures and created by local people with widely varying cultural positions had consequences for the nature of the stories they tell, and for the relationship of those stories to their immediate audiences, very different in each case. This closeness in place and time gave them both immediate political implications, with differently inflected meanings for their initial audiences and critics than for more distant observers and later audiences. Here I focus on two points about these two Far Western operas. One deals with the geographical proximity of their creators and audiences to their subjects. In addition, despite the sharply contrasting nature of these two operas,

---

[2]   Lawrence W. Levine, in *Highbrow/Lowbrow: The Emergence of Cultural Hierarchy in America* (Cambridge, MA: Harvard University Press, 1988) argues that opera had become an elite genre by the close of the nineteenth century; however, elite and popular versions of opera remained for several decades beyond that in most parts of the USA, lingering into the 1920s. Mormons as well as miners built public auditoriums for all-purpose use, including operatic ventures.

Composed and Produced in the American West, 1912–1913   189

Table 10.1   Indianist operas produced in the USA, 1907–1918

The "Western" Operas

Narcissa: or, The Cost of Empire
Composer: Mary Carr Moore
Librettist: Sarah Pratt Carr
Premiere: Seattle, WA, 1912. Revivals San Francisco 1926; Los Angeles 1945
Quasi-historical account of Whitman massacre/incident of 1847 in Oregon Territory
near present-day Walla Walla, WA, without added triangle

The Sun Dance Opera
Collaborators: William F. Hanson and Zitkala Sa (Gertrude Simmons Bonnin)
Premiere: Vernal, UT, 1913. Revivals Provo (Brigham Young University) and Salt Lake
City, UT, 1914; Provo 1935; New York City, 1938
Partial re-enactment of (post-contact Sioux) sun dance framed by romantic triangle
among Sioux, Ute, and Shoshone individuals; set in Ute country adjoining Vernal

The "Eastern" Operas

Poia
Composer: Arthur Nevin
Librettist: Randolph Hartley, on story by Walter McClintock
Premiere: Philadelphia, PA, 1907
Set in pre-contact Blackfeet country (western Montana); all-Blackfeet triangle

The Sacrifice
Composer: Frederick Shepherd Converse
Librettist: John Macy, on story by Converse
Premiere: Boston, MA, 1911
Set in rapidly Americanizing California, 1846; triangle among two Mexicans and one
"American" (i.e., Anglo-American)

Natoma
Composer: Victor Herbert
Librettist: Joseph D. Redding
Premiere: Philadelphia, PA, 1911
Set in Old California, 1820s; triangle among two "Americans" and one Mexican

Azora, Daughter of Montezuma
Composer: Henry Hadley
Librettist: David Stevens
Premiere: Chicago, IL, 1917
Set in the City of Mexico just before and at the moment of contact; triangle among two
Aztecs and one Tlascalan

Shanewis, or The Robin Woman
Composer: Charles Wakefield Cadman
Librettist: Nelle Richmond Eberhart
Premiere: New York Metropolitan Opera, 1918; revived 1919
Set in contemporary California and Oklahoma; triangle is one Pawnee, two "Americans"

---

each has somewhat unusual ethical, quasi-religious, even didactic aesthetic content.
This second point is at least partly a consequence of another common element
shared by these two operas, that women were heavily involved in their creation.

190   *Opera Indigene: Re/presenting First Nations and Indigenous Cultures*

The gender-based cultural baggage they carried is reflected in their work. Most prominently, one does not imagine religious conviction of any kind as a key factor in male-created stage treatments of Native Americans or of the winning of the West, yet such convictions, however different in each case, are fundamental themes for each of these two operas. As another consequence, romantic entanglements, so central to the plots of most of the standard operas, are played down (in *Narcissa*) or their potential racial and class implications sidestepped and neutralized (in *The Sun Dance Opera*). These characteristics are essential to the unusual kind of authenticity to be found in the creation and reception of each opera, for they engage both the nineteenth-century concept of the "women's sphere" and the twentieth-century notion of the "male gaze."

Despite these similarities, the two operas and the cultural situations of their creators could hardly be more different. I begin with Mary Carr Moore (1873–1957) and *Narcissa: or, The Cost of Empire*. Moore was a privileged white Western American whose grandfather had helped build and later manage the first transcontinental railroad, completed in 1869. She studied voice and composition in San Francisco, by far the most cosmopolitan city west of Chicago. Financial setbacks prevented her from finishing her vocal studies abroad, as her family had planned. Except for a few months in New York City in 1913, Moore made her career entirely in the Far West, singing, teaching, composing, and organizing community performances in several California cities and towns before and after her years in Seattle. For her, and for her librettist (her mother, Sarah Pratt Carr, who became an ordained Unitarian minister in mid-life), their choice of subject was inspired by Arthur Farwell's American Music movement, and their passionate, quasi-religious view of America's expansionist Manifest Destiny.[3] Wishing to portray Narcissa and Marcus Whitman's missionary passion as the opera's dominant element, they chose not to introduce a romantic triangle that might compete with this theme. Given their positions as Victorian ladies, neither Carr nor Moore wished to portray the Whitmans as publicly consumed by carnal love. Thus the text of their love duet carries a heavy religious burden: "All these I dare, for thee and God, / To Him in heav'n I pledge my faith, / And if He send or crown or rod, / To thee, my love, I give my heart." As Sarah Pratt Carr wrote in her Foreword to the libretto:

> The early part of the nineteenth century was marked by a missionary spirit that swept America as a frenzy ... Men and women canceled obligations and broke ties of home and love that they might carry the gospel to perishing souls ...
>
> Dr. Marcus Whitman was one of these ... To this passion soon was added that of patriotism. He saw the possibilities of that great domain [i.e., Oregon Territory,

---

[3]   Moore and Carr were both outspoken suffragists. The connection between American expansionism and the suffrage movement is explored in Allison L. Sneider, *Suffragists in an Imperial Age: US Expansion and the Woman Question, 1870–1929* (New York: Oxford University Press, 2008).

Composed and Produced in the American West, 1912–1913   191

including modern Oregon, Washington, and British Columbia] ... On the other
hand, ... it was the policy of the Hudson's Bay Company to keep the country
wild and the Indian a savage fur hunter unspoiled.... .

This missionary passion is the theme of the opera, with patriotism as the second
motive scarcely less powerful ... .[4]

This choice creates something of an operatic handicap for their protagonists,
one that both Moore and Carr willingly accepted, although it led some critics to
question whether this four-act, through-composed work was a real "opera."[5]

In contrast to *The Sun Dance Opera*, the sources for *Narcissa* are straightforward.
A piano-vocal score was published by Witmark in 1912, and two hand copies
of the full score with only minor differences are in the Moore collection at the
University of California, Los Angeles. A summary of the plot, which moves from
upstate New York to the West Coast to the mission site in the course of its four
acts, is found in Table 10.2.

The Whitmans' mission, undertaken before the boundary between the USA
and Canada west of Lake Superior was settled, held a mythically patriotic position
for the early white population of the Pacific Northwest, from which the opera's
first audiences were drawn. Seattle had become a city almost instantly when it
became the jumping-off place for the Klondike Gold Rush following the Yukon
discoveries of 1896. Moore began work on *Narcissa* only a decade after that.
The land on which the composer and most of the audience had recently settled
had once been intended by the British-owned Hudson's Bay Company as a
permanently wild reserve for "the Indian a savage fur hunter unspoiled" (Foreword
quoted above). The understanding that their newly acquired real estate had been
saved from becoming part of a designated Canadian wilderness only by Marcus
Whitman's heroic trip back east to Washington, DC in the winter of 1846–1847
had only been seriously challenged shortly before Moore and Carr determined to
construct an opera on the story. Answering that challenge in a way that kept the
Whitmans' contribution in a central position was almost certainly one of their
motivations. Thus the topic had not only "missionary passion" but also a very
local political significance for its creators and for its first audiences. Instead of
a romantic triangle, they managed to construct another kind of authenticity—an
early feminist one—with their sympathetic portrayal of Narcissa as she struggled
to fulfill her role as a missionary woman. The opera is full of characteristic musical

---

[4]   Carr, "Foreword to the Libretto," *The Cost of Empire* (Seattle, WA: Stuff Printing
Concern, 1912).

[5]   Catherine Parsons Smith and Cynthia S. Richardson, *Mary Carr Moore, American
Composer* (Ann Arbor: University of Michigan Press, 1987) contains more biographical
information as well as a catalog of Moore's compositions, which includes several other
operas as well as numerous songs and some instrumental music. See the Mary Carr Moore
collection, Music Library, University of California, Los Angeles.

192   *Opera Indigene: Re/presenting First Nations and Indigenous Cultures*

Table 10.2   Plot summary of *Narcissa: or, The Cost of Empire*

Act I, The Missionary Commitment
As the congregation of his home church in Rushville, NY, sings an anthem on Psalm 137 ("By the waters of Babylon, There we sat down, yea, wept, When we remembered Zion … How shall we sing the Lord's song in a strange land?") Marcus Whitman arrives from the Pacific Northwest and, accompanied by two (silent) Native Americans, interrupts the service to tell his story. He and Narcissa declare their love and their missionary commitment simultaneously ("All these I dare for thee and God …") They promptly marry and, with the congregation's blessing, set off to cross the continent to find the mission. The act concludes with Old Hundred and a patriotic missionary hymn ("Yes, my native land, I love thee, … Can I bid a last farewell?")

Act II, Arrival at Fort Vancouver, headquarters of the Hudson's Bay Company near the mouth of the Columbia River, 1836
Dr. John McLaughlin, the Company's factor, arrives by sea; fur traders and Indians arrive by canoe; and the missionary party arrives overland. Chief Yellow Serpent offers the Whitman party a site for the mission upriver; some Indians express doubt ("The Indians' fate is sealed.") Elaborate welcoming ceremonies. A tango represents the exoticism of the luxurious fort; a French-Canadian folk tune represents the trappers ("Malbrough s'en va-t-en guerre"); Native American dances and cries ("Woe," "Hai-ya") and chorales represent Indians and missionaries.

Act III, The Mission at Waiilatpu
After her anguished soliloquy ("Another weary day"), Narcissa recalls her duty and sings a lullaby to a settler's orphaned child (her own has died), then soothes the restive Indians by singing the Twenty-third Psalm. McLaughlin warns of trouble from the beleaguered Indians, represented by Waskema and Delaware Tom ("Woe! The Indians' fate is sealed.") Yellow Serpent's son Elijah sings a ballad in popular style to Siskadee, his beloved ("Southward now, the waning sun I'll follow.") Promising to return for her in the spring, he leads the young men south toward California for the winter. Marcus sets off for Washington, DC to prevent the USA from ceding Oregon Territory to Britain. New settlers arrive, combining suggestions of the Star Spangled Banner with a chorale ("We've come to take possession of this land.")

Act IV, The Tragedy, 1847
Marcus has returned. As the Indian women prepare to welcome the men returning from California ("Gone is the winter"), they learn that Elijah was murdered at Sutter's Fort by a white man. Waskema foretells catastrophe; Narcissa, understanding the danger better than Marcus, reminiscences about the mission ("Oh mother dear, how lightly I took on this mighty errand.") The Cayuse and Umatilla men are enraged and incited by Delaware Tom. Marcus, Narcissa, and several others are murdered. Dr. McLaughlin arrives, too late, and swears vengeance. The opera ends with a dirge ("Woe") sung by the Indian women.

---

references. The home congregation back in rural New York State is given a psalm and a missionary hymn; later on, the settlers arrive in Waiilatpu (the mission site) to suggestions of "The Star Spangled Banner." The French-Canadian trappers arrive singing "Malbrough s'en va-t-en guerre." Moore's use of a tango rhythm at the opening of Act II seems jarring until one considers the profound popularity of *Carmen* as a quintessential representation of cultural otherness in the late nineteenth century. Here it marks the exoticism of the setting at the mouth of the Columbia River, and heralds the encounter there of four separate cultures:

Composed and Produced in the American West, 1912–1913   193

the Hudson's Bay Company (aristocratic English), their client French-Canadian trappers, the local Indigenous Cayuse and Allied Tribes (here Cayuse, Walla Walla, and Umatilla) and the arriving American missionaries (pointedly more egalitarian than their English hosts).

Although she visited the site of the Whitmans' mission, Moore did not canvas local Native individuals for melodies she might adapt to her purpose. (A possible reason was that, by 1900, the Cayuse people had already abandoned their own tongue and adopted the Nez Perce language.) Where needed, she used stock "Indian" melodies, as in the motif that underlies much of Marcus's narrative account of his first trip to Oregon Territory; then reappears under the anxious dialogue in Act III as tension mounts. For the Indian dances and chants that appear at the end of Act II, she relied on her experience of an Apache demonstration she had observed on a trip to the Southwest.

Two music examples suggest Moore's expressive range. Example 10.1, the love duet, reveals Moore's lyric gift and her ability to write effectively for the voice, born of her early training as a singer. The character of Narcissa is the principal beneficiary of Moore's lyricism throughout the opera, not only here but also in the opening scene of Act III ("Another weary day," in which she longs for personal privacy and the comforts of her upbringing), and in Act IV ("Oh Mother dear," her meditation on the impending disaster). The closing dirge (Example 10.2), with its long diminuendo and its two-chord ostinato, is a moving representation of the "vanishing race" theory widely believed to be inevitable in Moore's time.[6]

The composer had ambitions for *Narcissa*. She recruited John Cort, a prominent West Coast theater manager recently relocated to New York, to promote the opera. Cort was unsuccessful in getting an Eastern production, but he recruited an experienced Eastern stage manager and two well-established opera singers for the lead roles in a Seattle production.[7] The sense of historical authenticity was heightened by the use of authentic Indian costumes and props. In addition, a survivor of the massacre was present in the opening night audience. (Hostages,

---

[6] David R.M. Beck, "The Myth of the Vanishing Race" (February 2001), on http://lcweb2.loc.gov/ammem/award98/ienhtml/essay2.html (accessed March 4, 2009). This is part of an extensive collection of sources on North American Indians found on the Library of Congress American Memory website.

[7] The stage manager was Edward P. Temple. Charles Hargreaves of the Metropolitan Opera sang the role of Marcus; Luella Chilson-Ohrman of the Chicago Opera sang the role of Narcissa. Other roles were taken by local singers. Cort was unable to recruit an experienced conductor. Moore herself eventually conducted all performances of the opera. Cort's failed efforts to get a New York production resulted partly from financial conditions, but also, in part, from prejudice. "New York managers looked upon a Westerner and a woman who had composed a grand opera in the light of a joke and refused her a satisfactory hearing," as Seattle commentator Helen Ross wrote in the Seattle *Town Crier* (April 13, 1912), p. 11. Arthur Farwell is credited with persuading Witmark to publish the piano-vocal score; very likely the expense was underwritten by Moore.

Example 10.1 *Narcissa*, excerpt from the Act I love/commitment duet between Marcus and Narcissa

Example 10.2 *Narcissa*, Act IV, dirge at end of opera. Ostinato fades away. The end of a way of life and of entire race as well as that of the missionaries. "The final brotherhood of all mankind" is to be achieved only in the afterlife

196   *Opera Indigene: Re/presenting First Nations and Indigenous Cultures*

some as young as seven years old, had been taken after the 1847 murders, so this was not an unreasonable claim.)

A preview and three scheduled performances were received with enthusiasm. The local critic wrote

> "Narcissa" ... is strikingly original and in some places startlingly so ... There is a solemnity and dignity pervading the whole which never loses its grip ... In "Narcissa" has been struck a note that is absolutely untouched. There does not come to mind any opera in the history of music which has very much in common with this one. Certainly it is American grand opera, and the only one worthy the name.[8]

The nationally distributed *Musical America* gave *Narcissa* most of a page, including a photograph of the set:

> in the light of a narration well told, ably constructed and given an adequate musical setting, the opera fills its purpose entirely. Regarding the music itself there can scarcely be a difference of opinion. The score is rich in free, spontaneous melody given excellent treatment and at no time forced. In using the original Indian melodies Mrs. Moore has shown wonderful skill. ... the handling of the chorus and the effectiveness of the ensemble show the composer to possess creative ability of the highest order.[9]

Although she composed other operas after *Narcissa* (generally quite different in character) and managed local ad hoc productions for most of them, Moore persisted in seeking more performances of this most "American" of her operas. She may have struck out with national companies, but she succeeded in engineering two Western revivals, one in San Francisco in 1925, and a second in Los Angeles in 1945. Both were received politely, but neither drew the consistent enthusiasm of the Seattle production. In neither case was she able to muster the resources for as polished a production. Very likely, too, the sense of historical immediacy had vanished with the passage of time. The lack of drama—always meaning the absence of a romantic triangle—was seen as an ever-more serious shortcoming. "Faithful as her book was to history, picturesque as it was with its colonial and Indian types, it was lacking in the qualities that persistently held attention. If it were to be compared with a really thrilling book like the one used by Bizet in 'Carmen,' its lack of dramatic incident and of variety would be made plain," wrote

---

[8]   Cyril A. Player, "'Narcissa' Sung: Well Received," *Seattle Post-Intelligencer* (April 23, 1912), p. 4.

[9]   Carl Presley, "Historical Opera of the Northwest," *Musical America* (May 11, 1912), p. 5.

one reviewer in 1925.[10] Its harmonic idiom, relatively conservative to begin with, probably seemed anachronistic as well.

The 1945 revival, given under the title *The Cost of Empire* (the originally intended title) was greeted with a certain impatience. It was said to have an "interesting" story but lack "glamour," and was criticized for lack of variety in its tempos, almost certainly an issue arising from the sketchy preparation.[11] Yet friendlier critics continued to admire its story and Moore's lyric and dramatic gifts. Clarence Gustlin, a pianist who had toured extensively with lecture-recitals on American music between the wars, wrote to Moore after that performance:

> Your excellent opera, "The Cost of Empire" ... I regret very much ... was not in my repertoire some years ago when I was touring the States, under auspices of the National Federation of Music Clubs, in a special effort to acquaint the public with the subject of American Opera ... . I can say, without hesitancy, that your work deserves a very high place among American compositions in this form. In fact, I have neither examined nor heard any other which I would consider its superior ... .[12]

The collaboration that led to *The Sun Dance Opera*, unlike that between Carr and Moore, was not a matter of the usual composer/librettist division of labor. The difficulties of sorting out the contribution of each of its creators are partly the result of their dramatically different backgrounds, their contrasting power positions, and their implicitly limited agreement about their goals for the project. Incomplete sources create further issues, as will be seen. William F. Hanson and Zitkala Sa were by any measure an odd couple. Hanson (1887–1969), the son of Mormon homesteaders, grew up near Vernal in Utah, and attended Brigham Young University (BYU) for two years before returning to his home town as a school teacher. As a young man, he had observed certain Ute ceremonial celebrations, such as the Bear Dance. He wished to represent the elements of Native culture he had observed in a way that would help preserve it, and that would secure greater sympathy for it from his fellow Mormons. Only later, in 1924, did he go east to study at the Chicago Musical College; in the same year he joined the BYU faculty, where he continued to pursue the same goals with respect to Ute culture, though,

---

[10]   John D. Barry, "Ways of the World," n.d., unidentified clipping in Mary Carr Moore Scrapbook no. 6, Mary Carr Moore Archive, UCLA.

[11]   Isabel Morse Jones, *Los Angeles Times* (March 17, 1945), p. A5. Jones and one other critic also complained about the sameness of tempo. It seems likely that Moore, by then 72, was unable to fully control what was clearly an under-rehearsed performance.

[12]   Clarence Gustlin to Mary Carr Moore, March 22, 1945 in Scrapbook no. 19, Mary Carr Moore Archive, UCLA.

198   *Opera Indigene: Re/presenting First Nations and Indigenous Cultures*

in the absence of further collaborations with Zitkala Sa, with ever-diminishing fidelity.[13]

Zitkala Sa (1876–1938), whose English name was Gertrude Simmons Bonnin, was a Yankton Sioux who was taken from her mother at age seven and sent to an Indian school. She later studied at Earlham College (Indiana) and the New England Conservatory (Massachusetts), before teaching at the Carlisle (Pennsylvania) Indian School and, in 1900, touring as a soloist with its band. The *New York Times* advertised one of its concerts thus:

> Carnegie Hall, Wed. Ev., March 28 / Prior to their departure for the Paris Exhibition, By approval of the U.S. Interior Department, Exhibition Concert of the U.S. Carlisle Indian Band. 55 Musicians and Zitkala Sa, Indian Girl Violinist, from the U.S. Indian School, Carlisle, Pa. / Mr. Dennison Wheelock, Musical Direc'r / Note—This concert is a repetition of that given at the White House, March 17th, by request of President McKinley. Seats, $1.00, 75c, and 50c. Now on sale at box office and Schuberth's, 23 Union Square.[14]

Contrary to any expectations generated by either her sex or her ethnic background, she was by far the more highly educated and musically experienced of the two collaborators who created *The Sun Dance Opera*.

Zitkala Sa thrived intellectually on her "white" education but was seldom far from her ongoing personal struggle over how to be true to herself in both white and native cultures. As an author, she is the subject of numerous dissertations in American literature, history, and politics, but she has escaped attention from musicologists until fairly recently. She is apparently the only Native American of her time who was involved in the composition of an "Indianist" opera.[15] Although

---

[13]   Hanson, *Sun Dance Land* (Provo, UT: J. Grant Stevenson, 1967) summarizes his knowledge of Ute culture. His description of the Bear Dance is contained in his master's thesis (BYU, 1937). His later operas, composed independently, include *Tam-man Nacup* (composed 1923, produced at BYU 1927, 1928) and *Bleeding Heart* (produced at BYU, 1938). He also gave a series of lyceum lectures in the area from 1925 under the title "Hanson's Wigwam." Hanson's papers and music are in the Department of Special Collections at BYU. (Only the last version of *The Sun Dance Opera*, as used for the 1938 revival, is preserved, however.) Hanson's papers are in Collection 299, Special Collections, Brigham Young University.

[14]   *New York Times* (March 25, 1900), p. 9. Zitkala Sa's papers are in the Raymond and Gertrude Bonnin Collection 1704, Special Collections Brigham Young University.

[15]   Zitkala Sa, *Old Indian Legends* (Boston: Ginn & Co., 1901), reprint ed. A.M. Picotte (Lincoln: University of Nebraska Press, 1985); *American Indian Stories* (Washington, DC: Hayworth Publishing House, 1921), reprint ed. D. Fisher (Lincoln: University of Nebraska Press, 1985), reprint ed. S. Dominguez (Lincoln: University of Nebraska Press, 2003); *Dreams and Thunder: Stories, Poems, and The Sun Dance Opera*, anthology ed. P.J. Haven (Lincoln: University of Nebraska Press, 2001); *American Indian Stories, Legends, and Other Writings*, ed. C.N. Davidson and A. Norris (New York: Penguin Books, 2003);

Composed and Produced in the American West, 1912–1913 199

she spent time studying piano at Otterbein College (Ohio) following the first production of *The Sun Dance Opera* in 1913, her life circumstances led her to abandon music soon afterward. Despite the success of numerous English-language publications dating back to the late 1890s, she chose to live among other Indians. In 1902, she married Raymond T. Bonnin, another Sioux and an employee of the Bureau of Indian Affairs (BIA), the federal agency that still administers Indian reservations, and went to live with him on the Uintah-Ouray Reservation from 1902 until 1917, when he left the BIA. It is possible that she decided to participate in the opera project as a result of early discussions of the Society of American Indians about how to counter the destructive stereotypical "wild Indian" images common to popular Wild West shows. In any case, for Zitkala Sa, representing "native culture" was a far more diverse and complex issue than it was for Hanson.

Besides involving such an unlikely collaboration and a location more isolated, even, than distant Seattle, *The Sun Dance Opera* has source issues. There are two very different scores, whose dates are more than two decades apart. The first is a rough piano-vocal version deposited in the US Copyright Office in 1912, about three months before the first production. This consists of a brief overture and twenty-three short numbers divided into three acts and five scenes. It includes some stage directions and the framework for a certain amount of spoken dialogue. No other copy of the 1913 version is known. The other score is a later revision, now at BYU, probably prepared for the 1938 New York revival. Its radical changes include added characters and events; the added magical "Love-Leaves," slightly reminiscent of the love potion in *Tristan und Isolde*, are the most prominent example. Some numbers are eliminated, others are extensively recomposed, and still others are added. Sections performed by Ute men in the early production(s) are written out for later performers taking their roles. All these changes were made by Hanson. How much was added for other revivals between 1914 and 1938 is

---

with C.H. Fabens and M.K. Sniffen, *Oklahoma's Poor Rich Indians: An Orgy of Graft and Exploitation of the Five Civilized Tribes—Legalized Robbery* (Philadelphia, PA: Office of the Indian Rights Association, [1924]). Many of her stories and essays, originally published in the *Atlantic Monthly, Harper's Monthly Magazine, Everybody's Magazine, The American Indian Magazine*, and *The Earhamite*, are available online at NetLibrary.com, for example "Why I am a Pagan," *Atlantic Monthly*, 90 (December 1902), pp. 307–310. A complete list of her essays appears in the register to the Raymond and Gertrude Bonnin, National Council of American Indians papers in the Department of Special Collections, BYU. The fullest statement of her cultural ambivalence is in her letters to Carlos Montezuma, in the Hayden Library, University of Arizona; copies are in the Bonnin collection. Susan Dominguez, "Zitkala Sa (Gertrude Simmons Bonnin), 1876–1938: (Re)discovering *The Sun Dance*," *American Music Research Center Journal*, 5 (1995), pp. 83–96. Unaware that an earlier version of the score exists in the Library of Congress, Dominguez based her conclusions on the 1938 score at BYU, which has very little in common with the early version. See also Catharine Parsons Smith, "An Operatic Skeleton on the Western Frontier: Zitkala Sa, William F. Hanson, and *The Sun Dance Opera*," *Women & Music: A Journal of Gender and Culture*, 5 (2001), pp. 1–30.

200   *Opera Indigene: Re/presenting First Nations and Indigenous Cultures*

unknown, since the scores for these intermediate versions are not in the Hanson collection. Table 10.3 outlines the two versions.

Table 10.3   *The Sun Dance Opera*: two versions

1912 deposit copy (Hanson and Zitkala Sa)	Late score [c. 1935–1938] (Hanson)
Overture: fanfare opening followed by a medley of tunes used later, ending with the "Sun Dance" theme	Overture: middle section extended with a "Medicine Chant" and Sweet Singer's "I gave her the love-leaves"
Act I Winona and Ohiya, separate numbers Duet Ohiya and mother Sweet Singer aria Hebo, Blue Necklace and Gossips poke fun at Sweet Singer Crier and chorus summon all to the start of the Sun Dance: "We must away"	**Act I** Winona and Ohiya, same numbers Ohiya-mother duet cut Sweet Singer aria cut Mother, new aria Hebo et al. scene expanded, chorus added New concluding chorus: "Away, away, away"
Act II Scene 1 Circle Dance War Dance ("Each tell [sic] of brave deeds. Capture Sun Dance poles. All in action while they dance.") Wa-ci-pe (Sun Dance) chorus Sun Dance enclosure erected (Most of this scene not written out)	**Act II** (Written out for performers playing roles of Indian dancers; expanded from four to twenty pages) Wa-ci-pe chorus cut Chorus added: "Tall Trees" (signed "Provo, Utah")
Act II Scene 2 Ohiya's Serenade to Winona Chorus: Witches of the Night	**Act III** (expanded from three to twenty-seven pages) Ohiya's Serenade expanded Winona: new aria Same chorus expanded
Act II Scene 3 Sweet Singer, "A Throbbing Heart Song" to Winona, who turns him down Winona and Hebo, duet Chorus ("Great Spirit Hear Our Prayers") Sun Set March (Braves) The Sun Dance proper begins and extends through the pause	**Act IV** (greatest divergence here) "Heart Song" cut Shoshone Maid (a new character, previously wronged) confronts Sweet Singer with two arias and a duet. New chorus ("Great Spirit Hear, Prayer") substituted The Sun Dance begins as before

In the opera as it was initially produced in Vernal in 1913 and in Provo and Salt Lake City the following year, fragments of the Sun Dance—a post-contact Sioux ceremony—were enacted by Native Americans—specifically Utes—who were residents of the neighboring Uintah-Ouray Reservation, for a largely white, Mormon audience. These ceremonial excerpts, with their powerful religious significance, were sandwiched among more traditionally Western operetta-like scenes depicting a romantic triangle. The triangle echoed Mormon sexual (i.e. "moral") values, and, very likely, a desire to dispel the cloud left by the Mormons' early practice of polygamy rather than any known Ute practice.[16] Yet it avoids sensitive issues of white-native contact; instead, the triangle addresses differences and rivalries among Sioux, Ute, and Shoshone individuals (this is almost certainly Zitkala Sa's choice). Even so, the European operatic tradition gives the work its overall shape and supplies a fatally colonialist framework. For his part, Hanson reported his motivation this way:

> We have tried to use the Opera as a medium to interpret the inner and human side of the Red man. He has been influenced in his forms, rituals and social customs by a heredity and environment so vastly different than ours, that we often mistake and call the Aborigine a being without heartthrobs, loves, social standards, or devotion.[17]

Zitkala Sa never wrote about her participation in this project. She is quoted, however, by N.L. Nelson, writing in the *Deseret News* (still the Mormon church-owned newspaper in Salt Lake City) at the time of the 1913 production, as saying, "I have been trained in the concepts of the Christian religion, but I do not find them more beautiful, more noble, or more true than the religious ideals of the Indian ..."[18] In the same essay, Nelson, a music professor at BYU, went on to characterize

---

[16] Donald Callaway, Joel Janetski, and Omer C. Stewart, "Ute," in *Handbook of North American Indians*, vol. 11, ed. Warren d'Azevedo (Washington, DC: Smithsonian Institution, 1978–), p. 352, report that marriage was "'a tenuous and temporary bond in all Ute groups.' Choosing a spouse was usually an individual decision although parents had some influence in the selection for first marriages." The interior quotation is from Anne M. Cooke Smith, "Ethnography of the Northern Ute," *Museum of New Mexico Papers in Anthropology*, 17 (1974), pp. 128–37.The *Handbook* also implies an unusual element of equality between the sexes, one that does not fit with Hanson's or the overwhelmingly Mormon audience's view: "Like other Great Basin tribes and unlike almost all the rest of western North America, the Ute had an equal proportion of men and women shamans." (*Handbook*, p. 354). This contrasts sharply with Mormon religious practice. Thus a Sun Dance ceremony would not have been undertaken for so personal a reason. Moreover, the notion that the bride's father must "give" the bride to her suitor was not an essential Ute practice.

[17] William F. Hanson, program for the 1935 production at BYU. Hanson papers.

[18] N.L. Nelson, *Deseret News* (March 29, 1913), and *Musical America* (April 26, 1913), clippings in Hanson papers. Mormons characterized North American Indians as "Lamanites." They were thought to be degenerate descendants of peoples dispersed at the Tower of Babel who emigrated from Jerusalem to the New World about 600 BCE. See Robert Wauchope, *Lost Tribes & Sunken Continents: Myth and Method in the Study of American Indians* (Chicago, IL: University of Chicago Press, 1974), pp. 59–60. Mormons generally characterize non-Mormons, including Christians, as "gentiles."

202   *Opera Indigene: Re/presenting First Nations and Indigenous Cultures*

Zitkala Sa as a properly domesticated and westernized female individual in spite of her origins:

> For Zitkala Sa—otherwise Mrs. R.T. Bonnin, who now lives in a modern home at Fort Duchesne (on the Uintah-Ouray Reservation), and whose husband is an employee of the United States government—is one of those rare spirits whom God sends, now and then, among lowly peoples to lift them to higher planes. As an Indian maiden—for she is a full blooded Sioux—she was educated in the best of Indian schools, ... finishing her studies of the piano and violin in the Boston Conservatory of Music. Gentle, refined, modest to a fault, and of a strongly intuitional cast of mind this woman has assimilated the best in American civilization, without losing any of her deep appreciation of the spiritual ideals of her own people.[19]

That such an explanation, laden with such obvious racial and gender stereotypes, was deemed appropriate by Nelson and his editors, makes clear the dimensions of Zitkala Sa's assumed cultural inferiority relative to her white collaborator and her white audience.

Given the lack of literal evidence about Zitkala Sa's and Hanson's separate contributions, some speculation is in order. Insofar as there are features of the "authentic" and the "exotic," we may safely ascribe the former to her and the latter to him. Hanson's initial idea had been to present an indoor, staged version of the Bear Dance, a Ute springtime ceremony. In an assertion of her own tribal identity, Zitkala Sa persuaded him that they should represent the Sun Dance, a post-contact Sioux religious ceremony, instead. There may have been other reasons for this choice. It may have been easier to persuade the Ute participants to perform portions of a recently borrowed ceremony before a white public, rather than a long-established one of their own. The Sun Dance had been outlawed by the United States government, endowing it with the charm of the forbidden for its Mormon audience, who had emigrated to Utah after suffering persecutions of their own. It seems likely that Hanson dreamed up the romantic triangle, and that Zitkala Sa, herself Sioux, avoided issues of contact by choosing a Sioux hero (Ohiya), who elects to undertake the five-day Sun Dance in order to win the hand of the Ute chief's daughter (Winona) in the face of competition from a renegade Shoshone visitor (Sweet Singer).

Hanson had collected a number of the melodic ideas that he adapted for the opera. (Curiously, none of them matches the melodies collected a year later by ethnologist Frances Densmore, although several of them assume the descending shape that Densmore found to be characteristic of Ute song, and they shared

---

[19]   Nelson, *Deseret News.*

Composed and Produced in the American West, 1912–1913   203

two informants.[20]) Of the Ute-derived melodies used in the opera, the one that definitely came from Zitkala Sa is "Ink-pa-ta," the third of Hanson's nine themes, a love song sung or played by several of the characters; it is the only theme that is scarcely extended or elaborated, always appearing with minimal changes to its initial four-part harmonization.[21] In Example 10.3 here, it appears following Ohiya's serenade with the love-flute.

Zitkala Sa supplied other details of Ute courtship practice, such as the carving of the love-flute. She very likely organized, rehearsed, and helped costume the Ute participants. To the Indian-generated tunes, Hanson added his own songs and choruses. Example 10.4 gives the opening of the chorus that concludes Act I, suggesting the extensive changes in the score between 1912 and 1938. In each case, a crier begins. In the first case "How now, why linger here," is given a waltz-like setting, "We must away." In the later, the waltz has been discarded; the crier begins with a more chant-like "Hail tribesman all, our chieftain comes," leading to a more formal chorus, "Away, away, away." However the division of labor worked, *The Sun Dance Opera*'s initial success depended much more heavily on Zitkala Sa than would have been the case for the usual librettist.

What is not speculation is that Zitkala Sa's share in creating the first version of *The Sun Dance Opera* was emphasized as an element of the opera's simultaneous authenticity and its exoticism. That is quite different from recognizing her as an equal collaborator, as becomes even more evident when one sees that Hanson copyrighted both surviving scores under his own name. He only assigned "an undivided half interest" in the opera to his Sioux collaborator a month after the first production, most likely at her or her husband's insistence on the suggestion of a revival in Salt Lake City or Provo. Only much later in his life, long after all the productions and after her death did Hanson give her credit as co-creator of the opera. In a shaky hand, he added "Zitkala Sa & W.F. Hanson" after the opera's title

---

[20]   Hanson's list of nine examples, now in the Hanson papers, is labeled "Part 2, Appendix B, Themes used in The Sun Dance Opera" and was intended for his book but omitted from the published version. Constructed long after the fact, it is limited to those themes actually used in the score. It is reproduced in Smith, "An Operatic Skeleton on the Western Frontier," pp. 11–14, as Example 1(a) through (i). Frances Densmore, *Northern Ute Music* (Washington, DC: Smithsonian Institution, Bureau of American Ethnology, 1922; reprint New York: Da Capo Press, 1972). Densmore visited the Uintah-Ouray reservation in 1914 and 1916. Quinance, one of Densmore's informants, was the leader of the half-dozen Ute men who participated in *The Sun Dance Opera* performances in 1913 and 1914, and in Hanson's later lyceum performances. John Archoop was also an informant to both Hanson and Densmore.

[21]   The possibility of a double meaning for "Ink-pa-ta" is raised by Tara Browner, who reports that a modern Sioux interpretation of its lyrics suggests the anger of a rejected male lover, who is labeling her a prostitute. This conflicts with the report of marriage as "a tenuous and temporary bond" in Ute practice (see note 16 above.) Whether Zitkala Sa and the participating Utes were enjoying a private joke, or whether the meaning has actually changed, is unclear.

Example 10.3 *The Sun Dance Opera*, "Ohiya's Serenade" and "Ink-pa-ta" from Act II, Scene 2, 1912 version

in his written account of the opera and of what he knew about the culture of his Ute neighbors. He also wrote that "she skeletoned the story."

Apart from the ownership issue, the power imbalance among the collaborators and participants has some features that we might not think about. In 1913, members of the Ute tribe who lived on the Uintah-Ouray reservation, including those who

Example 10.4 *The Sun Dance Opera*, chorus concluding Act I

took part in the early performances, were literally wards of the US government.[22] Much of their treaty/reservation land had been sold to whites, some very likely to members of the opera's early audiences. Often illiterate, the Ute were dependent on the Bureau of Indian Affairs through the local agency (at nearby Fort Duchesne) for their subsistence, given that they could no longer survive as hunters and gatherers. They were not recognized as American citizens, meaning that they were not allowed the right to assemble peacefully or to practice their religion, including the Sun Dance. Since federal policy was to turn them into farmers as quickly as possible, they were not allowed to leave the reservation for any reason, including

---

[22] The relatively few Utes who managed to survive nineteenth-century contact with whites were confined by 1913 to two reservations in Colorado and to the Uintah-Ouray reservation in northeastern Utah; these had been established by Lincoln in 1861. Many had gradually been pushed onto the reservations by white settlement in the decades after the Mormons were themselves driven west from Illinois in 1847. By the mid-1870s, the Utes were restricted to about 9 percent of their aboriginal range.

opera performances, until the crops were safely harvested. Letters from Quinance, one of the Ute participants, advise Hanson as to when they might be allowed to come to Provo for a production and complaining of the exorbitant prices they would be charged to be driven there.[23]

The Sun Dance Opera was enthusiastically received at its premiere, filling the hall in Vernal for three nights. The only published report is by N.L. Nelson, printed in the *Deseret News* and, in shortened form, in *Musical America*. His commentary dwells on the favorable impression the opera made on its audience and on the sympathy with which native peoples are represented. For Nelson, and very likely for the audience, the production enhanced his "understanding" and assuaged his "deeply imbedded" Western guilt. That, perhaps, was his measure of the opera's and the performance's "authenticity" for those early audiences. A review from the first production at BYU in May 1914 also stresses the "authenticity" of the proceedings: "the nearness to Indian life was little less than marvelous."[24]

What had pleased Utah critics in 1913 and 1914 was less successful in New York City a quarter-century later.[25] Despite Hanson's extensive revision of the score, New York critics had no trouble pointing out the awkward disconnect between the "ethnological" and the "popular" sections of the production. The difference in critical reception over that time period had less to do with the critics' relative musical sophistication, however obvious that is to us, and more to do with their relative distance in time and geographic location from the usual sites of the Native ceremonies. Both displayed a certain cultural voyeurism as part of their common interest in the "primitive." The claims of authenticity were intended at least partly to separate relatively elite genres such as opera and operetta from the cruder, cigarstore Indian stereotypes of popular culture. In neither set of critical responses was Zitkala Sa's probable intention addressed—that is, her concern to generate support for improving the lot of the opera's Native American participants.

Even in its later version, *The Sun Dance Opera* is, to say the least, dated. If it were to be reconstructed today, the solemnity of the Sun Dance might be enhanced by skipping the triangle entirely and using the opera's elements to address the pervasive dilemma faced by Zitkala Sa, and still faced by Native Americans (and, indeed, other minorities)—namely, how to adapt to the overwhelming pressures

---

[23]   Letters, 1926, Hanson papers, written out by a third party. Example: "Dear Friend, I found out here white man want $50 to take five of us out—$60 for 6 to ride. Five of us ready to go anytime. We want to go soon so can be here to work in the spring ... Maybe you can get a car to take us. $50 too much money. This car can't take all our things—it's too small ... ."

[24]   Unidentified clipping from a Provo paper, Friday May 22, 1914. Hanson papers.

[25]   The New York performance took place on April 27, 1938 at the Broadway Theatre. The New York Light Opera Guild was directed by John Hand, who had sung the role of Ohiya in the 1914 production at BYU. Critical commentary appeared in the *Herald Tribune* (signed by FDP), *Daily News*, *Musical America*, *Musical Courier*, and *New Yorker*.

and power of the dominant white culture while retaining any semblance of personal or group integrity. That is a struggle in which Zitkala Sa and the other native participants in the production were involved whether they wanted to be or not, but not one which Hanson or the white audiences, either in Utah or New York City, could easily have accepted as an operatic subject. Even in an age of *verismo* opera, that would surely have seemed dangerously realistic, even subversive, and nowhere nearly exotic enough for its audiences.

Zitkala Sa's later direction led decisively away from the complexities of theatrical make-believe, and she never did return to public music-making. In fact, there is no record of her further involvement with the opera or with Hanson's later, steadily more fantasy-laden Indianist projects. She found other ways to use her multiple gifts. In 1917 the Bonnins left Utah for Washington, DC, where she became a political activist, first through the Society of American Indians and later, the National Council of American Indians. Among the lobbying successes to which she could lay claim was a 1924 Act of Congress granting citizenship to all Native Americans, including those who had demonstrated a compelling, if necessarily not entirely authentic, version of Native American values in *The Sun Dance Opera*. Her later path serves to dramatize the contrast in the cultural situations of each of its creators, and the resultant divided character of the opera itself.

As a practical matter, *Narcissa* is sufficiently complete that a revival would be possible, though its naïvetés would have to be addressed in some way. Despite their radical differences, both *Narcissa* and *The Sun Dance Opera* are unique expressions of regional interests and attitudes that expand our perceptions and understandings of the cultures of the American West early in the twentieth century. The geographical closeness of each to the events they portray, and their nearness in time, is fundamental to their early, local success. Their (sharply contrasting) portrayals of racial difference and religious conviction were immediate for their creators and their early audiences. What we take for their exoticism was much less exotic at the time and more "authentic." Absent these qualities, and our view puts them in a more distant perspective, making them seem more similar to the better-known "Eastern" Indianist operas than they actually were to their initial audiences.

PART IV
Canadian Perspectives

Chapter 11

Assimilation, Integration and Individuation: The Evolution of First Nations Musical Citizenship in Canadian Opera

Mary I. Ingraham

Music as a location for the performance of social and political relationships has long been recognized in scholarly research. Opera in particular has been viewed as a productive site for the expression of political and social ideologies, in the promotion of nationalistic goals, or to relate an event or for the representation of individual and collective identities. The politics of music as citizenship in these studies historically has been applied to works composed within culturally influential national systems such as the *ancien régime*, the *Risorgimento*, Nazi Germany or Communist Russia and generally references a force external to the music: how a particular work is used to promote an ideology, a socio-political reality or an identity. With this study I am proposing instead to view musical citizenship from within an operatic work, to merge the politics of citizenship with the representative potential of music, and to consider music as an embodiment of contemporary perspectives on citizenship and tolerance of cultural difference. What I refer to as musical citizenship involves the dynamic relationship of representation in musical compositions and the role it plays in synthesizing the practices of one cultural community within another. The basis of this study is the consideration in six operas across the first hundred years of Canadian history (1867–1967) of the interplay of contemporary social and political issues of citizenship and of semiotic principles in textual and musical representation or signification.

The significance of examining musical citizenship in operatic compositions can be appreciated on some level in many Western musical products in the genre, but I find it to be particularly effective within postcolonial cultural communities in which collective identity has been more consciously—and in some cases more recently—considered. Operas composed in Canada, for which no canon of works can be identified,[1] requires such a conceptual framework, given the fact that issues

---

[1]   Very few Canadian operas are known outside of Canada. Notable exceptions are Harry Somers's *Louis Riel* and R. Murray Schafer's *Patria* series. Bourdieu's hypothesis regarding "cultural consecration" might be activated here, since references to other Canadian operatic works, if noted at all, appear primarily in academic discourse. Pierre Bourdieu, *The Field of Cultural Production: Essays on Art and Literature* (New York, 1993), p. 124.

212   *Opera Indigene: Re/presenting First Nations and Indigenous Cultures*

of nationality have developed simultaneously with issues of modernity in social and political practice. Original compositions written within this environment need a new approach, particularly with respect to the representation of First Nations peoples,[2] a cultural group previously unvoiced in operatic discourse. Musical citizenship of Indigenous Canadians, defined here briefly as the status or authority of the native voice within a musical work, is determined not simply as a conceit of composition or the result of adhering to extant texts. It extends beyond the stereotypical stories and sounds of native representation, involving the examination of hierarchies, where and how such stereotypes are employed in the music, and how they are manipulated to assert additional cross-cultural boundaries and relationships. Rewriting historical events and reducing Indigenous Canadians to musical stereotypes was common in the early years of Canadian opera, and musical exemplars from these years thus exhibit the capacity to serve as barometers of nation- and identity-building pressures within Canadian history.

This chapter explores specifically the intersection of government policy and opera creation in the first 100 years of Confederation. From the assimilationist policies of the consolidated Indian Act passed in 1876 to the integrationist strategies of its amendments in 1951 and subsequent multicultural discussions leading up to the federal policy on multiculturalism adopted in 1971, consecutive democratic governments in Canada have attempted to control and institutionalize social, cultural and political difference vis-à-vis Indigenous and non-Indigenous cultures.[3] Examination of the six works selected for discussion in this chapter reveals similarly constructed musical identities, in which an emphasis on cultural assimilation gives way to integration and, ultimately, to a form of parallelism and individuation.

In his introduction to *Citizenship, Diversity and Pluralism*, political scientist Alan Cairns dares to shift the definition of citizenship away from an administrative

---

[2]   In this paper, the terms First Nations peoples and First Nations are used except where direct quotations include the word "Indian," and in reference materials from Canadian legislative documents that consistently use the term "Indian". Various pieces of legislation governing First Nations peoples and lands reserved for them constitute what is referred to in this chapter as Canada's Indian Act, which underwent considerable change in the first 100 years of Confederation. For legal terminology relating to all Aboriginal Peoples in Canada, see *Words First: An Evolving Terminology Relating to Aboriginal Peoples in Canada*, reprinted online at www.ainc-inac.gc.ca/ap/tln-eng.asp (accessed July 10, 2009).

[3]   Eva Mackey's discussion on the role of state intervention in the culture of Aboriginal peoples in Canada portrays the government as passive-aggressive in their "benevolence" to First Nations peoples in this period. In institutionalizing culture for all Canadians through cultural policies and arms-length institutions, she explains, they simply "'institutionalize[d] various forms of difference, thereby controlling access to power and simultaneously legitimating the power of the state'." Eva Mackey, *The House of Difference: Cultural Politics and National Identity in Canada* (Toronto, ON: University of Toronto Press, 1999), p. 50. Following Cairns's definition of citizenship (see footnote 4, below), Mackey's critique emphasizes a top-down approach—that is, forced vertical integration.

focus on the evolutionary aspects of civil, political, and social rights and from a fixed view of it as an institution, and toward a view of citizenship as "a linking mechanism, which in its most perfect expression binds the citizenry to the state and to each other."[4] Cairns's definition emphasizes relationships, and he assigns to citizenship both "vertical" and "horizontal" properties: "vertical" referring to the relationship individuals have to the state (their sense of ownership or loyalty to a nation), and "horizontal" in their relationship to each other (a sense of community, if you will). Neither presupposes the other, and in the history of Canada since Confederation in 1867, Cairns proposes that these properties have not always been in balance and therefore true citizenship for all inhabitants has not always been achieved. In its most extreme manifestations, an emphasis on the vertical dimension of citizenship may lead to complete assimilation of difference, while an imbalance in favor of the horizontal dimension potentially results in divisive individuation. What lies in between these two poles, however, is a third and potentially more creative space in which contemporary forms and messages of social, political, and cultural concerns engage in a more integrated type of citizenship that balances vertical and horizontal relationships. Bhabha finds a similar "in between space" in hybrid cultures of postcolonial societies, proposing this as a distinctive place for the examination of reflection and resistance in cultural objects.[5] In such a space there exist the heterogeneous identities of state, communities, and individuals as well as their cultural practices. Precisely such an understanding enables us to write a more effective history of Canadian culture. While simply examining the role of diverse identities in the creation, production, and consumption of the dominant narratives of Canada's history in terms of the citizenship model is an obvious approach, a more critical exploration of them from within works of art has the potential to stimulate a greater capacity for understanding multiple narratives. The medium of opera, as a complex cultural object within the postcolonial narratives of history, then becomes a vehicle for both overt and covert expressions of identity and citizenship.[6] Although exploring the myriad of potential influences

---

[4] Cairns writes: "Citizenship has both a vertical and a horizontal dimension. The former links individuals to the state by reinforcing the idea that it is 'their' state: that they are full members of an ongoing association that is expected to survive the passing of generations. Their relation to the state is, accordingly, not narrowly instrumental, but supported by a reservoir of loyalty and patriotism that gives legitimacy to the state. The horizontal relationship, by contrast, is the positive identification of citizens with each other as valued members of the same civic community. Here, citizenship reinforces empathy and sustains solidarity by means of official statements of who is 'one of us'." Alan Cairns, John Courtney, Peter MacKinnon, Hans Michelmann, and David Smith (eds.), *Citizenship, Diversity and Pluralism: Canadian and Comparative Perspectives* (Montreal and Kingston: McGill-Queen's University Press, 1999), p. 4.

[5] Homi Bhabha, *The Location of Culture* (London, Routledge, 1994), p. 2.

[6] Discussing citizenship enacted in staged dramatic music in Canada is itself uncharted territory; however, studies in American cultures by Reily, Corse, and Pisani, among others, provide a strong foundation for such interdisciplinary work. As distinctive signifiers of

214   *Opera Indigene: Re/presenting First Nations and Indigenous Cultures*

on musical composition in Canada across 100 years is beyond the scope of this study, I offer below an overview of important social and political events in the creative environs of opera as a means of contextualizing musical citizenship, first by establishing an historical setting for the changing modes of representation of Canada's native peoples and second by examining select musical compositions within this context.

The theoretical foundation for this study is derived from several sources: postcolonial theories of the colonizer and colonized, literary theories of narrative and representation,[7] discourses in political theory such as is found in Cairns, and the theoretical and analytical perspectives of studies in cultural anthropology, sociology, musicology, and ethnomusicology.[8] The latter have been accessed specifically for their perspectives on understanding the lived experiences and aesthetic concepts of "space" and "place" and the relationship of society, politics, history, and music to constructions of identity, nationhood, and, ultimately, to citizenship. Benedict Anderson's observations on the utility in postcolonial society of "the census, the map, and the museum" as important "institutions of power"[9] are also germane to a

---

cultural tolerance, textual and musical features of key operas viewed through the lens of relevant political and historical contexts encourages an exploration of the role that these materials play in reinforcing, resisting, and re/presenting contemporary political and social goals of identity and citizenship. Opera's role in this discourse is as both mediator and mediated of social, cultural, and political values. Deprived of any direct influence on any of these political and cultural endeavors, Canadian First Nations peoples appear, as Eva Mackey suggests, primarily as "supporting actors" (*The House of Difference*, p. 39). See also Suzel Ana Reily, "Macunaima's Music: National Identity and Ethnomusicological Research in Brazil," in Martin Stokes (ed.), *Ethnicity, Identity and Music: The Musical Construction of Place* (Oxford: Berg, 1994); Sarah Corse, *Nationalism and Literature: The Politics of Culture in Canada and the United States* (Cambridge: Cambridge University Press, 1997); Michael Pisani, *Imagining Native America in Music* (New Haven, CT: Yale University Press, 2005).

[7]   This specifically refers to Peirce's Sign Theory, an overview of which can be found in Albert Atkin, "Peirce's Theory of Signs," in *The Stanford Encyclopedia of Philosophy*, ed. Edward N. Zalta, http://plato.stanford.edu/archives/spr2009/entries/peirce-semiotics (accessed November 3, 2010). Following Peirce's theory, in *Imagining Native America* Pisani indexes nearly thirty different items under "musical devices as ethnic markers" in First Nations musical representation. See also Tara Browner, *Transposing Cultures: The Appropriation of Native North American Musics, 1890–1990* (PhD dissertation, University of Michigan, 1995), p. 17.

[8]   These include: Benedict Anderson, *Imagined Communities* (London and New York: Verso, 1983); Bhabha, *The Location of Culture*; Bourdieu, *The Field of Cultural Production*; Adam Krims, *Music and Urban Geography* (London, 2007); Edward Said, *Culture and Imperialism* (London: Vintage, 1994); and Martin Stokes (ed.), *Ethnicity, Identity and Music: The Musical Construction of Place* (Oxford: Berg, 1994). Mackey (*The House of Difference*) also discusses the correlation between national goals, government policies, and representation of Aboriginal Peoples.

[9]   Anderson, *Imagined Communities*, pp. 163–85.

study of opera creation in Canada, and might be seen to cross the political-cultural divide often left unexplored in traditional musicological discussions, extending the reach of Anderson's important work beyond his discussion of the historical privileging of print and literacy. In Canadian history, such "institutions of power" established immigration policies that impacted census-making, encouraged westward expansion that influenced geographical boundaries, and created cultural institutions that ultimately affected who and what was included in cultural activities, such as the museums and collections movements directed at constructing a national identity for the country's citizens. To Anderson's institutional triumvirate might also be added the social programs and cultural policies affected by Canadian federal legislation, through which particular examples of cultural expression have been advantaged. That these "forces" of postcolonial power continued to modify the goals for nationhood in the first 100 years of Canadian society supports a closer examination of changes in the rules of musical engagement, rules that contributed to music's role in the establishment of what Daniel Francis has referred to as the "Imaginary Indian."[10]

Between 1867 and 1967, approximately 127 original operas[11] were composed in Canada: forty-six before World War One, thirty-four between the beginning of World War One and the end of World War Two, and forty-seven works from the end of World War Two to the Centennial Year of 1967. Of these, only twelve currently are known to overtly display First Nations characters and historical events, real or imagined (see Table 11.1).

What links all of these works is their narration of an event in Canadian history and their integration of signifiers of First Nations cultures into an established form of Western art music.[12] Diverse cultures such as those of First Nations peoples, denigrated or ignored by non-Indigenous Canadians in the early years following Confederation, gained popularity in Canadian opera beginning in the late nineteenth century, initially as an indigenous exotic other. Such voices were important to the construction of a common history for Canadian citizens, even though their voices might be neutralized in operatic composition by their location

---

[10] Daniel Francis, *The Imaginary Indian: The Image of the Indian in Canadian Culture* (Vancouver: Arsenal Pulp Press, 1992).

[11] The paucity of evidence for early Canadian composition makes it impossible to give a definite number here. My decision to define the genre of opera broadly as staged dramatic and musical works enables compositions to be included in the total that are not specifically designated as operas: works described as burlesques and pageants, for example. Issues of locating resources and genre definition are just the beginning of problems working with this repertoire. For a discussion of some of these issues in relation to Canadian opera studies, see Mary Ingraham, "Something to Sing About: A Preliminary List of Canadian Staged Dramatic Music Since 1867," *Intersections*, 28/1 (2007), pp. 14–77.

[12] The scope of native representation in these operas is varied. Over 100 years, cultural artifacts became more accessible to a broader society and to composers specifically, aided in no small way by advances in technology and communications.

216   *Opera Indigene: Re/presenting First Nations and Indigenous Cultures*

Table 11.1   Canadian operas incorporating First Nations characters and events, 1867 to 1967

PIN*	Title	Represented Nation(s); event
Lavallée 1865	The Indian Question	Sioux; 1860s rebellions
Clappé 1879	Canada's Welcome: A Masque	"Indian" Chief; fictional
Broughall 1885	90th On Active Service or, Campaigning in the Northwest	Cree, Métis; 1869–1885 rebellions
Dixon 1886	Halifax to Saskatchewan: "Our Boys" in the Riel Rebellion	Cree, Métis; 1869–1885 rebellions
Aldous 1895	Ptarmigan: A Canadian Carnival	"Indian"; fictional
Vézina 1912	Le Fétiche	Iroquois; eighteenth-century conflict with French
Willan 1929a	An Indian Nativity Play	"Indian" (lost; probably Huron); biblical
Willan 1943	The Life and Death of Jean de Brébeuf	Iroquois, Huron; seventeenth-century religious conflict
Morrison 1950	Tzinquaw	Coast Salish: Cowichan Band; Legend of the Thunderbird and Killer Whale
Pentland 1952	The Lake	Okanagan; 1870s settler relations
Adaskin 1967	Grant, Warden of the Plains	Cree, Métis; early nineteenth century
Somers 1967	Louis Riel	Cree, Métis; 1869–1885 rebellions

* PIN stands for Preliminary Ingraham Number, and reflects the catalogue number created for individual operas in Mary Ingraham, "Something to Sing About: A Preliminary List of Canadian Staged Dramatic Music Since 1867," *Intersections*, 28/1 (2007), pp. 14–77. As the PIN is constructed from the composer's name and the date of the premiere performance of a work, the addition of an "a" or "b" tag reflects a situation in which more than one opera appeared within a single year.

in a sometimes invented past. On the surface much of the music used to represent First Nations characters in this period seems simply to reflect a romanticized colonial view of Francis's "Imaginary Indian," juxtaposing musical stereotypes of "primitivism" with "civilizing" elements of the music of Western traditions. However, witnessing the cultural practices of native Canadians through such representation also illuminates the role of music in constructing and maintaining the fictions of cultural tolerance and control. Evocations of native peoples in all of these works therefore ultimately are seen to reflect issues of identity and hegemony embedded in the vertical and horizontal aspects of citizenship.

Federal Policy and First Nations Cultures in Canada, 1867–1967: An Overview

Canada's Confederation into a Dominion in 1867 and the immediate political drive for ideological unity provided the earliest and most direct influence on cultural expression. Table 11.2 provides an overview of relevant politics and policies in Canadian history between 1867 and 1967, and forms the basis of my discussion in this area. Furthermore, the principles of assimilation of all Canadians into one citizenry arguably affected First Nations—at the time, "Indian"—cultures the most dramatically. Indeed, their classification as "Origin: Indian; Nationality: Canadian" in the 1901 Census, although a resolution not unique to Canada, was determined with little if any consideration for the multiple internal nations of aboriginal communities or to the individuals' understanding of citizenship or relationship to "foreign" governance.

Legislation post-Confederation remained largely based on a belief that First Nations peoples would be assimilated. A consolidated Indian Act in 1876 reflected contemporary concerns of status, land, and governance, with an emphasis on policies that supported and rewarded enfranchisement for First Nations peoples as full citizens of Canada, along with the correlative reduction of benefits to them as "Status Indians." In 1880, Prime Minister Sir John A. Macdonald redefined his government's First Nations policy as intending to "wean them by slow degrees, from their nomadic habits, which have almost become an instinct, and by slow degrees *absorb* them or settle them on the land."[13] The word "absorb" is important here, as policies and legislation fell out of this position that greatly impacted the interpretation of citizenship for many decades.

The government's case for removing First Nations peoples to reserves in these years was founded on a widely held belief that not just First Nations cultures, but the First Nations peoples themselves were dying out from disease and starvation caused in part by advancing civilization. "This sense of urgent mission controlled the way First Nations peoples were portrayed in the work of White artists," Francis writes, "who became amateur ethnographers seeking to record Indian life as it was lived before the arrival of White people. Artists ignored evidence of Native adaptation to White civilization and highlighted traditional lifestyles. Often the result was an idealized image of the Indians based on what the artist *imagined* aboriginal life to have been *before contact*."[14] At the same time as the government was trying to stamp out vestiges of traditional First Nations culture in everyday life, it was creating a new institution devoted to the preservation of that culture: the national museum. The force of the Canadian museum movement and the collecting

---

[13] House of Commons Debates, May 5. 1880. Cited in Kahn-Tineta Miller, George Lerchs, and Robert G. Moore, "The Historical Development of the Indian Act," in *Canada: Treaties and Historical Research Centre*, ed. John Leslie and Ron Mcguire (Ottawa, ON: Indian and Northern Affairs, 1978), p. 192. (My emphasis).

[14] Francis, *The Imaginary Indian*, p. 24. (My emphasis).

218   *Opera Indigene: Re/presenting First Nations and Indigenous Cultures*

Table 11.2   Related events in Canadian history and politics, 1867–1967

1867	Dominion of Canada formed, including the provinces of Nova Scotia, New Brunswick, and Canada (Quebec and Ontario) (population: 3.2 million)
1868	Indian Act (IA) passed, for the "protection, assimilation and Christianization" of "Indians" and the management of their lands
1869	Extension of IA with new Enfranchisement Act establishes municipal-style government reserves; Immigration Act passed
1870	Purchase of Rupert's Land and North-Western Territory from Hudson's Bay Company; Manitoba joins Confederation
1871	British Columbia enters Confederation with promise of railway; Canada's first National Census (thereafter by decade)
1873	Prince Edward Island joins Confederation
1876	Consolidated Indian Act passed that established the definition of "Status Indian"
1880	Independent Department of Indian Affairs established
1884	IA Amendments banning Potlatch festivals and the Tawanawa dance; Indian Advancement Act passed to provide limited forms of self-governance
1885	Métis uprising and execution of Louis Riel; Canadian National Railway (CNR) completed
1890	IA Amendments prohibiting all tribal dances
1895	IA Amendments prohibiting First Nations festivals
1898	Creation of the Yukon Territory
1901	IA Amendments further restricting the celebration of tribal festivals and dances
1905	Alberta and Saskatchewan join Confederation
1906	New consolidated IA and consolidated Immigration Act passed
1910	New Immigration Act
1914	IA Amendments restricting participation in dances, rodeos, and exhibitions
1919	New Immigration Act passed with guidelines based on ethnicity
1920	IA Amendments allowed government to ban hereditary rule in bands
1936	Department of Indian Affairs made a branch of the Department of Mines and Resources
1940	National Registration of Census (previously a provincial activity)
1947	Canadian Citizenship Act
1949	Indian Affairs Branch transferred to the Department of Citizenship and Immigration; Newfoundland and Labrador join Confederation
1951	New Indian Act ends the ban on Potlatch festivals; Massey-Levèsque Commission Report on the Arts, Letters and Sciences
1952	Amendments to Immigration Act; Canadian Broadcasting Corporation Television (CBCTV) established
1957	Canada Council for the Arts, Humanities and Social Sciences established
1960	First Nations peoples receive federal vote in Canada
1965	Transfer of Indian Affairs Branch to the Department of Northern Affairs and National Resources
1967	EXPO 67—Canada celebrates its Centennial (population: 20 million); points system established and incorporated into Immigration Act

of artifacts for it, combined with the newly constructed First Nations cultural identities, assisted in solidifying perceptions into institutionalized stereotypes. The work of Canadian anthropologist-ethnographer Marius Barbeau,[15] begun in 1911, provided the earliest and most extensive body of material on Canadian First Nations cultures. However philanthropic Barbeau's personal goals, his work might therefore be viewed as a further example of cultural hegemony founded on the widely held belief that First Nations peoples were in fact dying out and that their culture needed "saving."

The Canadian government continued to enforce restrictions on First Nations peoples up to World War One by legislating bans on tribal dances and ceremonies between 1885 and 1951, claiming that such forms of self-expression were antithetical to assimilation. Examples include the 1884 ban on Potlatch festivals and participation in the "Tawanawa" dance (punishment was two to six months' imprisonment), and the prohibition of traditional practices that were considered by local government officials and clergy to be "barbaric" and "immoral," and to constitute "debauchery of the worst kind."[16] More persuasively, the Department of Indian Affairs officials convinced the government that these events "offered 'evil' temptations to Indians and disrupted work schedules on reserves."[17] In 1914, additional bans were placed on "participation in dances, rodeos and exhibitions," and successive leaders continued to perpetuate the belief that the ceremonies themselves "encourage[d] barbarity, idleness and waste, interfered with more productive activities and generally discouraged acculturation."[18] In a country determined to extinguish diversity in pursuit of national unity, the uncooperative "other" was best kept at a safe distance, an attitude that is echoed in both texts and music of early Canadian operas.

Leading up to and following World War One, restrictions on First Nations cultures were relaxed somewhat, enabling First Nations peoples to perform and ethnographers such as Barbeau to document further cultural practices. By this time, however, First Nations peoples had changed, becoming less "Indian" through decades of enforced assimilation. Francis explains: "Canadians did not expect Indians to adapt to the modern world. Their only hope was to assimilate, to become White, to cease to be Indians ... To the degree that they changed, they

---

[15] Marius Barbeau was an employee of the Museum Branch of the Geological Survey of Canada (after 1927, the National Museum). His legacy survives in the form of research notes, photographs, recordings, and publications now mostly held at the Canadian Museum of Civilisation. Barbeau's groundbreaking work, including stories, artifacts, and folksongs collected from French Canadians and First Nations peoples across Canada, remained culturally central for Canadian composers throughout most of the twentieth century.

[16] Miller et al., *Canada*, p. 82.

[17] Ibid., p. 111.

[18] Francis, *The Imaginary Indian*, p. 99.

220   *Opera Indigene: Re/presenting First Nations and Indigenous Cultures*

were perceived to become less Indian ... The Imaginary Indian, therefore, could never become modern."[19]

Despite increased restrictions on their freedoms, fewer First Nations peoples than expected opted out of land entitlements in order to accept the so-called benefits offered by the government as the rewards of enfranchisement.[20] In response, the Canadian government again revamped their First Nations legislation, altering the law to promote the integration of First Nations peoples into Canadian society first, with "gradual enfranchisement" as the ultimate goal.[21] The language and intent of the 1951 Indian Act is echoed in Minister of Citizenship and Immigration Walter E. Harris's remarks that: "More emphasis is being laid on greater participation and responsibility by Indians in the conduct of their own affairs ... The ultimate goal of our [new] Indian policy is the *integration* of the Indians into the general life and economy of the country."[22] Despite continuous amendments and attempts by some communities to have the Act repealed and the Department of Indian Affairs phased out when the Canadian government was moving to even more inclusive policies and multicultural recognition in the 1960s, it appeared that there was no better solution—or at least none that was worth pursuing at the time and at the expense of existing programs and policies.

Issues of First Nations citizenship in Canada thus consumed government officials and agencies for much of the first hundred years of Canadian history, and the status of First Nations peoples in policies and cultural domains in some ways distracted many from the goal of welcoming citizens of many cultures into a new nation. Following Cairn's citizenship paradigm, although challenged by federal legislation, communities of First Nations peoples nevertheless continued to exist in these years in the horizontal perspective on citizenship, but certainly not all of them revered the federal government or behaved as expected of loyal citizens in the vertical aspect. While both relationships to citizenship were nonetheless in play, the balance or in-between space of tolerance in this case was clearly unstable, and real citizenship, as Cairns notes, was not achieved.

Musical Citizenship in Canadian Opera

Opera is an extremely fertile place in which to interpret aspects of musical citizenship: text, music, and visual aspects of production offer multiple sites

---

[19]   Ibid., p. 59.

[20]   "The Government's aggressive 'assimilation' and 'citizenship' policies after 1880 had not been as successful as expected. ... [M]ost Indians refused to surrender their separate legal status, treaty rights, and privileges to take on the responsibilities of citizenship." Miller et al., *Canada*, p. 151.

[21]   Ibid., p. 122.

[22]   House of Commons Debates, June 29, 1950. Cited in Miller et al. *Canada*, p. 192. (My emphasis).

of signification as well as multifarious and promising potentialities for the consideration of relationships, whether vertical, horizontal, or in the space in between. But when and how do these reflect citizenship?

Semiotic theory is especially helpful in conceptualizing the various sites of representation and in understanding or interpreting their meaning: who and what is included or excised, and the placement of signs and symbols vis-à-vis each other in the musical and textual drama, become sites of inquiry on issues of citizenship. Theories of signification founded on Peircean logic classify the signs of representation as iconic (having a qualitative connection to the object), indexical (having a physical or existential connection), or symbolic (signification that is successful only through social or cultural consensus).[23] Citizenship is enacted in music therefore through the interpretation of signs, first through the reading of a sign as representative of a particular identity (in this study, of First Nations peoples or Whites), and then by examining the relationship of a particular sign to other signs in the work. Based on Cairns's expression of the dimensions of citizenship, signs can serve as markers of community or local relationships in the horizontal dimension, and cross-cultural relationships in the vertical. Combined, these relationships will confirm or deny further aspects of citizenship.

Literal signs in the text of opera are often the easiest to interpret within this framework, but occasionally the ground that links a text with a specific identity (such as associating specific animals or behaviors with a specific culture) needs elucidation or even another sign or signs to make its relationship sensible.[24] Consideration of the fields of representation of First Nations peoples in the Americas have established connections with a body of original textual and musical compositions that would have constituted contemporary practice for new works, and, for Canadian composers between 1867 and 1967, musical models might just as readily have been Western European or US American works, given the exchange

---

[23] For Peirce, the theory of signs is irreducible from these three stages and the power of signs themselves lies in their potential for multiple interpretations determined as a synthesis of thought by a community of assessors. Signs also have the capacity to mediate identity and thus construct communities of representation. "Representation," W.J.T. Mitchell declares, "is exactly the place where 'life', in all its social and subjective complexity, gets into the literary work," an assertion that also may be applied to opera texts and, I would argue, music. William J. Thomas Mitchell, "Representation," in *Critical Terms for Literary Study*, ed. Frank Lentricchia and Thomas McLaughlin, (Chicago, 1995), p. 15.

[24] Interpreting the historical practice of musical signs to represent specific individuals or communities is not the goal in this chapter: others such as Pisani and Browner have completed comprehensive research in this area and prepared extensive materials for linking features of melody, harmony, and rhythm (as well as the actual melodies, harmonies, and rhythms themselves), to American First Nations communities: Pisani, *Imagining Native America* and Browner, *Transposing Cultures*. See also Michael Pisani, "'I'm an Indian Too': Creating Native American Identities in Nineteenth- and Early Twentieth-Century Music," in *The Exotic in Western Music*, ed. Jonathan Bellman (Boston, MA: North Eastern University Press, 1998).

222   *Opera Indigene: Re/presenting First Nations and Indigenous Cultures*

of traveling performers and repertoire in these years. What I am interested in exploring here, then, is how known or accepted signs might have been used in text and music to construct identities and how their organization suggests truths, perspectives, and meaning in the context of establishing musical citizenship.

With over a century of examples of Indigenous representation in composed music, few contemporary listeners would have difficulty identifying musical features associated with the translation of First Nations cultures into Western art music: suitably rendered, elements such as accented and repeated rhythmic patterns (often including a drum), the use of minor tonalities, pentatonic scales, open fifths, and grace notes provide powerful evocations of First Nations. As Bellman, Browner, and Pisani explain, these and other "ethnic markers" such as drones, echo effects, inflections, intervallic tendencies, and cross-rhythms, are shared among North American First Nations peoples in general (since they are often of the same cultural groups).[25] The primary space in which Canadian representation of First Nations peoples might be viewed as noticeably different than other North American representation is in the area of musical citizenship. Opera as an established high-culture expression and "Indianisms" as distinct and prominent cultural signifiers provide a potent location in which to consider this. Of the twelve operas noted in Table 11.1 above, I will focus on six works as the basis of my discussion of literary signifiers, and two of these (Lavallée 1865 and Somers 1967) as exemplars of musical citizenship through brief case studies. The six works are: Lavallée's *The Indian Question*, Clappé's *Canada's Welcome*, Vézina's *Le Fétiche*, Pentland's *The Lake*, Adaskin's *Grant, Warden of the Plains*, and Somers's *Louis Riel*.

By Cairns's socio-political definition, musical citizenship in the works studied might be seen to better represent the realities of the horizontal aspects of citizenship than the vertical: that identifiable communities exist is understood, but whether they are welcomed into vertical relationships is not. What is iniquitous in the horizontal representation of First Nations peoples in music is that, for the most part, "Indian" is considered homogeneous, as if a single nationhood could be described. For instance, although *Louis Riel* provides the clearest example of cultural integration of actual First Nations music, Somers too is accountable for homogenizing cultures. In the score to Marguerite's lullaby "Kuyas" (published separately from the opera), Somers describes his musical material as based on motifs "from the song of the Skateen, the Wolfhead tribe of a Nass River tribe ..." and set to words of the Cree, or Plains Nation taken "from a story told by an Indian on Sweetgrass [sic] reserve ..."[26] Nass River First Nations peoples are Nisga'a and are located on the northwest coast of British Columbia; their language is either Nisga'a or Gitskan; the Sweet Grass Reserve, which is however Cree, is located near Battleford, Saskatchewan. The coastal tribe invoked in music is thus about

---

[25]   Jonathan Bellman (ed.), *The Exotic in Western Music* (Boston, MA: North Eastern University Press, 1998); Browner, *Transposing Cultures*; Pisani, "'I'm an Indian Too'."

[26]   Harry Somers, *Kuyas* (Scarborough, ON, 1971), p. iii.

2,000 km away from the source of the textual material and, correspondingly, from anywhere near Riel's home. Is this music, then, an iconic or a symbolic marker? Or is it simply another location for interpreting contemporary attitudes toward First Nations peoples in which anything that sounds First Nations will do?

A map of selected symbols of indigeneity found in the text and story of each the six operas studied is presented in Table 11.3. In this table, textual signs are listed as either literal or behavioral for the purpose of comparing works. Literal symbols include names of characters (or are descriptive of the characters themselves, such as the "Indian Chief"), location names, languages, and symbols or specific attributes that clearly situate a text in the actual space of First Nations communities. In addition to place names, several of these works situate First Nations characters simply "in nature." For operas such as Clappé's *Canada's Welcome* (1879), this association binds the Edenic myth of nature as paradise with the cultural myth of basic goodness, acknowledging (as it does in Somers's *Louis Riel*) the potential for civilization to corrupt.[27] In the literal group are also included specific animals that may be interpreted as cultural icons of First Nations heritage such as the raven and the thunderbird, and lifestyle and traditional objects (teepees, wigwams, canoes, hatchets, etc.). Most of the literal signs are self-explanatory. The most remarkable change in the works studied over the period is the incorporation in the text of languages other than English: first French (Clappé 1879, Vézina 1912, Adaskin 1967, and Somers 1967), then native languages or dialects such as the Red River Bungay (Adaskin 1967) and Cree (Somers 1967). Pentland's gesture to language discrepancy (Pentland 1952) is represented in the faulty English spoken by her First Nations characters.

Cultural practices evidenced in spirituality, rituals and fetishes, belief systems, and legend-telling are shown in the table as behavioral signs, as are character traits understood as First Nations through historical agency such as a propensity for non-violence, faithfulness, innocence, and naïveté. These types of behavioral signifiers and representations of spirituality and native superstition appear in texts across the period. More noticeable, however, is the emphasis on savagery, scalping, blood-thirstiness, and head-hunting rituals that begin to appear in the works towards the end of the nineteenth century and that, not coincidentally, emerged as natives were increasingly marginalized in society, their cultural practices restricted, and their identity historicized through ethnographic research.[28]

Further aspects of citizenship are enacted in the interaction between characters and communities, including establishing social hierarchies, constructing historical "fictions" for dramatic or political effect, and representing disparities in issues

---

[27] Mackey suggests that there is "a version of history which depends on constructions of Aboriginal people as child-like, trusting, and ultimately friendly to their Canadian government invaders ... ." Mackey, *The House of Difference*, p. 35.

[28] The popularity of cultural "Indianisms" at this time, it must be remembered, was at least partially dependent on representations of them as unrefined, savage, and needing to be "civilized."

Table 11.3   Selected First Nations cultural signifiers in the texts of Canadian operas

	Lavallée 1865 *The Indian Question*	Clappé 1879 *Canada's Welcome*	Vézina 1912 *Le Fétiche*	Pentland 1952 *The Lake*	Adaskin 1967 *Grant, Warden of the Plains*	Somers 1967 *Louis Riel*
Literal						
Characters	Sitting Bull Tenino	Indian Chief The Four Seasons Chorus of Indians and Hunters	Pied-Léger Pérusse Técumseh Chief Bison-Borgne Saika	Maria Johnny Mac Yacumtecum Cherumchoot	Grant Maria Narrator Pierre Falcon	Louis Riel Marguerite Ambroise Lépine, Delorme, Ritchot Goulet, Naul, Baptiste, Léptine, Lagimodière, Wandering Spirit, Poundmaker (and others)
Locations	in nature	in nature	Quebec in nature Wolf Tribal Camp	Okanagan Lake Squally Cove Indian Camping Ground	Red River	Red River Border Crossing Fort Garry Frog Lake Batoche
Languages	English	English French	French	English (Indians speak faulty English)	English French Bungay	English French Cree Latin
Animals/ objects (selected)	fish horn wigwam hatchet raven	canoe wigwam buffalo	Canoe snowshoes tomahawk	Na'aitka, lake monster moccasins berry dyes hides	moccasins pemmican bannock buffalo	drums reserves arrows buffalo
Behavioral						
Spirituality		Manitou Spirit	Manitou Spirit	spirits	spirits	
Ritual and fetish	superstition	superstition fetishes	superstition	superstition	superstition	superstition
Social	non-violence	fairness subsistence living	savagery scalping	legend-telling	legend-telling	non-violence scalping

Assimilation, Integration and Individuation 225

such as gender and religion. Socially, First Nations peoples are placed in several of the libretti in service positions: as domestic help (Maria in *The Lake*), as nature guides (Johnny MacDougall [Mac] in *The Lake*), or as powerful First Nations leaders who are, unfortunately, on the wrong side of the law (Sitting Bull in *The Indian Question*, Grant in *Grant, Warden of the Plains*, or Louis Riel in *Louis Riel*). Truth in narrative also becomes a citizenship issue in stories of both historical fact and historical fiction. For example, the libretto of *The Indian Question* links the Sioux leader Sitting Bull with Colonel Carter, two men who likely never met or battled, but who might have been known to the composer in the 1860s as having opposing sympathies during the American Civil War.[29] Pentland's *The Lake* is based on the memoirs of a nineteenth-century pioneer woman in British Columbia's Okanagan Valley.[30] Representation of historical details in the libretto of *Louis Riel* expose significant areas of revision to English histories of the period, including sympathizing with the Métis leader to whom history has not been kind and portraying the Prime Minister as a drunkard driven by his own political agenda.[31]

Gendering of space and objects appears to varying degrees in the text and music of all of the operas and presents a third location for the examination of representation. In Clappé's opera, Canada appears "dressed as an Indian maiden" and is described (and ultimately "she" sings as such) as innocent, female, and fully assimilated. Additionally, First Nations daughters and wives are positioned in these operas in roles of service as maids, cooks, and infatuated girls, and are musically characterized with lyrical, emotional, and wailing melodies. Examples of such gendered melodies include Saika's wailing "Ou-hé! Ou-hé!" in measure 15 of Act II, scene 1 of *Le Fétiche*; Maria's emotional narrative in "A Long Time Ago" in *The Lake*, with an added dissonant musical outburst when she considers the monster of the lake, Na'aitka, in measures 70 and 74; Maria's lyrical "Autumn Song" in *Grant, Warden of the Plains*; and Marguerite's chant, "Hano, hano," in *Louis Riel*. Gendering of space as female frequently coincides with the textual articulation of superstition, linking First Nations spiritual beliefs with a sense of naïveté.

Expressions of religious difference are common in these texts. Many texts focus on the superstitious nature of First Nations values and lifestyle and introduce, through non-First Nations characters, the logic and "superiority" of a Christian approach. In two of the texts, First Nations characters express their spirituality

---

[29] Lavallée was living south of the border from 1860 to 1862 and also fought in the Civil War as a Unionist.

[30] Livesay's libretto was inspired by the characters and accounts described by Susan Allison in her memoirs, edited by Margaret Ormsby and published by UBC Press in 1976 as *A Pioneer Gentlewoman of British Columbia: The Recollections of Susan Allison*.

[31] Ironically, the opera presents both men as ambitious, as first Riel, and then Macdonald exclaims: " I cannot let one man stand in the way of a whole nation." The nation referred to by each, of course, is different, and a different outcome would have been likely if Riel's plan for self-determination had been successful.

226   *Opera Indigene: Re/presenting First Nations and Indigenous Cultures*

coincidentally with their dismay at the loss of indigenous lifestyles through contact with white society: Clappé's *Canada's Welcome* includes an Indian Chief who invokes the Manitou, or Spirit, and laments the passing of the First Nations way of life in "The Manitou Has Spoken," and (the character) Canada sings of nature as the location of indigenous spirituality; Pentland's Maria sings of the corruption of the First Nations way of life, invoking the legend of the lake monster Na'aitka as society's recompense.

Another layer of complexity in the works studied, although not exclusively reserved for First Nations peoples, is the ubiquitous dominant culture humor (puns and put-downs, irony and bathos). Humor is used to establish hierarchy in the juxtaposition of choruses (Soldiers and Indians) in Lavallée's "Uncle Sam is Very Much Dissatisfied," in which American soldiers request that the First Nations peoples give in to their demands peacefully ("Now do try, lay down and die"), and Vézina's scalping song that mimics cries of pain ("Och! Och! J'ai vingt scalps à ma ceinture") for comedic effect.

Applying Peircean semiotics further to musical signs themselves involves investigating the iconic features of materials directly inspired from native music, the symbolic representation of music inspired by native cultures, and the indexical markers that are interpreted through historical practice as symbolic of native culture. As noted above, *Louis Riel* is the only opera studied that overtly incorporates authentic First Nations music into its structure.[32] However, the impact on musical citizenship in this example is complicated by the composer's construction of new music from it, on which more will be said later. Despite the hundred-year span of the operas examined, musical indicators of Canadian First Nations peoples are fairly consistent and correspond to Pisani's definition of "markers" of ethnicity: metrical and rhythmic associations, modal and harmonic elements, instrumental associations, and so on are commonly found across the works. If any generalization is possible, it would appear from the works studied that the musical style of indigenous representation in early operas studied is largely gestural, with minimal semiotic inflection: settings are romantic and Western European-styled, with few musical markers of local identity. Works composed in the dynamic early years of the twentieth century, such as Vézina's *Le Fétiche*, incorporate iconic and symbolic semiotic materials, using dance rhythms, chanting, and vocables, as well as instrumental associations to represent First Nations characters or characteristics, but it is not until after World War Two that musical representation of First Nations peoples in Canadian opera begins to consider more overt authenticity, albeit through the contemporary lens of cultural integration. To consider the ramifications of these elements as a reflection of musical citizenship requires an understanding of the organization of materials and the construction of characters across textual

---

[32]   The inclusion of this material within the genre of opera reflects an increased accessibility to materials as well as a greater sensitivity to their innate value as cultural signifiers, both indicative of contemporary Canadian society in the 1960s.

Assimilation, Integration and Individuation 227

and musical domains. Lavallée's *The Indian Question* and Somers's *Louis Riel* are used below as exemplars of such aspects of musical citizenship.

Lavallée's libretto for *The Indian Question*, written by Will F. Sage, centers on the peaceful resolution of a conflict over land between the leaders of the Sioux Nation and the United States Army, Sitting Bull and Colonel Carter, respectively. Although actual events are implied in the story, the meeting of these two men in the events described and the surprising outcome (that of a peaceful settlement) are historically inaccurate. The narrative nonetheless focuses on conflicting identities of Whites, here portrayed as controlling, forceful, and misinformed about their opponents, and First Nations peoples, who display dignity, non-violence, and compassion. Tenino, Sitting Bull's (fictional) daughter ultimately agrees to marry the soldier Walter Wingate, at last settling the question of ownership of disputed lands. In addition to these unexpected examples of social and political equality, Sitting Bull mimics a reversal of religious conversion (Act I, Scene 2: "Auspicious the day for devotion, to convert the poor misguided white") and he inverts the typical humor hierarchy to mock the Americans (Act I, Scene 2: "You to the wigwams follow where warm wigs will furnish your hair"). The distinct identities of First Nations peoples and Whites in the opera also are further distorted by Lavallée's use of Western musical idioms for all characters. Although appropriately dignified in tone, Sitting Bull's solo in Act I, Scene 2 is lyrical, diatonic and founded on triadic harmonies, and no distinct First Nations markers are voiced. The music of the chorus of Indians in Act I, Scene 7 ("Now hear their cry lay down and die") is similarly Western: homophonic and with a stately air that belies the artificial sincerity of their text. In contrast, Act II, Scene 22 attempts musical representation through a distinct "wailing" melody sung by Indian maidens on the word "Ah" in measures 30–38, an imitative drum rhythm, and a pulsing quarter-note rhythm danced by the Indians while "blow[ing] on fish horns" in measures 39–46. First Nations peoples and Whites are given more clearly delineated melodies in this scene in general, and their close interaction makes the articulation of "difference" more pronounced. This number opens with an agitated G-minor section, and includes musical markers of open fifths on tonic and dominant notes in the bass in a repeated eighth-note pattern, grace note embellishments in the upper voice on third and fifth scale degrees, and, in measure 19, the introduction of the Chorus of Braves on the text "Oh we never tell a lie, for if we did 'twould make us cry." Carter and his men enter in measure 47 with a G-major operetta-styled melodic dialogue, followed by an appeal to be set free ("But let us free and we will be most peaceful in the nation"), still in the major key. However, the Chorus of Braves closes the number with a repeat of earlier material in G minor, thus asserting their control; the ABABA' pattern in the music literally has Carter and his men surrounded by the "Indians." Nonetheless, in the final musical resolution of the story in Act II, Scene 23, "The Flower Song," the young lovers Tenino and Walter revert to singing a charming waltz in A major, and musical dominance is reasserted. Although suggestive of First Nations identity with textual references (Tenino wages her love on superstition and nature: "The daisy tells my fate"), Lavallée's

228 *Opera Indigene: Re/presenting First Nations and Indigenous Cultures*

music clearly favors Walter, who responds by disabusing her of this "silly" notion and moving the melody harmonically into C major for four measures (measures 42–45) before reasserting E major with a new text/sub-text: "The daisy cannot tell the strife. The heart alone is right."

Somers's *Louis Riel*, undoubtedly the best-known Canadian opera of this period, is also the most musically eclectic. It tells the story of significant events in the life of the Métis leader Louis Riel, and his actions and reactions to the federal government's push to remove the threat of First Nations peoples who stand in the way of national expansion. At the end of the opera, as in reality, Riel is hanged for treason. Musically, the opera contains folk materials (from French, English, Scottish, and First Nations origins), hymns and popular songs of the period, and original atonal, electronic, and neo-romantic (often tonal and diatonic) music. Its multilingual and multicultural expression represents many facets of the French, English, and Métis conflicts in the late nineteenth century associated with Louis Riel. Religious and social power struggles, regional versus national ideology, constitutional tensions, and other dualities complicate the libretto and are signified in Somers's score using the various musical materials. Many elements come into play when considering musical citizenship in this opera, as musical characterization and leitmotivic representation are central to the portrayal of the drama. Marguerite's solo "Hano, hano" was discussed above for its representation of the lyrical, feminine First Nations peoples, and her solo "Kuyas" for its obvious link to authentic cultures. The opening section in *Louis Riel* evinces additional features of First Nations representation in a more abstract, electronic musical setting. It is in two parts, both of which are pre-recorded for performance: the first includes a rhythmic timpani and tom-tom section in which each player first performs an interpretation of similar material, followed by a duo in which they perform independent musical lines that, again, perform similar patterns. Instrumental association of the tom-tom with First Nations peoples (Riel and his followers; Métis were considered "Indians" in Canadian law until 1879) suggests that timpani—similar but Western instruments—are then connected to the government. The two identities mediated throughout the musical and textual drama of the opera are evoked more overtly in the tenor vocal solo of the second part of this opening section. Here, additional cultural signifiers of First Nations identity are heard in grace notes and an extensively ornamented melody, "sliding pitches",[33] flexible rhythm and unmetered progression of the vocal line, in the use of the minor mode, and in a limited vocal range that rises and falls in an arc with each phrase. Emotions are intensified in melodies throughout the opera through the integration of First Nations "markers" into Somers's contemporary, atonal compositional style such that the same characteristics may also be considered representative of progress, perhaps for the First Nations peoples as well as for the French and English in the drama. As a reflection of the realities of history, however, in the final scene Riel's lyrical rural, western, Métis, Catholic idealism literally is silenced by Macdonald's declamatory urban, eastern, English, Protestant nationalism.

---

[33]   Pisani, *Imagining Native America*, p. 6.

Each of the works examined here reflects features of First Nations cultures, whether its message is complicit with contemporary White political viewpoints or contrary; whether it perpetuates an historical fact or revises history to emphasize a predominant cultural concern or stereotype; or whether it is composed specifically to communicate a previously silenced voice or situation. These works express diversity through textual references to contemporary events, reiteration of contemporary concerns, or stereotypes about First Nations peoples and symbolic musical stereotypes based on historical models. What links each composer's expression of cultural diversity and citizenship is grounded on both the power of the signs to signify and our interpretation of them according to a set of complex, unique processes of which historical understanding of the dominant culture's view of the First Nations peoples in Canadian society is but one. However, it is clear from these few examples that it was well into the twentieth century before iconic musical markers become evident in original operas in Canada, not only due to the challenges of access to materials, but also (and perhaps more importantly) because of societal and political views of the value of First Nations cultures. Even in middle of the twentieth century, when French Canadian cultures were exposed to broad public discussion, the status of First Nations peoples remained underrepresented in Canadian opera. The three works written after World War Two illustrate an attempt to present the First Nations peoples more appropriately by incorporating ethnographic texts and music: legend-telling in *The Lake* and *Grant, Warden of the Plains*, and the use of First Nations stories in *The Lake*, *Grant, Warden of the Plains*, and *Louis Riel*, and the incorporation of First Nations music in *Louis Riel*. The sophistication of the musical integration of these materials into the Western operatic genre speaks as much to the maturity of the nation as to the composers themselves.

Conclusion

Musical citizenship in Canadian opera in the early years after Confederation was superficially granted just for showing up—a sort of cultural tokenism implicit in Clappé's *Canada's Welcome*, perhaps, with its indistinct "Indian Chief" character. In addition to the stereotypes of representation commented on briefly here, paradigms of musical citizenship in these operas can be seen further in the stylistic contrasts in characterization: in the vocal parts, between singing and speaking; melodically, between lyrical and more abstract styles; harmonically, as the shift from tonal to modal (and later to atonal) and between diatonic and chromatic inflection; and timbral, using instruments and (by the end of the period) acoustic and electronic means. Additionally, these works can be studied for influences from and incorporation of folk songs of French- and English-Canadian traditions, and by hymns, marching songs, and popular songs of the period. The transformative use of these elements ultimately suggests dramatic liaisons that, taken together with the literary and musical characterizations just discussed, establish operatic identities

230   *Opera Indigene: Re/presenting First Nations and Indigenous Cultures*

consistent with contemporary concerns. And so the complexity of First Nations representation in Canadian opera is hardly surprising and the evolving nature of their musical citizenship as a reflection of their status in political and social arenas easier to comprehend. The intersection of cultural signifiers in literary and musical domains may then present (or represent) the most accurate location of cultural citizenship. Earlier works which, granted, may no longer be considered musically interesting, demonstrate a deliberate assimilation in the European style used by Lavallée and Clappé;[34] symbolic assimilation followed in Vézina's opera. But by the end of the period studied native representation in musical drama can best be described in terms of integration of individuals, historical texts and musical styles that similarly reflect composers' contemporary cultural environs.

The year 1967 was important in Canadian history and ultimately inspired the creation of a plethora of materials for a discussion of cultural identity (a topic for another study). In 1967, Canada embarked on a major "cultural binge"[35] in the form of a World Exposition. The issue at hand for government and society alike was then not *whether* but *where* First Nations peoples fit.[36] Ultimately, they were included in EXPO celebrations with their own pavilion and grants for production projects.[37] And, if Adaskin's *Grant, Warden of the Plains* and Somers's *Louis Riel* were any indication, the tides of musical citizenship with respect to First Nations cultures had also turned. Now fully integrated into Western genres, the First Nations voice desired—like the French of the time—to be distinct. In the climate of multiculturalism following 1967, individuation was the only way forward.

---

[34]   Writing on Clappé's *Canada's Welcome*, Dorith Cooper notes that the music is "reminiscent of Bellini ... [and] hardly appropriate for a native." Dorith Cooper (ed.), *The Canadian Music Heritage*, Vol. 10, *Opera and Operetta Excerpts I* (Ottawa, ON: Canadian Musical Heritage Society, 1991), p. x.

[35]   Keith MacMillan, "The Editor's Desk," *musicanada*, 6 (November 1967), p. 2.

[36]   "They were stuck between two conflicting goals and strategies," Mackey writes. "On the one hand, the [1964 policy paper called 'Participation in Canada's Centennial by People of Indian Ancestry'] claims 'the Indians' could not be 'lumped with the rest of the citizenry.' *Not* giving them *special* treatment would be politically unacceptable, because of public opinion. ... On the other hand, ... 'it would be *dangerous* for the Commission to declare the Indian as a *special* group' without a good rationale for doing so." 1964 policy recommendation by A.J. Courmier, cited in Mackey, *The House of Difference*, pp. 60–61; emphasis Mackey.

[37]   "On the schedule of native events were those that focused on the rich heritage of native customs, legends, stories, songs and dances. These were displayed in pow-wows, sports meets, pageants, exhibitions and ceremonials." Peter H. Aykroyd, *The Anniversary Compulsion: Canada's Centennial Celebrations, A Model Mega-Anniversary* (Toronto, ON: 1992), p. 113. Cited in Mackey, *The House of Difference*, p. 60.

Chapter 12
"Too Much White Man In It": Aesthetic Colonization in *Tzinquaw*

Alison Greene

In June 2007 I traveled to Salt Spring Island, just off the southeast coast of Vancouver Island, British Columbia, to visit a private museum which houses the Akerman family memorabilia. The main purpose of this visit was to hear the recording of a radio broadcast of an opera written in 1950 by a relative of the family, Frank Morrison. The work, titled *Tzinquaw*, was devised and produced in the Vancouver Island town of Duncan by Morrison, a local school teacher and church musician. Morrison had collaborated with members of the Cowichan Tribes First Nation, and had created an "Indian opera"[1] using the traditional culture of the Cowichan people.

At the museum, the recording of *Tzinquaw*, a copy of the Canadian Broadcasting Corporation recording of the first performance, was played for me. Although I knew already that the work was a strange mix of musical cultures, I could not have anticipated what I heard. The first extract from the opera was a solo piano piece reminiscent of a nineteenth-century piano concerto cadenza. What followed was a traditional Cowichan song. There was then a choral piece that evoked choruses of Gilbert and Sullivan. The final excerpt was a solo that, in spite of its use of a Cowichan melody, sounded like it had been lifted straight from the Church of England hymn book. With the exception of the traditionally performed song the music sounded predominantly as if it had been composed by a nineteenth-century European composer. Given the examples I had just listened to, this "Indian opera" did not, for the most part, sound "Indian" at all, and it seemed that the Cowichan music had been invaded or rather, colonized, by the Western tastes and standards of the man responsible for creating it. A look at Morrison's program notes also seemed to confirm a paternalistic attitude to the Cowichan people and their culture. Morrison described himself as someone who appreciated the Cowichan music and wanted "only to try to show them how to share it, to their own advantage, with the outside world."[2] The music I had heard did not show the Cowichan music to their advantage, but rather showed Morrison's ability to

---

[1]   Ellen Harris, "*Tzinquaw* – The Story of an Indian Opera" (unpublished: Ellen Harris Fonds, University of British Columbia, Special Collections, 1950).

[2]   Frank Morrison, "Music and Drama With the Cowichan Indians," *Tzinquaw* performance program (Duncan, November 22, 1950).

232   *Opera Indigene: Re/presenting First Nations and Indigenous Cultures*

"sanitize" the performance into something palatable for the Western audience. An examination of the process by which *Tzinquaw* was developed in its music, text, and stage production aspects shows how this act of colonization was realized by the opera's creators, and then condoned by the positive reactions of most of those who witnessed its performances.

Tzinquaw was first performed on the stage of the Cowichan High School Auditorium on November 22, 1950. At this point in Canadian history The Indian Act continued to regulate how and where First Nations culture could be performed. Frank Morrison, conscious of the possible disappearance of the Cowichan traditions, wanted to show the non-native Canadians of Duncan the artistic wealth of these people, and many who saw the opera praised *Tzinquaw* as a moving exaltation of a marginalized culture. However, others took issue with what they considered a Western cultural imposition in the approach Morrison took to incorporating Cowichan material in the opera. These critics, including writers, musicians, composers, and ethnomusicologists, considered Morrison's approach as one that made the Cowichan culture subservient to his own values in an act of aesthetic colonization, thus deforming the native material. The opera was then staged according to Western theatrical tastes and styles in order to make it accessible for the anticipated white audience. Cowichan cultural practice was re-structured into an entertainment to be consumed by the very Canadians whose federal and provincial governments were in the process of abolishing the traditional practices of the Canadian First Nations.

The Genesis of *Tzinquaw*

The Original Project

Tzinquaw the opera was the end result of a long musical project undertaken by Frank Morrison and members of the Cowichan First Nation during the 1940s. In 1942, Abel Joe, a member of the Cowichan Nation, approached Morrison with a request for help in preserving the traditional songs of his people.[3] Morrison was an amateur pianist and director of music at the local Anglican church, and coached the Cowichan on the hymns they sang. For eight years Morrison, Joe, and many other interested members of the Cowichan First Nation worked together on piano transcriptions of Cowichan songs. Abel Joe would sing the melodies and Morrison would pick out the pitches until both were satisfied they were accurate. Morrison would then harmonize the songs with piano accompaniments. When he played the results back to the tribal members, the Cowichan were described as surprised and full of pride that this music, with European harmonies and played on a piano,

---

[3]   "Cowichan Indian Opera to Make Stage History," *Daily Colonist*, November 12, 1950, p. 33.

was their own music.[4] The compositions that Morrison played back for his native colleagues, however, were not their own songs but rather versions that deformed their songs by forcing them into the structures and vocabulary of Morrison's musical aesthetics.

Native Myth Becomes Opera

When enough material had been gathered and written down in Western music notation, Abel Joe asked Morrison to write a musical theater piece about the legend of the Tzinquaw, the Thunderbird, using the piano transcriptions of the Cowichan songs. The legend details the fight between Tzinquaw and Quannis, the Killer Whale. In Coast Salish tradition the Thunderbird is a mythical bird with enormous strength who causes the sound of thunder by flapping his wings and causes lightning by flashing his eyes. The story takes place in Cowichan Bay where Quannis, a supernatural killer-whale, takes up residence at the mouth of the Cowichan River and begins to scare away all the salmon which are food for the Cowichan people:

> Quannis, for many weeks, swam back and forth and to and fro in the quiet waters and by his evil spells drove all the fish away. Then came the months of the fishing and there were no fish for the Indian people to catch. And the people grew weak from hunger. But so powerful were the evil spells of Quannis the Killer-Whale that not even the bravest men of the band were able to take the spear and rope and kill him ... The days went by. The sun rose over the Island and went down behind the mountains, and still Quannis the Killer-Whale swam back and forth and to and fro, and the little ones wailed from hunger ... and the old ones fainted from hunger ... and the strong ones grew weak from hunger ... the stricken Cowichan people at last believe ... that man alone, with his paddles and spears and ropes, is not strong enough to kill the evil whale. So ... they kneel on the on the clam-shell beach and pray to the great Tzinquaw to come to their aid ... Then, with rolling of thunder and flashing of lightning, comes the Tzinquaw to the help of his Cowichan people. He kills the evil whale and casts his body on the beach so that his people may have food.[5]

The Format of the Opera

Morrison chose an operatic format for *Tzinquaw*, writing a libretto with four scenes, and included his own poetry which interpreted the meanings of the original songs. Traditionally each song belonged to a specific Cowichan family who explained the

---

[4] Frank Morrison, "Music and Drama With the Cowichan Indians," *Tzinquaw* performance program (Duncan, November 22, 1950).

[5] Frank Morrison, "Synopsis," *Tzinquaw* performance program (Duncan, November 22, 1950).

234 *Opera Indigene: Re/presenting First Nations and Indigenous Cultures*

meanings of the songs to him and gave him permission to include them in the opera.[6] Morrison harmonized all the transcribed songs, wrote piano accompaniments for them, and composed several pieces of solo piano music which underscored dramatic episodes in the narrative. The original Cowichan songs are included in the opera; each Cowichan song title is first given in Hul'q'umi'num, and under each title the original melodies are notated and followed by Morrison's versions of them. The songs are taken out of their traditional contexts and are placed in the opera's scenario in order to suit Morrison's dramatic version of the *Tzinquaw* narrative. Each of the four scenes of the opera begins with a piano introduction with a spoken voice-over narrating the story, followed by songs tailored to suit the story. *Tzinquaw* also includes traditional rituals; a burial ceremony is performed, and several traditional dances including a Paddle Dance, a Visitors' Dance, a Stick Game, and a Rabbit Dance are added to flesh out the story.[7] The rituals and dances are placed in the opera's narrative at appropriate dramatic moments but are frequently noted in the staging script in the manner of Western theatrical blocking instructions.[8]

Once the score was completed, Morrison handed it to Cecil West, the stage director of the performance. West was originally from England and had been production chief and a director at the Montreal Repertory Theatre during the 1930s. The company produced mainly European classical works, and West had been part of the programming team.[9] West's staging rehearsals of *Tzinquaw* took two years, with a cast of twenty-five members of the Cowichan Nation. West also designed the production's set and costumes from research material at the British Columbia Provincial Museum.[10] The audience at the first performance was predominantly citizens of the city of Duncan, and several Government dignitaries were in attendance, including the Superintendent of Indian Education for the Department of Indian Affairs, and the local Member of Parliament.[11]

The Reception of *Tzinquaw*

Tzinquaw was a moving experience for many who saw it at the Duncan premiere, and the critical response was hugely positive, if not rapturous. The reviewer for

---

[6]   Ida Halpern, "On the Interpretation of 'Meaningless-Nonsensical Syllables' in the Music of the Pacific Northwest Indians," *Ethnomusicology*, 20/2 (May 1976), p. 262.

[7]   Frank Morrison, *Tzinquaw Piano/Vocal Score* (Duncan, 1950).

[8]   Cecil West, "*Tzinquaw* Setting and Stage Effects, Floor Plans, and Running Order" (unpublished: Cowichan Historical Society, Duncan, 1950).

[9]   Herbert Whittacker, *Setting the Stage: Montreal Theatre 1920–1949* (Montreal: McGill_Queen's University Press, 1999), p. 62.

[10]   "Legend of Tzinquaw," *Vancouver Daily Province*, magazine section (November 18, 1950): p. 7.

[11]   Ron Baird, "Indians Present Legend of Thunderbird and Killer Whale," *Daily Colonist* (November 23, 1950), p. 8.

the *Daily Province*, Van Perry, called the work "an epochal smash-hit."[12] Another reviewer stated that the opera was something more than entertainment, it was "an emotional experience which must be seen to be believed."[13] Mamie Moloney, a columnist with the *Vancouver Sun*, was even more fulsome in her praise, describing *Tzinquaw* as an "emotional experience that few white people have been privileged to enjoy." She went on the state that this work presented audiences not with the stock "Hollywood Indian" but rather with "the Indian of history, of a culture and tradition, of a dignity and pride that fills his fellow Canadians with admiration and love."[14]

Not everyone was convinced, however, and the critics who were not so enthusiastic were noted professionals in the fields of music and literature. The ethnomusicologist Ida Halpern acknowledged that the opera was "a great event" and agreed that the task undertaken by Morrison must be accorded the "highest regard and respect,"[15] but she considered that this kind of cultural documentation was "a job which required professional advice from anthropologists and musicologists."[16] Vancouver composer Barbara Pentland similarly praised the "authentic" sections of *Tzinquaw*; however, she criticized Morrison's own writing, calling his music "superimposed accompaniment."[17] In a letter to the Editor of the *Vancouver Sun*, writer and poet Dorothy Livesay suggested that Morrison should perhaps remove his "improvements," asking "do we send white artists into Stanley Park to touch up the totem poles?"[18]

First Nations Rights and *Tzinquaw*

Although the critical response to *Tzinquaw* was divided, the opera heightened awareness of the perilous state of First Nations culture in Canada of the 1950s. From the 1876 Indian Act, for almost seventy-five years, the Government of Canada, with the intention of "civilizing" the natives, had systematically reduced the rights of First Nations people to perform the songs, dances, and ceremonies that constituted their spiritual worldview.[19] By the 1940s, when Morrison and Joe were working together, the Indian Act was so stringently applied that it had become a

---

[12] Van Perry, "Cowichan Indian Opera Wins Audience Acclaim," *Vancouver Daily Province* (November 23, 1950), p.11.

[13] Stanley Bligh, "Indian Operetta Packs Big Punch," *Vancouver Sun* (March 27, 1953), p. 19.

[14] Mamie Moloney, "Tzinquaw," *Vancouver Sun* (December 11, 1950), p. 21.

[15] Ida Halpern, "B.C. Indian Opera 'Tzinquaw' called 'Exciting experience.'" *Vancouver Daily Province* (March 27, 1953), p. 4.

[16] Ibid.

[17] Barbara Pentland, letter to the editor, *Vancouver Sun* (April 1, 1953), p. A4.

[18] Dorothy Livesay, letter to the editor, *Vancouver Sun* (April 25, 1953), p. A4.

[19] Richard H. Bartlett, *The Indian Act of Canada* (Saskatoon: University of Saskatchewan Native Law Centre, 1980), p. 5.

236 *Opera Indigene: Re/presenting First Nations and Indigenous Cultures*

criminal offense to perform traditional songs and dances anywhere but on reserve lands without official permission. First Peoples had to apply to the Indian Affairs Department for the right to perform at events like stampedes or fairs.[20] The cast of *Tzinquaw* were able to circumvent these laws by forming a private limited liability company under the title of the Cowichan Indian Players Limited with the Duncan Kiwanis Service Club serving as the official booking agents for the organization.[21] The fact that the production was an opera, produced by non-natives in a white cultural setting, may have given legitimacy to the off-reserve performance of traditional native music and dance.

The opera's fans and detractors alike commented on these oppressive laws endured by the First Nations and applauded Morrison's contribution to raising awareness of native culture. Mamie Moloney made a distinct reference to government policy toward the First Nations, stating that *Tzinquaw* had put an end to the notion held by some Canadians that the Canadian native was an "inferior specimen with little pride or ambition ... who must be cared for and protected by a paternalistic government."[22] Ida Halpern's ethnomusicological fieldwork had involved years devoted to the preservation of First Nation songs, and she acknowledged the fact that Morrison had increased the Cowichan peoples' awareness of their heritage with his work.[23] Regardless of their differing views of *Tzinquaw*, these writers were making important statements which drew attention to the fact that the songs and dances, which had so excited them in the performance of the work, had almost disappeared through government legislation and the attitudes that produced such laws.

Cultural Salvage and Colonization

Marcia Crosby states that "when a culture is represented as going through *fatal* changes, the natural thing to do is save or salvage it."[24] This concept, known as the "salvage paradigm," was a prevalent view held largely, but not exclusively, by early ethnographers and ethnomusicologists wherein a member of a dominant culture endeavors to save what is perceived to be a dying one. An unequal relation is created between the two cultures with the dominant one choosing what is worth salvaging from the subordinate one. The dominant culture proceeds on its own aesthetic values, with a well-meaning but paternalistic attitude, and the end result

---

[20] Ibid.

[21] *Tzinquaw* performance program (Duncan, November 22, 1950).

[22] Moloney, "Tzinquaw."

[23] Halpern, "B.C. Indian Opera."

[24] Marcia Crosby, "Construction of the Imaginary Indian," in *Vancouver Anthology: The Institutional Politics of Art*, ed. Stan Douglas (Vancouver, BC: Talonbooks, 1991), p. 274.

is "produced authenticity."[25] This so-called authenticity describes, for example, the early Indian paintings of Canadian artist Emily Carr, who devised one such salvage project when she attempted to make a visual record of every one of the Northwest tribal totem poles, where they were and as they were. Carr intended these paintings to be historical, documentary representations of totem poles and Indian villages constructed, she believed, by a race of people in the process of disappearing.[26] Carr, like Morrison, sought out and collected information about the art and traditions of the Northwest First Nations peoples.[27] Carr's evident admiration for their totem poles created a trust between her and the natives, and a sympathy for them on her part.[28] Her paintings were created as a record of what she believed to be a vanishing people; early proponents of Carr's painting often constructed her work as "a valuable record of a passing race."[29] Morrison too, certainly had sympathy and respect for the Cowichan peoples and their culture while at the same time practising his own version of the salvage paradigm in collecting the Cowichan music and saving it from what he considered to be certain disappearance. He believed the natives shared his view that their music could be adapted to what he called the white man's standards, but there was a colonialist assumption in Morrison's words that Cowichan music needed to be adapted to suit the tastes of its designated non-native audience.

The Music of *Tzinquaw*

Morrison's aesthetic was significantly informed by his experience as a church musician. In composing the score for *Tzinquaw*, Morrison took the piano transcriptions he had made of the Cowichan songs and further adapted them for Western music notation by adding key signatures, time signatures, bar lines, and perfect cadences to the end of the Cowichan melody lines. The musical settings of these songs reflect Morrison's musical tastes, and such settings force the asymmetrical Cowichan melodies into the conventions of church music; many of the transcribed songs are constricted into the four-measure, four-phrase structure of the standard chorale format with a four-part chordal accompaniment that follows the melody. In addition, a number of the original songs were changed or adjusted metrically. For example, a song titled *The Wanderer's Song*, initially transcribed by Morrison in three-quarter time, is rearranged in four-quarter time

---

[25]   James Clifford, "Of Other Peoples: Beyond the Salvage Paradigm," in *Discussions in Contemporary Culture*, ed. Hal Foster (Seattle, WA: Bay Press, 1987), p. 129.

[26]   Crosby, "Construction of the Imaginary Indian," p. 276.

[27]   Greta Moray, *Northwest Coast Native Culture and the Early Indian Paintings of Emily Carr, 1899–1913* (PhD dissertation, University of Toronto, 1993), p. 216.

[28]   Ibid., p. 221.

[29]   Ibid., p. 128.

238   *Opera Indigene: Re/presenting First Nations and Indigenous Cultures*

to better fit the English text written for it.[30] Other songs demonstrate influences of the Gilbert and Sullivan operettas in their melodies and arrangements. These influences are apparent in character songs sung by the warriors in the *Tzinquaw* narrative, especially the chorus of the rollicking, boastful song, *In Great Canoes*. This example echoes Gilbert and Sullivan's drinking choruses, and in particular the opening chorus of *The Pirates of Penzance*.[31] Both the operetta chorus and Morrison's chorus have distinct similarities in the use of metrical designation, musical introduction, melody line, cadence points, and accompaniment. Other operetta influences are apparent in a mournful duet for a male and female voice titled by Morrison as *The Trouble Song*. The duet is strophic with two verses and a refrain which is echoed by a chorus of women.[32] This particular song received a critical plaudit from the *Daily Colonist* writer, who considered that the duet rivaled "Puccini for sheer emotional appeal and melody".[33] Throughout the score, Morrison uses Western musical terms and he dictates performance instruction in the standard European music languages of Italian and French. The chorus from *In Great Canoes* is to be performed in a sprightly waltz rhythm which is marked *sforzando-marcato*, and an interpretation entitled *Weeping for the Dead* is described as a *marche funebre* designated *Largo dolorosa, mezzo-forte, marcato legato*. The refrain of this song, which is sung in the original Hul'q'umi'num is given the performance instruction *Lacrimoso*.[34] Morrison also composed incidental music to underscore dramatic moments in the opera. These entr'actes are written in a nineteenth-century bravura piano style, more like a cadenza, with fast scale and arpeggiated figures, rapid double-octave passages and glissandi. The instrumental scoring for *Tzinquaw* is for piano and Western drums. Other instruments indicated are traditional percussive rattles and drums that were utilized in the dances onstage.[35]

Morrison's use of time signatures is limited, and the predominant metrical marking is four quarter beats to the bar. He frequently uses an ostinato figure that approximates drumbeats, a pattern that appears throughout the score. However, this pattern is written in polyphonic chords and played on a piano instead of an untuned wood or skin drum, or two sticks hit together as was typical of Cowichan practice.[36] The simplicity of the single pitch of the drum is lost and the polyphonic effect of so many notes being played together results in a thick, almost symphonic texture.

---

[30]   Morrison, *Tzinquaw Piano/Vocal Score*, p. 14.

[31]   Arthur Sullivan, *The Pirates of Penzance* (London: Chappell & Co., n.d. [1880]), p. 12.

[32]   Morrison, *Tzinquaw Piano/Vocal Score*, pp. 15–16.

[33]   Don Ingham, "Legend of Cowichan Indians 'Tzinquaw' Makes British Columbian Stage History," *Daily Colonist* (November 23, 1950), p. 8.

[34]   Morrison, *Tzinquaw Piano/Vocal Score*, p. 12.

[35]   Ibid.

[36]   A.E. Pickford, *Coast Salish: British Columbia Heritage Series Vol. 2*, ed. A.F. Flucke (Victoria, BC: A. Sutton, Provincial Archives, 1965), p. 51.

The Text of *Tzinquaw*

The texts that Morrison wrote to the transcribed melodies are also informed by his experience as church musician as well as by his experience in the kind of amateur community-theater presentations, musical theater, and operetta that flourished in Canada during the postwar years. His poetry is very far from the traditional text in ritual songs of the Coast Salish and Western First Nations. Many First Nations songs use vocables, historically considered "meaningless" by ethnomusicologists, but which can in fact have a mnemonic relationship to the specific song. Although the dances that accompany the songs tell their story, a knowledge of the meaning of the syllables aids the choreography and the dance performance. Ida Halpern gives an example of how this works by describing the Salish Medicine Dance. The dancer, attempting to cure a woman who is unable to move her legs, rubs his thighs with downward rubbing motions while the syllables of the accompanying song are "An na na" which means pain.[37] Text in Coast Salish songs is often highly repetitive, a practice believed to bring spiritual power to the singer. The repetitive pattern of the text has also been said to induce a trancelike state to the singer and listener that allows for communion with the supernatural: "The outstanding feature of traditional Indian verse construction is repetition, which conveys the accumulation of power. Refrains, reiteration of phrases in part or in whole, meaningless vocables, and parallel phrasing all give the effect of rhyming thoughts and incremental repetition. For the Indian this effect is hypnotic and magical."[38] An English translation of a song by another Northwest Coast First Nation, the Haida, shows this repetitive style:

> The used to be plenty, there used to be plenty, chief,
> There used to be plenty in your house, chief;
> There used to be plenty, there used to be plenty, chief,
> There used to be plenty, there used to be plenty, chief,
> You cry and move about to see them come by canoe (to the potlatch), great chief.
> There used to be plenty, there used to be plenty chief;
> There used to be plenty, there used to be plenty, chief.[39]

Morrison, in contrast to this repetitive form, wrote his opera text in a poetic style reminiscent of nineteenth-century English poetry, and of the English hymnal. There is no repetition of the words as in traditional practice, and Morrison employs the use of verses and stanzas with rhyming patterns. There is much use of apostrophe, dramatic invocatory style, and religious incantation similar to that of Western

---

[37] Ida Halpern, "On the Interpretation of 'Meaningless-Nonsensical Syllables'," p. 260.

[38] Penny Petrone, *Native Literature in Canada: From the Oral Tradition to the Present* (Toronto, ON: Oxford University Press, 1990), p. 22.

[39] John Swanton, *Haida Songs, Tsimshian Texts, Vol. 3* (Leiden: E.J. Brill, 1912), pp. 46–47.

240   *Opera Indigene: Re/presenting First Nations and Indigenous Cultures*

religious ceremonial texts. The text also contains such archaic, highly formal words as "thee" and "thou." For example, Morrison's version of the Invocation of the Thunderbird is comparable to nineteenth-century Anglican hymn texts:

> Ah, Tzinquaw, Ah Tzinquaw, Mighty one
> The sound of thy wings is the thunder
> And flashing of fire from thine eye is lightning
> That shatters the sky
> Now thou art nigh – O hear our cry
> . . .
> Ah Tzinquaw. Ah Tzinquaw. To thee we call
> . . .
> O Mighty one
> King of the sun, send us thine aid
> We are afraid.[40]

Morrison was very clear that his English versions of Cowichan songs were not direct translations but interpretations he devised from the meanings of the dances that accompanied the songs, saying of his interpretations that "it was always a delight to satisfactorily tell the Cowichan stories in words that could be sung"[41] The implication here is that non-English words were not singable.

The Stage Production of *Tzinquaw*

Tzinquaw's staging was entirely Western in practice and technical execution. Although he claimed that the staging was in adherence with authentic First Nation traditions, Cecil West's designs were an interpretation of Cowichan culture viewed through a Western lens. West's statement, that complete authenticity would be difficult, "since records of the period are almost non-existent or at the very best fragmentary, complete authenticity in design has been impossible," is somewhat ironic, considering that the historical record was contained in the Cowichan song and oral traditions that were a part of *Tzinquaw*.[42] The production took place on a proscenium stage with the accompanying instruments placed on the floor below the stage. The set, using the single-point perspective, comprised a painted backdrop of Cowichan Bay with painted canvas flats on stage right and left, representing trees and an Indian house. The Tzinquaw and the Killer Whale were flat cutouts painted with copies of Coast Salish designs. Both animal units were designed to be flown;

---

[40]   *Tzinquaw* performance program (Victoria, March 1951).

[41]   *Tzinquaw* article, *CBC Times*, 1/21 (November 26, 1950), p. 3.

[42]   Cecil West, Designer's Notes, *Tzinquaw* performance program (Duncan, November 22, 1950).

the Tzinquaw hooked itself onto the whale during the climactic storm scene and both pieces were flown out together.

West's scenic designs followed Western conventions of illusion and perspective used in stage design practice since the sixteenth century, and the use of flying creatures has a direct connection with British pantomime, which used flying dragons and mythical beasts in the productions of the eighteenth and nineteenth centuries.[43] In contrast, the Cowichan used neither the picture-frame presentational style of the proscenium theater nor the kind of painted scenery that was traditional in these theaters. Their performances were site-specific, the tribal longhouse, and in a format similar to theater-in-the-round where performers and observers interacted. Sometimes the entire space of the longhouse became a performance venue; outer walls, doors, and roof were utilized, depending on the ritual and the dance associated with it.[44]

Despite the re-situation of traditional practice from longhouse to the proscenium stage, West and Morrsion seem sincerely to have believed that the native performers were living their roles "with all the intensity of their nature."[45] West's production notes show, however, that every detail of staging and interpretation was imposed on the native performers and that they were given acting and blocking instructions, even in their own traditional dances and rituals.

The Critical Response

The positive responses to the music of *Tzinquaw* were as enthusiastic about Morrison's own musical transcriptions as they were about the traditional Cowichan music. One writer approved of the "grand opera construction" of the work as well as his view that the opera could be compared to those of Puccini.[46] Some of the reviewers excused Morrison for altering the Cowichan songs to suit his audience. The *Daily Colonist* reasoned thus: "The only modern touch is the addition of White Man's music, which is used essentially to interpret to the White Man's ears, the Indians' story."[47] In contrast to the positive reviews, composer Barbara Pentland and ethnomusicologist Ida Halpern's responses were particularly unforgiving. Pentland criticized the piano accompaniment which forced the performers to sing their songs "against an arbitrary and much too loud" piano accompaniment which resulted in "either the singer conforming and ruining his melody or sounding out

---

[43]   David Mayer, *Harlequin in his Element: The English Pantomime* (Cambridge, MA: Harvard University Press, 1969), p. 110.

[44]   Halpern, "On the Interpretation of 'Meaningless-Nonsensical Syllables'," p. 254.

[45]   "Legend of *Tzinquaw*," *Vancouver Daily Province*, magazine section (November 18, 1950), 7.

[46]   Ingham, "Legend of Cowichan Indians."

[47]   "Hit Indian Opera Appears Thursday," *Daily Colonist* (May 5, 1953), p. 6.

242 *Opera Indigene: Re/presenting First Nations and Indigenous Cultures*

of tune when he tried to retain it."[48] Halpern questioned Morrison's use of musical devices like waltzes, arpeggios, and European harmonies, and she took special exception to Morrison's use of the piano, which, as a fixed-pitch instrument, could not replicate the smaller micro-tones found in the melodic line of native songs.[49]

The approving critics applauded Morrison's literary style; the *CBC Times* was very complimentary, finding his text nothing short of "inspired."[50] Of the opposing reviews, Dorothy Livesay was the harshest critic of Morrison's text, taking issue with the English words, "quite unsuitable to the native rhythms and vowel sounds, which were put into the mouths of the Indian actors." Yet, she wrote, "in the moments when they were allowed to use their own language ... the dramatic effect was intense."[51] Livesay would have agreed with scholar Penny Petrone, who has said of the translation of First Nations' story into foreign idioms that: "In translating a narrative or song ... the translator must consider not only linguistic fidelity but also the connotive and denotive meaning of words and the cultural matrix informed by the attitudes, beliefs, and customs of the tribe of which the original is an organic part."[52] Morrison's language and literary style were completely alien to the traditional language and practice of the Cowichan people. In *Tzinquaw* the songs became commodified entertainment for an audience of non-natives consumers. The admirers of *Tzinquaw* were captivated by what they considered "authentic" performance and believed the opera depicted real native life and culture: "as real and as authentic as an Indian village."[53] Perhaps the most direct negative critical point was made by two natives who saw a performance of *Tzinquaw* in Vancouver. When asked how they liked the show, they replied: "Too much white man in it."[54]

Questions of Authenticity and Aesthetic Colonization

It is evident that Frank Morrison and Cecil West's own Western cultural aesthetics were imposed on the musical and spiritual culture of the Cowichan First Nation. It was an act, albeit an unwitting one, of aesthetic colonization. However supportive the dissenting artist-professionals were of Morrison's preservation attempts, they nevertheless argued that this was an imposition of alien values on a culture that had already been subjugated enough by the Government of Canada. They argued against the claims of authenticity and that the imposition of the white man's aesthetics on the First Nations material rendered it inauthentic. Even the traditional

---

[48]   Pentland, letter to the editor.

[49]   Halpern, "B.C. Indian Opera."

[50]   "*Tzinquaw*," *CBC Times*.

[51]   Livesay, letter to the editor.

[52]   Petrone, *Native Literature in Canada*, p. 7.

[53]   "Cowichan Tribe Pitches Camp," *Vancouver Daily Province* (March 26, 1953), p. 11.

[54]   Elmore Philpott, article, *Vancouver Sun* (March 30, 1953), p. 4.

material presented in the opera was claimed inauthentic since its presentation was alien to the spiritual practices of the Cowichan people.

In all the controversy surrounding the production of *Tzinquaw*, many hailed the work as innovative, and as a milestone in the history of Canadian culture. Audiences who had never been to any kind of opera or who had never seen traditional First Nations performance were captivated by what they saw. The Vancouver radio reviewer Ellen Harris claimed that "*Tzinquaw* isn't like anything else ... Here is a new creation which has grown directly from the old."[55] The opera was performed in Victoria, Vancouver, and in towns in the lower Vancouver Island region to eager, appreciative audiences. The admirers of *Tzinquaw* were so excited by the fact that this opera was based on native culture and performed so well, to their great surprise, by native performers, that they were unable to see the colonization of First Nations traditions that the opera enacted. The Cowichan people were lauded for having "established themselves as professional entertainers thus achieving a new civilized distinction for their ancient race."[56]

It must be said, though, that without Frank Morrison and his sympathetic relationship with the Cowichan people, the collaboration between him and Abel Joe that led to the creation of *Tzinquaw* would not likely have occurred. Nobody else would have been trusted and granted the honor of being allowed to transcribe and collect songs that belonged to families who had to give permission for the transcription and performance. Morrison had presented unfamiliar material in an entirely familiar way, something he intended when he devised the opera in an aesthetic the audiences could understand. *Tzinquaw*, artistically conservative though it may have been, was, at the time, the only attempt to preserve the Cowichan culture, and the opera gave a new impetus to the Cowichan people in the preservation of their cultural traditions. In August 1979, *Tzinquaw* was restaged for two performances at the opening of the new Cowichan Theatre.[57] The production, an exact copy of the original staging, was generally well received, but projected further performances did not take place. Lack of funds may have contributed to this, but one reviewer commented on the fact that it had taken almost thirty years to build up enough momentum to restage the opera which gave "some idea of the cultural inertia resisting a performance such as this."[58] In spite of the fact that *Tzinquaw* the opera seems consigned to history, the culture that was showcased in the work lives on. The Cowichan First Nation Tzinquaw dancers and singers maintain the performance traditions of their culture and perform regularly in Duncan and at cultural celebrations across Vancouver Island and British Columbia to this day.

---

[55]   Harris, "*Tzinquaw* – The Story of an Indian Opera."

[56]   "Tzinquaw Draws 3,000 in First Run at New Auditorium," *Cowichan Leader* (November 30, 1950).

[57]   Max Wyman, "Indian Drama Evokes Powerful Images," *Vancouver Sun* (August 7, 1979).

[58]   "*Tzinquaw* Alive and Well, 30 Years Later," *Daily Colonist* (August 4, 1979).

Chapter 13

Peaceful Surface, Monstrous Depths:
Barbara Pentland and Dorothy Livesay's
The Lake

Dylan Robinson

Introduction

The history of the arts in Canada is marked by instances of heroic settler figures battling against inhospitable environments and fierce elements toward the settlement of the land. These narratives have been no less present in the history of Canadian opera. Examples include Healy Willan's *The Life and Death of Jean de Brébeuf* (1943), Harry Somers's *Louis Riel* (1967), Murray Adaskin's *Grant, Warden of the Plains* (1967), Istvan Anhalt's *Winthrop* (1983), and John Estacio's *Frobisher* (2007). In contrast to these heroic settlers figures, Barbara Pentland and Dorothy Livesay's chamber opera *The Lake* paints a picture of John and Susan Allison, pioneers in British Columbia's Okanagan valley, in which these settler characters are far from infallible. In the following chapter, I demonstrate how Pentland and Livesay use the settler figure in *The Lake* to voice a critique of the relationships between settlers and First Peoples, drawing out tensions between the Okanagan First Nations characters' views regarding care for the land, and the settlers' views of its productivity and development.

This chapter offers a discursive analysis of *The Lake* that examines the disjunctions between Susan Allison's statements, and the language in which these are spoken. This analysis reveals the conflicting nature of the characters' words and actions that, in turn, undercuts the foundational myth of Canadian identity, the myth of 'white settler innocence'.[1] Such disjunctions between word and deed are numerous in *The Lake*. Susan's respect for the Okanagan First Peoples is put into question by her persistent use of language that references concepts of commodity

---

[1] My analysis of the myth of "white settler innocence" is here informed by Eva Mackey's research on critical multiculturalism in *The House of Difference: Cultural Politics and National Identity in Canada* (Toronto, ON: University of Toronto Press, 2002). Mackey notes how historical relationships representing the "… 'positive,' 'generous,' and 'tolerant' treatment of Native people" by Canadian settlers "have been interpreted and re-shaped within a national tradition in order to create a mythology of white settler innocence" in Canada. Mackey, *The House of Difference*, p. 26.

246 *Opera Indigene: Re/presenting First Nations and Indigenous Cultures*

and ownership, a language that exposes the settlers' underlying motivation to possess the land and increase its productivity. The portrayal of Susan's friendships with the Okanagan people (her "love [of] every one") is undermined by her inability to listen and respond to Marie's story while they reminisce about the day the settlers arrived. Despite Susan's keen interest for Marie to re-tell the story of Susan and John's arrival in Okanagan territory, Susan does not take this opportunity to engage with Marie as a partner in dialogue but instead uses the moment to overlay her own more peaceful narrative upon Marie's story. Significantly, Susan's narrative overlay focuses upon an image of the landscape's picturesque beauty—a landscape in which there is notably "no life, only the silent flying of a few late swans," a landscape devoid of the Okanagan peoples' very presence.[2]

Such examples, as we will see, illustrate that while Susan endeavors to respect the beliefs and stories of the Okanagan people, the language and manner in which she expresses these sentiments is ultimately at odds with the integrity of the statements themselves. This chapter considers these disjunctions between the denotative content of the characters' statements and the connotations suggested by Livesay's choice of language, and the particular emphasis Pentland places upon this language in her musical setting of it. I will analyze two instances of this disjunction in particular detail: Susan's opening aria, and the duet between Susan and Marie that opens the second half of the opera. My analysis of these sections illustrates Pentland and Livesay's construction of the encounter between the Okanagan peoples and the settlers as one in which relationships are mediated through the troubled rhetoric of Canadian "inclusion" and "tolerance" of First Peoples.[3] At its worst, such a rhetoric of implied consensus claims (and even celebrates) a reciprocity of dialogue through its elision of dissenting perspectives about less-than-heroic occupation of First Nations' territories. Reading *The Lake* as a critique of this rhetoric reflects both Livesay's inclination to explicitly address social issues in her poetry, and Pentland's tendency toward dealing with political and social causes in compositions including *News* (1970) about the Vietnam War, and in *Ice Age* (1975) and *Tellus* (1981–1982), both dealing with topics of environmental destruction.

The History of *The Lake* / *The Lake* as History

In June of 1951, Gordon Jeffrey, a lawyer and amateur organist from London, Ontario, commissioned Barbara Pentland to compose a chamber opera suitable

---

[2] Susan's reminiscence of the empty and lifeless landscape is here a great irony, since their duet is a simultaneous reminiscence of the same day, each character from their own perspective, and at which they were *both* present. Indeed, most ironic is that Marie stands directly *beside* Susan (in the present) as she tells the story of how there was "no life" in the Okanagan valley at the time of the settlers' arrival.

[3] For further discussion of this rhetoric of inclusion and tolerance see Mackey, *The House of Difference*.

Peaceful Surface, Monstrous Depths 247

for a small ensemble and four amateur singers. Following a successful organ concerto he had previously commissioned from Pentland, Jeffrey's commission stipulated that the new opera that be "Canadian-themed," last no longer than twenty-four minutes, and be suitable for an ensemble of varying musical abilities. The resulting opera, *The Lake*, was written and developed in collaboration with poet Dorothy Livesay, and completed in 1952. Despite Pentland's efforts to follow the parameters set by Jeffrey, the opera was never performed, a fact undoubtedly due to the work's degree of difficulty in performance.[4]

Livesay's libretto is based upon the Okanagan pioneers John and Susan Allison, their First Nations maid, Marie, and the "half-breed" farmhand Johnny MacDougal, who in the opera is referred to as "Mac." Completing this cast is the unseen Na'aitka, the monster of Okanagan Lake known to many Canadians today as the "Ogopogo." While the central characters are based upon the actual settlers and Okanagan First Peoples from the area now known as the town of Summerland, British Columbia, the story itself is less historically accurate. Dorothy Livesay, in possession of some of Susan Allison's writings, adapted several sections of this memoir for the libretto.[5] The central event of the opera, John's crossing the lake during a fierce storm, in fact conflates the Okanagan peoples' story of Na'aitka with a separate incident Susan Allison relates in her memoir, in which John's boat is crushed in an ice jam while crossing the lake, causing him to jump back across pieces of ice in order to make it safely back to shore. Each event in the libretto and memoir is narrated similarly. In each Susan describes watching the boat cross the lake during the storm, seeing something hit the boat (a piece of ice in the memoir / Na'aitka in the opera), and then running down to the lake to ensure John has survived.

Elaborating this event for the opera, Livesay constructs the premise that John must make a trip across Lake Okanagan to "old Okanagan Mission" during a fierce storm in order to retrieve essential supplies for the approaching winter. A pregnant Susan, afraid that Na'aitka may attack her husband, tries unsuccessfully to persuade John not to go. As the boat departs on its journey across the lake, Susan thinks she sees Na'aitka undulating amongst the waves. Against Marie's appeals, Susan runs down to the shore to find out if the monster has attacked the boat. Shortly after Susan's departure, John and Mac are shown upon the shore, arguing whether, as Mac believes, their boat

---

[4] From a performance perspective, the work is relatively straightforward by today's standards of contemporary compositional practice. In 1950, however, Pentland's developing interest in serialism along with the rhythmic complexity of the vocal lines would have made the work challenging for many performers, let alone Jeffrey's amateur ensemble. The "foreign" serial style of the work would have been a deciding factor in Jeffrey's decision not to perform the work. Indeed, in the first presentation of the work by the Canadian Broadcasting Corporation radio, the professional singers were similarly unable to sing their parts as written.

[5] These memoirs have since been compiled and published by Canadian historian Margaret Ormsby as *A Pioneer Gentlewoman in British Columbia: The Recollections of Susan Allison* (Vancouver: University of British Columbia Press, 1976).

248   *Opera Indigene: Re/presenting First Nations and Indigenous Cultures*

was attacked by the monster or whether, as John believes, the boat hit an object or rock in the water. Upon their return to the house, they learn from Marie that Susan, despite the storm, has run down to the shore to search for them. After searching for and eventually locating Susan in the woods, John proceeds to scold her for being so impetuous, and concedes that Susan and Marie's "little game has worked" to keep him home. The opera concludes with the reunited couple returning to the homestead with Mac and Marie just as Susan feels the first signs of labor.

Although the opera remains to have a fully staged production, it received a Canadian Broadcasting Corporation (CBC) radio broadcast performance in 1954 organized through Livesay's efforts, and a concert performance by students at the Vancouver Academy of Music organized by the long-time Pentland advocate and interpreter, mezzo-soprano Phyllis Mailing. This lack of interest in the opera might here be considered consistent with the more general apathy held by both the local and national musical community toward Pentland's "uncompromising style"—a frequent euphemism used by critics to describe her atonal musical language and commitment to serialism.[6] However, the continued disinterest in the production of this opera might also be understood as the result of the opera's break with traditional nation-building narratives that portray Canadian pioneers as heroic figures who bring civilization and productivity to the untamed Canadian wilderness.

While contemporary Canadian operas that deconstruct Canadian history have become far more prevalent in the late twentieth and early twenty-first centuries, in the historical context of 1952 an opera such as *The Lake* that does not celebrate Canada's history through the settler figure would more than likely be received by its audience as unpatriotic. And while *The Lake* might seem loyal to the Canadian narrative of the pioneer's efforts in "giving to the land," and demonstrates the settlers' efforts to make the land productive, Livesay and Pentland problematize this settler myth in their critical portrayal of the settler characters. John Allison relates to the First Peoples as a source of labor ("I've got to get the Indians to work faster"), demeans Marie by chastising her for not being able to stop the pregnant Susan from running down to the lake during a fierce storm, and is domineering and condescending toward his wife. John's very first words of the opera, "Susan! Susan! Where are you, wife?", accentuated by a melody that with each call of her name rises higher and higher, emphasizes his impatience at not knowing where Susan is. John also speaks condescendingly about the Okanagan peoples: "My dear wife, whatever the Indians say delights you. But you must not forget your common sense!" This statement both discounts the First Nations characters'

---

[6]   The opera is particularly interesting as one of Pentland's earliest efforts toward integrating serialist principles with her already tightly controlled compositional technique focusing on economy of thematic and motivic material. Though Pentland does not apply serial techniques rigorously in *The Lake*, the opera demonstrates her attempt to integrate serialism with her pan-diatonic style, influenced by her study with Aaron Copland at Tanglewood. The overture demonstrates a loosely constructed opening ten-note row, with several pitches repeated, while emphasizing perfect fourths throughout. See Example 13.1.

traditional knowledge as little more than fantasy, and is patronizing toward Susan, who is deemed foolish for believing in such stories.

Susan's character, in turn, is depicted as opportunist in her collecting of stories from the Okanagan First Peoples to write about for a London newspaper. She sensationalizes one story she is told by focusing on the otherworldly appearance of "the little people." In addition, as I will shortly demonstrate in my analysis of the Susan and Marie's duet, Susan is portrayed as self-absorbed. While she seems to listen and respond to Marie's story of the day the settlers arrived, and Na'aitka's wrath, she is in fact more immersed in her own memory of the picturesque Okanagan landscape, a reminiscence very much at odds with Marie's "warning" to take care of the land. Susan's character, moreover, is at times portrayed as gossipy. When John asks Susan where he found one of the Okanagan men who was supposed to be "haying" ("Where do you suppose I found him [Cherumchoot] this time?") Susan responds with the phrases "I couldn't guess!" and "Good heavens, had he murdered someone?" John then explains that he found Cherumchoot sitting in the Indian camp "Naked as God made him, hugging his bones ... he had gambled his clothes away" to which they both burst into *sprechstimme* laughter while Susan condescendingly notes "what a lovely joke" it is. That such issues of alcoholism in First Nations communities in the 1950s (not to mention present-day native communities across Canada) are here treated as no more than a "lovely joke" is perhaps the most damning of Livesay and Pentland's negative depictions of the settler characters. In such a context of Livesay and Pentland's unsympathetic depictions of Susan and John Allison, it is perhaps less surprising that *The Lake* has not received the attention of those interested and able to produce new work, particularly during the years of celebratory nationalism leading up to and including Canada's 1967 centennial year. To speculate on the motivations behind Livesay and Pentland's choice to unfavorably depict the settlers, we might return to Alison Greene's discussion in the previous chapter of Pentland and Livesay's critical responses to the opera *Tzinquaw*, a collaboration between members of the Cowichan Nation and the amateur composer Frank Morrison that was performed the year prior to *The Lake*.[7] By situating these two projects side by side we might better understand Livesay and Pentland's opera as a counterbalance to the exoticized representation of First Nations culture they perceived in *Tzinquaw*.

Blurring Ownership, Possessive Itemization, and the Language of Commodity

From this overview of the opera's history and Livesay and Pentland's characterization of the settlers, I will proceed to analyze in greater detail how Livesay's language choice and Pentland's musical setting situate Susan and John Allison in contrast to the Canadian myth of "white settler innocence." This is

---

[7]   See Alison Greene, Chapter 12 in this volume.

250   *Opera Indigene: Re/presenting First Nations and Indigenous Cultures*

achieved, in part, by emphasizing the settlers' focus on ownership, possession, and treatment of the Okanagan people as a means toward achieving their own objectives. Indeed, from the very first word of the opera, "item," this importance of ownership in the settlers' lives and making the land productive is immediately revealed.

As the opera begins, we see Susan cataloguing items that have been traded— products of the land including huckleberries, a rose, and a hat woven from the meadow grass. Despite this fairly straightforward organizational activity, the opening aria in fact does not emphasize a sense of order through Susan's cataloguing. Instead, the lack of grammatical consistency in Livesay's libretto *increases* narrative ambiguity. Each statement is an entry in Susan's notebook that here presumably acts as a ledger to keep track of what items have been traded, to whom the items are traded, and what labor the Okanagan people have undertaken in trade for the specific item Susan gives:

> Item, to Yacum-Tecum, for bringing me a hide to tan: one bag of sugar.
> To Jacob one-leg,--huckleberries---
> One hat woven with my own hands from the meadow grass.
> Item to Dumby--for helping me plow a field----
> A pair of my best wool socks---
> Item, to Marie's granddaughter Suzanne---
> My thanks, and a rose for taking care of the children this morning.[8]

The opening of the aria here demonstrates a lack of grammatical consistency through Livesay's careful avoidance of parallel sentence structure to describe each of Susan's exchanges. Consequently, it becomes difficult for the listener to discern what items Susan has given and received, to whom they have been given, and from whom they were received. Musically, Pentland makes the trading activity in Susan's first ledger entry increasingly complicated for the listener to follow by segmenting and elongating the statement. Pentland breaks "Item, to Yacum-Tecum, for bringing me a hide to tan: one bag of sugar" into segments that sound more like individual sentences in themselves: "Item. To Yacum-Tecum. For bringing me a hide to tan. One bag of sugar."

For Susan's second entry, Livesay reverses the order of information Susan enters in the ledger's columns. To read the libretto we might deduce that that Susan is now speaking out of ledger-column order, and that "--huckleberries---" were not received but *given* to Susan by Jacob one-leg, since we can safely surmise that Susan gave Jacob one-leg the hat woven with her "own hands." Yet Pentland here reverses her earlier choice to elongate and segment the sentence, and instead places the two parts of the entry in close proximity. In listening, the statement is thus heard as "To Jacob one leg: huckleberries," and leaves the listener wondering to whom the hat belongs.

---

[8]   *The Lake*, libretto (Pentland Fonds, National Library of Canada), p. 1. The original formatting and punctuation have been retained in this quotation.

Peaceful Surface, Monstrous Depths 251

Thus the listener is left puzzled as to what the results of trading and cataloguing have been in Susan's accounting aria. This confusion is all the more significant because Susan's note-making is an activity presumably meant to *increase* the sense of order in trading. The very purpose of precise accountability in the activity itself is distorted by grammatical dis-ordering and musically elongating and segmenting Susan's statements of trading activity. Despite the intention of the activity, the overall result of this cataloguing is a blurred sense of ownership. The scale of such trading might here seem small—a hat, huckleberries, a rose. Yet the implications of Susan's puzzling accounting practices will not be lost on contemporary readers who are familiar with Canada's history, and ongoing debates, regarding the ownership of natural resources and land treaty negotiations, negotiations which are understood by many First Peoples as a history of coercive trading for "trinkets of little value."[9]

While the relationships in giving and trading become confused in Susan's opening aria, the itemization—the products themselves and the possessive connotations of ownership—remains an emphasis. In this portrayal of the land's productivity, the settlers are engaged (*pace terra nullius*) in the process of making the land "useful." In many of Susan's exchanges an item of the land is given in return for First Nations labor toward making the land productive. Such productivity is emphasized in the language Susan uses from the first word of the opera, "item," and its subsequent repetitions through the opening aria. This emphasizes the driving force of settlement: making the land productive, and harnessing its resources as commodities. The word "item" begins three out of the aria's five phrases, and is accentuated by augmenting its duration while the words that follow are all set syllabically to short rhythms. Additionally, Pentland uses a series of rising perfect fourths and a gradual crescendo to increase the tension each time the word is repeated. As each item is noted, the music amplifies Susan's increasing excitement, and effectively highlights Susan's possessive desire (Example 13.1).

The possessive connotations are further emphasized musically in Pentland's setting of the word "item." The first syllable of the word, "I", is lengthened while the second syllable, "tem," remains short. The contour of the interval also works to emphasize the "I": the pitches of the two syllables span a descending perfect fourth, placing further emphasis on the "I" while de-emphasizing the "tem."[10] Other than the lengthened "I's" of "Item", this emphasis is again noticeable at the

---

[9]   I here refer to Jacques Cartier's trading with the people of the "new world" in which he notes, "we gave them knives, glass beads, combs, and other trinkets of small value at which they showed many signs of joy ...": Ramsay Cook, *The Voyages of Jacques Cartier* (Toronto, ON: University of Toronto Press, 1993), p. 24.

[10]   The notes for these repetitions of the word item are B♭ to F, C♯ to G♯, and F to C. It is interesting to note that the first three notes of these repetitions (B♭, C♯, [D♭] F) form a B♭-minor triad, a tonal center of the work. It might even be generalized that implicit narrative structure of this pervasive triad also works to focus our attention toward these commodity-oriented words. Additionally, the opening motif, first heard at the beginning of the short overture to the opera and then repeated at each mention of "the lake," joins "item,"

Example 13.1 *The Lake*, Susan's opening aria

end of the aria, at which point Susan sings "I wish," in which the "I" is held for three counts. This final instance of emphasis on "I" this time conspicuously links "I" of the "Item" and the subjective "I" together in a musical statement of possession (see Example 13.2).

---

representing product, and "the lake" representing nature, consequently providing a musical link between the two to signify the commodification of the land.

Example 13.1 *concluded*

Example 13.2 *The Lake*, conclusion to Susan's opening aria

Ownership continues to be emphasized as the opera progresses, with significant repetitions of the word "own." Susan speaks of "socks knit from our own wool," and says "I suppose we can take our own wheat, our very own" over to the mill for grinding. In this last phrase "own" is emphasized the second time it is sung, and elongated with a half-note that comes at the end of a crescendo. To Jacob one-leg, Susan gives a hat woven with her "own hands from the meadow grass." The word "own" is here emphasized with a rising glissando, and is the only word in the

254   *Opera Indigene: Re/presenting First Nations and Indigenous Cultures*

phrase that is given more than one beat per syllable, which works to distinguish it from the surrounding words. Since this statement already implies that Susan wove the hat with hands that were most likely her own (it would be strange if she wove the hat with hands that were not her own), the redundancy might be heard (with the help of the rising glissando), to imply a kind of greed; the "tone of voice" Susan takes might here be considered similar to that of a petulant child.

In addition to Susan's focus on cataloguing the products of the land that she owns, she also describes the land itself in terms of value. For instance, she wants to "enrich; from sandy soil to grow a green life, where like gold the peaches blow." Yet while Susan's statement expresses her good intentions to keep the land beautiful and lush with "green life," her words reference images of wealth and currency. Moreover, Susan not only emphasizes ownership of items through the language she uses, but also describes the Okanagan people in commodity-oriented terms by calling them "a recompense," a description that denotes payment or compensation. The most troubling reference to ownership arises, however, when Susan recounts her trip to visit Yacum-Tecum:

> Susan: … I slipped off to the Indian camping ground and wrote down the legend of the little people (they are so tiny old Yacum-Tecum said, with round heads, black eyes and long black hair. Half fish, half men … suckling their children halfway out of the water). Oh, such a tale to write about to London! I think I can hardly wait till evening to set it down.

This text is spoken in *sprechstimme* as an almost confidential whisper in which Susan becomes increasingly excited. Susan's excitement is intensified by the acceleration of tempo and increased dynamic level, and reaches its climax as she sings "Oh, such a tale to write about to London." The musical accompaniment is here briefly reminiscent of circus music, or an out-of-tune organ-grinder's music, further adding to the story's exotic appeal. Susan sensationalizes Yacum-Tecum's story by exaggerating the strange physical appearance of the little people, and avoids any reference to the actual narrative of the story itself. Heard in the context of the rising musical intensity given to successive repetitions of "item," this tale becomes yet another product. As an aside that occurs within Susan's aria, Yacum-Tecum's tale is simply the next item in the list of items Susan documents, another object that can be "set down." The itemization thus continues, as the legend becomes fetishized, rendered an exotic object whose cultural cache may potentially increase Susan's status when she sends it to England to be published.[11]

---

[11]   As detailed by Margaret Ormsby (*A Pioneer Gentlewoman*), Susan Allison published several articles about the Similkameen people and their stories in British journals.

Storytelling Together, Apart

While Susan's opening aria demonstrates what we might categorize as a "settler worldview" that emphasizes ownership and possession, the disjunctions between the settlers' and Okanagan peoples' perspectives are most clearly highlighted in a duet between Susan and her First Nations maid, Marie. Once John has left on his trip across the lake, Susan enters into a reverie about the campfires and stories on the day of the settlers' arrival in the Okanagan. She then asks Marie to recount the story of Na'aitka. Marie agrees, but instead tells the story as one in which the settlers' arrival disrupted Okanagan cultural traditions, where "Okanagan Indian grew up with scornful glance, he sneered at games, at Chief, left campfire, would not dance." For Marie, this is not a story of the picturesque landscape, but one in which "white man led him wrong, gold burned in his head, he sought no quiet life but 'Chikamin' [greed for gold] instead." It is a story that recounts Na'aitka's arrival in conjunction with the settlers' arrival.

Despite the differences in perspective, both characters appear on the surface to engage in dialogue and describe their respect for the land. However, like the description of the lake itself as a peaceful and placid surface beneath which lurks a monstrous presence, this duet exemplifies a seemingly peaceful "surface" interaction between settler and Okanagan characters beneath which lies a more troubling elision of Marie's warnings to take care of the land. While Susan's responses to Marie's story seem as if they are voiced in agreement with Marie's statements, further analysis reveals them to be Susan's own reverie overlaid upon Marie's story. In sum, Susan and Marie's duet illustrates an invitation for First Nations history to be spoken (Susan after all *asks* Marie to tell her story) that then denies that history an auditor as it becomes a mere pretence for Susan's own nostalgia. Below the duet's placid surface we thus encounter a disturbing example of Susan's exscription of Marie's voice through the *semblance* of dialogue. Such a reading is supported by examining the displacement between synchronic and diachronic alignment of Susan and Marie's statements.

When Marie states that "before the white man came, Okanagan Indians knew no shame" Susan, in quick succession to Marie's statement sings "O can we keep it so," but immediately follows this with "this valley cool, in winter white with snow, in summer a blue bowl." Consequently, it is unclear for the listener whether the statements should be understood as "can we keep the Okanagan Indians from living lives without shame?" or "can we keep this valley cool, beautiful, and fruitful?" The answer is given at the opera's conclusion, at which point Susan repeats this phrase, but in reverse order, singing "this valley cool. In winter white with snow, in summer a blue bowl. O can we keep it so?" The inversion of the statement works to confirm that Susan is indeed more concerned with retaining the beauty of the lake than with helping the Okanagan First Nations characters from living lives "without shame."

Susan's interest in keeping the valley picturesque and productive is further evidenced when we consider the language by which Livesay has Susan articulate this perspective. Susan's hope that their arrival in the valley has not created a negative

256   *Opera Indigene: Re/presenting First Nations and Indigenous Cultures*

disturbance is moderately positive, but she voices this statement in tentative, uncertain language: "but I hope we come here not to destroy, greedy for gold," as if she is unsure of her own intentions. Susan also responsibly declares that "the future of this land lies in our hand." While at first glance this statement reinforces the sense of responsibility that Susan feels, musically, emphasis is placed on the ending of the statement, elongating the words "... *land ... our hand*," and thus reinforces a sense of possession. Additionally, the phrase's ending is set in a higher range than the rest of the phrase, with a crescendo and pitch climax on the word "our." The statement also links the words "land" and "hand" in rhyme, and consequently constructs a possessive image of the land held within the pioneer's grasp. Lastly, the statement is sung simultaneously with Marie's phrase "up rose Na'aitka" suggesting an association between Na'aitka's arrival and the Allison's possession of the land (see Example 13.3).

Pentland notates the vocal parts in a way that further reinforces the discontinuity of the relationship between the Okanagan people and pioneers. That the vocal lines are written in two different time signatures, with Susan singing in 2/4 while Marie

Example 13.3   *The Lake*, "Up rose Na'aitka"

sings in 6/8, suggests that the characters are singing simultaneous arias (in contrast to a shared duet). Moreover, this form of notation provides an apt metaphor for the split between the characters' worldviews. Just as the characters' narrative perspectives are in contrast, each character's melodic line here emphasizes time in a different way. Although each measure could be said to contain the same total amount of "time"—that that the characters share the same objective reality, or have the same amount of time to express themselves—the way time is apportioned by each character emphasizes the distinctiveness of each voice or worldview. While Susan divides her time into double meter (emphasising her statements in groups of two), Marie divides her time into triple meter.

In conclusion, I would like to address the resistance this work has faced in receiving a full staging. Prospective producers seem to have rejected proposals that would see the premiere of this work on grounds that its simplistic depictions of the Okanagan First Nations characters endorses a negative portrayal of First Nations culture in general. Producers may likely have been reluctant to stage the work for fear of offending audience members by the derogatory representations of First Peoples. However, I would like to reiterate here that the lack of interest in producing this work may have less to do with the unfavorable characterization of the First Nations characters Marie and Mac than with the unfavorable characterization of the settlers themselves, and Pentland and Livesay's critical representation of settlement history. Susan and John Allison are, as I have described, quite far from the typical heroic, infallible characters encountered within pre-centenary Canadian artistic practices that depict pioneers' struggles in taming the Canadian landscape. In the Canadian mythological imaginary that prides itself on the hardship and struggle of Canadian settlers battling against nature, Pentland and Livesay's *The Lake* stands out as a work that does not idealize Susan and John Allison nor present their interaction with First Nations characters as fully positive. *The Lake* instead provides us with a critical portrait of Susan and John's inability to enter into dialogues in which they listen to and reflect on Marie and Mac's beliefs. This disjunction is perhaps most evident in the opera's conclusion, in which Susan and John sing about their future on the land: "And let our children grow to [love and] nurture it from wilderness to golden fruitfulness." Here John's avoidance of the word "love" betrays his continued desire to make the land productive at the expense of respect for the Okanagan peoples' perspectives. We are left with the persistence of a settler worldview that separates knowing the land from a love and respect for it. *The Lake*'s conclusion in fact encapsulates the sharp contrast between word and deed that I have sought to examine in this chapter. The audience is presented with an idyllic portrait of the settlers, standing together looking over the lake as the sun rises and Susan feels the first signs of labor. Yet this image, full of hope, once again contrasts the connotations of John's statement that separates knowing the land from a love and respect for it, and here stands again as a final index of the disjuncture between word and image that Livesay and Pentland seek to effect throughout the opera.

Chapter 14

The Politics of Genre: Exposing Historical Tensions in Harry Somers's *Louis Riel*

Colleen L. Renihan

We [do not create] tension. We merely bring to the surface the hidden tension that is already alive.

Martin Luther King Jr.

In previous analyses of historically based operas in Canada, very little has been made of the ways in which the operatic genre creates, enhances, subverts and/ or distorts the historical narratives brought forth in these works. In the words of historian Hayden White, "narrative, far from being merely a form of discourse that can be filled with different contents, real or imaginary as the case may be, already possesses a content ... ; this 'content of the form' of narrative discourse in historical thought [must be] examined."[1] If we follow White's advice and unpack the political and cultural content of the operatic genre in Canadian operas based on First Nations history, several previously controlled tensions are revealed, and previously silenced historical voices are heard. Through an examination of one of Canada's most historically and culturally significant operas, *Louis Riel*, written by playwright Mavor Moore and "Canada's darling of composition"[2] Harry Somers for the Canadian Centennial in 1967, I examine the ramifications of genre on the representation of this extraordinary figure in Canadian history.[3] I approach *Louis Riel* with an ear tuned to issues of hegemony, and to the tensions between Riel's First Nations anti-hero status and the conventions of the operatic genre itself. What does this operatic representation offer Riel's memory? Do questions regarding the inherent implications of operatic convention limit the way in which

---

[1]   Hayden White, *The Content of the Form* (Baltimore, MD: Johns Hopkins University Press, 1987), p. xi.

[2]   Harry Somers, Composer Portraits Series CD. Centrediscs Canada, 2007.

[3]   The opera *Louis Riel* is based on John Coulter's 1950 play entitled *Riel: A Play in Two Parts* (Toronto, 1962), which, incidentally, has been credited with starting what historian Albert Braz has termed the infamous and still thriving "Riel Industry." Based on the success of the former play, Coulter produced two later plays, *The Crime of Louis Riel* and *The Trial of Louis Riel*, both in 1968—a year after *Louis Riel* the opera was premiered at the O'Keefe Centre in Toronto.

260   *Opera Indigene: Re/presenting First Nations and Indigenous Cultures*

we can approach works such as *Louis Riel* in contemporary Canadian society? In what follows, I argue that by isolating the tensions produced by the juxtaposition of operatic convention and Riel's identity as a Métis anti-hero we might begin to interpret the elements of conflict and convergence between First Nations and Western cultural voices in the opera. By unveiling the sites of tension in the work where expressions of Riel's Métis heritage and the operatic genre's conventions conflict, we can begin to view *Louis Riel* as part of an ongoing project of decolonization in Canada—as a site where the tensions between past and present, East and West, French and English, First Nations and European are not obscured, but rather positioned in such a way that they might be creatively explored and thus newly understood.

Louis Riel and Canadian History

The story of the opera is based on the post-Confederation Métis uprisings of 1867–1870 and 1884–1885 in what were Canada's Northwest Territories (what are now the provinces of Manitoba and Saskatchewan). This is one of the most contested chapters in Canadian history, primarily because the country entered into Confederation in 1867—an event preceded and followed by a time when the relationship between Canada's First Nations peoples and European settlers was most disastrously strained, the effects of which still resonate powerfully with Canadians. Both groups had differing views on land ownership and, most importantly, on the nature and conditions of national unity. Louis Riel was the charismatic leader of the Canadian Métis[4] peoples on the prairies—a mystic, who was central to their establishing a provisional government for the province of Manitoba. Because of his strong opposition to Canada's first Prime Minister, John A. Macdonald, and to Confederation, Riel was exiled to Montana for several years, but eventually returned, passionately raising Métis grievances to the Canadian government in 1885. This unsuccessful mission led to the tragic Northwest Rebellion, where British and French soldiers arrived from the East in a deadly attack on the Métis people at Batoche. Riel was eventually hanged for high treason, but his impassioned legacy looms large in the Canadian national imagination.

    Louis Riel is one of the most popular and complex figures in Canadian history, a man whose conflicting representations in literature, painting, sculpture, poetry, music, and theater render him a strangely appropriate representative of the fragmented and conflicted Canadian identity. According to Canadian composer R. Murray Schafer, Louis Riel is the archetypal Canadian hero because of the fact

---

   [4] The Métis people are descendants of interracial marriages between Indigenous peoples and Europeans (the word Métis is derived from the Spanish *mestizo*, meaning "mixed race"). They are one of the many Indigenous groups that make up the First Peoples of Canada.

The Politics of Genre   261

that he "personifies the dissonance at the root of the Canadian temperament."[5] He also, as I will argue, demonstrates the dissonance at the root of many operatic historical representations, and also the veiled tensions in operatic juxtapositions of First Nations culture and Western culture. In the opera, we gain insight into the man's inner conflict, and into its broader social implications, as the historical Riel inhabits and also resists the tropes of operatic characterization. The operatic Riel is presented simultaneously as both hero and anti-hero, as Canadian and non-Canadian, and, curiously, as both operatic and non-operatic. For the purpose of my discussion, I will seek out moments of genre-related tension in the work, moments where Riel's operatic nature somehow defies his own cultural and political beliefs. Historian Dominick LaCapra makes a related argument for the isolation of sites of resistance in historical works, insisting, "it must be actively recognized that the past has its own 'voices' that must be respected, especially when they resist or qualify the interpretations we would like to place on them. A text is a network of resistances."[6] The resistances within the historical narrative of *Louis Riel* might suggest, as La Capra intimates, that there are voices in the story that have yet to be heard.

Redefining Nationalist Formulations: *Louis Riel* in Context

Canada's cultural and economic goals in 1967 affected not only the cultural prominence of the work at the time of its creation, but also its meaning in national terms. The most significant cultural force surrounding the work's production and reception was the Canadian Centennial celebration in 1967, for which *Louis Riel* was created. The opera was commissioned by the Floyd S. Chalmers Foundation, produced by the Canadian Opera Company, and supported through financial assistance from the Canadian Centennial Commission, the Canada Council and the Province of Ontario Council for the Arts. Because of these sanctioned political associations, audiences and critics carried lofty expectations for the opera's ability to be representative of Canada at a time when looking carefully back and hopefully forward were central to the process of defining a national identity. Geographical unity was still of primary importance in Canada in the 1960s, as was the issue of establishing a common ground between Anglophone and Francophone groups— Canada's competing colonizers. With the perilous situation in Quebec, national unity was paramount.[7] *Louis Riel* highlights issues of national cohesion and

---

[5] R. Murray Schafer, *On Canadian Music* (Indian River, ON: Arcana Editions, 1984), p. 49.

[6] Dominick LaCapra, *Rethinking Intellectual History: Texts, Context, Language* (Ithaca, NY: Cornell University Press, 1983), p. 64.

[7] Quebec experienced the famous "Quiet Revolution" during the 1960s, which resulted in a modernization and secularization of French Canadian society, followed by an increase in confidence and the desire for independence. The terrorist group Front de

262 *Opera Indigene: Re/presenting First Nations and Indigenous Cultures*

regionalism, and exposes the tensions in the very idea of Canadian nationalism, by placing East and West in opposition, and by resonating loudly with First Nations concerns about the nature of this national unity. Intriguingly, through a multifaceted resistance to the traditional marginalization of Indigenous cultures in the image of our national identity, the opera relates uneasily to the nationalist project for which it was created. Riel's mission, after all, involved orchestrating a defiant opposition to Canadian Confederation, rendering his heroic role in the 1967 Centennial opera highly ironic. Mary Ingraham duly notes that the domains affecting Canadian cultural production in general demand consideration of... [the contradictions inherent in] the production and consumption of culture in relation to power structures and the tensions of conflicting [political] interests [...]."[8] While the relationship between political influence and artistic creation in *Louis Riel* seems at first to be one of compatibility, the creators managed, subversively as I propose, to use the work as a vehicle for cultural and political commentary at this significant historical moment. Other reactions to the revisited issue of Canadian unity in 1967 were less subtle; events of the Centennial celebrations—specifically Montreal's *Expo 67* at which *Louis Riel* was performed—were sites of protest for minority groups including First Nations peoples, who insisted that the Centennial celebrations represented a further indoctrination of British land claims, merely a reminder of past struggles.[9] As Linda and Michael Hutcheon have noted, "it was [undeniably] a moment of high English-Canadian nationalism," their statement flagging the most prominent problem concerning many cultural products of this era.[10] As *Louis Riel* demonstrates, the political concerns surrounding Canada's Confederation of 1867 found parallels in the concerns of the Centennial, and go to the heart of First Nations issues in contemporary Canadian society as well. The unique contradictions between the commissioned nature of the opera and the cultural work that *Louis Riel* engages in suggests that we have more to gain in confronting, rather than suppressing, the work's inherent tensions.

Libération du Québec (FLQ) gained momentum during this time, leading to the fateful October Crisis in 1970.

[8] Mary Ingraham, "Something to Sing About: A Preliminary List of Canadian Staged and Dramatic Music Since 1867," *Intersections*, 28/1 (2007), p. 20.

[9] Olive Dickason, *Canada's First Nations: A History of Founding Peoples from Earliest Times* (Norman: University of Oklahoma Press, 1992). Dickason describes how *Expo 67* in Montreal provided First Nations peoples with a forum at which to "publicly express for the first time on a national scale, dissatisfaction with their lot" (p. 375).

[10] Linda Hutcheon and Michael Hutcheon, "Imagined Communities: Postnational Canadian Opera," in *The Work of Opera: Genre, Nationhood, and Sexual Difference*, ed. Richard Dellamora and Daniel Fischlin (New York: Columbia University Press, 1995), p. 3.

The Significance of Operatic Convention

The tensions between genre and subject in *Louis Riel* are indicative of the inherent promise of investigating the nature of the historical narratives created in Canadian opera. They also suggest that historical opera in Canada may operate differently than it does and has in other national traditions. Somers and Moore seem to have approached the work not only with a fascination for certain aspects of Riel's story, but also with an interest in exploring operatic convention. Like Riel, they had a mission. In the words of Moore, "The goal was not simply to put Riel's story to music, but, rather, to use the conventions and traditions of Grand Opera as a form of nation-building, a platform for discovering who we are."[11] This is deeply telling; since both Somers and Moore were interested in the Riel story for its potential to make national statements via the operatic genre specifically, it seems only fitting to consider the success of these goals based on a close analysis of opera's conventional features. "I would love to create legend," said Somers, intimating some level of belief in unconventional narrative constructs, and in the possibilities that he saw in opera for this purpose.[12] While Riel is established as a hero, however—as Linda Hutcheon points out—"From the very first scene, Canada is the villain of the piece."[13] Creating a narrative structure by which Canada itself is the anti-hero is of course exceedingly problematic, to say the least, in an opera commissioned to celebrate the nation's Centennial, and supported by the Canadian government. Between Riel's apparent status as hero and his revolutionary desire to oppose British colonial structures, the opera's protagonist is a conflicted historical character. The genre, as I will argue, is directly—yet curiously—implicated in this conflict.

Historians such as Alun Munslow, Keith Jenkins, and Hayden White have recently argued for the importance of a close analysis of genre in historical narratives—in the actual *mode* of historical telling.[14] As an extension of their work, we might consider the operatic genre, the actual "story space governing its mode of expression,"[15] to offer important cultural clues to the stories it tells. Many of the tensions within *Louis Riel* arise from the norms of a genre that is itself an immigrant on Canadian soil, through elements that govern the identity of

---

[11] Mavor Moore, quoted in Richard Turp, "Louis Riel: Harry Somers' Canadian Grand Opera Revived at McGill University," *Opera Canada*, 46/1 (Spring 2005), pp. 24–7, p. 24.

[12] Somers, quoted in Eitan Cornfield, "A Documentary of Harry Somers," *Composer Portraits Series* CD (Centrediscs, 2006).

[13] Linda Hutcheon, "Opera and National Identity: New Canadian Opera," *Canadian Theatre Review*, 96 (Fall 1998), p. 6.

[14] See Keith Jenkins, *Re-thinking History* (New York: Routledge, 1991); Alun Munslow, *Deconstructing History* (New York: Routledge, 2006); and White, *The Content of the Form*.

[15] Alun Munslow, *Narrative and History* (New York: Routledge, 2006), p. 28.

264   *Opera Indigene: Re/presenting First Nations and Indigenous Cultures*

the genre itself. In order to define these elements, I adopt Herbert Lindenberger's framework from *Opera the Extravagant Art*, in which he associates the notion of the operatic "with such terms as histrionic, extravagant, gestural, ceremonial, and performative ..."[16] I would add a history of nationalist tendencies, as well as a direct affiliation with the European tradition, to Lindenberger's list. This self-reflexive employment of genre, what Linda Hutcheon has identified as a parodic mode of self-conscious representation, is evident on many levels in *Louis Riel*.[17] In Act II, Scene 4, for example, Somers notes in the score that the character playing Dr. John Schultz, a leader of the governmental troupe sent to arrange the settlement of the Red River valley, is to sing with "a voice at times melodramatic lieder, at times declamatory grand opera."[18] Associating the unfavorable character of Schultz with an ostentatious style of singing demonstrates that Somers and Moore were undoubtedly conscious of the genre's political and cultural implications, and that, to them, the genre may well have reached an inescapably self-referential point, prompted here by the need to express historical voices that can no longer be silenced. In this way, opera is revealed as a fraught cultural product, its aesthetic conventions being repeatedly and purposefully challenged in *Louis Riel*. For this reason, I pause to consider the problematic nature of representing Métis history through a genre that creates meaning by way of its unavoidably Western narrative constructs. Canadian composer R. Murray Schafer has suggested that "Opera is an aristocratic experience, far removed from the hearts of a people working close to the land in an attempt to open up a new country ... it seems thrust on [people] from 'above' or 'abroad'."[19] How, then, can we interpret Riel's interaction with the genre in a way that advances both the unifying, nationalistic goals of the work as well as the identity-affirming goals of Riel for his people? I will continue my consideration of the ways in which the genre contributes to these narratives by examining additional points of tension in the work, and how the implications of genre take on new meaning in each instance, beginning with an examination of Somers's use of musical quotation.

Quotation: Reinterpreting Subaltern Voices

The musical quotations that Harry Somers has employed in *Louis Riel* inadvertently highlight the work's operatic elements, and increase the complexity of the work's

---

[16]   Herbert Lindenberger, *Opera the Extravagant Art* (Ithaca, NY: Cornell University Press, 1984), p. 76.

[17]   Linda Hutcheon, *A Poetics of Postmodernism* (New York: Routledge, 1988).

[18]   Harry Somers, *Louis Riel*. Libretto by Mavor Moore with Jacques Languirand, score, 1967, photocopies of manuscripts in the possession of the Canadian Music Centre, Full Orchestra. Act II, Scene 4.

[19]   R. Murray Schafer, *The Public of the Music Theatre, Louis Riel: A Case Study* (Vienna: Universal Edition, 1972), p. 7.

The Politics of Genre   265

meanings; they render the work intertextual, even intercultural, aligning it in some ways with the concept of the Canadian mosaic. These non-operatic references suggest that Somers and Moore were interested in broadening the meaning of the work, and in reforming or at least questioning the historical narrative by bringing other voices into it. The quotations simultaneously challenge the nature of the genre and highlight it by setting the atonal musical "ground" (as Andrew Zinck has referred to it)[20] as well as characteristic operatic elements, along with their aesthetic associations, against a contrasting idiom—a folk one, in many instances. The opera begins with an adaptation of "Riel sits in his chamber o' state," an unaccompanied folksong that is not sung live, but broadcast into the theater on pre-recorded four-track quadraphonic tape.[21] The melody, written by Alexander Hunt Murray, was originally sung by Canadian soldiers marching on Fort Garry in 1870.[22] In Somers's adaptation, the lively march becomes a slow, modal, and haunting melody sung by a solo tenor, and the recording features electronic sounds that distort the simple tune. Native-inspired ornamentation such as lower grace notes, *trillo* figures, and descending glissandi at the ends of phrases are specified in the score, rendering the song's origins ambiguous through a tension that involves both its textual and musical layers. The tape medium contradicts what we interpret to be the traditionally authentic goals of the folk aesthetic (as well as operatic convention). In the folk genre, we expect an intimate encounter with the song, and we expect the song to be delivered in a personalized manner by an individual folksong singer, both of which are betrayed by the taped and electronically broadcast nature of the song. The aforementioned Native-inspired layer of ornamentation also seems strange, foreshadowing the problematic combination of First Nations and European traditions in the opera, and setting up the cultural and historical tensions in the work (see Example 14.1).

Additional quoted material appears throughout the work, such as Ontario hymn tunes, and two Indian dances in the introduction to Act II, Scene 6, the second of which is the "Buffalo Hunt" from Margaret Arnett MacLeod's collection in *Songs of Old Manitoba* (see Example 14.2). [23] In addition to the words being translated into English for MacLeod's collection, the song was also musically altered from its original in order to render the dance more "primitive." The additive metrical organization, the modal setting, the a-metrical accents of the hand-clapping in the second system, and the composer's indication that it should be sung by "a lyric

---

[20]   Andrew Zinck, "Music and Dramatic Structure in the Operas of Harry Somers" (PhD dissertation, University of Toronto, 1996).

[21]   Interestingly, Harry Somers himself appeared as the singer on the tape used in the original production.

[22]   Margaret Arnett MacLeod, *Songs of Old Manitoba* (Toronto: Ryerson Press, 1960), p. 50.

[23]   "The Buffalo Hunt" uses a text written by Pierre Falcon, renowned Métis songwriter who was known as the "bard of the Prairie Métis" (Lillian Buckler, "The Use of Folk Music in Harry Somers's opera Louis Riel." MMus. thesis, University of Alberta, 1984, p. 26).

Example 14.1 *Louis Riel* Introduction ("Riel sits in his chamber o'state")

baritone with a tenor quality" demonstrate the composer's intentions to evoke a primitive indigenous culture.[24]

Somers also situates the opera's story historically through music by quoting several popular songs from the era, such as the uniquely tonal Métis song "Est-il rien sur la terre (Le Roi Malheureux)" in Act I, Scene 2 and Act II, Scene 2, and "Orangemen Unite" in Act II, Scene 4, which features an onstage band that is instructed to play very badly. The song "We'll Hang him up the River"—which was included even in John Coulter's original play, on which the opera was based—appears in numerous instances, including Act II, Scene 4 and even in a concealed canon in the orchestra in Act II, Scene 5, creating an Ivesian effect of altering the folk aesthetic by transforming it through a heavily manipulated compositional device.

---

[24] Somers, *Louis Riel*, Act II, Scene 6. The choice to use a baritone for this high-tessitura piece was likely an attempt to imitate the high-pitched, falsetto singing voices of First Nations powwow singers through the indications in the score. Its performance by a trained operatic singer further highlights the tensions between operatic convention and First Nations culture.

Example 14.2 *Louis Riel* Act II, Scene 6 (Dance: "The Buffalo Hunt")

The most notable external musical reference—because of its length and its significance as actual First Nations cultural property—is the lullaby, "Kuyas," which Marguerite, Riel's American wife, sings to her baby in Act III, Scene 1.

268 *Opera Indigene: Re/presenting First Nations and Indigenous Cultures*

"Kuyas" is based on a five-note motif from the "Song of Skateen," a Nisga'a song from northern British Columbia—not of the Montana Métis, as the opera implies.[25] Aside from "Kuyas," the non-operatic quotations are mostly tonal, creating contrast in their juxtaposition with the atonal "ground," as well as with each other. The juxtaposition of musical languages from contrasting geographical milieus and characters demonstrates the larger-level cultural tensions with which the opera is concerned.

Operatic Lyricism Reclaimed?

Perhaps the most significant aspect of Riel's interaction with the generic conventions of opera is through the highly lyrical mode of self-expression given to him by Somers, which supports the image of Riel as an obstreperous religious fanatic. Of the hundreds of representations intended to capture the essence of Riel, this image seems to be the most prominent, since it is used to explain Riel's erratic behavior, that of a "mystic madman" as he has often been represented.[26] Many authors have been drawn to this particular rendering of the Riel story, perhaps more than any other interpretation, but none has validated it to the extent that the opera does. Steeped in a tradition where presenting supernatural elements, divine inspiration and emotional expressiveness are the norm, the opera expresses this particular aspect of Riel perhaps too easily, inevitably endorsing his emotionalized character.[27] In contrast to Eastern Canadian characters such as Prime Minister Macdonald and Thomas Scott, who express themselves in a rhythmic speech-song style, Riel often succumbs to an exaggerated and effusive vocal style in his arias, characterized by highly lyrical and melismatic vocal lines.[28] In an aria from Act I, Scene 4, Riel sings in a raw emotional manner, with virtuosic exclamations that push the

---

[25]   The "Song of Skateen" was collected and notated by Sir Ernest MacMillian and Marius Barbeau. In an interview about Somers's composition of the opera, Barbara Chilcott recalls the choice of the piece for this scene, explaining how she convinced Somers to use it because of "the Indian connection; it's in Cree; and it's talking about long ago..." Incidentally, Somers did not feel that this was problematic. The piece features accents by flute, sleigh bells, tom-tom, and bass drum (Somers, Composer Portraits Series).

[26]   Thomas Flanagan's controversial *Louis 'David' Riel: Prophet of the New World* expresses an anti-Métis agenda similar to Donald Creighton's account in *The Story of Canada*, positing Riel as a religious fanatic who is motivated by his own greed. See, for example, Thomas Flanagan, *Louis 'David' Riel: 'Prophet of the New Worl'* (Toronto, ON: University of Toronto Press, 1996); and Donald Creighton, *The Story of Canada* (Toronto, ON: Faber and Faber, 1975).

[27]   The negative connotations of Riel's effusive lyricism echo Catherine Clément's argument in her book *Opera, or the Undoing of Women*, trans. Betsy Wing (Minneapolis: University of Minnesota Press, 1988).

[28]   Brian Cherney, *Harry Somers* (Toronto, ON: University of Toronto Press, 1975), p. 132.

Example 14.3 *Louis Riel* Act I, Scene 4 (Aria: "Dieu! O mon Dieu!")

limits of the singer's vocal range (see Example 14.3). Carolyn Abbate's argument for the inherently triumphant nature of the pure, unaccompanied operatic voice attributes it the power that I believe it holds here, as we witness Riel's "undefeated voice speak across the crushing plot."[29] Although Riel's emotionalized expression is primarily focused on religious fervor here, his zealousness is understood to also

---

[29] Carolyn Abbate, *Unsung Voices: Opera and Musical Narrative in the Nineteenth Century* (Princeton, NJ: Princeton University Press, 1991), p. ix. The parallels with

270   *Opera Indigene: Re/presenting First Nations and Indigenous Cultures*

address the national cause to which he is equally devoted. His religious zeal and national passion are one in the opera, and most significantly, they are normalized by the genre.

In this aria, as Riel imagines himself to be the reincarnation of the prophet David, he both reaffirms his identity as religious fanatic, and also aligns himself with a lineage of operatic heroes who are driven by passion or madness to sing themselves into a frenzy.[30] Donna Zapf has identified similar incidents as representative of the opera's tendency to universalize the character of Riel beyond historical specificity, thereby, I would argue, confirming the strangely heroic and operatic nature of his mission and of his character.[31] This aria demonstrates how lyricism, a vehicle of subjectivity in operatic expression, presents an important source of genre-related tension in Riel's operatic expression. The reclaiming of Riel's effusive and emotional character is one of the most significant revisionist contributions of the opera to the so-called "Riel industry."

Electronic Music: Operatic Traditions Reconfigured

Riel's operatic nature is established further through the contrast between his lyrical vocal expression and the electronic elements in the score. The use of electronically mediated voices and recorded sound in the opera exemplifies Somers's manipulation of both the foundations and limits of the genre, in an attempt to create genre-related tension at moments of high dramatic tension, such as the prologue and battle scene. His original intention involved "presenting the audience with a totally unfamiliar sound,"[32] and also rendering operatically trained voices powerless when confronted with electronic sound. These pre-recorded sounds, subversive of operatic subjectivity, place Riel in a position where he is forced literally to compete with them, rendering his operatic lyricism more traditional by comparison. At one point during the creation of the opera, in fact, Somers had

---

Catherine Clément's argument in *Opera, or The Undoing of Women*, transl. Betsy Wing (Minneapolis: U. Minnesota Press, 1988) are instructive here.

[30]   In fact, the operatic mad scene exemplifies a very typical convention of the genre. These infamous mad scenes to which I refer appear in many bel canto works such as Donizetti's *Lucia di Lammermoor* and *Anna Bolena*, Bellini's *I puritani* and *La sonnambula*, Verdi's *Macbeth*, and even Britten's *Peter Grimes*. The tensions arising from the predominantly female gendered nature of this trope are striking, and they contribute, I would argue, to Riel's othering in the work. I am grateful to Professor Emeritus Andrew Hughes at the University of Toronto for sharing his research and ideas on operatic madness with me.

[31]   Donna Zapf, "Singing History, Performing Race: An Analysis of Three Canadian Operas: *Beatrice Chancy*, *Elsewhereless*, and *Louis Riel*" (PhD dissertation, University of Victoria, 2005).

[32]   Quoted in Cherney, *Harry Somers*, p. 134.

The Politics of Genre 271

hoped to pit Riel against a cacophony of electronically sampled sounds in what would (if it had materialized) have been a true operatic nightmare:

> In the Trial Scene, I want to achieve something Kafka-ish rather than literal: the prosecuted man who really doesn't understand the frame of reference he's in. I want voices from the speakers, sometimes totally distorted, to sound various statements and accusations, while Riel keeps trying to sing over and through them to make his statement.[33]

This quotation again shows Somers's forthright desire to place the genre itself at the center of the conflict. Similarly, in the final scene of the opera, the chorus, undeniably the driving center of nationalist tendencies in nineteenth-century operatic works (and in nationalist works), is entirely removed and is replaced by a taped chorus. Genre-subverting manipulations such as these only serve to render Riel's emotional, subjective, and undeniably heroic actions increasingly operatic. Through the manipulation of musical and genre-related tensions, Somers and Moore are able to destabilize, and thereby vindicate, the character of Riel in the opera.

New Essentializing Toolboxes? Issues of Musical Representation

Critiques of the musical representation of First Nations peoples in art music have been relatively few, and most have been directed at the lexicon of essentializing primitive musical elements that have been used to depict indigeneity.[34] Although "primitive" musical signifiers—from the "ready-made toolbox of exotica," as Michael Pisani has defined it—were employed to a certain extent by Somers (for example, the musical modifications made to the "Buffalo Hunt," as mentioned above), I would like to suggest that these musical elements are not the most prominently problematic in terms of their representation of the Métis people.[35]

---

[33] Harry Somers, *Discussing the Score to Louis Riel*. LP booklet (CMC 24/25/2685), National Arts Centre Orchestra, (Washington, 1975), p. 9.

[34] I am thinking, for example, of the work of Michael Pisani and Tara Browner. In Browner's "'Breathing the Indian Spirit': Thoughts on Musical Borrowing and the 'Indianist' Movement in American Music," *American Music*, 15/3 (Autumn 1997), pp. 265–84, she identifies three varieties of Native American musical representation: symbolic, indexical, and iconic. In *Louis Riel*, we find all three: the tom-toms in the Introduction are indicative of battle and therefore symbolic; the Indian dances in Act II, Scene 6 attempt to approximate Native sounds and are therefore indexical; and the Tsimshian lullaby, "Kuyas," from Act III, Scene 1, is appropriated, using actual materials from Native music, and is therefore iconic.

[35] Michael Pisani, "'I'm an Indian Too': Creating Native American Identities in Nineteenth- and Early Twentieth-Century Music," in *The Exotic in Western Music*, ed. Jonathan Bellman (Boston, MA: Northeastern University Press, 1998), pp. 229–30.

272   *Opera Indigene: Re/presenting First Nations and Indigenous Cultures*

Rather, the atonal and serial techniques employed to represent Riel and his people seem to create equally problematic historical and genre-related issues. All scenes with Métis characters are depicted through an atonal musical "ground," and several of the principal characters, including Riel, are depicted through a serial language. Atonality and serialism, with their undeniable ties with the institutionalizing power of Western modes of thought and organization, resonate with a sense of cultural loss or assimilation of the First Nations peoples' own forms of cultural expression.[36] At first glance, the association of Riel and his people with an atonal musical language would seem appropriate, given that atonality originated as a musical approach that resisted conforming to the system of tonal hierarchies that characterized Western music between the seventeenth and nineteenth centuries.[37] Furthermore, Somers's employment of an avant-garde compositional technique in much of his music from the 1960s might also lead us to assume a sympathetic attitude toward his First Nations subjects, since it was an idiom that inspired him in many compositions from this time.[38] Despite this, however, we cannot dismiss the association of atonality with European values and power structures, and thus we cannot leave the atonal and serial representation of Riel and his people unquestioned. Its role in the high-modernist project, legitimized by the academy

---

[36]   Atonality and serialism were musical systems adopted by composers who were disenchanted with the tonal system of harmony at the beginning of the twentieth century. While compositional freedom was central to both techniques, both atonality and serialism (in particular) proved to be equally as restrictive for composers, and, more importantly, less accessible for the listener. These techniques, relegated to elite educational institutions in the United States, were thus regarded as the European-based trends that contributed to the creation of the utmost elite compositional stream in America in the early twentieth century.

[37]   Timothy Taylor's *Beyond Exoticism* (Durham, NC: Duke University Press, 2007) attributes the origins and structure of both tonality and opera (and their inherent conceptions of self and other) to the problematic enterprise of European colonialism. To quote Taylor, "Tonality arose to a long supremacy in western European music in part because it facilitated a concept of spatialization in music that provided for centers and margins, both geographically and psychologically" (p. 25). Interestingly, Taylor does not account for the representation of the "other" in modern musical idioms such as serialism, but one might infer its liberating or democratizing potential from his argument.

[38]   Parallels between *Louis Riel* and Schoenberg's *Moses und Aron* from the 1950s are limited, but striking nonetheless. The latter work was first staged in Zurich in 1957, and it is likely that Somers would have known about the event. Like *Louis Riel*, *Moses und Aron* is also concerned with the liberation of an oppressed people by a visionary figure. Though Somers didn't have the same kind of personal investment in the Métis narrative in *Louis Riel* that Schoenberg had in the Jewish message in *Moses und Aron*, both approached their subjects sympathetically, and both acknowledged and strategically manipulated the issues that atonality and excessive lyricism posed for their protagonists. The serial musical language and lyrical singing of Riel in Somers's opera, however, results in a more politically charged cultural product (in musical terms) than Schoenberg's, given the associations of these styles with those of the imperialistic cultural power that Riel felt was inimical to his people's identity.

in the mid-century, cannot be denied. According to Georgina Born, the musical avant-garde, "being no longer marginal and critical of the dominant order as in the early period of modernism, [has] failed to achieve wider cultural currency, [and therefore] remains an elite form of culture."[39] This particular manifestation of the musical avant-garde in opera, therefore, inhabits several hefty political contradictions. In a highly political opera about the struggles against imperialist expansion and influence, the atonal "ground" and Riel's serial language in the very least pose critical challenges for the work.

Riel's first row (Example 14.4) is characterized exclusively by interval classes 1 and 3, and is employed in a very vocally restrictive and relatively stringent construction in his arias, particularly in his first aria, "Au milieu de la foule" (see Example 14.5). It encompasses several of the more prominent motifs in the opera, most importantly the "lonely leader" motif, as Somers referred to it, which consists of a rising minor third followed by a falling semitone. This motif appears often in the flute (as it does in this excerpt), creating a dissonance between the serial organization of the musical language and the "primitive exotic" of its instrumentation, as Donna Zapf has observed.[40] In this aria, Riel's serially organized—yet operatically lyrical—lines thus create a tension that resonates politically and culturally.

Example 14.4   Riel Row 1

The musical characterization of Riel and his antithesis, Prime Minister Macdonald, presents perhaps the ultimate instance of Somers and Moore's sympathetic inclinations toward Riel. Somers initially pointed out the contrast between Riel's and MacDonald's style of delivery: "What I've done essentially is juxtaposed Riel and MacDonald. Riel always sings – I think the Romantic always sings. I think the political realist sings when necessary, but he uses a political form of speech."[41] Interestingly, though the Prime Minister's musical language is also atonal, his rhythmic profile defines him very differently than Riel's, in a more stylized and (foolishly) playful way (see Example 14.6).[42] The Prime

---

[39]   Georgina Born, *Rationalizing Culture: IRCAM, Boulez and the Institutionalization of the Musical Avant-Garde* (Berkeley: University of California Press, 1995), p. 4.

[40]   Zapf, "Singing History, Performing Race," p. 131.

[41]   Somers, Composer Portraits Series.

[42]   The musical depiction of MacDonald in contrast with Riel is important for my purposes. In the opera as a whole, the Canadian government in the "East," particularly Prime Minister Macdonald, is represented in tonal, popular music of the time—often in banal dance meters. As Eleanor Stubley has suggested, this music imitates "the intricate footwork of the dance that sustains the political machinery of Ottawa." Riel himself once

Example 14.5 *Louis Riel* Act I, Scene 2 (Aria: "Au Milieu de la foule")

Minister's vocal material, thought to reference a Victorian vaudeville mode, suggests a primarily popular style, whereas Riel's resonates within the more lyrical convention of operatic expressivity—Somers considered him, after all, to be "The Romantic."

---

observed that Cartier was "deceitful, false ... one mastered in the political waltz": Eleanor Stubley, *Louis Riel 2005, The Story*. Program notes for Opera McGill (Faculty of Music, McGill University, 2005).

Example 14.6 *Louis Riel* Act I, Scene 3 (Aria: Macdonald's "Sugar Aria")

276 Opera Indigene: Re/presenting First Nations and Indigenous Cultures

Conclusions: Reconceptualizing Tensions in Politicized Operatic Narratives

These points of conflict in *Louis Riel* raise aesthetic and historical questions regarding the complexities of the opera and the equivocal cultural work that it performs. The tensions that I have highlighted deny the work narrative closure, insisting that the intersection of nationalist agendas and First Nations culture in *Louis Riel* remain an open and fluid site for reflection and debate. As Jennifer Reid observes, "Across the broad range of ostensibly contradictory Riels, we find a myth that bears a distinct resemblance to the man ... and we may well discover that both the man and the myth provide an aperture through which we can discern the foundations for a collective narrative."[43] Notably, the operatic genre, as I suggest, is not an apolitical platform on which to examine this narrative; as David Levin has argued, "opera [as a genre] is unsettled."[44] Contemporary historical opera, rife with contradictions, frictions, and representational issues, has the ability to comment on cultural relationships and tensions, to present more subjectively focused and therefore sympathetic historical figures, and to further illuminate our conservatively constructed Canadian history. Indeed, acknowledging the cultural and political nature of the tensions in *Louis Riel* reveals new aspects to this chapter in Canadian and Métis history, thereby illuminating the advantages of examining our history through the operatic lens.

---

[43] Jennifer Reid, *Louis Riel and the Creation of Modern Canada* (Albuquerque: University of New Mexico Press, 2008), pp. 242–3.

[44] David J. Levin, *Unsettling Opera* (Chicago, IL: University of Chicago Press, 2007), p. 1.

PART V
New Creation and
Collaborative Processes

Chapter 15
Creating *Pimooteewin*

Robin Elliott

As I write this article about *Pimooteewin* (*The Journey*), the first opera set to a libretto in the Cree language, a touring production of the work is completing its ten-day tour of Northern Ontario.[1] On this tour, the opera has played to mixed First Nations and non-First Nations audiences, whereas the premiere production in Toronto played to a cosmopolitan but largely non-First Nations audience. The website of Soundstreams Canada, the Toronto-based company which commissioned *Pimooteewin* and brought it to the stage, has tracked the progress of the northern tour via a blog, an online video diary, and links to reviews, educational materials, and the libretto for the work.[2] *Pimooteewin*, then, is a vehicle that has allowed traditional Cree culture and storytelling to fuse not just with opera, but also with online social media and information sharing networks.

The tour of Northern Ontario has been accompanied by workshops for audiences ranging from pre-school children to high school students; the educational mandate is a central focus to the opera. The workshops are about music, storytelling, movement, and dance. In the course of this tour, hundreds of new stories about *Pimooteewin* and its own journey have emerged, some of them personal and known only to the individuals involved, and others attracting more attention. One

---

[1]   I wish to acknowledge with thanks the help provided by Lawrence Cherney and the Soundstreams Canada administrative team (in particular Catherine Boudreau and Leonie Hentschel) while I was writing this article. Cherney kindly agreed to speak with me about *Pimooteewin* over breakfast at By the Way Cafe on Bloor Street in Toronto on April 6, 2009. The Soundstreams team provided me with a copy of the score and libretto of the work, a DVD of the premiere production in Toronto (which I had attended in person on February 15, 2008), and other publicity and information materials including photos, reviews, biographies of the artists, and two versions of a study guide to the work – one prepared for workshops in Toronto schools, and a slightly different version used for schools in northern Ontario. The touring production opened in Moosonee on May 5, 2009, and continued to May 14, 2009 with visits to Moose Factory, Cochrane, Kapuskasing, Timmins, and Iroquois Falls. After this article was completed, a second tour of Northern Ontario opened on 23 April 2010 in Red Lake, and continued to 7 May 2010 with visits to Sioux Lookout, Thunder Bay, Wawa, and Red Rock. To date (May 2010), the opera has been performed in 14 communities before 7,500 audience members. In addition, 330 workshops have been presented to 6,000 school children in dozens of schools.

[2]   The URL for the web site is www.soundstreams.ca; the materials cited were available as of September 4, 2009.

280 *Opera Indigene: Re/presenting First Nations and Indigenous Cultures*

story that received widespread notice is that of Miyopin Cheechoo, an eight-year-old student at Bishop Belleau School in Moosonee, a town of 3,000 people on the southwestern shore of James Bay. Her mother tongue is Cree, and she enjoyed the fact that the opera was sung in her language, even though it is in a dialect quite different from her own. But she was interested in one aspect of the opera in particular. As an article in the *Toronto Star* newspaper reported, "Two and a half years ago she lost her little sister, and then her grandfather. In the opera, the spirits of the deceased are shown dancing and enjoying themselves on the far side of a river. On the car ride home after *Pimooteewin*, Miyopin told her mother that she thought her sister was probably 'dancing with her Mooshum (grandfather) on the other side of the river'."[3] Miyopin's response to the opera is, as we shall see, remarkably similar to a dream vision which led to the creation of the work.

Introduction

Pimooteewin (*The Journey*) was billed as "the first Cree opera" when it was premiered in Toronto in February 2008. It is sung in the Cree language, with a spoken narration in English and also surtitle projections that give a translation of the Cree text. The story concerns Weesageechak, the Trickster figure, who decides to visit the land of the dead with his best friend, Migisoo (the Eagle), to visit the spirits of those they love and bring them back to the land of the living. The spirits of the dead are captured in a basket, but on the long journey back they escape one by one. When Migisoo remarks that they should be allowed to bring the spirits back to life, Weesageechak replies:

> Mawch. Ig'wani igoosi, n'choowam. (No. Let it be, my friend)
> Igwani igootee tageeayachik. (They should stay there.)
> Ita kayachik kayasitinoowuk. (Where live the ancient ones.)
> Kitooteeminawuk. Kayasitinoowuk. (Our people. The ancient ones.)[4]

The work was created by the librettist Tomson Highway (Cree-Canadian,[5] the country's best-known First Nations playwright, and also a classically trained pianist), the composer Melissa Hui (born in Hong Kong, raised in North Vancouver from the age of eight, now living Montreal; a graduate of Yale University and from 1994 to 2004 a faculty member at Stanford University), and the choreographer Michael Greyeyes (Plains Cree, a former professional ballet dancer, and a faculty

---

[3] Paul Lantz, "The Spirit of the Opera is There, in Moosonee," *Toronto Star* (May 9, 2009), online edition.

[4] Tomson Highway, *The Journey (Pimooteewin)*, libretto (typescript, 2005), p. 10.

[5] Highway self-identifies as Cree-Canadian on the website of the Canadian Lesbian and Gay Archives, at www.clga.ca/npc/HighwayT-095.shtml (accessed December 21, 2010).

member at York University). This chapter examines the creative process that brought this work to the stage, and some of the genre issues that it raises.

Background

In 2003 Soundstreams Canada sponsored a Northern Voices Festival that was devoted to the theme of music theater and opera for young audiences. As part of the festival, there was a performance by Sandra Laronde's Red Sky theater company of *Caribou Song*, a play based on a children's book by Tomson Highway.[6] There were also panel discussions as part of the festival; one was on cross-cultural collaborations, and Tomson Highway and Melissa Hui were participants. Lawrence Cherney, artistic director of Soundstreams, has written that "It was obvious during the panel that the creative sparks were really flying between them. I had already asked Tomson if he would adapt an aboriginal myth that could be set to music, and on the spot Tomson, Melissa and I decided to collaborate to create and produce what would eventually become *The Journey*."[7]

Highway went on to write the libretto for the work in 2005,[8] drawing upon Cree storytelling traditions but also on a dream that he had had. In October 1990, his brother René, a professional dancer, was in a Toronto hospital, dying of AIDS-related causes. Highway held René in his arms, fell asleep, and had a dream that they were both in a boat heading toward a mist-enshrouded island. "On that island, only one of us was allowed to get off and it was him," Highway recalls. "I had no choice but to go back to the mainland in that boat by myself … [The dream] was a very powerful experience and I believe with every ounce of my being that René is still on that island, which is here, just in a different psychological space. I live every single day of my life for him."[9]

---

[6]   Tomson Highway, *Caribou Song / atíhko níkamon* (Toronto, ON: HarperCollins, 2001). Red Sky is "is a Toronto-based international performing arts company [that] shapes contemporary Aboriginal performance in dance, theater and music." www. redskyperformance.com. Information about the company's production of *Caribou Song*, with music by Rick Sacks, is available at http://www.redskyperformance.com/caribou-song-tomson-highway-family-theatre (accessed December 21, 2010).

[7]   Lawrence Cherney, "*The Journey*: Working with Long-Time Soundstreams Collaborators," *emuse* 14 (January, 2008), online at www.elmerisclersingers.com/pr_ emuse_jan08.html (accessed September 4, 2009).

[8]   There are two versions of the libretto, an initial longer version, and a final ten-page-long typescript that is labeled "second draft" (January 20, 2005). I have only seen the second, shorter version, which was kindly supplied to me by Soundstreams Canada. This version is also included in the Study Guide cited in n. 24.

[9]   Victoria Ahearn, "Tomson Highway's Libretto for Cree Opera Inspired by Real Life" (April 26, 2009). This Canadian press article appeared in *Macleans* and in numerous other print and online media, and is available at www.soundstreams.ca/press_area/in_the_ news_detail.php?id=34 (accessed December 21, 2010).

Much of Highway's creative work is bound up with the memory of his brother. Together, the two men created *The Sage, the Dancer and the Fool* (1984), a danced play about native mythologies and sexualities. Highway created the music for the play, and, as he told Noah Richler, "Now I play this piece each morning as part of my prayer for him. My brother dances with seagulls."[10] Similarly, Highway's novel *Kiss of the Fur Queen* is an evocative and compelling *roman à clef* that relates the story of two Cree brothers from northern Manitoba—Champion, later renamed Jeremiah (based on Highway himself), and his brother Ooneemeetoo, renamed Gabriel (base on René).[11] In the novel, as in real life, the boys are abused by priests at a residential school,[12] but go on to fulfill their destiny as artists: Champion/Tomson as a pianist and writer, Ooneemeetoo/René as a ballet dancer who dies young in a Toronto hospital. The Fur Queen character in the novel is one of many Trickster figures that appear in Highway's writings. Highway himself has often been described as a Trickster because of his often outrageous sense of humor, but it was his brother René who created the role of Nanabush, the Trickster in *The Rez Sisters*, the play that brought Highway to widespread attention when it was first performed in 1986.[13] In one sense, then, Weesageechak in *Pimooteewin* is an autobiographical portrait, and in another sense it is a tribute to Highway's brother René.

The Trickster and the Libretto

The Trickster figure is central to most Native North American storytelling traditions and belief systems. Highway notes that the Trickster is known as "Weesageechak in Cree, Nanabush in Ojibway, Itkomi in Sioux, Raven on the West Coast, Glooscap on the East, Coyote on the Plains."[14] Half-god and half-human, male and female simultaneously, the Trickster in modern First Nations literature is "at once a spiritual entity and a literary device for introducing narrative twists, jokes, and

---

[10]   Noah Richler, *This Is My Country, What's Yours: A Literary Atlas of Canada* (Toronto, ON: McClelland and Stewart, 2006), p. 126.

[11]   Tomson Highway, *Kiss of the Fur Queen* (Toronto, ON: Doubleday, 1998).

[12]   Highway alludes to this autobiographical fact—his sodomization by a priest at the age of eight—in the pointed conclusion to his otherwise light-hearted essay "Why Cree is the Sexiest of All Languages," in *Me Sexy: An Exploration of Native Sex and Sexuality*, ed. Drew Hayden Taylor (Vancouver, BC: Douglas & McIntyre, 2008), p. 40.

[13]   Tomson Highway, *The Rez Sisters: A Play in Two Acts* (Saskatoon, SK: Fifth House, 1988). This was Highway's sixth play, but the first to garner significant national and international attention. It won the Dora Mavor Moore Award for best new play and was nominated for a Governor General's Award. Nanabush is the Ojibway name for the Trickster.

[14]   Tomson Highway, "Why Cree is the Funniest of All Languages," in *Me Funny*, ed. Drew Hayden Taylor (Vancouver, BC: Douglas & McIntyre, 2005), p. 165.

Creating Pimooteewin 283

word games."[15] Highway has been a central figure in establishing the Trickster as one of the defining features of contemporary First Nations writing; together with Daniel David Moses and Lenore Keeshig-Tobias he founded the ironically titled "Committee to Re-Establish the Trickster" in 1986.[16] In his play *The Rez Sisters*, the Trickster (Nanabush) is a male dancer and the other seven main characters are all females; in *Dry Lips Oughta Move to Kapuskasing*, the sequel to *The Rez Sisters*, Nanabush is portrayed by a woman, and doubles with the one female role, while the other seven main characters are all men.[17] Despite recent critical controversies about the role of the Trickster in First Nations culture, the figure remains central to the work of Highway in general, and *Pimooteewin* in particular.[18]

Although the Trickster is in essence a humorous character, the humor is difficult to translate across cultures. A personal anecdote may help to demonstrate this. When I first read the Cree writer Paul Seesequasis's story "The Republic of Tricksterism," I found it to be a richly entertaining and amusing story which explores the comic potential of the conflicts and contradictions of those holding First Nations status in Canada.[19] However, after reading an essay by Janice Acoose and Natasha Beeds in which they explain—also in a very humorous fashion— their interpretation and understanding of Seesequasis's story, I realized that the humor of the story works on several different levels, and some of those levels are inaccessible to non-First Nations readers.[20]

---

[15] Penny van Toorn, "Aboriginal Writing," in *The Cambridge Companion to Canadian Literature*, ed. Eva-Marie Kröller (Cambridge: Cambridge University Press, 2004), p. 25.

[16] Daniel David Moses, "The Trickster's Laugh: My Meeting with Tomson and Lenore," *American Indian Quarterly*, 28/1–2 (2004), pp. 107–111.

[17] Tomson Highway, *Dry Lips Oughta Move to Kapuskasing* (Saskatoon, SK: Fifth House, 1989).

[18] The book *Troubling Tricksters: Revisioning Critical Conversations*, ed. Linda M. Morra and Deanna Reder (Waterloo, ON: University of Laurier Press, 2010) is a collection of essays that "provokes a re-visioning of trickster criticism in light of recent backlash against it." www.wlupress.wlu.ca/Catalog/morra.shtml (accessed July 15, 2009). Criticisms of trickster discourse have been wide-ranging; contentious issues include reductive generalizations that amount to essentialism ("all First Nations writers are trickster figures"), the prioritizing of cultural, as opposed to political, First Nations agendas ("let's talk about trickster figures instead of land titles"), and the facile conflation of trickster discourse with postmodern theories about the instability of all knowledge.

[19] Paul Seesequasis, "The Republic of Tricksterism," in *An Anthology of Canadian Native Literature in English*, ed. Daniel David Moses and Terry Goldie (Toronto, ON: Oxford University Press, 1998), pp. 411–16.

[20] Janice Acoose and Natasha Beeds, "Cree-atively Speaking," in *Me Funny*, ed. Drew Hayden Taylor (Vancouver, BC: Douglas & McIntyre, 2005), pp. 85–97. Their discussion of Seesequasis's story is on pp. 89–96. As a non-First Nations writer, I did not think it appropriate to call this essay "Cree-ating *Pimooteewin*," but after reading this essay by Acoose and Beeds, the temptation was certainly there.

284   *Opera Indigene: Re/presenting First Nations and Indigenous Cultures*

Highway himself is keenly aware of this untranslatable quality of Cree humor. He cites the Cree phrase "Neee, awi-nuk awa oota kaa-pee-pee-tig-weet," which can be translated into English as "Hey, who is coming in the door?" As Highway notes, the English version is not at all funny, "But in Cree, the sentence is not only funny, it is hysterical; one might even say there is a cartoonish quality to it ... And that is the visceral reality of the Cree language."[21] This may be one reason that the humor of *Pimooteewin* was largely lost on non-First Nations audiences. As one Toronto critic complained, "if you're expecting Highway's exuberant, rollicking humor, you will be disappointed. Lines such as 'I am walking' and 'I am flying' seemed pretty thin—at least in translation ... Although a Cree-speaker might appreciate qualities that went over my head, to me both the libretto and music suffer from emotional coolness."[22] In light of this criticism, the role of the Narrator can be seen as decidedly ambivalent. On the one hand, the Narrator helps to explain the text to non-Cree-speaking audience members, but, on the other hand, the lack of comprehension of the non-First Nations audience of the nuances of the humor in the libretto highlights the cross-cultural divide that no translation can surmount.

The text of *Pimooteewin* can be seen as fitting into two quite different literary traditions—that of the opera libretto and that of Cree narrative tales. It is the Cree oral storytelling tradition that is evidently the more pertinent of the two. In this connection, Highway has observed that there are three distinct terms for the concept of narrative in the Cree language:

> The first term is *achimoowin*, which means "to tell a story" or "to tell the truth." The second is *kithaskiwin*, which means "to tell a lie," meaning "to weave a web of fiction," as it were. And the third, which lies at a point exactly halfway between these first two is *achithoogeewin*, which means "to mythologize." Meaning that the visionaries of my people, the thinkers who gave birth and shape to the Cree language as we know it today, chose the exact halfway point between truth and lie, non-fiction and fiction, to situate mythology.[23]

Thus in terms of Cree oral literature, *Pimooteewin* is an example of *achithoogeewin*—stories which are neither true nor false, and are draw on elements of both fiction and non-fiction to tell essential truths about Cree culture.

In terms of its relationship to the European operatic libretto tradition, the most striking thing about *Pimooteewin* is that it is about a voyage to the land of the dead, just as several of the foundational works in the European operatic repertoire

---

[21]   Highway, "Why Cree is the Funniest," p. 163.

[22]   Tamara Bernstein, "A Chilly Cree Journey to the Afterlife," *Globe and Mail* (Toronto), February 18, 2008, online at www.elmeriselersingers.com/rev_18Feb08.html (accessed September 4, 2009).

[23]   Thomson Highway, *Comparing Mythologies* (Ottawa, ON: University of Ottawa Press, 2003), pp. 21–2.

are: Peri's *Euridice*, the earliest opera for which music survives (1600), Caccini's setting of the same libretto by Rinuccini (1602), and Monteverdi's *Orfeo* (1607). It is not clear whether or not Highway consciously drew on these European precedents in fashioning his libretto. But given his extensive training in classical music, I am inclined to think that he was well aware that he was placing *Pimooteewin* within a tradition of operatic tales of voyages to the land of the dead.

The Music

Once Highway's libretto had been completed, it was sent to Melissa Hui to be set to music. "The libretto was my direct source of inspiration and material," Hui notes. "I needed to listen intently to the rhythm of the Cree language so that I emphasize the right syllables in each word and I create the music that complements the rhythm of the text."[24] Initially Hui tried to set the libretto without having heard the Cree language spoken, using pronunciation guidelines that she got from Highway. But her concerns about capturing the correct rhythms, inflections, and durations of the text led her to request a recording of the text. "Tomson Highway read the whole libretto into my computer at a Montreal cafe while he was in town for an unrelated cabaret performance as the pianist of his trio," Hui has stated. "I believe Michael Greyeyes' father, a native Cree speaker, came to the performance and did understand it! So I was really gratified."[25]

The terms of the commission determined the instrumentation of the work: tenor and soprano soloists, narrator, SATB choir, flute/alto flute, oboe, percussion, violin, viola, cello, double bass. Included in the percussion complement are both non-Aboriginal instruments (tam-tams, gongs, cymbals, lion's roar) and Aboriginal ones (an Aboriginal drum and ankle rattles, the latter worn by choir members).

Initially, Hui thought of casting Weesageechak as a soprano soloist, but the role ended up being written for the tenor voice. This gender switch is entirely appropriate, given the nature of the Trickster. As Highway notes, "In Cree, the male-female-neuter hierarchy is entirely absent ... [Weesageechak] is theoretically neither exclusively male nor exclusively female, or is both simultaneously."[26] The composer's decision to make Weesageechak a tenor and Migisoo a soprano arose because of a duet in the opera when the Trickster sings "I am walking" and the eagle sings "I am flying." As Hui notes, "It occurred to me that the eagle had to sing the higher part and needed to be the soprano rather than the tenor. Sometimes the practicalities of the work determine the solutions."[27]

---

[24]   Leonie Hentschel, "An Interview with Melissa Hui," *Pimooteewin / The Journey: Study Guide* (Toronto, ON: Soundstreams Canada, 2009), p. 21, www.soundstreams.ca/images/Study_guide_The_Journey_final.pdf (accessed December 21, 2010).

[25]   Melissa Hui, email communication to the author, July 13, 2009.

[26]   Tomson Highway, "A Note on Nanabush," *Dry Lips*, p. 12.

[27]   Hentschel, *Pimooteewin* 2009, p. 21.

Hui created a haunting, somber score for the work which evokes the land of the dead. The instrumental scoring is sparse; the warm sounds of the violin and viola are absent from much of the work. Michael Greyeyes notes insightfully that "the music for this piece cannot be categorized easily. It is Canadian. It is northern ... this music is full of winter. The austerity of the music is like winter itself."[28] The work opens with sustained single-pitch pedals in the cello and viola, activated by a complex and recurring rhythmic pattern played pizzicato by the double bass; Hui states that her intention is "to create a lonely forlorn atmosphere ... the tone suggests grief and loss."[29] This opening music recurs at the end of the opera, some fifty minutes later. While one might be tempted to view this return to the opening music at the end of the opera as expressing the First Nations concept of time as circular rather than linear in nature (another example of essentializing and simplifying the variety and complexity of First Nations cosmologies), it could equally well be interpreted as arising from Hui's Chinese background. Mary Ingraham has noted that "[Hui] specifically acknowledges the role her Chinese heritage played in the "cyclical perception of time" expressed in her music. Hui's music is generally not goal-oriented or harmonically-based, as is much of our Western music."[30]

The Staging

Michael Greyeyes was charged with the responsibility of bringing *Pimooteewin* to the stage as the director/choreographer. He is Plains Cree, born and raised in Prince Albert, Saskatchewan. His parents spoke Cree at home, but did not teach the language to Michael, a fact about which he is philosophical rather than bitter. "A subtle twist of consciousness" is how he describes the loss of Cree language in his generation—he regards it as a legacy of the mindset instilled by the residential schools which his parents attended.[31] As he does not speak Cree, he sought help from his father about how to pronounce and understand the libretto of *Pimooteewin*. Highway's Swampy Cree dialect is different from the Plains Cree spoken by Greyeyes's parents; his father understood the libretto, but termed it "bush Cree" (as opposed to his own more "urbane" Cree).

---

[28] Hentschel, "An Interview with Michael Greyeyes," *Pimooteewin / The Journey: Outreach Study Guide* (Toronto, ON: Soundstreams Canada, 2008): 12–13. This earlier version of the study guide was supplied to me in hard copy by the publisher.

[29] Hentschel, *Pimooteewin* 2009, p. 21.

[30] Mary Ingraham, "Hui's Cultural Influences: Hong Kong to Canada," *Influences of Many Musics*, Canadian Music Centre web site, at www.musiccentre.ca/influences (accessed September 4, 2009).

[31] Michael Greyeyes, in conversation at a public talk about *Pimooteewin* hosted by Soundstreams Canada and held in the Bata Shoe Museum, Toronto, March 25, 2009.

Greyeyes, who trained as a dancer with the National Ballet of Canada and later as an actor (he has an MFA degree from Kent State University), decided that to make the action of the myth understandable to an audience who does not speak Cree, he would use the *kuroko* from Japanese kabuki theater. The *kuroko* are dressed in black, and so too are the singers in the choir, as they usually represent the souls of the dead. The three *kuroko* figures also manipulate props and puppets to portray physical elements (autumn leaves, the river, the basket) and characters (Weesageechak and Migisoo). "At times they're kind of enablers to Trickster and Eagle; other times they're kind of extensions to the Elmer Iseler Singers; other times they're working with puppets," Greyeyes notes.[32] In the northern Ontario touring production, which played in larger spaces than Toronto's Jane Mallett Theatre, the *kuroko* were given an enhanced dance role as well (see Figure 15.1). "Unusual means of staging might help audiences see our stories, our mythology in new ways. Mixing Japanese traditions with Cree mythology, to me, seems perfectly logical and natural."[33] Adding to the eclecticism of the production are the costume designs of Shawn Kerwin and the set and prop designs of Teresa Przybylski, both of which are modernist and not specific to any time period or cultural group.

Genre Issues

Calling *Pimooteewin* "the first Cree opera" was no doubt intended to target the work to as wide an audience as possible—to those interested in new music theater, in First Nations contemporary artistic performances, and in intercultural collaborations.[34] But was it really an opera? Those involved in the creation of the work seem to have divergent opinions.

In Hui's opinion, the work is an oratorio rather than an opera: "I'm not sure this is a new art form. I think of *The Journey* as an oratorio, a semi-staged dramatic work."[35] Hui had only written one short opera before *Pimooteewin*, a fifteen-minute-long work titled *The Cellar Door* (2002) created for Toronto's Tapestry New Opera Works; it is also scored for soprano and tenor soloists and chamber ensemble (though without choir). The word "opera" does not appear anywhere in the score of *Pimooteewin* that she produced.

Nor, for that matter, does Highway's libretto use the term opera; it simply gives the title of the work, without genre designation. Highway was drawn initially

---

[32]   CBC News staff, "Cree Opera *Pimooteewin* to Tour Northern Ontario: Huge Cast Hits the Road for Timmins, Cochrane, Moose Factory," *CBC News* online edition (April 3, 2009), www.cbc.ca/canada/toronto/story/2009/04/03/cree-opera.html (accessed December 21, 2010).

[33]   Hentschel, *Pimooteewin* 2008, p. 12.

[34]   The exoticization entailed in calling the work a Cree opera also played a crucial role in the marketing and reception of the work.

[35]   Hentschel, *Pimooteewin* 2009, p. 21.

Figure 15.1   From the Toronto premiere production of *Pimooteewin* at the Jane Mallet Theatre, February 2008: Tenor Bud Roach as Weesageechak, soprano Xin Wang as Migisoo, and two *kuroko* figures, with the Elmer Iseler Singers in the background

toward oratorio, rather than opera. When first approached by Cherney in 2003, Highway related that "he had always wanted to write a Cree oratorio."[36] While he did not object to calling *Pimooteewin* an opera, when asked shortly before the premiere of the work if he would consider writing another opera libretto, he responded "Well, I've never had any ambition to become an opera librettist. It was an interesting experience [writing *The Journey*], I loved every second of it, but I don't think I'll write another one."[37]

An early version of the Study Guide produced by Soundstreams Canada for the educational workshops in Toronto refers to the work as "a new music drama," "a Cree music drama," and "new music theatre."[38] The final version of the Study Guide also uses these terms, but adds a section that defines opera and oratorio, notes that *Pimooteewin* contains elements of both art forms, and asks the students "What do you think after having seen the performance? Is *The Journey* an oratorio

---

[36]   Cherney, "*The Journey*."

[37]   Martin Morrow, "Journey Man: The Nomadic Tomson Highway Talks about Writing the First Cree Opera," *CBC News.ca* (February 13, 2008), www.cbc.ca/arts/theatre/highway.html (accessed December 21, 2010).

[38]   Hentschel, *Pimooteewin* 2008, pp. 4, 5, 6.

or an opera? Which elements did you see from each of the art forms?"[39] For his part, Michael Greyeyes has stated that the work is like an oratorio but with a movement/dance component and costumes; in his words, the artistic team "highjacked" opera for its own purposes.[40] Lawrence Cherney, who was ultimately responsible for marketing the work as "the first Cree opera," defends his choice of the term. He states that to call it an oratorio would give a staid impression that is at odds with the nature of the work, and although it may be somewhat static in terms of its staging, he feels that the term opera does represent the work accurately.[41]

Although in one sense the terminological scruples about whether *Pimooteewin* is an oratorio or an opera, or some other kind of music/theater combination are not all that important, they do nevertheless have an impact on the reception of the work. The definition of oratorio from *Grove Music Online* reads as follows:

> An extended musical setting of a sacred text made up of dramatic, narrative and contemplative elements. Except for a greater emphasis on the chorus throughout much of its history, the musical forms and styles of the oratorio tend to approximate to those of opera in any given period, and the normal manner of performance is that of a concert (without scenery, costumes or action).[42]

The chorus in *Pimooteewin* does indeed have a large role to play and the text is from what can be considered the sacred domain of Cree storytelling. The work was performed in a semi-staged production with costumes, however, which is not characteristic of the oratorio tradition. Opera is more broadly defined in *Grove Music Online* as

> a drama in which the actors sing throughout ... since all operatic works combine music, drama and spectacle, though in varying degrees, all three principal elements should be taken into account in any comprehensive study of the genre, even though music has traditionally played the dominant role in the conception and realization of individual works.[43]

Beyond these stylistic considerations, there are broader cultural issues at stake. In Canada the term "opera" is associated in the minds of many with elitist cultural circles, even though many opera companies receive generous subsidies from the federal government. Thus terming *Pimooteewin* an opera rather than an oratorio gives it greater cultural capital, as opposed to the quasi-religious connotations of

---

[39]   Hentschel, *Pimooteewin* 2009, pp. 18–19.

[40]   Greyeyes, in CBC News staff, "Cree Opera."

[41]   Lawrence Cherney, in interview with the author, April 6, 2009.

[42]   Howard E. Smither, "Oratorio," *Grove Music Online*, www.oxfordmusiconline. com (accessed December 21, 2010).

[43]   Howard Mayer Brown, "Opera," *Grove Music Online*, www.oxfordmusiconline. com (accessed December 21, 2010).

290   *Opera Indigene: Re/presenting First Nations and Indigenous Cultures*

oratorio or the liminal status of more obscure generic designations such as "new music theater" or "new music drama."

Having considered the question of whether or not *Pimooteewin* is a Cree *opera*, we might turn now to ask in what ways is it a *Cree* opera? What possible meanings can be unpacked from the first half of that term? Does it refer to the cultural background of the librettist, the composer, or other members of the creative team, to the singers and performers, or only to the language of the libretto? Do we expect a certain style of music in a Cree opera? If so, what kind of music? One can imagine a sliding scale of "Cree-ness," ranging from, at the one end, a case where all of the creative team and the performers are Cree, the libretto is in the Cree language, and the music is in traditional Cree style to, at the other end, a case where the Cree content is minimal. At what point on this scale does a work earn bona fide qualification as a *Cree* opera? What percentage of the creative team must be Cree to warrant designation as a Cree opera?[44]

Perhaps out of sensitivity to this very issue, or in reaction to criticisms voiced at the time of the Toronto premiere, the poster for the northern Ontario tour of *Pimooteewin* made a subtle but significant change to the term, calling the work "the world's first Cree language opera."[45] The fact that Hui is Chinese-Canadian may have led some to question the legitimacy of calling *Pimooteewin* a Cree opera, even though no such qualms would be voiced about calling *Don Giovanni* or *Rinaldo* Italian operas. Although Hui does, as noted above, use some Aboriginal percussion instruments, her musical style, according to Greyeyes, is "unlike music from anything I understand as traditional native music—which makes it perfect for *The Journey*."[46] For Cherney, Greyeyes, Hui, and Highway, the collaborative aspect of the work is paramount, so that while it is termed a Cree opera, the Cree aspect is simply the most important of several cultural and musical heritages that are blended in the work, including European music and drama, Japanese *kabuki* theater, contemporary theater, and Cree storytelling traditions. Cherney states that these diverse influences "are combined to create something new without giving up their own identity ... cultures encounter each other and enter into a dialogue, thereby creating new relationships."[47]

Of the performers in the cast for the Toronto production only one, Cara Gee, the Narrator, was of First Nations descent (she is Ojibway). For the Northern Ontario tour the role was assumed by Meegwun Fairbrother, who is also of Ojibway descent. It was a curious feature of the opera that the (non-First Nations) Elmer Iseler

---

[44]   These questions inevitably shade over into highly contentious issues of who is granted, and who has the power to grant, First Nations status in Canada.

[45]   An image of this poster is online at the website of Meegwun Fairbrother: http://meegwun.blogspot.com (accessed December 21, 2010). The poster also gives the title of the work in Cree language symbols, as well as in English and in Cree using the Latin alphabet.

[46]   Hentschel, *Pimooteewin* 2008, p. 12.

[47]   Hentschel, *Pimooteewin* 2009, p. 6.

Singers and the two soloists (also non-First Nations singers) sang the Cree text of the work, while the only First Nations performer provided the spoken narration in English. Indeed, the question of how to determine whether *Pimooteewin* is a *Cree* opera can quickly shade over into issues of cultural appropriation, essentialism, and political correctness—issues about which Highway, for one, has very outspoken opinions. He has argued that "saying that only Native actors have the right to play Native roles—on stage, anyway, as opposed to film ... would be like saying to someone like Canadian filmmaker Atom Egoyan, 'you have the right to work with Armenian actors only,' which, of course, would automatically bring his career to a standstill ... What we all need is diversity! That's what makes Canada work as a society; precisely its diversity. If we—all of us—were Cree, I would have had my head macheted off a long, long time ago!"[48]

Nevertheless, it is the Cree aspects of the work—the language, the story, and the participation of Highway and Greyeyes—which have received the most attention and make the work stand out from other similar recent new operas. According to Highway, the Cree language not only embodies a particular worldview, but is also an inherently musical language— "a wonderful language to set to music because the sounds are not rigid, but very flexible."[49] In addition, Highway feels that the character of the Trickster cannot be properly explained in English: it is a creature whose temperament and subtle nuances can only be properly related in the Cree language.[50] In this sense, then, *Pimooteewin* is not only a Cree opera, but an untranslatable one at that.

Re-creating *Pimooteewin*

Loretta Todd has noted that "Traditional oral history accommodated difference, ritualizing the telling of histories and stories though the act of witnessing. There was not one story, or one song, or one dance."[51] In First Nations oral culture, the story was fashioned anew each time it was retold, taking into account the different context of each retelling. For *Pimooteewin*, which arose out of Cree oral storytelling traditions, the decision to mount a tour to northern Ontario resulted in some minor but nevertheless important changes to the work that can be seen in the light of Todd's observations about the oral transmission of traditional stories.

---

[48] Tomson Highway, "Should Only Native Actors Have the Right to Play Native Roles?' *Prairie Fire*, 22/3 (2001), pp. 20–26; reprinted as an afterword to his play *Rose* (Vancouver, BC: Talon Books, 2003), pp. 152–60 (quoted passage is on pp. 158–9).

[49] Hentshel, *Pimooteewin* 2009, p. 8; this is Cherney recalling what Highway told him about the Cree language.

[50] Hentshel, *Pimooteewin* 2009, p. 15.

[51] Loretta Todd, "Notes on Appropriation / L'appropriation," *Parallelogramme*, 16/1 (Summer 1990), pp. 29–33; the cited passage is on p. 32. I am grateful to Dylan Robinson for bringing this article to my attention.

292   *Opera Indigene: Re/presenting First Nations and Indigenous Cultures*

For the version of *Pimooteewin* that toured northern Ontario, the small chamber ensemble was reduced to keyboard and percussion, and the choir was slightly reduced, from twenty to sixteen singers. The two soloists (Bud Roach and Xin Wang) were the same in both productions, as was the conductor (Lydia Adams), but the narrator changed, as already noted. During the leadup to the Toronto premiere, there were over fifty educational workshops offered in Toronto schools, in the Native Canadian Centre, in the Centre for Indigenous Theatre, and elsewhere. The educational workshops were also an important part of the northern Ontario tour. Michael Greyeyes and Melissa Hui participated in the workshops in Toronto; Greyeyes and Meegwun Fairbrother (who performed the role of the Narrator) took part in the workshops in northern Ontario.[52] As noted above, the role of the *kuroko* was expanded for the northern Ontario performances, with a stronger emphasis on dance.

Although the changes to the work itself were noteworthy—Cherney likens it to a Broadway show, altering and improving as it develops in performance[53]—the changes in the audience and the locales were even more important. The Soundstreams company members were often in awe of the scenery that they encountered. Moose Factory and Moosonee are situated across the Moose River from each other. When the company performed in these two locales in early May, it was "breakup season"—the river was choked with ice making its way to James Bay. As a result the performers had to travel from Moosonee to Moose Factory by helicopter—something the locals take for granted, but an exciting experience for the southerners, who were in awe of the aerial views of the river filled with ice floes.

In the smaller northern communities, the ratio of First Nations to non-First Nations audience members was much higher than in Toronto, which also gave the performances an added significance. As Greyeyes noted, "What's unique about touring in the North is that for the entire community—unlike in Toronto where there are eighty shows going and you've never heard of any one of them—this is somewhat of a big deal. Everyone turns out."[54] Cree members of the audience experienced aspects of their culture new to them, while many in the audience were no doubt witnessing a live operatic performance for the first time.

Having won success in Toronto and in small-town venues in northern Ontario, *Pimooteewin* is set now to continue its journey. Future plans include tours to western Ontario and Quebec, to Vancouver for performances during the 2010

---

[52]   Tomson Highway was in Brazil at the time of the Toronto performances and in southern France at the time of the northern Ontario tour; he did not participate in the workshops and has never seen the work in live performance. Some touching video diaries of the northern Ontario school workshops are available online at www.soundstreams.ca/behind_the_scenes/detail.php?id=22 (accessed December 21, 2010).

[53]   Hentschel, *Pimooteewin* 2009, p. 6.

[54]   CBC News staff, "Cree opera,"

Olympic Games, and perhaps even to Scandinavia.[55] As it makes its way in the world, *Pimooteewin* will continue to grow and develop, and to demonstrate to new audiences that Cree culture and the traditions of European opera can be joined to create a fertile hybrid art form.

---

[55] The projected performances during the Vancouver Olympic Games in 2010 did not take place, but as of late 2010 plans are underway to tour *Pimooteewin* in New Zealand

Chapter 16

After McPhee: Evan Ziporyn's
A House in Bali

Victoria Vaughan

Opera is often touted as the definitive interdisciplinary performing artform. This is especially true when multiple cultural intersections enrich the genre through varied musical traditions and performance practices, and are given the added experimental dimension of multimedia technology. Such a work is exemplified in the new operatic collaboration, *A House in Bali*, by American composer Evan Ziporyn[1] and librettist Paul Schick. This chapter discusses the complex interplay between Balinese characters and the protagonist of the piece, Canadian composer Colin McPhee, using some historical and analytical examples alongside details of the upcoming premiere production. It acknowledges three elements of the opera in relation to the story's inherent colonial history and its upcoming presentation as a cross-cultural collaboration in multiple venues and for diverse audiences (first in Bali in 2009, then in the USA and beyond in 2009 and 2010). First, it aims to evaluate the musicological background to the work's inception through Colin McPhee's autobiography, his own transcriptions and compositions, and his personal and musical experiences in Bali. Second, it addresses some of the associated cultural issues, not least the re-telling of McPhee's story and those of his colleagues and friends, some of whom remain important figures in present-day Bali. Finally, the chapter elaborates upon practical considerations regarding the production of the opera, many of which are heavily impacted by the nature of Balinese performing arts versus the *modus operandi* of Western opera theater.

The 2004 paperback edition of Carol Oja's 1990 biography of Colin McPhee begins with a short quote from a CD-liner: "Before Evan Ziporyn, before Lou

---

[1]   Special thanks to Evan Ziporyn for advance copies of the full score, piano/vocal reduction, and MP3 files for A House in Bali © Airplane Ears Music (ASCAP) 2009. Additional thanks to Dewa Ketut Alit, Kadek Dewi Aryani, David Bengali, I Nyoman Catra, Jody Diamond, Desak Made Suarti Laksmi, Damen Mroczek, Larry Polansky, and Paul Schick.

Evan Ziporyn is a Western-trained composer, Grammy-winning performer, and long-time student of Balinese gamelan music. In addition to many years spent in the tuition of the island's pre-eminent teachers and performers, Ziporyn was a founding member of Gamelan Sekar Jaya in the San Francisco Bay Area, and is the founder and director of Gamelan Galak Tika in Boston.

296 *Opera Indigene: Re/presenting First Nations and Indigenous Cultures*

Harrison, there was Colin McPhee."[2] It is no surprise that Oja's opening line and this author's own title both mention major figures in the research and composition of music related to and inspired by Bali, but there is a more wide-reaching implication of a musicological "timeline" which works in both directions when it comes to things Balinese. Writing about his 1956 visit to Asia, Benjamin Britten observed that the Balinese "have been living cut off from the Western world."[3] Certainly, when he visited the region in the mid-1950s, the musical and cultural performances that Britten experienced were like nothing that was being represented in Europe at the time. Indeed, one could say that until recently the island was relatively culturally isolated even from the rest of Indonesia. As a small, predominantly Bali-Hindu island, Bali is nestled in the middle of the largest Muslim country in the world. The Indonesian archipelago's most populous island, Java, is considerably closer to Bali than the Isle of Wight is to Portsmouth, and yet Bali's geographical and cultural isolation has helped it to maintain its uniqueness, musical and cultural, thus increasing its charm for composers like McPhee, Britten, Harrison, and now Ziporyn.

In the case of this new work, an examination of its "timeline" also allows us to study a Western history of the reception of Eastern musical forms (and dance and drama), while investigating our own reception of others' receptions. The source for *A House in Bali* is the autobiographical memoir of the same name by composer Colin McPhee,[4] who spent several years during the 1930s living in Bali and documenting the music, concerned about its destruction by the web of forces inexorably entangling the Eastern world, as the plot outline below illustrates.

Synopsis

As the opera begins, we see McPhee setting about to secure a plot of land in Gianyar province and building his accommodation. The presence of a Westerner occasions heated meetings among the town's elders, and the villagers barricade the entrance to McPhee's lot in an effort to seal him off. Rather than seek official authorization to continue building, he opts to solve the conflict through village channels. This considerate and noble attitude gains him acceptance into the community.

We are then introduced to German-Russian artist Walter Spies, a resident of Bali at the time, and American anthropologist Margaret Mead, who serve as interlocutors to McPhee throughout the story, commenting on and elaborating its central themes according to their own different points of view. McPhee also makes the acquaintance of a ten-year-old peasant boy, Sampih, swimming in the river by his house, and hires him as a domestic. One evening he comes home to

---

 [2] Carol Oja, *Colin McPhee: A Composer in Two Worlds* (Smithsonian Institution, 1990), p. xi.

 [3] M. Cooke, *Britten and the Far East* (Bury St Edmunds: Boydell Press, 1998), p. 71.

 [4] Colin McPhee, *A House in Bali* (New York: Oxford University Press, 1987).

find Sampih improvising a dance to the wild syncopations of a Gamelan record. McPhee subsequently resolves to sponsor Sampih's study of Balinese dancing. He finally presents the fruits of his learning at a great feast to an enchanted audience, including the regent, and representatives of a number of prominent families.

A series of *Topeng* (masked fables) and the arrival of more international characters in Act III portend the unraveling of the dream that is/was McPhee's Bali. He learns from villagers that ghosts have been abroad, and that their visits will only increase in frequency. The very same night, the composer is awakened by a bright specter framed in the doorway of his bedroom, and the next day a Japanese visitor appears and is suspected of being a spy (for what would soon be the Japanese occupation of Indonesia). Finally, Spies is arrested by a Dutch policeman and McPhee understands that he must leave the island, never to return.[5]

Background

Colin McPhee was the first transcriber of Balinese *gamelan* music into Western notation, which he chanced upon when hearing an Odéon 78rpm recording in New York City in 1928.[6] Inspired by these early field recordings, McPhee traveled to Bali in 1931, ostensibly to study and document gamelan music, but his journey was also very much in reaction to the current state of Western music, as well as growing uncertainty with the political climate in Europe. Pursuing a kind of "synthesis" between Eastern tradition and Western experimentation, McPhee sought inspiration in Balinese traditions in order to focus his compositional process. In particular, he began to transcribe gamelan music, perhaps as an exercise in "musical cultural awakening" and to bolster his lagging compositional output.

A study of McPhee's transcriptions now shows them to be remedial at best, especially when viewed from today's global armchair. The fact that we have early recordings from the same time period that McPhee encountered this music allows us to be highly critical of what could be considered his limited listening and transcription skills. We can hear the same recorded materials that McPhee was working with, and yet with modern ears, we hear the "gaps" between the transcribed notes or see the mistakes in his approximation of the pitch and rhythm. Certainly, McPhee's two-piano transcriptions are fairly straightforward to play (albeit at quite a pace), and while they give a vague approximation of the sound and structure of Balinese music, they are entirely lacking in the intricacies of tuning between instruments. The "legend" that was published alongside his transcription of *Pemoengkah* (c.1940) lists the pentatonic notes in a *gendér* scale (calling it a

---

[5]   Summarized from the libretto for *A House in Bali* by Paul Schick.

[6]   Much of this original recording is now available on the CD: *The Roots of Gamelan* (World Arbiter, 2001) which also contains footnotes by McPhee and additional recorded material from 1941, including five of McPhee's gamelan transcriptions performed on two pianos by Colin McPhee and Benjamin Britten.

298   *Opera Indigene: Re/presenting First Nations and Indigenous Cultures*

Balinese "solfeggio") and a very approximate correlation with Western tuning. In documenting the music for piano, McPhee attempted to classify Balinese music within a musical and cultural language with which he was comfortable, albeit a language that, in the application of Western, even temperament, "flattens" the shimmering effects of *ombak* (literally "waves") typical to the systematic tuning of two sets of Balinese *gendér* (gnde:ɐ) the instrumentation for which *Pemoengkah* is intended, which plays interlocking patterns (*kotékan*). While gamelan instruments are tuned to be performed together, to offset each other's resonances they are never tuned to the exact same pitch. The difference in tuning between a pair of *gendér* will normally be between five to eight beats per second, and the tuner will try and make the pairing sound aesthetically pleasing rather than aiming for a specific pitch frequency.

McPhee's documentation technique thus seems painfully remedial today and indeed insulting, considering that the careful, exact tuning of a piano would sound dull to a Balinese audience. To take the beautifully formed and carefully "mistuned" instruments and stick them into the straitjacket of an equal temperament keyboard distorts the music in the process of documenting it. If synthesis is what McPhee aimed for in transcribing *gendér* music, his approach seems dreadfully off course.

McPhee did himself play the gamelan often and would "ask a gendér player to move aside while I took his place for a while."[7] He goes on to say "I knew the melodies by heart, and as I played, I felt both peace and exhilaration..."[8] But when asked about McPhee's playing, the master gamelan player and teacher, I Madé Lebah, said that McPhee "couldn't play the actual gamelan instruments. He knew the music but he couldn't play the instruments."[9] This noticeable contradiction suggests that perhaps McPhee knew, at some level, that his proficiency and training in annotating Western music might be the only reliable way for him to effectively document Balinese music.

Cultural Considerations

In narrating the life of the man and his Western colleagues, McPhee's "otherness" in this tropical paradise, both cultural and musical, is of vital importance to the opera. How he relates to the musical material as its transcriber is illustrative of how separate he felt from the Balinese people, and that, while he sought musical and cultural synthesis, he would ironically never fully achieve either while residing in Bali. These various layers of "otherness" and separateness also demand further investigation. As one considers the notion of the observer (the transcriber, the diarist) being changed by the process of observation, it is important to realize

---

[7]   Oja, *Colin McPhee*, p. 87.

[8]   Ibid.

[9]   Ibid., p. 91.

After McPhee: Evan Ziporyn's A House in Bali

that the evolution of *A House In Bali* not only changes the Western participant as observer of the East, but that there is relative motion between the observer and the observed as the piece is created. This is borne out in the senses of time within the piece. Just as moving vehicles have different speeds and rates of events occurring within them, there are varied tempi of collaborative artistic creation. Additionally, there are time dilations experienced in East/West interaction that relate to cyclic versus diachronic time (myth versus history), and in a musical work such as *A House in Bali*, colotomy versus teleology. Thus McPhee's dilemma as transcriber only scratches the surface of cultural and musical differences between his personal history and the world of Bali.

Evan Ziporyn's opera *A House in Bali* is the culmination of a 27-year-long project which not only tackles the issues associated with combining Balinese performing arts with Western musical tradition (the "square peg in a round hole" scenario that McPhee was struggling with) but also truly embraces it. The fact that McPhee is the subject matter makes the narrative that much more interesting, as a vehicle for Ziporyn's own musical autobiographical reflections. The world premiere production of *A House in Bali* was commissioned and devised by Real Time Opera, working closely alongside the composer and librettist, and created for two locations: the intimate *Puri Saraswati* (Water Palace) in Ubud, Bali, close to McPhee's actual residence in Sayan, and the expansive Zellerbach Hall at the University of California's Cal Performances in Berkeley, USA, for the summer and autumn seasons of 2009, respectively.

The first musical theme in Ziporyn's opera borrows directly from a piano composition by McPhee called *Kinesis* (Example 16.1a) written in New York in 1930, after McPhee had heard the Odéon 78rpm recordings, but before his first visit to Bali. Ziporyn's application of *Kinesis* for the opening scene of the opera (Example 16.1b) uses thematic melodic material but it is now accompanied by a slower but more restless bass-line. In this scene, McPhee is in Paris, having already spent some time in Bali, then returning to the West in the hopes of being inspired, but actually finding himself more frustrated by the Western musical climate than ever before. It goes without saying that, in the minds of most historians, the 1920s and 1930s were exciting times for musical development in the West. For McPhee to appear bored and frustrated says a lot about how he felt the existing musical community could not or would not accept him, or perhaps that he himself did not "fit in." This could have been as much a facet of latent homosexuality as his musical compositional taste (as will be later discussed in more detail) but, whatever the reason, McPhee apparently felt that neither New York nor Paris sated his frustration and wanderlust.

Thus, the opera's opening scene in Paris functions both as a cultural backdrop before his journey to Bali, and also a foundation for McPhee's emotional journey, providing the audience with an overture comfortably orchestrated in a Western musical palette. It is firmly rooted at A=440 with a sextet orchestration of violin,

Example 16.1a McPhee's score of *Kinesis*, mm. 1–5

Example 16.1b Ziporyn, *A House in Bali*, Act I, Scene 1, mm 1–7

cello, double bass, guitar, percussion, and keyboard, and acts as a foil to the Balinese music that comes in subsequent scenes.

As the first scene progresses, Ziporyn introduces the character of McPhee himself; in this production, seated at table, trying in vain to compose. His first vocal entrance, accompanied by the "restless" bass-line, then returns to the frenetic upper theme as McPhee fruitlessly scribbles away (Example 16.2). The accompaniment then begins to move away from the original *Kinesis* and becomes more frantic, until McPhee reaches an impasse and the entire score stops. This moment is a realization of writer's block in the most extreme way, and it seems to take a bit of jump-starting to get the music up and running again (Example 16.3).

But the short, opening scene is where the colonial origins of the story ends. Scene 2 uses very different musical language from Scene 1, and the story begins to unfold into its new Balinese location, which remains the setting for the rest of the opera. Ziporyn blends traditional Balinese rhythmic and melodic patterns with jazz influence and syncopation native to Balinese music, introduced by gamelan. Slowly the Western instruments rejoin the ensemble, starting with the electric bass, at the bottom of the texture, functioning much like the gong in a gamelan ensemble.

McPhee sings again in this scene, in a conversation with two local men who perform in traditional Balinese vocal style. The direct translation of these Balinese character-types is more akin to "clown" than actor or singer, a parallel that works well when one thinks of *commedia dell'arte* characters, or British pantomime stereotypes. They also draw on comic types from traditional Hindu epics as manifested in Balinese plays (*wayang wong*) and shadow puppet plays (*wayang kulit*).

Scene 3 (parts 1 and 2) introduces the "character" of the House itself. As it happens, McPhee has chosen a location that transgresses by a few feet onto the official burial ground for that village, and this triggers the village elders to seal off McPhee in his own property. McPhee handles this delicate situation, in his first

Example 16.2 Ziporyn, *A House in Bali*, McPhee composing in vain, Act I, Scene 1, mm. 36–44

Example 16.3 Ziporyn, *A House in Bali*, Realization of McPhee's writer's block, Act I, Scene 1, mm. 112–122

real introduction to Balinese society, by avoiding bureaucratic entanglements and negotiating directly with the elders of the *banjar*, and through this action respect is earned on both sides.

Here, musical form serves as dramaturgy, with gamelan percussive sound effects notated in the score as "hammering" (Example 16.4). The gamelan players themselves become the builders, and each armed with a "hammer" (actually, a gamelan mallet, or *pongul*), they step out from the ensemble to construct the house vertically, piece by piece, by hammering stock patterns in time with the music. In this particular production, the finials and roofs are then flown down to complete the vertical construction already created by the players.

Example 16.4 Ziporyn, *A House in Bali*, The "hammering" rhythms, Act I, Scene 3

Because gamelan is taught by ear, there is no additional music-learning required, as one would expect with Western operatic chorus members or supernumeraries; the Balinese players simply step out from behind their instruments, collect a "building block", arrive at their destination on stage, and join in with a physical representation of the musical score, hammering their newly placed block in perfect time with the rest of the seated ensemble.

This aspect of the performance is of particular interest for the stage director, because it affords a level of musical accuracy in performance that is more of a parallel to Western concert-hall virtuosi than the on-stage musicians in Western opera, due to the exemplary musical/percussive skills required of the cast. In Ziporyn's own words, the rhythms required of the players as they hammer are standard Balinese gamelan sequences that any player would know intimately, but they sound incredibly complex (especially to unaccustomed ears) and the overall effect is stunning. Even to musically trained ears, as in the case of Benjamin Britten:

> ... the music is fantastically rich—melodically, rhythmically, texture (such orchestration!!) & above all formally. It is a remarkable culture ... at last I'm beginning to catch on to the technique, but it's about as complicated as Schoenberg.[10]

This concept of utilizing standard repertory techniques from Balinese music as a staging device is entertaining but has an additional historical and cultural element that deserves mention. In today's Bali, construction sites use modern techniques alongside master-craftsmen and stonecarvers. Instead of pile-driving machinery, builders use long, bamboo sticks to square out a site and pour concrete, combining native plants for simplicity (and cost) and modern materials for strength and longevity. Additionally, in creating McPhee's House (the structure/the opera/the metaphor/the physical fact) it is vital to consider the placement of the buildings in relation to the village, the main temple, and, ultimately, the large volcanic mountain Gunung Agung, which is the spiritual center of the Balinese world. Each part of a family's individual housing complex relates to different parts of the body, perhaps echoing the strict formal structures of family and caste in Balinese society—the temple is the head, while the "trash" area is the anus. Even on a microcosmic scale, architectural measurements themselves relate directly to the human body (in a slightly more free-form way than the strict 12 inches of a "foot") Finally, all

---

[10] Cooke, *Britten and the Far East*, p. 70.

After McPhee: Evan Ziporyn's A House in Bali   303

buildings are constructed in a highly methodical manner, starting with the vertical element or pillar that is closest to the Gunung Agung mountain, and adding the other structural elements in a strict order, all depending on the number of vertical poles and so on. All of this plays an important role in any theatrical staging of the building process as a main "character" of this opera, the House itself, is revealed.

In Act II we begin to see another side of Colin McPhee, the Balinese side, the "other" that he would continually refer to for the rest of his life. During a trip to Bali in January of 2008, already well into the project, composer Evan Ziporyn and librettist Paul Schick decided that, as it then stood, the story of McPhee didn't allow them to explore this sense of "otherness" to its fullest. The solution they arrived at was to add two pivotal characters from McPhee's life in Bali, the anthropologist Margaret Mead and the artist Walter Spies. For a while, Schick was working on the first scene for McPhee, Spies, and Mead to be based around a gamelan piece called *Alus Harem (Fragrant Forest)*, which McPhee mentions in his other best-known book, *Music in Bali*.[11] *Alus Harem* traditionally occurs during a scene in which the *dalang* (puppeteer and narrator) sets up his shadow puppets and places them according to their essential natures. McPhee, Spies, and Mead are thus classified within this story in the same way, and already embedded into Balinese dramatic form. The piece has very short phrases, and the libretto text would have been easily interspersed with the short segmented phrases on *gendér*, but after a few months of working on this change, Ziporyn suggested instead a series of tableaux. Specifically Ziporyn favored the three Western characters co-existing but not interacting quite as closely as an "ex-pat" community would; more like the displaced individuals that they appear to be when their works and books are analyzed. The tableaux solution is also a brilliant way to keep McPhee's interaction with Westerners very separate from the way he interacted with Balinese characters in the quotidian Bali-Hindu way of life, and brings their intellectual, analytical, and anthropological relationships into relief. These tableaux link us to the introduction of the most important character, certainly for McPhee, the young boy called Sampih.

Sampih represents so many aspects of Balinese life to McPhee. He is the naïve child in an idyll who is playing naked in the water when McPhee first encounters him, untamed, and, in the words even of Sampih's own parents, a "wild child." McPhee develops a homosexual obsession with Sampih, following the incident where Sampih discovers gramophone recordings and begins dancing wildly.

At the start of Act II, Scene 4, Spies analyzes a trip they had all made in McPhee's new car, of which Sampih was afraid. Spies sings:

> The excursion marked a step
> in your relationship,
> You took him to a foreign land
> and brought him safely back.

---

[11]   Colin McPhee, *Music in Bali: A Study in Form and Instrumental Organization in Balinese Orchestral Music* (New Haven, CT: Yale University Press, 1966).

We can assume that Spies, in this instance, offers the audience a Western viewpoint of the event, that the native child (who would most likely never leave the island) has a safe foreign experience without leaving home. McPhee listening to gamelan music from his apartment in New York is perhaps a close parallel, as a sensory experience of the Other. "Technology" here equates with "foreign."

Later in the story McPhee, in an unchallenged demonstration of ownership, or paternalism, decides that Sampih needs training in traditional Balinese dance technique. A teacher is hired and Sampih learns dancing in preparation for a public performance. Again under the strange impression that he is somehow expert in these matters, McPhee then decides that Sampih should learn from another, better teacher. This time it is a female teacher, who instructs him in the "new" dance technique, and the public performance is bigger and better.

In these events, our observer-cum-transcriber-cum-diarist determines the outcome of a student whose dancing skills he seems to imagine as being triggered by the sounds of a gramophone; once again, foreign technology, the Western world, triggers McPhee's "interjections." Surely Sampih had heard *live* gamelan on an almost daily basis. Why did the wind-up mechanism make him dance? It seems that McPhee perhaps imagines himself as the "sound source," but also the "provider."

From what we gather from the first teacher, Sampih is *not* a natural dancer. Again quoting from the libretto, I Nyoman Kalér, the dance teacher says:

> It's like this. He is not what you might call stupid.
> But he has the body of a peasant.
> He will never be very graceful.
> This one is a wild animal, rough like a strong wind.
> But his mouth is good, and his eyes are beautiful.
> He will never dance well, but he could be perhaps
> an actor of strong parts.
> If you wish I will teach him for a while,
> for an actor must know how to dance.

It is possible that McPhee felt some competition here from Spies, who himself commissioned the famous *Kecak* dance by appropriating existing trance chant, which is performed by sometimes hundreds of men, naked to the waist, writhing together in a elaborate patterns and singing complicated interlocking rhythmical chants. These foreigners initiated and witnessed the evolution of a dance that would have certainly raised eyebrows in the West. Another indicator of the flow of ideas and flexibility of our "timeline" is that the *Kecak* has been wholeheartedly adopted by Balinese performers and makes up a staple part of the dance repertory today.

The ultimate goal of McPhee's actions in relation to Sampih is difficult to unpack. Nothing about this aspect of the story is written down; it remains a mystery despite the wealth of other information contained his diaries and books. What is clear, however, is that his fascination for Sampih is closely tied with a

Balinese culture that has a certain unwritten and unspoken openness to sexual relations. Sampih here stands for the Bali that McPhee cannot ultimately control, tame, or master. Three days after McPhee left Bali for the last time, Walter Spies was arrested by the Dutch authorities in Indonesia, for, as the records indicate, "homosexual activities." Before then, Spies and McPhee and others had enjoyed pretty free relations with whomever they chose. Margaret Mead recalls: "Walter Spies's choice of Bali and of a continuing light involvement with Balinese male youth, seemed part of his repudiation of the kind of dominance and submission, authority and dependence, which he associated with European cultures. The very disassociated impersonality of Bali gave him the kind of freedom that he sought."[12] Mead's considerable written output, along with that of more recent anthropologists, clearly documents the nature of these interactions and the effects of the sexual freedom experienced by these early visitors to the island.[13] From a Balinese perspective, it was seen as a good thing for a young boy to be close, physically, emotionally, and educationally, with a "great artist," which is what Spies was (and still is) seen as to be by the Balinese.

Sampih continued to be trained in dance after McPhee's departure from Bali, and he is well known among dancers. For this production, this author and choreographer Dewi Aryani have been devising the scenes where she plays the role of the female teacher. Aryani is particularly interested in the concept of creating a dance which illustrates a dance lesson; where the teacher stands behind the child and moves his limbs, much like a puppet (but also a mirror) and in the earliest scenes when Sampih is young, also very feminine in dance style.

Balinese children begin dance lessons almost as soon as they can walk, and gamelan ensembles of young boys (and more recently young girls) are incredibly exciting and humbling to observe in action. They use the same fundamentals as the Orff method, focusing on rhythmic material, use of pentatonic patterns, and so on, with teaching and memorization of vast amounts of musical material entirely based on aural and visual-kinaesthetic learning, rather than written text. Dancing is developed in the same way, and in the process of casting singers and dancers around the island, the production team came across sizeable *Bale Banjars* (village halls with open walls) with huge mirrors along the back wall, so that what seemed like the entire village population under the age of twelve could participate in communal dance classes. These classes are very often free; given to the Banjar by a teacher who happens to live in the village as part of his or her expected contribution to the community.

---

[12]   H. Rhodius (ed.), *Schönheit und Reichtum des Lebens: Walter Spies* (The Hague, Boucher: Maler und Musiker auf Bali, 1965), p. 359, cited in J.A. Boon, *Verging on the Extra-Vagance: Anthropology, History, Religion, Literature, Arts ... Showbiz* (Princeton, NJ: Princeton University Press 1999), p. 86.

[13]   It is worth noting that if McPhee had staying on the island just a few days longer than he did, he would most certainly have suffered the same fate as Spies.

Practical Considerations

Performing alongside Aryani (as dancer/choreographer) will be the young dancer playing Sampih, three Balinese singer/dancer/actors, three Western opera singers (performing the roles of McPhee, Walter Spies, and Margaret Mead) an eighteen-man gamelan and the Western sextet, all of whom appear onstage. Finally, there is our *dalang* and his puppets. The sung and spoken text is predominantly in English, but there are several languages in the show and much improvisation by *dalang* and the two male actors, using English and Bali-Indonesian interchangeably, as well as variations of Sanskrit, and Kawi (Old and Middle-Javanese) alongside modern colloquialisms. In a normal shadow-puppet play there would also be ethical and cosmological references alongside jokes about current events and politics.

In this production of *A House In Bali*, scenic designer Damen Mrozcek and video/lighting designer David Bengali were especially interested in creating a visual language that worked as well for performance in Bali as for subsequent performances on the Western stage. The Flood Scene in Act II, for example, raised special questions regarding scenic technology, and some ingenious solutions were devised. The first was to use long swathes of Balinese printed cloth, laid down across the stage and manipulated by the gamelan players to represent the waves. The cloth in question uses a traditional pattern called "clouds" that seems almost *Art Nouveau* in its stylized undulating pattern abstracted from nature (see Figure 16.1). In motion, this pattern closely resembles waves and would allow Sampih and his friends to rise and fall through the slowly rising water. In a Western theatrical setting, this scene would also be enhanced by the use of multiple scrims (huge pieces of netting, covering the entire proscenium opening) which allow light to reveal or hide any action occurring upstage of the scrim. When backlit, the swimming boys and the cloth would be entirely visible, but with front-projections fading in and out, the boys would appear and disappear behind the scrim, as if lost in the waves. From McPhee's position downstage of the scrim, they would seem ghost-like, unattainable, there and gone again in a moment.

Bengali's video design went further still in using scrims to create the Balinese landscape. Starting with the famous image of a man in a triangular hat leading a donkey (painted by Walter Spies in many of his Balinese works, such as *Die Landschaft und ihre Kinder* of 1939) the designer devised multiple layers of video projections that created Spies's two-dimensional "repeating horizons" in 3D space. In animating the image, Bengali adds time to a two-dimensional canvas. Spies, himself also a musician, very much thought in terms of musical correlations (e.g. tonality and themes) when he painted. Using video projections to paint the beauty of Bali onto a Western stage allows scenic designer Mroczek to link the more tangible, physical scenic elements into a familiar visual vocabulary, which he then enhances with foliage and intricate details taken from the stylized patterns of the ubiquitous "Tree of Life" (*Kayon*) that begins and ends every Balinese *Wayang Kulit*. In some senses this production takes *Gesamtkunstwerk* into a new and international cross-cultural dimension.

Figure 16.1   Photo of Cloud Fabric used in production of *A House in Bali*

Conclusion

In his book *Marvellous Possessions*, Steven Greenblatt recalls his first night on a trip to Bali, walking by moonlight to a tiny village and, with some disappointment, discovering that the light emanating from the local *bale banjar* was not in fact a shadow puppet piece, playing out the *Ramayana* or *Mahabarata* by lamp oil, but, instead, that the villagers were watching an elaborate temple ceremony on the communal VCR. Greenblatt began to recognize that some of the viewers were themselves participants in the ceremony on the screen, then in a trance-like state, now whooping with delight at the television. His definition of this event, which he leaves deliberately ambiguous, is of witnessing "the assimilation of the other,"[14] not only the television and the VCR, but even his own presence at the event illustrates the imposition of Western technology into the oft-hailed pure and unadulterated art-forms and traditions of the island.

Perhaps Balinese performing arts are already multimedia enough, multilinguistic enough, assimilated into "normal life" enough, that the addition of foreign singers to tell the story of another foreigner somewhere down (or up) the "timeline" is simply another way of telling a story about the island; that its inhabitants are transient characters, however one looks at it. It is appropriate to end this discussion with a quote from Idanna Pucci's translation of the stunning painted ceiling at Kerta Gosa in central Bali, which depicts a telling of the *Bhima Swarga* that dates back to 1710. Kerta Gosa is often referred to as the "Sistine Chapel of Bali," but in content is more closely related to Dante's *Inferno*. The paintings are a catalog of human behaviors that should be avoided if the viewer is to avoid going to hell in the afterlife, and they range in severity from incest to gossiping and farting.

---

[14]   Steven Greenblatt, *Marvelous Possessions: The Wonders of the New World* (Chicago, IL: University of Chicago Press, 1991), p. 3.

308   *Opera Indigene: Re/presenting First Nations and Indigenous Cultures*

Pucci's description of Balinese life both illustrates a core underlying theme of *A House in Bali*'s development from page to stage, and also encapsulates to a degree what so entranced Colin McPhee as he sought emotional and musical refuge:

> Balinese life is still permeated by belief in a divine, omnipresent force. In every gesture of a musician playing his gamelan instrument, in every whirl of a temple dancer, in every shadow cast by a puppet in a shadow play, the Balinese perceive a manifestation of this super-natural power. The paintings and wood carvings, the stone sculptures and temples that dominate the landscape of daily life, are not merely artistic reflections of a rich cultural heritage but are, in fact, an organic outgrowth of the people themselves, a special dimension of their being – as natural a part of them as their hands or eyes. In Bali, the gap between "myth" and "reality" does not seem to exist.[15]

McPhee's own book, *A House in Bali*, is a cautionary tale to warn against any production striving toward a simplified cultural mixing-pot paradigm, a musical, dramatic, or choreographic mélange that fails miserably in telling the actual story. Not least, the fact that synthesis ultimately and tragically eluded McPhee is a large part of the story itself ,and in this new telling it is important to assess carefully our modes of integration between the constituent elements of multimedia in the dance opera, just as it is vital to evaluate the various levels of cross-cultural interactions and assimilations. By premiering at the *Puri Saraswati* in Ubud, this production will bring high-tech production into an ancient palace, and yet by creating the work just yards from the original memoir's inception we have somehow come full circle again.

---

[15]   I. Pucci, *Bhima Swarga: The Balinese Journey of the Soul* (New York: Bulfinch Press, 1992), p. 9.

Chapter 17

West Coast First Peoples and *The Magic Flute*: Tracing the Journey of a Cross-Cultural Collaboration

Robert McQueen Interviewed by Dylan Robinson, with Responses by
Cathi CharlesWherry and Tracey Herbert, Lorna Williams, and
Marion Newman

This chapter consists of an interview conducted by Dylan Robinson with Robert McQueen, director of Vancouver Opera's Coast Salish adaptation of Mozart's *Magic Flute*. After this interview concluded, members of the collaborative process and audience were invited to respond to the interview. Respondents were Cathi Charles Wherry (Anishnabeque, Rama Mnjikaning) and Tracey Herbert (Shuswap, Bonaparte) from the First Peoples' Heritage, Language, and Culture Council, Dr. Lorna Williams (Lil'wat), the Canada Research Chair of Indigenous Knowledge and Learning at the University of Victoria, and Marion Newman (Kwagiulth), a mezzo-soprano who performed in the production.

Dylan Robinson: Hi Robert. First, let me thank you for taking the time to discuss this rich and complex production with us for *Opera Indigene*. I'd like to begin by spending some time discussing the stages of the creation process and the various collaborative partnerships that emerged over the course of the production. From what I understand, the development process for the Vancouver Opera's Coast Salish *Magic Flute* was significantly longer than usual for the production of an opera. Where did the initial idea to view Mozart's *The Magic Flute* (and Coast Salish culture through the lens of *The Magic Flute*) come from?

Robert McQueen: Early in the spring of 2004 I met with James Wright and Randy Smith at Vancouver Opera to discuss my interest in directing a new production for their company. The idea, which came from the opera company, was to invite First Nations artists from a variety of disciplines to join with a group of seasoned theater professionals to create a new production of *The Magic Flute*. While I was intrigued by the idea, I realized that to bring one of Mozart's best-known scores together with the traditional and contemporary culture and artistry of Canada's West Coast First Peoples and to achieve a satisfying result, either artistically or politically, would be profoundly challenging.

310 *Opera Indigene: Re/presenting First Nations and Indigenous Cultures*

DR: Did you have any apprehension about working on such an enormous adaptation that brings together different First Nations cultural practices drawn from the many nations whose territory lies along the west coast with one of the most firmly entrenched operas within the operatic canon? What were your primary concerns at the beginning stages of the process?

RM: Certainly, my immediate concern was—how appropriate was it for me, a non-First Nations person, to helm such a complicated production? I asked for time to think about it. Vancouver Opera Association gave me a month.

During this time I approached friends and colleagues, both First Nations and non-First Nations, for their advice and consideration. Of all these conversations perhaps the most important was my meeting with Brenda Crabtree. Brenda is a Stó:lõ artist and serves as the First Peoples advisor at the Emily Carr University of Art and Design in Vancouver. To summarize our almost two-hour meeting cannot be done, but, briefly, her principal advice was simple and profound:

> Seek guidance;
> Don't assume;
> Ask permission.

At the end of our meeting she commented on how she felt there was much merit to the work, and, as with every path worth pursing, how it was important to know that, regardless of what is done, someone will find fault with it. She reminded me to treat each aspect of the production with absolute respect while being inventive and engaging the deepest imagination of the whole team.

It was advice that I held close over the next two and a half years of work that went into creating this production of *The Magic Flute*.

Lorna Williams: On a cold February night I saw the West Coast People's version of *The Magic Flute*, an opera I am very familiar with and one of my favorites. I remember the anticipation—both dread and excitement. I knew the right people were involved in the production from the First Nations side, and my friends assured me that it was the same on the Opera production side. But, so many times in the past I had been disappointed in so-called collaborations. The opening was right, with a welcome to Coast Salish territory. I settled into my seat. By the end of the performance, I was moved and thrilled with the work; my thought was that lots of teaching and learning had occurred in both directions; it was a cross-cultural collaboration.

The conditions to bring this project to life were a long time coming, conditions in both the Vancouver Opera Company (VOC) and in the First Nations communities. I recall discussions in the 90s exploring ideas for collaboration. The talks broke off, but there was movement forward, such as the recognition and acknowledgment that VOC is on Coast Salish land and their involvement was unequivocal in any project. At the same time, it was acknowledged that the creative expertise could not be found in any one First Nation and that there needed to be collaboration between First Nations, Inuit, and Métis peoples.

LW *continued* One of the questions discussed was whether there would be an adaptation or a new opera—who are the artists who would be involved? What would the story be, from which First Nation? At the time there was no centralized body such as the First Peoples' Heritage, Language, and Culture Council familiar with First Nations, Inuit, and Métis artists and who could act as an intermediary between the artists and other institutions.

Opera is not new to First Nations, especially not to the Coast Salish. I remember attending education conferences in the late 60s and 70s when the gathering would request that the Cowichan tenor Abel Joe sing from his opera *Tzinquaw* written in the 40s and based on one of his family's stories. Opera is storytelling, music, and theater, all part of First Nations tradition. If anyone has ever attended a Northwest Coast potlatch or a family celebration they would be part of a web of stories told in recitation, song and dance—some simply shared, others in elaborate and complex productions. The stories are always full of surprise, wisdom, wit, and awe; humorous and insightful. Stories told to be remembered.

Reading the interview with Robert McQueen demonstrated the time was right for this project. It is evident deep listening occurred on both sides, each took each other seriously and respected their point of view. A principle of Indigenous leadership is "to treat each aspect ... with absolute respect while being inventive and engaging the deepest imagination of the whole team." This was good advice, Robert heard it and was able to lead from that perspective. He succeeded because I suspect it is his way of being generally. When speaking with members of the production I saw this principle at work throughout.

RM: By the time I accepted Vancouver Opera's invitation that spring, they had already been engaged in a year-long dialogue with the First Peoples' Heritage, Language, and Culture Council in Victoria to begin the complex inquiry into this work—and during the development process leading up to *The Magic Flute*'s premiere at the Queen Elizabeth Theatre in early 2007, a principal team of fifteen artists, theater makers and language specialists were engaged in creating the production's set, costume designs, and choreography, and in the adaptation of the libretto.

Cathi Charles Wherry and Tracey Herbert: Vancouver Opera came to the First Peoples' Heritage, Language, and Culture Council (the First Peoples' Council) to talk about developing an interpretation of *The Magic Flute* that was specific to British Columbia, and that would somehow include First Nations. We are frequently asked for guidance or to partner in projects, and are selective about where we invest our resources and energy. These relationships don't work when what begins as a partnership transforms, as one party overpowers the other, becomes autocratic or simply takes ownership of the ideas and work. Initially we were cautious about validating the project with our involvement, and hesitant to invest our reputation and good community relationships. However, we were interested to hear more.

312   *Opera Indigene: Re/presenting First Nations and Indigenous Cultures*

CCW and TH *continued* At the time, we appreciated Randy Smith's sincerity and openness, and Jim Wright's admission that they didn't know how to proceed or if this was even appropriate. Their humility about what they were exploring gave promise to the possibility of working together. At the same time, we were very honest and direct about our concerns and priorities. This shared attitude and dynamic set a tone that remained for the duration of the project.

A significant first step was to develop a *Reciprocal Benefits Document*, which directly stated the benefits and expectations for all involved, including the First Peoples' Council, the communities we serve, and Vancouver Opera. The process of creating this document allowed us to evaluate the project's worth to our mandate and constituents, while also serving to establish an organization-to-organization relationship based on clear intentions and purpose. During the three years we worked together, this document reminded us all of these priorities.

Within this climate, protocol concerns and political issues were dealt with globally and almost always preventatively, and communication was very good. With the First Peoples' Council doing this pre-emptive work and carrying responsibility for most advocacy and related communication, it was possible for the artists to do their work without becoming burdened with power politics and confusion.

DR: I have to be honest here and say that I'm made slightly apprehensive by James Wright's statement that Vancouver Opera "wanted a new production of *The Magic Flute* that reflected our lives here in British Columbia,"[1] and wonder who exactly the "our" he was referring to is. It seems like there might be some conflation here—that First Nations culture represents "our [who, Vancouver Opera season subscription holders? Those who live on Coast Salish territories?] lives" seems to me dangerously close to historical and contemporary narratives of the arts in Canada that have historically sought to inscribe First Nations culture as a part of "our" Canada's heritage. I think we need to be attentive to language that elides First Nations and Canadian identities.

So yes, I'm interested in the inception of this project, and wonder if you could tell me what the initial impetus for bringing these worlds into relationship with one another was.

RM: The work had, as mentioned, already been in process for a year prior to my coming onboard as the director so, as to the initial impetus for creating the production, that might best be answered by the opera company. Having said that, I must note that from my first meeting with them I felt that the opera company was fully aware of the enormity of the venture they were undertaking and were engaging all means by which to ensure the authenticity of its unfolding.

---

[1]   Quoted in Robert Jordan, "West Coast Magic: Vancouver Opera Looked to B.C.'s First Nations Heritage to Conjure Classic Mozart," *Opera Canada* (March/April 2007), p. 18.

West Coast First Peoples and The Magic Flute

RM *continued* Perhaps the most significant first-step was the partnership Vancouver Opera forged with The First Peoples' Heritage, Language, and Culture Council in Victoria. The First Peoples' Council's principal mandate is to assist British Columbia First Nations in their efforts to revitalize their languages, arts, and cultures. Between the two organizations great attention was placed on creating a platform for dialogue within the Indigenous artistic, academic, and political communities.

In May 2004, immediately following my acceptance of the contract offer, the First Peoples' Council and Vancouver Opera hosted a meeting with an advisory council comprised of senior members from within the West Coast First Nations community. For me this was an important gathering in that it allowed me to engage the expertise and experience of a remarkable group of artists, educators, and community leaders. This meeting provided the opportunity to seek counsel in how to best honor the issues of cultural protocol and to create a system of communication that would allow us to deal with the concern of appropriation, particularly in the areas of set and costume design, language, and choreography.

DR: And once you had decided to take part in the project, how did you go about deciding on the approach you would take in adapting the opera? I'd like to know about some of the motivations behind your decisions as to how and what would be adapted in *The Magic Flute*'s story, and decisions regarding the degree to which the libretto and music would be altered.

RM: The development of our libretto adaptation was perhaps more about evolution of process, rather than imposing immediate directorial decisions. What I mean by this is that it was by taking Brenda's advice to heart and seeking and asking that the form of the production began to emerge, rather than it being something I arrived at the table with already complete.

Let me give you an example with regard to the decision to create a libretto adaptation. From the beginning it was decided that the production would be sung in English. Early in our work we facilitated a series of meetings with a group of artists and academics from within the city's First Nations community to begin an in-depth examination of both the possibilities and the considerations that surrounded the project. In advance of each gathering the participants were sent a recording and a complete score of the opera with an invitation to study the piece and to offer their immediate response to both the material and the project. Through the course of these conversations it became clear very quickly that to present the libretto without alteration would cause considerable confusion for a First Nations audience.

There were two principal issues that emerged surrounded Schikaneder's text. The first was the use of the multiple gods of Egyptian mythology in a piece drawing its influences from monotheistic cultures. The second concern of our advisory was the patriarchal tone taken by Sarastro and his gang. There are ten major nations that sit on the coastal land called British Columbia, which are largely matriarchal

314   *Opera Indigene: Re/presenting First Nations and Indigenous Cultures*

RM *continued* cultures, and our council felt that it would be held as very strange indeed to hear male elders speak with such contempt about women.

Since the score was to be sung in English it became clear that, while guarding the dramaturgy of Schikaneder's text, there would have to be some consideration given to these concerns. This led to Vancouver Opera asking if I would be interested in writing a new libretto adaptation.

In the initial draft of the adaptation I focused my attention on the areas of the libretto that had prompted concern. For example, in the original translation Sarastro refers to the Queen of the Night as:

> A haughty woman, only a man should guide your hearts.
> Without him, woman is accustomed to wend her way out of her sphere.

In the adaptation this became:

> Yet, she is too proud. By me your path must be decided.
> The Queen deceives and she misleads and by her lies you are misguided.

Adapting the libretto also allowed me the exciting opportunity to create a text that would bring into focus the specifics of this unique production, and which could, I felt, include some of the Hul'q'umi'num language. Hul'q'umi'num is the traditional language of the Musqueam people, on whose ancestral territory the Vancouver Opera house sits. Through the efforts of the Musqueam community, in partnership with the University of British Columbia's First Nations Language program, the critically endangered language of Hul'q'umi'num has largely been revitalized, and while creating the text adaptation for this production I spent over a year and a half working with Jill Campbell and Larry Grant, both Musqueam band members, and Dr. Patricia Shaw, who is the director of the language program at the university, with the goal to include Hul'q'umi'num words and phrases in the spoken text of the libretto.

As to the question about what motivated our decisions, there were two concerns that were at the forefront of the entire process. The first was to create a production that both protected and honored the contemporary and traditional practices of the artists invited to participate in its creation and the other was to guard the integrity of Mozart and Schikaneder's work. Each aspect of the decision-making process was examined through the lens of these two points of consideration.

DR: It's interesting that, from what I understand, the primary aspects of the opera that were adapted to stage the work seem to be those that are most often adapted in opera: the visual design of costume and set, language of the libretto, and choreography. Did the production team ever consider altering the instrumentation, asking First Nations singers and musicians to collaborate on the adaptation?

RM: Vancouver Opera was clear in their directive that the piece was to be played without alteration to the score. And it followed that, in creating the libretto adaptation, all efforts were made to preserve the music exactly as written. While it would have been very exciting to introduce Coast Salish instrumentation and sound into the piece, that would have created a production that was not in line with the intent and vision set forth by the producing company.

DR: The collaborative processes that occurred between Vancouver Opera's production team, First Nations artists, and the First Peoples' Council seem to me to make this production successful as a piece that is as much an expression of First Nations cultural practices as it is a production of *The Magic Flute*. I was particularly struck by Michelle Olson's choreography, and am interested to know more about how she approached developing this aspect of the production with you.

RM: Michelle's engagement in the project was a great gift, both to the piece and certainly for me personally. Although she is currently Vancouver-based, Michelle's family background is Han First Nation, from the interior Yukon. In our initial conversations one of her primary concerns was that we find someone of Salish background with a traditional dance practice to partner with her in the creative process. When I asked who she might consider having work with us Michelle's immediate response was that Bob Baker would be her first choice.

Taken from the artist's statement she made as part of our *Opera Indigene* presentation in London here is how Michelle described her creative relationship with Bob:

> A significant part of the success of this venture was the work of Bob Baker. It was his generosity in sharing his dance and traditions that really allowed the production to land in a place of integrity. I requested that Bob Baker come on board as cultural dance advisor; it was imperative that Bob be a part of the forming of the choreography because of his extensive knowledge of his own West Coast dance traditions. Being from interior Yukon, I am an observer of West Coast First Nations culture not a part of it and I knew that I needed the guidance of Bob in the forming of the work. He had clear guidance around protocol and what can and cannot be shared.

As part of our rehearsal preparation, Michelle, Bob, and I met over several weeks in the autumn of 2006. During our work-sessions we would listen to a piece of music from the score that we felt might include choreography in the staging. First I would describe the key narrative elements in the piece of music—a sort of "here is what I think is going on"—and then I would ask both Michelle and Bob to respond to what the description and listening evoked in each of them and how we might articulate their response using both traditional and contemporary dance.

Perhaps one of the most significant results of this process was the staging at the top of the second act. The beginning of this scene marks the arrival of Sarastro and

316   *Opera Indigene: Re/presenting First Nations and Indigenous Cultures*

RM *continued* his advisors at a council meeting where the fate of Tamino is to be discussed. We decided that the feeling of place, or location, that best fit the environment of the scene was a long-house meeting. Michelle then asked Bob if there was a dance in the Salish tradition that would take place before an important meeting or council and Bob told us about the Snowbird dance. Traditionally, the Snowbird is danced to sweep the floor of a meeting room of all negative energy so that the work to be done can be accomplished in a clear and positive way. After we had been assured we could have permission to use this dance as part of the production, Bob taught it to Michelle in its traditional form and then Michelle began to abstract it to create a contemporary version. As the Snowbird dance is done by women, and the music at the top of Act II is very male in its tone and musicality, it was clear that we would have to find a way of creating the choreography without the use of the score. What evolved was one of our most exciting moments on stage. The curtain rose on the second act as three of our female dancers cleansed the meeting space by dancing Michelle's beautiful contemporary version of the Snowbird—in complete silence. As their dance neared completion and the space was prepared, maestro would give the downbeat of the music and the men would begin to make their entrance. It was a very satisfying marriage of traditional and contemporary dance form and practice coming together to create something that beautifully illuminated the intent and vision of the production both in its form and through the creative process that got us there.

DR: And while you were working with Michelle Olson and Bob Baker on the choreography, yet another set of collaborations was occurring in the visual design aspects of the opera: the set, lighting design, the costumes, and even the magic flute itself. Who, specifically, were the artists that were involved in planning and creating the visual design, and in what ways were you involved in these collaborations?

RM: Over the two-year development period our set and costume designs evolved in unique ways, each quite different from the other. The costumes were co-created by John Powell, who is Kwak'waka'wakw, from Vancouver Island, and non-Native Vancouver Opera designer, Christine Reimer (Figures 17.1 and 17.2).

Beyond the protocol and cultural considerations, one of my primary concerns was how we were going to bring together the sensibilities of two very extraordinary artists to find a unified voice in the design. After much dialogue it became clear that the answer lay in encouraging a freedom of imagination from each of the designers—a championing that released both Christine and John to draw on the influences of their cultural background and practice, without feeling that they had to try and create (or re-create) costumes that were based literally and solely on west coast traditions, which would have been both artistically and politically impossible. Christine took on Tamino, Pamina, The Queen of the Night, the Three Ladies, Monostatos and his gang, and the dancers. John was responsible for the creation of Sarastro, Papageno, and Papagena, as well as the priests, Speaker, the

Figure 17.1   *The Magic Flute*, produced by Vancouver Opera, Sarastro and his men, costumes designed by John Powell. Each of the nations on the coastal land of British Columbia was represented in costumes designed and created by John Powell

RM *continued* Three Spirits, the chorus, and the Ten Elders, who were drawn from within the male chorus.

Here, John felt that it was very important to represent each of the ten nations who live on coastal British Columbia. To give an example of each designer's research and development process here is John's description of how he created these ten costumes:

> In the world's eyes the art forms most studied and illuminated via anthropological, ethnological and archeological means have mainly been the work of The Haida or Kwak'waka'wakw Peoples. This is not a true representation of our coastal peoples and I wanted to include all of the ten major Nations which make their homes here. To my disadvantage I was Kwak'waka'wakw, and so although I had lived all my life around other peoples of the coast I felt unqualified to design in the art forms and cultures which we had now agreed upon. So the time was consumed over a period of seven months visiting museum collections of old textiles, reading seventy-two books from cover to cover on all the various nations and speaking to people of those nations. Initially I thought that I would

Figure 17.2 *The Magic Flute*, produced by Vancouver Opera, The Queen of the Night, costume designed by Christine Reimer

approach elders and speak with them hypothetically and ask them if they were responsible for dressing a nobleman in their fashion "what would that look like?" The responses were so vast and so varying and so no attempt was made to fulfill these. But now it became necessary to do the research to learn of all the peoples in order to work in forms which were both pleasing and respectful and not overstepping any issues of privilege or personal prerogatives. The whole of this production aimed at being respectful and doing it properly. My initial contract was simply to design these and have the wardrobe department of the Opera House build them. I was however not willing to give up my designs to someone else's interpretation and so I also was contracted to oversee the building and to cut all of the art work. My main concern in doing this was that because I was already borrowing from nine other cultures it had to be made exactly as I had researched and been advised or I was going to have to answer for it.

RM *continued* Throughout the process of creating our set design Kevin McAllister, who is non-Native, worked along side Carey Newman, who is a Kwagiulth and Salish

RM *continued* carver, visual artist, and jewelry designer. In addition to designing and carving the flute and bells which were the production's most prominent and important property pieces, Carey also served as the scenic design consultant on the piece.

Unlike many operas which have one setting for each act, *The Magic Flute* moves constantly from one environment to another. In the original score and libretto the descriptions of location include:

- "A rocky landscape"
- "Outside the palace"
- "A grove with three temples"
- "An unknown place near or inside the temple"
- "A garden"
- "A hall within"
- "Two mountains. Within one a waterfall rages. The other spits fire"

Early in our examination we freely explored how we might use "the land where we are" to serve the narrative of each scene as suggested by these libretto locations.

Here is how Kevin described our process:

> Conceptually, we approached *The Magic Flute* from a perspective of the West Coast environment. The land, the water, and the sky and their associated textures and colors served as our initial inspiration. These were elements we could respond to as artists and weren't dependent on a specific cultural background.

As the design developed, we began to simplify, stripping elements away, to provide a contrast between clean lines/surfaces and organic textures. Our approach became about using selection, choosing only a portion rather than the whole, so the design would be representative but non-specific.

This stylized base became the jumping-off point for the involvement of our First Nations collaborators. It allowed opportunities to engage a variety of contributors, from all backgrounds, each bringing his or her own unique background and point of view. My job in the beginning of this collaboration was to serve as gatherer and facilitator, listening and recording ideas for future use.

I then worked with each collaborator, guiding them as they refined their own contributions, ensuring a cohesive production with a strong conceptual vision.

The creation of our set and costumes was a remarkable collaboration. While holding onto the vision of their contribution each artist willingly engaged in a rigorous process of examination and re-examination throughout. It was an exciting, challenging, and deeply satisfying process and I feel it culminated in a design that represented each individual voice coming together to create the whole.

DR: By way of conclusion, I'd like to discuss the reception of the opera. It seems to me that the work is community-specific in the collaborative aspects of its development with primarily Coast Salish artists and the First Peoples' Council. Do

320   *Opera Indigene: Re/presenting First Nations and Indigenous Cultures*

DR *continued* you think that the production, as it stands now, could be presented in other parts of Canada, or even internationally? What challenges would emerge in touring this production?

RM: Perhaps the greatest resource in bringing this piece to the stage was the level of intention and commitment the entire team brought to their work. The production required a wakefulness and inquiry that by far exceeds any other project I have ever participated in. Without the level of engagement each person gave—and we are talking about a large gathering when you consider the number of people involved in the creative, production, administrative, advisor, and educational aspects of building this piece—we would never have been able to achieve what we did.

So, I think that the greatest challenge that would emerge in preparing this piece for either another sit-down production or for a tour would be whether we could re-create the same devotion to purpose we had on the first production. Without this I feel that it would be almost impossible to maintain the level of integrity that was the foundation of each aspect of the work.

Certainly, there was a huge learning curve for all of us involved and much that would be carried forth in building the piece again, but this will never be a simple re-mount, and so while it would be very exciting and gratifying to present the work in other communities in North America or internationally I would want to be certain that we could all recommit to the level of intent that first brought the production into being.

DR: Do you think that this devotion to purpose came from a commitment toward respecting protocol between Nations and knowing that this work was going to be seen both by regular Vancouver Opera patrons, but also the First Nations community here on the west coast? I'm thinking here that some of the commitment comes from First Nations artists engaging with cross-Nation traditions and the desire to respect those traditions in adapting it for the opera.

I'm also wondering if perhaps it might also be possible to consider touring this work not, then, as a piece, but rather as a *process* for bringing together First Nations artists and cultural organizations like the First Peoples' Heritage, Language, and Culture Council from other regions with opera companies? Say, a Six Nations confederacy collaboration with the Canadian Opera Company perhaps?

RM: This is a wonderful idea. There was a great deal of debate and an extraordinary level of excitement that was generated around the project. To not carry forward the opportunity for continued investigation into the possibilities of cultural collaboration would be a terrible loss.

DR: To take a more critical perspective for a moment, I'd like to talk about the political and social context of this collaboration. Despite the high level of collaborative engagement enacted in the variety of relationships between Vancouver Opera's production team and the First Nations artists involved, the

DR *continued* production does seem to favor an emphasis on the aesthetic contributions over conceptual ones. Notably, the production seems to me to explicitly avoid addressing specific First Nations social and political topics. To an audience not privy to the collaborative processes, the piece might seem to simply use the beauty of First Nations traditions—in both visual and choreographic aspects—as a new coat of paint on an old opera. Without such attention to the more challenging questions and concerns of First Nations communities, I wonder if such a focus on the visual and choreographic might inadvertently re-inscribe what Mohawk scholar Taiaiake Alfred has called the celebratory "paint and feathers and Indian dancing" form of exoticism in largely visual presentations of First Nations culture.[2]

Notwithstanding this critique, *The Magic Flute* is *The Magic Flute*, and there is perhaps only so far that the opera's story can accommodate such politically oriented additions. My larger question in all of this is what you feel the larger contribution of this production has been toward the First Nations communities that have engaged in its creation and reception?

RM: While it is a glorious piece of opera theater, *The Magic Flute* would never truly be able to serve all of the important considerations you have articulated in your question. One of the greatest hopes I hold for our production is that it might lead to a commission for the creation of a new opera. An opera written by a First Nations composer and librettist. An opera that would include the instrumentation and First Nations sound world we discussed earlier in the interview. An opera that would engage the extraordinary skills of our creative team members John Powell, Cary Newman, Michelle Olsen, and Bob Baker, and singers like Marion Newman to bring it to the stage. An opera that could address specific First Nations social and political questions in a way that our production never could.

As to the larger contribution the production may have made perhaps I will close with a few observations.

Shortly before we went into rehearsal for *The Magic Flute*, the Vancouver Opera

CCW and TH: The First Peoples' Council knew it was important to proactively communicate with the arts community, and invite discussion through community meetings. Socio-politically, there is so much to be remedied and this can bring the expectation that any large public project should be all things. A project like this engages participants with each other, moving them beyond just thinking and talking, to working toward something better. In many ways it is the artists and creators who risk invention and envision new ways and new relationships that can be modeled in other realms.

In many of our languages, nouns are predominated by verbs and words of action. With a project like this, we value the actions involved with creation, artistic processes, and especially community development as the "project"; the production is the outcome that is shared with a larger community as audience.

---

[2] Taiaiake Alfred, *Peace, Power and Righteousness: An Indigenous Manifesto* (Toronto, ON: Oxford University Press, 2008), p. 59.

322   *Opera Indigene: Re/presenting First Nations and Indigenous Cultures*

RM *continued* hosted a series of forums to introduce the production to the city. During the first of these meetings, which I was on the panel for, one of my colleagues stated that she felt the project was romantic in its aims, and unachievable in its ambition.

About halfway through the run of our production I was standing backstage shortly before the curtain was called out. Michelle Olson was speaking with someone across the deck and when she saw me she beckoned me over. Leonard George—who is the son of the well-known film and theater actor Chief Dan George and succeeded his father as chief of the Burrard Inlet Band—had been present at several of the performances to offer a front-of-the-curtain, pre-show blessing, and that night he had lingered behind to have a brief visit with Michelle backstage. Once we were introduced Leonard looked at me and said that it is important for me to know that this production and the work we had all achieved would open doors of trust that have never been budged. Although this was, without doubt, the most important comment I received during the entire run of the production I do not offer it here as a pat on our collective backs, but instead as a means by which to measure what was achieved.

Given the political, cultural, and artistic complexities of this project there were surprisingly few detractors during the course of creating this piece. This was due to several factors: First, we were given proper time to do the work. Almost three years were allotted us for investigation, consideration, hitting walls, finding a way into and through, or choosing another route all together. Additionally, the team that came together to create this production, in both the creative and advisory capacities, participated from a deep place of possibility. Perhaps the piece was romantic in its aims. But what we did achieve was a coming-together of a diverse group of extraordinary people who shared the vast resources of their collective knowledge, talent and experience to create a production that uniquely reflected the landscape of the home we all share.

Marion Newman: Any project that tries to combine European theatrical ideas with First Nations Culture is known to be a good bet when it comes to receiving grant money. I've been told on a number of occasions that I should consider making a CD with some aboriginal music incorporated somehow, because it's easy to get grants for anything that professes to "preserve" or "bring to light" the mysteries of my Kwagiulth and Salish cultural background. I've been asked to participate in a number of projects, where I was made to feel that my participation was needed more so that my name and cultural background could be placed on the grant applications, more than for my talents as a singer/performer. Of course, people don't actually come right out and say this, but the suspicion is there and I think for good reason. I also have English, Scottish, and Irish in my background and I've never once been asked to sing in a piece that was about any of those stories. Often the people running these projects are not aware of the protocol and sensitivities of the people of the area in which they are performing … or the people that they are professing to tell a story about. Often one is expected to have braided hair and to

MN *continued* speak softly yet profoundly, and some sort of regalia is always much appreciated. I am not actually bitter or confused by any of this, but I do tend to shy away from anything of the sort, preferring to make my way, in the music world, just like anyone else of European descent. I prefer to honor my First Nations heritage, and my family, in a more personal way.

So, initially, I was slightly guarded about how the idea of combining a German opera with Northwest Coast Native culture was going to be handled. I knew that it could be a very impressive and meaningful mix, but only if people knew to ask the right questions, who to ask those questions of, and which answers to take seriously and which ones to let go. However, the excitement of working on such a grand scale, in an art form (opera) that I've spent my life preparing for and working at, with a director who seemed genuinely caring, interested and sensitive about the entire project, made me think that it was worth the risk of possible embarrassment and shame.

The first five minutes of *Magic Flute* rehearsal in Vancouver completely erased any fears I still had lingering about how my colleagues would take this version of such a well-known opera. Robert McQueen welcomed everyone, explaining that we were on Native territory and that we had a spiritual person here to do an opening prayer song and to consult with us about Coast Salish protocol and traditions throughout our process. The prayer song, with accompanying drumbeat, was solemn and I could feel the mood of the room relaxing as we all realized that this was a safe place to explore, ask questions, sing the beautiful music of Mozart, and learn something that not many people have the fortune to find out about in such a manner.

There was a scene during one of the dress rehearsals of the opera, when I wasn't on stage, and I took that opportunity to take a look from the audience at how the set and costumes all looked on stage. This was the moment when the chorus came in wearing different regalia, ranging from the North to the West, as if they were arriving at a potlatch. They all came forward in a half circle as the curtains parted and I was completely taken aback at the emotion I felt come over me. I realized that this was the closest I'd ever come to seeing just how beautiful it must have been to see the different villages arriving at a special event, back in the day of my great-grandparents and before. An event that I have never had the chance to experience because for a long time the potlatch was outlawed, the masks and regalia confiscated, and people were forced to give up their religious ceremonies, their form of government, and their way of keeping a record of the important moments in life. I also realized at that moment how special this was going to be for my father as well, and I felt grateful to the Vancouver Opera and all of its team for taking the risk of mounting such a unique and special version of *The Magic Flute* so that all the people that came to the opera would be able to see what a rich and wonderful culture there is on the West Coast of Canada.

Up until this particular *Magic Flute* production, I'd always wondered if there would ever be a way of combining my two very different worlds: classical music, and my Kwagiulth and Salish heritage. I've always thought that it wasn't much

MN *continued* of a stretch that I've become an opera singer, because there is a long tradition of theater in the potlatch ceremonies of the Kwagiulth people. There were puppets and masks and trap doors and tunnels in the floor … all in order to tell stories dramatically and as realistically as possible. All done with song and dance, it sounds a lot like opera to me. This production fulfilled that need, far beyond my most elaborate expectations. The entire process was done with such care and attention and sensitivity to a culture that is struggling to stay alive, as well as make sense of how it fits into the world today. I am proud to be able to say that I was a part of this and will treasure the experience for the rest of my life and career.

Chapter 18

Pecan Summer: The Process of Making New Indigenous Opera in Australia

Deborah Cheetham and Daniel Browning, interviewed by
Pamela Karantonis

Pamela Karantonis: To begin with the interview, I thought I would start with a provocative statement: Some might say that opera is a dying art which needs to recruit new audiences, particularly in a multicultural place like Australia. What do you see as the advantages and limitations of opera as a creative form?

Deborah Cheetham: I think that the notion of opera being a dying art is nothing new. The point is that opera is not *one* thing and it keeps being reborn through new works, new audiences, and new generations. And I think what is important is to make opera accessible, while not actually impacting on its own integrity. For instance, you may see in theaters all over the world, even in Australia, where the effort to engage new audiences leads to a "dumbing down" of the art form. I don't think that's necessary. I think that quality theater experiences will always engage people. But accessibility is about how you brand yourself in a way. What the cost is for the … well, nowadays they're called a "consumer" but I still call it "audience." And education programs also. So in a way I don't consider opera a dying art form—but it hasn't been well!

PK: How much of a place is there for traditional forms of song and dance in your work? Similarly, for the music, as the composer of this work, what is your relationship to formal traditions? Who have been your inspirations?

DC: In *Pecan Summer*, the entire opera begins with a prelude that is a creation story from the Yorta Yorta mythology and so, for me, putting that right at the beginning, at the very first instance of the opera—that, for me, really makes it central. But that is an ancient story. But I suppose in a sense maybe audiences coming to see *Pecan Summer* will be expecting that, demanding it to a certain degree. I suppose if you're going to call this an indigenous opera then we want to see what *we* [i.e. the audience] think is indigenous culture. But of course as we know in the twenty-first century, indigenous experience, while it is anchored to that tradition, is fed by that tradition, is much broader than that experience. And indeed, for someone like myself, having been a member of the Stolen Generation and being taken from my culture, my reconnection to that culture has perhaps been

Figure 18.1   Deborah Cheetham

a much longer journey than for someone living in a community, where there are grandmothers and aunties who are available to tell the stories. So I've had to seek out those stories and be at a position in my life where I am at a point to receive those stories. And I'm very fortunate that in the last three or four years of my life, a lot of that has come together. So the traditional stories, the mythology, the beliefs ... of the spirituality, if you like, because I do see myself as a very spiritual person ... . The spirituality of the work is very firmly rooted in the Yorta Yorta tradition and the opera grows from there. Because what I wanted to do, Pamela, in particular with *Pecan Summer*, I wanted to tell a story, that took audiences back to a time before what they know right now and when I say "they," I mean Australian audiences—let's say the general, Australian, opera-going public. If they think "Aboriginal," the next word they usually think is "issue," You know, "Aboriginal issues"! What are the Aboriginal issues? Health, education, and so on; the conditions that Aboriginal people live in now, two hundred years on from settlement. That's what people are familiar with—not *all* people, unfortunately— but if they are aware, most people are familiar with Aboriginal people as they are *now*, since those two hundred years. What I really wanted to do was to say to audiences, "I know that you are going to value this experience of Aboriginal [culture] even more, if you could go back to a time when everything is as it should be." So I wanted to take the story back to a point and I thought that Creation was a good place to start!

The Process of Making New Indigenous Opera in Australia 327

PK: What makes the historical events behind *Pecan Summer* so readily expressed through opera?

DC: Well!

PK: Great drama?

DC: Yes, *great* drama! Well the pivotal moment in the story is when—and I have to be careful here as there were other language groups apart from the Yorta Yorta people who were herded onto the mission—so I will say the Aboriginal people of the Cummergunja Mission—decided to leave that mission. So they decided to leave that mission because of the harsh treatment and the degradation they endured. So two hundred men, women, and children left their land, the land of their ancestors of 60,000 years and crossed the river into Victoria, and so the symbolism of that—it's practically Biblical. It's an Exodus, that's what it is! And so last year [2008] when I ran the Spring Intensive [for the cast], the choral work I chose for them to perform was the Hebrew Slave Chorus. Because there are the Hebrews on the shores of the Euphrates, longing for the hills of their homeland, sending their thoughts on golden wings over the hilltops and they've hung up their lyres on the willow trees and I think "My God, the resonances for the people of Cummeragunja"—with that exile and that exodus. That's huge! It is an epic story. Therefore opera is the logical genre. And I've said before, in printed form, that opera is storytelling through music, and so storytelling through music and dance has been the practice of Indigenous peoples all around the world since the world began.

PK: Where does the title for the work come from? "*Pecan*" Summer—are pecans indigenous to Australia?

DC: No, pecans are not indigenous to Australia. It is actually a secret relating to one of the main characters, Alice, whose nickname is "pecan." Her father called her "pecan" as a little girl. I've had this title swimming around in my brain for four years, long before I've had the story, actually. I had this title *Pecan Summer*— which is often the way when I'm writing … I often have the title and then the story will find me. And I think where the title came from was that when I was growing up, my adoptive parents were at pains to tell me "you're not that dark" and that I "could pass for something else," like an Islander and I'd say "well, what island? What are you talking about? Australia's an island." So I didn't have that Aboriginal identity growing up and people were trying to project upon me a more suitable, or more acceptable identity. The Aboriginal experience in the 1970s was a pretty negative one … . And so I can remember someone saying to me: "oh look, your skin is the color of pecan!" or maybe I thought it and I wondered, "what *is* the color of my skin?" and it ["pecan"] must have been a word someone had suggested to me or I had thought of myself. Unfortunately, in Australia, there's

328   *Opera Indigene: Re/presenting First Nations and Indigenous Cultures*

a sort of reverse kind of discrimination going on, where if you don't look like you've just wandered in from the Western desert, then you're barely considered to be Aboriginal! You've really got to fight for your Aboriginality.

PK: Some European theater scholars have said that Aboriginal writings for the stage appear to be preoccupied with "the past as present," often in ways that seem supernatural in the Western sense. Is there a productive tension for you between past and present beyond the historical events of 1939 in *Pecan Summer*?

DC: This is an interesting question. There is an ever-so-slight tinge of superiority in that view of "you're so preoccupied," well yes! We are still teaching Shakespeare to our Year Twelve students [final year of secondary schooling] here, so preoccupation about certain things? ... I don't think anybody should be calling that card. It's *not* a preoccupation, it's a celebration of—if you have a look at how much Aboriginal theater there is or has been the opportunity to make, then I think that preoccupation is far too strong a word. I think we're still exploring the possibilities. And really, theater for Aboriginal people in the traditional sense is not removed from everyday life – theater or ceremony (and opera to me is both of those things) is part of the way Aboriginal people live. You can't divorce your experience of your everyday life as an Aboriginal person from the times that you want to express yourself in whatever artistic medium there is. So we need to rethink that term, "preoccupation." For me, it was important to start with that Creation story because it is about context, not preoccupation, depending on whatever context we might have in our lives—for instance, you could well say that Puccini was "pre-occupied" with *tonality*, which seems like a ridiculous thing to say!

PK: That's a really good point.

DC: So the story of *Pecan Summer* moves into the present, directly after this Creation story. We're thrust into 2004, then we're taken back to 1939 and then we're brought right up to the present day.

PK: So this is a narrative structure that you might say is not particular to any one culture.

DC: Well you want to tell a good story; otherwise the opera won't have legs. You can't move an audience unless they can engage in the story in some way. I think to understand a story which is outside of your own experience (which opera often is), you need a good story—though there are strong resonances [for me and for many] with *Pecan Summer*. The Aboriginal experience will be outside the experience of the average opera-goer in Australia, so you have to give context, so they can understand it, so that it's comprehensible.

The Process of Making New Indigenous Opera in Australia

PK: How important is the place of "the autobiographical" in the narratives of new indigenous opera? Do you think that artists need to tell their own stories as part of telling their culture's story?

DC: I think everyone tells their own story. I would defy *any* author of any book to resist this. You can create your own characters but you base this on something you've observed that is part of your own experience. I don't think it is possible to really create a narrative that is totally outside your own experience. But what you are talking about is the autobiographical. I've written an autobiographical work *White Baptist Abba Fan* and that has enjoyed some success. And what's interesting is that it was a play—an autobiographical work—and that's about a gay Koori opera singer and yet that play did just as well in Switzerland as it did in Sydney, so what is that saying about universal experience? I think as people, we have more in common than we have differences. So I have already written about myself. I think that autobiography is a very truthful way of telling a story. You don't necessarily need to talk about yourself. I mean *White Baptist Abba Fan* was when I wrote about first meeting my Aboriginal mother as a part of the circumstances of learning the truth of being a part of the Stolen Generation, also coming out as a lesbian, also being turfed out of the church, and all of these things. I've done that! I don't need to do that again. And that was a one-woman play and I don't need to do that again either. I want an ensemble piece and I want to write in a medium I understand best and love, and that is opera. The short answer to your question is that I think it is a *logical* expression. It is not the only expression, though. So what I am saying is, to a certain extent, I think that with anything you write some of your own experience is in there and it informs the way you write it. I mean, look at Richard Strauss. He is one of my great influences, in terms of music. Richard Strauss wrote the most glorious music for the soprano. Why? Because his wife was a soprano. He loved sopranos—for all I know, all his mistresses were sopranos. He was in love with "soprano." In a sense, in writing for that, he was exploring his experience of the soprano voice. Similarly, he wrote magnificently for the French horn, as his father was a great French horn player. So autobiographical doesn't necessarily mean: "Hi, my name's Deborah Cheetham and I am an Aboriginal opera singer"; I could just as well say that "Joan Sutherland was the most brilliant voice that the world has ever known." That's autobiographical, because it is something that I think. Or I am saying in *Pecan Summer* that there was something to be valued in the Aboriginal way of life pre-settlement, pre-colonization, and if we can value that then we can empathize much better than we do—as a nation. It is also autobiographical—but not as obvious.

PK: Of the culture?

DC: Yes.

PK: That's great—so we have moved beyond that limitation, by saying that all cultures express their identities through the personal and the collective experience—Aboriginal writing is not limited to a strict genre of the personal autobiography.

DC: Sure.

PK: Are there any specific examples in *Pecan Summer* where you think the influence of Yorta Yorta culture extends and redefines the possibilities of opera?

DC: OK, extends, yes, because the Biami Creation story will be sung in Yorta Yorta language, so that's new, that's never been done—so that's an extension and also will be danced, in traditional dance, which is not brand new to opera but it is an extension. ... What we need to get over in Australia is that once we get *one* of something, the response is: "great novelty value. OK. Been there, done that." And that's ridiculous! That's not an acknowledgment or a representation of indigenous talent. Or the comment: "oh yes. We've *had* one of those. There's only *room* for one of those. There's only room for one indigenous singer, one indigenous actor, one indigenous character in a cop show." That's so tokenistic. We need to move beyond that, and we *are*—we are slowly moving beyond that.

PK: Who is the ideal audience for this piece? Do you think that local and other regional, traditional communities need to see this work?

DC: I'd like them to. I am looking to take this to the opera-going public and then, and most importantly, my whole mission, my whole life as a performer is to bring *new* people to opera—always. I think it was because I was brought up as a Baptist—and that whole evangelical, missionary thing that's been indoctrinated into me my whole life—and so that drive to bring people into the fold—so that opera *isn't* a dying art and won't ever be. That's been a great passion of mine. I will be looking to bring people to opera that don't *see* themselves as opera-goers. I just feel that given the right quality of work, I think that opera is *the* most intense expression because it is the coming together of all the art forms—and so it should be able to reach any audience. But sadly it has had an elitist reputation. I was brought up by working-class people with middle-class aspirations, who really didn't listen to classical music. My adoptive parents were not really into listening to music at all and listened to talkback radio. So why should I fall in love with opera?

PK: How did you fall in love with opera?

DC: I was very fortunate. I had some high school music teachers who are still good friends to this day, who offered me the opportunity when I was in Year Nine to see Joan Sutherland in *The Merry Widow*, and you might say, "well that's just

The Process of Making New Indigenous Opera in Australia 331

operetta" but the following week I saw *Jenůfa* and fell in love with it and saw it twice that season. For me it was not such a leap from Lehár to Janáček because I just loved the medium. Now why should I love that? Because it was a quality theatrical experience and I was a student and could get $4 rush tickets. So I could *afford* to go as many times as I liked. I could become addicted to that, the way that kids these days are addicted to their X-box games! But I was actually going somewhere, doing something. I was living a vicarious experience for an hour and a half. By the time I was in Year Ten and deemed old enough to travel to the city on a train by myself, I would go to the opera three times a week. Because it was accessible because of price and there was quality and this was the 80s, and I think many would agree, though perhaps not everybody, that the 1980s was the real, golden age of opera for our national company. But I'm really not in favor of opera being dumbed down for audiences. I think that's an insult to the audience, let alone the composer.

PK: You speak in very nurturing terms about "growing a cast." How intense is the process for the cast and the creative team in collaborating on something which expresses the story of something that might be new to them? How much of a learning curve is it for those not familiar with either Yorta Yorta culture or opera?

DC: Well the process of growing the cast began with the talent identification program this year [2008]. To bring Indigenous singers who have had some classical training to the VCA (Victorian College of the Arts) in Melbourne and have them participate in our opera intensive course. Now that was a very short course ... that was like: "Here's the introduction. Let's see what we can do in this time." From that, two of the five participants have successfully auditioned and will commence, this year, their Bachelor of Music at the VCA.

PK: Fantastic.

DC: Now that is a phenomenal result. That means we have gone from *zero* Indigenous, classically trained singers at the VCA to three (as one is doing her Masters) ... and well, I work there, so including myself and I guess since I'm doing my PhD there, so: four. So we've got three out of the five studying here and they will work with the very finest teachers that we can offer here in Victoria. Another, a dramatic soprano from Western Australia, is now studying with one of the classical teachers at WAAPA (Western Australian Academy of Performing Arts)—Pat is studying with a wonderful teacher, called Linda Barcan, who will also be in the cast of *Pecan Summer*. I also brought Linda to Victoria to participate in the Spring Intensive, as I wanted her involved from the ground level, even before I knew I had a participant from Western Australia. So that worked out really well and Pat is having lessons with her back home [in Perth] every week. There's also Shedeena Black, who lives in New South Wales and is studying with a singing teacher now. So the Intensive was the first step in growing the cast.

332   *Opera Indigene: Re/presenting First Nations and Indigenous Cultures*

During this year, I will be visiting all of those participants and also auditioning new participants for the 2009 Spring Intensive and then I intend to have my cast locked in by the end of the Spring Intensive this year [2009], which will run from September 14 to 24. Basically I will have the Indigenous cast locked in [chosen] and then from there, it will be a series of rehearsal periods and then a workshop development period in 2010 and then production. So it is very intense, but each of those singers is with their individual teacher now and those teachers are in contact with me. And so we're doing everything we can to get them to a point to make sure they have the confidence and strength in their voices to carry the parts that I write for them.

PK: Of the people in the cast, how many would you say knew of this story of the mission walk-off? Was it all new to them?

DC: It was new to some of them. But I am very humbled because actually one of the cast members, a young man by the name of Tiriki Onus ... my first encounter with him ... I was introduced to him as the son of the great Yorta Yorta artist Lin Onus, and Tiriki's an artist in his own right, he's a sculptor. Tiriki and I were talking one day about his father's art and I expressed an interest in including some his design and concepts in the design of the opera and we started to talked about opera and Tiriki revealed to me that he had trained for five years to be an opera singer and it was his heart's desire as a young man to be an opera singer, but when his father passed away, he had to give it up to take on the art business. So that was amazing. But more amazing than that, his grandfather, Bill Onus, actually led the people off Cummeragunja mission!

PK: That's amazing. I've just gotten a chill.

DC: So what I'm saying is that this story had to be written. I'm just the person who is doing it and all the people who need us to be there, are there. So no one is more connected to it than Tiriki. And so this year, when we have our Spring Intensive, for the first week of it, we'll be at the VCA again, doing all the workshops and masterclasses and so forth. But in the second week, we're going up to Cummergunja and we're gonna re-enact that walk-off. So it's been incredibly enriching for everybody, including myself, to have Tiriki's knowledge and experience and direct link to that history. For the other Indigenous cast members, it has been .... only one or two of them hadn't heard of it at all. Anybody from the East Coast Aboriginal communities has some knowledge of it. So it is a familiar story. It just happened to be the first instance when Aboriginal people walked off a mission. It wasn't the last. But it began something, which I believe ultimately led us to the 1967 Referendum, which gave us the right to be counted as citizens and no longer counted under the Flora and Fauna Act. So what it has done for Indigenous cast members is a real strengthening and belief in the importance of that story. But what it has done to non-Indigenous cast members has been phenomenal! They have been so moved and these are people who have worked in the opera world the whole of their adult careers and never have they been so moved by a week that had such … I don't know … such *meaning*, really. This story has really touched people and given them a thirst for knowledge.

PK: Why do you think it has taken so long for a work like this to emerge and where do you see the future for Aboriginal artists' collaboration and creation in opera in this country?

DC: Well it's taken so long for all of the obvious reasons. I guess this is one of the last frontiers for Aboriginal experience. Maybe I'm being unrealistic, maybe there are many more frontiers. I think that opera is a rarefied world; I think that Opera Australia [the national company] has a lot to answer to. They have no Indigenous talent development program at all—on *or* off stage. Forgive me, but I think that most of the big companies that are federally funded to a degree have to [offer such a program]. I think that there has been a high level of discrimination—not active but … what can I say? …

PK: Institutionalized?

DC: Yes, well, institutionalized, it is. And so in the same way that Indigenous people have been excluded from many endeavors … do you see any Aboriginal cricket players? I'm looking at our "first eleven" [national team] and I'm not seeing any Aboriginal faces. They're playing South Africa and they've got a South African Indigenous bowler Makhaya Ntini who has taken quite a few wickets this test series. We don't see any Aboriginal wicket takers …

PK: You're right. I read in the *National Indigenous Times* about the current situation and the caption was that "you know we're in trouble when the South African team is more multicultural than ours."

DC: Absolutely! It's institutionalized discrimination and it's not from want of talent. I've always had the belief that there could be … I could not *possibly* be the *only* Indigenous soprano. I couldn't! It's just not possible. It's what we do. Singing is what we do. I think it's through lack of opportunity. You know it's a really elite development, the classical voice. It's very, *very* expensive. Who can afford it? Only a few people. I mean only a handful of non-Indigenous people do this … so we're … what, 2 percent of the population? So of course it is going to be a small number of people who actually dedicate themselves to it because only a small number of people do. I think it's taken this long, because, oh God, there are so many basic human rights that Aboriginal people have not had: education, health, you know, a life span that's as long as everybody else in the country. So I think that opera would not be high on the list of priorities! *We're* closing the gap because *my* world, *my* community is the arts community. So that's where I can

334　*Opera Indigene: Re/presenting First Nations and Indigenous Cultures*

[close the gap]—in education and that's where I can do the most good. So what does the future hold? We'll see after the premiere of the opera next year. We just march forward. We've been going for 60,000 years, so in the context of that, the last two hundred years have been something to move on from really, so hopefully we can do that together, but if not? We'll just do the best we can.

Pecan Summer: The Process of Making New Indigenous Opera in Australia and its Contexts, Daniel Browning interviewed by Pamela Karantonis

PK: From the perspective of documenting the process of Deborah Cheetham's work in creating *Pecan Summer*, what marks this work as significant within Australia?

Daniel Browning: It is the first opera to be composed by an Aboriginal composer and featuring Aboriginal artists, who tell an Aboriginal story. It reminds me of the African-American example of *Porgy and Bess*—where the cultural adaptation of what was a primarily European language and medium relates to a [different] culture for the first time. In Australia, opera might be forbidding to Aboriginal people because it excludes them. There are many examples of Indigenous opera. For instance, Aunty Delmae Barton from Mount Isa works on what she calls "Dreamtime Operas." Her son, William Barton, is a didjeridu player and they work on classicizing traditional music and creating contemporary classical music. The singing is very distinct and inspiring.

PK: Tell me something about how you have approached documenting Aboriginal collaboration and creation in opera in your recent radio documentary.

DB: The documentary is biographical—I interview the artists involved and find out what opera means to them; if it is about the performance or the sound. I look at Harold Blair and his complex life and career. He was a source of inspiration to aspiring Aboriginal opera singers, but it is also critically important that he was treated as an anomaly. I also hope to interview his daughter, Nerida Blair, who is a lecturer at the University of Western Australia. Harold Blair had to assimilate into a white Australian world. The idea of being assimilationist is now unpopular and his legacy is problematic because of that.

PK: It is interesting that Harold Blair sang on a US tour with Paul Robeson.

DB: Yes and Paul Robeson visited Australia before the 1967 Referendum to give inspiration to that cause.

PK: How much do you think that non-Aboriginal audiences and viewers of contemporary Aboriginal performance need to be educated to appreciate creative ideas and belief systems originating from ancestral culture?

The Process of Making New Indigenous Opera in Australia 335

DB: Of course this kind of education is important. However, the audience needs to be impressed with the work itself as much as they need to be educated, as representatives of Australian society, about the cultures involved in the work.

PK: We speak in this book about a "salvage ethnography" —when a culture seems under threat, scholars can speak of it in terms that it is dying out and over-compensate in their isolated study of ancestral culture, in ways that might seem inaccurate or out of touch with Indigenous peoples today. Is this something that you are aware of in discussions about Australian Aboriginal performance?

DB: Yes! There are people engaged in that kind of ethnographic work about song and dance in Arnhem Land. In Aboriginal culture things die out because people let them. I hate that way of representing Aboriginal culture [as if it is dying]. We should support culture as it is happening—supporting and maintaining culture as it exists. It's an anthropological afterthought to document performance, preserving it—because performance evolves. A good example of this is the Chooky Dancers [from the traditional Yolgnu community]. They wanted to farewell their Greek dance teacher and so "Yolgnu Zorba" [now a "youtube" sensation] was a tribute to him. It showed that their culture is evolving and responsive to change, not static. They were even invited to Greece, so it became a matter of cultural exchange. Another example would be the traditional performances in Arnhem Land, which respond to modern changes, such as the presence of the Indonesians and the arrival of aircraft to the region.

PK: Are there too many clichés about Aboriginal cultures in popular narratives? I'm thinking of Hollywood and the recent Australian Tourism Commission screen commercial about going "walkabout"?

DB: Absolutely—no question!

PK: How does it affect you as an Aboriginal person?

DB: It is distressing in that the visual language used is very limited. It is mythological and Aboriginal people are depicted as mystical and not real and therefore they are negated as people. It degrades their status as human beings and it means that you the viewer, negate any real relationship with Aboriginal people.

PK: How significant do you think it is that creative input, management, and direction of projects, at all levels, such as *Pecan Summer* involves Aboriginal Australians? If this isn't possible, what sort of consultation and collaboration is ideal to make work that is culturally sustainable within both traditional and urban Indigenous worlds?

DB: It is critical to maximize Aboriginal creative control on such projects, in order to keep things relevant. By this I mean an honest portrayal of an ever-developing culture.

PK: What do you think the difference is between creative work that is tokenistic as against work that is inclusive and, furthermore, giving a fair voice to Indigenous artists and the stories they need to tell, even if they are politically unpopular?

DB: Well a work that might be considered politically sensitive because it involves community health is the play *Chop Liver*, which was created with the Ilbijerri community in Victoria. It informed audiences about the risks of contracting Hepatitis C. But on the much wider scale, there is a lot of political, Aboriginal writing for the stage. Every Aboriginal Australian story is hard to hear for most audiences, if it's true to itself. For instance Wesley Enoch's work *Black Medea*. In television broadcast, there is the Aboriginal current affairs program *Message Stick*.

PK: Why do we need new work that teaches non-Indigenous audience members about the specific importance of particular landscapes and linguistic diversity, for instance Yorta Yorta culture?

DB: All audiences need to be educated about the pre-invasion linguistic diversity and cultural practices that exist on this continent [Australia]. If not, they are depriving themselves of the true history.

PK: Who do you wish to touch most with your documentary about the making of *Pecan Summer*?

DB: Ultimately an audience. I hope that it includes non-Indigenous and mainly Indigenous communities. It is about creating a culture by which we set things into motion and foster new creativity—a new culture. I want Indigenous audiences to know that opera is an OK form through which to express oneself, not just pop music.

Bibliography

Secondary Works

Abbate, Carolyn, *Unsung Voices: Opera and Musical Narrative in the Nineteenth Century* (Princeton, NJ: Princeton University Press, 1991).

Agnew, Vanessa, *Enlightenment Orpheus: The Power of Music in Other Worlds* (Oxford: Oxford University Press, 2008).

Anderson, Benedict, *Imagined Communities* (London: Verso, 1983).

Appleford, Rob, *Aboriginal Srama and Theatre* (Toronto, ON: Playwrights Canada Press, 2005).

Ashcroft, William, Gareth Griffiths, and Helen Tiffin, *The Empire Writes Back: Theory and Practice in Post-Colonial Literatures* (London: Routledge, 1989).

Australian Music Centre, *Dramatic Music: Australian Compositions – Catalogues of Australian Compositions – Part 5* (Sydney: Australian Music Centre, 1977).

Aykroyd, Peter H., *The Anniversary Compulsion: Canada's Centennial Celebration, A Model Mega-Anniversary* (Toronto, ON: Dundurn Press, 1992).

Bartlett, Richard H., *The Indian Act of Canada* (Saskatoon: University of Saskatchewan Native Law Centre, 1980).

Bashevkin, Sylvia, *True Patriot Love. The Politics of Canadian Nationalism* (Toronto, ON: Oxford University Press, 1991).

Bates, Daisy, *The Passing of the Aborigines* (London: Panther Books, 1972).

Bellman, Jonathan (ed.), *The Exotic in Western Music* (Boston, MA: Northeastern University Press, 1998).

Berger, Harris, M. and M.T. Carroll, *Global Pop, Local Language* (Jackson: University Press of Mississippi, 2003).

Bhabha, Homi K., *The Location of Culture* (London: Routledge, 1994).

Bloechl, Olivia A., "Protestant Imperialism and the Representation of Native American Song," Musical Quarterly, 87/1 (Spring 2004): 44–86.

—— *Native American Song at the Frontiers of Early Modern Music* (Cambridge: Cambridge University Press, 2008).

Brofsky, Howard, "Rameau and the Indians: The Popularity of Les Sauvages," in *Music in the Classic Period: Essays in Honor of Barry S. Brook*, ed. Allan Atlas (New York: Pendragon Press, 1985), pp. 43–60.

Brown, James N. and Patricia M. Sant (eds.), *Indigeneity: Construction and Re/Presentation* (New York: Nova Science Publishers, 1999).

Browner, Tara, "Transposing Cultures: The Appropriation of Native North American Musics 1890–1990" (PhD dissertation, University of Michigan, 1995).

—— "'Breathing the Indian Spirit': Thoughts on Musical Borrowing and the 'Indianist' Movement in American Music," *American Music*, 15/3 (Autumn 1997): 265–84.

—— "An Acoustic Geography of Intertribal Pow-wow Songs," in *Music of the First Nations: Tradition and Innovation in Native North America*, ed. Tara Browner (Chicago: University of Illinois Press, 2009).

Buckler, Lillian, "The Use of Folk Music in Harry Somers's Opera Louis Riel" (MMus thesis, University of Alberta, 1984).

Burton, Frederick Russell, *Hiawatha* (Boston, MA, New York, and Philadelphia, PA: Oliver Ditson Company, 1889).

Butler, Kevin, Kate Cameron, and Bob Percival, *The Myth of Terra Nullius* (Sydney: Board of Studies New South Wales, 1995).

Cairns, Alan C., John C. Courtney, Peter MacKinnon, Hans J. Michelmann, and David E. Smith, (eds.), *Citizenship, Diversity and Pluralism: Canadian and Comparative Perspectives* (Montreal, QC, and Kingston, ON: McGill-Queen's University Press, 1999).

Canadian Music Centre, *List of Canadian Music Inspired by the Music, Poetry, Art and Folklore of Native Peoples* (March, 1990).

Cheyfitz, Eric, *The Poetics of Imperialism: Translation and Colonization from The Tempest to Tarzan* (Oxford: Oxford University Press, 1991).

Clifford, James, "Of Other Peoples: Beyond the 'Salvage Paradigm'," in *Discussions in Contemporary Culture*, ed. Hal Foster (Seattle, WA: Bay Press, 1987): 121–30.

Coetzee, J.M., *Waiting for the Barbarians* (Johannesburg: Ravan Press, 1981).

Cohen, Hart, "Repertoire, Landscape and Memory: Schultz's and Williams's Journey to Horseshoe Bend Cantata," in *Intercultural Music: Creation and Interpretation*, ed. Sally Macarthur, Bruce Crossman, and Robaldo Morelos (Sydney: Australian Music Centre, 2006): 116–23.

Cooke, M., *Britten and the Far East* (Bury St. Edmunds: Boydell Press, 1998).

Cooper, Dorith (ed.), *The Canadian Music Heritage*, Vol. 10: *Opera and Operetta Excerpts I* (Ottawa, ON: Canadian Musical Heritage Society, 1991).

Corse, Sarah M., *Nationalism and Literature: The Politics of Culture in Canada and the United States* (Cambridge: Cambridge University Press, 1997).

Covell, Roger, *Australia's Music: Themes of a New Society* (Australia: Sun Books, 1967).

Crosby, Marcia, "Construction of the Imaginary Indian," in *Vancouver Anthology: The Institutional Politics of Art*, ed. Stan Douglas (Vancouver, BC: Talonbooks, 1991): 267–91.

Darian-Smith, Kate and Paula Hamilton (eds.), *Memory and History in Twentieth Century Australia* (Melbourne: Oxford University Press, 1994).

Dean, Bartholomew and Jerome Levi (eds.), *At the Risk of Being Heard: Identity, Indigenous Rights, and Postcolonial Studies* (Ann Arbor: University of Michigan Press, 2003).

Bibliography 339

Deloria, Philip. J., *Indians in Unexpected Places* (Lawrence: University Press of Kansas, 2004).

Diamond, Beverly and Robert Witmer (eds.), *Canadian Music: Issues of Hegemony and Identity* (Toronto, ON: Canadian Scholars Press, 1994).

Dickason, Olive, *Canada's First Nations: A History of Founding Peoples from Earliest Times* (Norman: University of Oklahoma Press, 1992).

Dominguez, Susan, "Zitkala Sa (Gertrude Simmons Bonnin), 1876–1938: (Re)discovering The Sun Dance," *American Music Research Center Journal*, 5 (1995): 83–96.

Dunbar-Hall, Peter and Chris Gibson, *Deadly Sounds, Deadly Places: Contemporary Aboriginal Music in Australia* (Sydney: University of New South Wales Press, 2004).

Elder, Bruce, *Blood on the Wattle: Massacres and Maltreatment of Aboriginal Australians Since 1788* (Sydney: New Holland, 1998).

Featherstone, Mike, *Undoing Culture: Globalization, Postmodernism and Identity* (London: Sage, 1995).

Francis, Daniel, *The Imaginary Indian: The Image of the Indian in Canadian Culture* (Vancouver, BC: Arsenal Pulp Press, 1992).

Gaski, Harald, "The Secretive Text: Yoik Lyrics as Literature and Tradition," in *Sámi Folkloristics*, ed. J. Pentikäinen (Turku: NFF Publications, 2000), pp. 191–214.

—— "Indigenous Interdisciplinary Internationalism: The Modern Sámi Experience, with Emphasis on Literature," in *Circumpolar Ethnicity and Identity*, ed. T.I. and T. Yamada (Osaka: Senri Ethnological Studies, 2004), pp. 371–87.

Geertz, Clifford, *The Interpretation of Cultures* (New York: Basic Books, 1973).

Gilbert, Helen, *Sightlines: Race, Gender and Nation in Contemporary Australian Theatre* (Ann Arbor: University of Michigan Press, 1998).

Grattan, Michelle, *Reconciliation: Essays on Australian Reconciliation* (Melbourne: Bookman Press, 2000).

Greenblatt, Stephen, *Marvellous Possessions: The Wonders of the New World* (Chicago, IL: University of Chicago Press, 1991).

Haberly, David T., *Three Sad Races: Racial Identity and National Consciousness in Brazilian Literature* (Cambridge: Cambridge University Press, 1983).

Halliwell, Michael, "'A Comfortable Society': the 1950s and Opera in Australia," *Australasian Drama Studies*, 45 (October 2004): 10–29.

Harrison, Klisala (forthcoming), "Musical Form as Theatrical Form in Native Canadian Stage Plays: Moving through the Third Space," in *Aboriginal Music in Canada*, ed. Anna Hoefnagels and Beverley Diamond (Montreal, QC: McGill-Queens University Press, 2011).

Hayden Taylor, Drew, "Alive and Well: Native Theatre in Canada," in *Aboriginal Drama and Theatre 1*, ed. Rob Appleford (Toronto, ON: Playwrights Canada Press, 2005), pp. 61–8.

Healy, Janet. "Cry 'Havoc!' and Let Slip the Dogs of War: The Genesis of Moya Henderson's Opera, Lindy," in *Encounters: Meetings in Australian Music:*

340   *Opera Indigene: Re/presenting First Nations and Indigenous Cultures*

Essays, Images, Interviews (Brisbane: Queensland Conservatorium Research Centre, 2005), pp. 56–9.

Hutcheon, Linda, "Opera and National Identity: New Canadian Opera," *Canadian Theatre Review*, 96 (Fall, 1998): 6.

Hutcheon, Linda and Michael Hutcheon, "Imagined Communities: Postnational Canadian Opera," in *The Work of Opera: Genre, Nationhood and Sexual Difference*, ed. Richard Dellamora and Daniel Fischlin (New York: Columbia University Press, 1995), pp. 235–52.

Ingraham, Mary I., "Something to Sing About: A Preliminary List of Canadian Staged and Dramatic Music Since 1867," *Intersections: Canadian Journal of Music*, 28/1 (2007): 14–77.

Johnston, Peter Wyllie, "'Australian-ness' in Musical Theatre: A Bran Nue Dae for Australia?" *Australasian Drama Studies*, 45 (October 2004): 157–79.

Jones, Eugene H., *Native Americans as Shown on the Stage, 1753–1916* (Metuchen, NJ: Scarecrow, 1988).

Jones, Howard Mumford, *O Strange New World: American Culture: The Formative Years* (London: Chatto and Windus, 1965).

Jordan, Robert, "West Coast Magic: Vancouver Opera Looked to B.C.'s First Nations Heritage to Conjure Classic Mozart," *Opera Canada* (March/April 2007): 18.

Keillor, Elaine, *Music in Canada. Capturing Landscape and Diversity* (Montreal, QC, and Kingston, ON: McGill-Queen's University Press, 2006).

Kirk, E.K., *American Opera* (Urbana: University of Illinois Press, 2001).

Kirshenblatt-Gimblett, Barbara, *Destination Culture: Tourism, Museums and Heritage* (Berkeley: University of California Press, 1998).

Langton, Marcia, *Well I Heard it on the Radio and I Saw it on the Television – An Essay for the Australian Film Commission on the Politics and Aesthetics of Filmmaking by and about Aboriginal People and Things* (Sydney: Australian Film Commission, 1993).

Lavie, Smadar and Ted Swedenburg, *Displacement, Diaspora and Geographies of Identity* (London: Duke University Press, 1996).

Lea, Tess, Emma Kowal, and Gillian Cowlishaw (eds.), *Moving Anthropology: Critical Indigenous Studies* (Darwin: Charles Darwin University Press, 2006).

Lehtola, Veli-Pekka, *The Sámi People: Traditions in Transition* (Fairbanks: University of Alaska Press, 2004).

Lush, Paige Clarke, "The All American Other: Native American Music and Musicians on the Circuit Chautauqua," *Americana: The Journal of American Popular Culture*, 7/2 (2008). Online.

Mackey, Eva, *The House of Difference: Cultural Politics and National Identity in Canada* (Toronto, ON: Toronto University Press, 1999).

Magowan, Fiona and Karl Neuenfeldt (eds.), *Landscapes of Indigenous Performance: Music, Song and Dance of the Torres Strait and Arnhem Land* (Canberra: Aboriginal Studies Press, 2005).

Bibliography 341

McGrane, Bernard, *Beyond Anthropology: Society and the Other* (New York: Columbia University Press, 1989).

McNally, Michael D., "The Indian Passion Play: Contesting the Real Indian in Song of Hiawatha Pageants, 1901–1965," *American Quarterly*, 58 (2006): 105–136.

Meglin, Joellen A., " 'Sauvages, Sex Roles, and Semiotics': Representations of Native Americans in the French Ballet, 1736–1837, Part One: The Eighteenth Century," *Dance Chronicle*, 23/2 (2000): 87–132.

Mignolo, Walter D., "Rethinking the Colonial Model," in *Rethinking Literary History*, ed. Linda Hutcheon and Mario J. Valdès (Oxford: Oxford University Press, 2002).

Miller, Kahn-Tineta, George Lerchs, and Robert G. Moore, "The Historical Development of the Indian Act," in *Canada: Treaties and Historical Research Centre*, ed. John Leslie and Ron McGuire (Ottawa, ON: Indian and Northern Affairs, 1978).

Morgan, George, "Indigenous Wannabes," *Meanjin*, 60/1 (2001): 83–90.

Morra, Linda M. and Deanna Reder , *Troubling Tricksters: Revisioning Critical Conversations* (Waterloo, ON: Wilfrid Laurier University Press, 2010).

National Archives of Australia, *Fact Sheet 112 – Royal Commission into Aboriginal Deaths in Custody* (Canberra, 2004).

Oja, C., *Colin McPhee: A Composer in Two Worlds* (Washington, DC: Smithsonian Institution, 1990).

Petrone, Penny, *Native Literature in Canada: From the Oral Tradition to the Present* (Toronto, ON: Oxford University Press, 1990).

Phillips, Ruth B. and Christopher B. Steiner (eds.), *Unpacking Culture: Art and Commodity in Colonial and Postcolonial Worlds* (Berkeley: University of California Press, 1999).

Pisani, Michael, " 'I'm an Indian Too': Creating Native American Identities in Nineteenth- and Early Twentieth-Century Music," in *The Exotic in Western Music*, ed. Jonathan Bellman (Boston, MA: Northeastern University Press, 1998).

—— *Imagining Native America in Music* (New Haven, CT: Yale University Press, 2005).

Power, Anne, "Voiced Identity: A Study of Central Characters in Seven Operas from Australia 1988–1998" (PhD dissertation, University of Wollongong, 1999).

Pratt, Mary Louise, *Imperial Eyes: Travel Writing and Transculturation* (London: Routledge, 2008).

Presley, Carl, "Historical Opera of the Northwest," *Musical America* (May 11, 1912): 5.

Reece, Bob, *Daisy Bates: Grand Dame of the Desert* (Canberra: National Library of Australia, 2007).

Reid, Jennifer, *Louis Riel and the Creation of Modern Canada* (Albuquerque: University of New Mexico Press, 2008.

Reily, Suzel Ana, "Macunaima's Music: National Identity and Ethnomusicological Research in Brazil," in *Ethnicity, Identity and Music: The Musical Construction of Place*, ed. Martin Stokes (Oxford: Berg, 1994).

Richards, Fiona (ed.), *The Soundscapes of Australia: Music, Place and Spirituality* (Burlington, VT: Ashgate, 2007).

Robertson, Boni, Catherine Demosthenous, and Hellene Demosthenous, *Stories from the Aboriginal Women of the Yarning Circle: When Cultures Collide* (Brisbane: Hecate Press, 2005).

Robertson, Carol E. (ed.), *Musical Repercussion of 1492: Encounters in Text and Performance* (Washington, DC: Smithsonian Institution Press, 1992).

Root, Deborah, *Cannibal Culture: Art, Appropriation, and the Commodification of Difference* (Boulder, CO: Westview Press, 1996).

Said, Edward, *Culture and Imperialism* (London: Vintage, 1994).

Savage, Roger, "Rameau's American Dancers," *Early Music* 11/4 – Rameau Tercentenary Issue (October, 1983): 441–52.

Schechner, Richard, *Between Theater and Anthropology* (Philadelphia: University of Pennsylvania Press, 1985).

Simpson, Adrienne, *A History of Professional Opera in New Zealand* (Auckland: Reed, 1996).

Smith, Catherine Parsons, "An Operatic Skeleton on the Western Frontier: Zitkala-Sa, William F. Hanson, and The Sun Dance Opera," *Women & Music: A Journal of Gender and Culture*, 5 (January, 2001): 1–31.

—— "Composing Wild Indians: Reflections on Race and Place in a Western Opera," unpublished paper (Eugene, OR: Annual Meeting of the Society for American Music, February 17, 2005).

Stokes, Martin (ed.), *Ethnicity, Identity and Music: The Musical Construction of Place* (Oxford: Berg, 1994).

Straw, William, "Pathways of Cultural Movement," in *Accounting for Culture: Thinking Through Cultural Citizenship*, ed. Caroline Andrew, Monica Gattinger, M. Sharon Jeannotte, and William Straw (Ottawa, ON: University of Ottawa Press, 2005).

Symons, David, "The Jindyworobak Connection in Australian Music, c.1940–1960," *Context*, 23 (Autumn 2002): 33–47.

Syron, Liza-Mare, "'The Bennelong Complex': Critical Perspectives on Contemporary Indigenous Theatre and Performance Practice and the Cross-Cultural Experience in Australia," *Australasian Drama Studies*, 53 (October 2008): 75–83.

Tacey, David, *Edge of the Sacred* (Melbourne: Harper Collins, 1995).

Taussig, Michael, *Mimesis and Alterity: A Particular History of the Senses* (New York: Routledge, 1993).

Taylor, Timothy, *Beyond Exoticism: Western Music and the World* (Durham, NC: Duke University Press, 2007).

Todd, Loretta, "Notes of Appropriation," *Parallelogramme*, 16/1 (Summer 1990): 29–33.

Bibliography 343

Todorov, Tzvetan, *The Conquest of America: The Question of the Other*, trans. Richard Howard (New York: Harper and Row, 1984).

Tomlinson, Gary, *Music in Renaissance Magic: Toward a Historiography of Others* (Chicago, IL: University of Chicago Press, 1993).

—— *The Singing of the New World: Indigenous Voice in the Era of European Contact* (Cambridge: Cambridge University Press, 2007).

Treece, David, "Caramuru the Myth: Conquest and Conciliation," *Ibero-americanisches Archiv*, 10/2 (1984): 139–73.

—— "The Indian in Brazilian Literature and Thought: 1500–1945" (PhD dissertation, University of Liverpool, 1987).

Trinh, T. Minh-ha, *Woman, Native, Other* (Bloomington: Indiana University Press, 1989).

Tuhiwai Smith, Linda, *Decolonizing Methodologies: Research and Indigenous Peoples* (London: Zed Books Ltd., 1999).

Turner, Victor, *Drama, Fields and Metaphors: Symbolic Action in Human Society* (Ithaca, NY: Cornell University Press, 1976).

van Toorn, Penny, "Aboriginal writing," in *The Cambridge Companion to Canadian Literature*, ed. Eva-Marie Kröller (Cambridge: Cambridge University Press, 2004).

Von Glahn, Dennis, *The Sounds of Place: Music and the American Cultural Landscape* (Boston, MA: Northeastern University Press, 2003).

Warrington, Lisa, "Brave 'New World': Asian Voices in the Theatre of Aotearoa," *Australasian Drama Studies*, 46 (April 2005): 98–116.

White, Patrick, *Voss* (Harmondsworth: Penguin, 1960).

Winchester, Kate, "Moon Music: Musical Meaning in One Night the Moon," in *Reel Tracks: Australian Feature Film Music and Cultural Identities* (Southampton: John Libbey, 2005).

Zapf, Donna, "Singing History, Performing Race: An Analysis of Three Canadian Operas: *Beatrice Chancy*, *Elsewhereless*, and *Louis Riel*" (PhD dissertation, University of Victoria, 2005).

Zitkala Sa, *Dreams and Thunder: Stories, Poems, and The Sun Dance Opera*, ed. P.J. Hafen (Lincoln: University of Nebraska Press, 2001).

Primary Works

Antill, John, *Corroboree: Symphonic Ballet Score* (Sydney: Boosey and Hawkes, 1956).

Australian Government Culture Portal, "Reconciliation," www.cultureandrecreation. gov.au/articles/indigenous/reconciliation (accessed on June 23, 2009) .

Australian Human Rights Commission, *Bringing Them Home: The 'Stolen Children' Report* (1997), www.hreoc.gov.au/social_justice/bth_report/index. html (accessed on June 9, 2009) .

344 *Opera Indigene: Re/presenting First Nations and Indigenous Cultures*

Beck, David R.M., "The Myth of the Vanishing Race" (February 2001), http://lcweb2. loc.gov/ammem/award98/ienhtml/essay2.html (accessed March 4, 2009).

Cadman, Charles Wakefield, *Shanewis: The Robin Woman* (Boston, MA: White Smith Publishing Co, 1918).

Cheetham, Deborah, *Wilin Spring Intensive – Pecan Summer Introduction* (Melbourne: Victorian College of the Arts, September 27–28, 2008).

Chi, Jimmy and Kuckles, *Bran Nue Dae*, libretto and selected score (Sydney: Currency Press, 1991).

City of Sydney, "Barani Indigenous History of Sydney," www.cityofsydney.nsw. gov.au/barani/themes/theme1.htm (accessed March 11, 2009).

Clappé, Arthur A., *Canada's Welcome: A Masque*, in *The Canadian Musical Heritage*, Vol. 10, *Opera and Operetta Excerpts I*, ed. Dorith Cooper (Ottawa, ON: CMHS, 1991), pp. 17–26.

The Commonwealth Citizen and Nationality Act. 1948 www.dreamtime.net.au/ indigenous/timeline3.cmf (accessed August 22, 2008).

Coulter, John, *Riel: A Play in Two Parts* (Toronto, ON: Ryerson, 1962).

Glass, Philip, *Waiting for the Barbarians* (New York: Dunvagen Music Publishing, 2005).

Henderson, Moya (composer and co-librettist) and Judith Rodriguez (co-librettist), *Lindy: An Opera in Three Acts* (Church Point, Sydney: Henderson Editions, 1997).

Highway, Tomson, *The Journey (Pimooteewin)*, libretto typescript, 2005.

Lavallée, Calixa, *TIQ: The Indian Question Settled at Last* in *The Canadian Musical Heritage*, Vol. 10, *Opera and Operetta Excerpts I*, ed. Dorith Cooper (Ottawa: CMHS, 1991), pp. 27–54.

Meale, Richard, *Voss* (Sydney: Sounds Australian, 1987).

Monteverdi Claudio, *L'Orfeo – Favola in Musica; Lamento D'Ariana, Tomo di Monteverdi – XI. XII, Opere*, ed. G. Franscesco Malipiero (Bologna: Ventura, 1930).

Morrison, Frank, *Tzinquaw*, piano/vocal score (unpublished: Cowichan Historical Society, 1950).

Pentland, Barbara, *The Lake* (Canadian Music Centre manuscript).

Schultz, Andrew (composer) and Gordon Kalton Williams (librettist), *Journey to Horseshoe Bend Symphonic Cantata* (Sydney: Australian Music Centre, 2003).

Somers, Harry, *Louis Riel* (Canadian Music Centre manuscript).

Strehlow T.G.H., *Journey to Horseshoe Bend* (Sydney: Angus and Robertson, 1969).

—— *Songs of Central Australia* (Sydney: Angus and Robertson, 1971).

Sutherland, Margaret (composer) and Maie Casey (librettist), *The Young Kabbarli* (Australia: Albert Edition, 1972).

Vézina, Joseph, *Le Fêtiche*, in *The Canadian Musical Heritage*, Vol. 10, *Opera and Operetta Excerpts I*, ed. Dorith Cooper (Ottawa, ON: CMHS, 1991): 180–202.

Recorded Works

Antill, John, *Corroboree*, conducted by John Lanchberry, Sydney Symphony Orchestra (1977): CDOASD 793060.

Chi, Jimmy and Kuckles, *Bran Nue Dae*, CD recording and programme notes (Polygram: 1993): BNDCD002.

Cohen, Hart (director and producer) *Cantata Journey A Documentary* (Research Decisions, 2006).

Henderson, Moya, Judith Rodriguez, and Opera Australia, *Lindy*, sound recording, Australian Broadcasting Corporation, including "The Composer on the Spot' About *Lindy* (CD Liner Notes)," (ABC Classics, 2005): CD ABD476 7489.

Perkins, Rachel, *One Night the Moon* (Siren, 2001): DVD SVE550.

Schepisi, Frederic (director) and John Bryson (author), *Evil Angels* (Metro Goldwyn Mayer, 1988).

Schultz, Andrew, *Black River* (MusicArtsDance, 1990): CD MADCD0001.

—— *Journey to Horseshoe Bend*, conducted by David Porcelijn, CD recording (Australian Broadcasting Corporation, 2004): CDABC 476 2266.

Schultz, Andrew (composer) and Kevin Lucas (director), *Black River* (Lucasfilms, 1993).

Somers, Harry, *Discussing the Score to Louis Riel*, LP booklet, National Arts Centre Orchestra (Washington, 1975): CMC 24/25/2685.

—— *Composer Portraits Series* (Centrediscs Canada, 2007): CMCCD 11306.

Sutherland, Margaret, *The Young Kabbarli, Anthology of Australian Music on Disc: Dramatic Vocal Music, Sutherland and Whitehead* (Canberra School of Music, Australian Music Centre and National Film and Sound Archive, 1999): CSM:32.

Whitehead, Gillian, *Outrageous Fortune*, CD and booklet (Sounz Wellington, 1998).

Zubrycki, Tom (director), *Bran Nue Dae*, VHS cassette (Ronin Films, 1991).

Index

Note: References to Figures and Music Examples are in **bold**.

Abbate, Carolyn 65, 269
Abel Joe *see Tzinquaw*
Aboriginal Deaths in Custody, Royal
    Commission on 84
Aboriginal Dreaming 144, 155
Aboriginal Land Rights and Native Title
    105
Aboriginality
    and the didjeridu 87
    as process 88
    representation 76
Abu Ghraib prison 63
Adaskin,Murray, *Grant, Warden of the
    Plains* 216, 222, 230, 245
    cultural signifiers 224
Agnew, Vanessa 28
Alencar, José de, *O Guarany* (novel) 165,
    166
    Il Guarany, comparison 167–8
Alfred, Taiaiake 321
America, Vespucci's discovery **22**
American Indian Dance Theatre 34
American Indians, Society of 207
Anderson, Benedict 214, 215
Anhalt, Istvan, *Winthrop* 245
Antill, John 94
    Corroboree 97, 98–9, 101
Apianus 22, 24
Appleford, Rob, *Aboriginal Drama and
    Theatre* 44, 45
Aranda
    culture 110
    language 100–101, 106
Ashby, Arved 65
Ashcroft, William, *The Empire Writes Back*
    58
astronomy, Indigenous 144

Atwood, Margaret & Christopher Hatzis,
    Pauline 11
Austin, J.L. 75
Austin-Broos, Diane 110, 112
Australia
    Indigenous opera 83–8
    Stolen Generations 139
    as *terra nullius* 144
authenticity
    examples 77
    meaning 75

Bach, J.S., *Karrerrai worlamparinyai*
    ("Wachet Auf") **107**
    in *Journey to Horseshoe Bend* 111–12
Bacon, Francis
    on Icarus 20
    on the Irish 26
    on Orpheus 24, 25–6, 27
    on science 24, 25
    works
        The Advancement of Learning
            20–21
        De sapientia veterum 20, 24
        Instauratio Magna 21
        The Masculine Birth of Time 21
        The New Atlantis 21, 24
        "Orpheus; or Philosophy" 7, 24
Bailey, Garrick 181
Baker, Theodore 173
Bali
    Kerta Gosa building 307
    music 296
Bangarra Dance Theatre 84
    Black River 4
Barambah, Maroochy 83
Barbeau, Marius 219

Bartoli, Daniello 20
Barton, William 100
Bates, Daisy 8, 95–6
    The Passing of the Aborigines 95, 97
Bax, Arnold, Sir 104
Beaivváš Sámi Theater 37
    Min duoddarat 35
Bengali, David 306
Beyond Eden 11
Bhabha, Homi 213
Biko, Steve 63
Blake, Christopher, Bitter Calm 81–2
Bloechl, Olivia 28, 32
Bodin, Jean 22
    De la démonomanie des sorciers 26
BONES (Buck) 4, 5, 7, 31, 36, 45–54
    dance 4
    embodiment 52–4
        English 46
        invented 47–9
    genre shifts 49, 51
    language, vocables 48
    music examples 50, 51
    narrative 46
    physicality 53
    production process 52
    repetition 50
    Skuvle Nejla, comparison 55–6
    staging 46, 47
Bonin, Gertrude Simmons see Sa, Zitkala
Born, Georgina 273
Boyd, Anne 7
Braga, Francisco, see also Jupyra
Brant, Joseph 11
Brazil
    Abolition of Slavery 160
    national foundation myth 165
    Proclamation of Republic 160
Britten, Benjamin 296, 302
Browner, Tara 9
Browning, Daniel 11, 334, 335, 336
Bryson, John, director, Evil Angels/A Cry
    in the Dark 116, 118, 139
Buck, Sadie see BONES
Burton, Frederick R., Hiawatha 184–5

Cabot, Sebastian 28
Cadman, Charles Wakefield 174, 184

The Sunset Trail 183
    see also Shanewis
Cairns, Alan
    Citizenship, Diversity and Pluralism
        212
    citizenship paradigm 212–13, 221
Campanella, Tommaso, Città del sole 23
Canada
    Cartier's discovery of 21
    chronology 1867–1967: 218
    Confederation (1867) 213, 217, 260,
        262
    First Nations
        assimilation policy 217
        bans on cultural activities 219, 236
        integration policy 220
    Indian Act (1876) 212, 235
    Indigenous operas 216, 220–29
        authenticity 226
        humor 226
        religious differences 225–6
        space, gendering 225
        symbols of indigeneity 223, 224
    multiculturalism 10, 212
    'white settler innocence', myth 245, 249
Carmody, Kev 86, 87
Carr, Emily 237
Carr, Sarah Pratt 190–91
Carter, Tim 17, 18
Cartier, Jacques, discovery of Canada 21
Casey, Maie 95
Chafe, Eric 16
Chamberlain, Lindy
    and frontier nationalism 119–20
    Marcus on 119–20
    wrongful conviction 8, 115–16
    see also Lindy
Charles V, King of Spain 19
Chautauqua touring circuit 33
Cheetham, Deborah 325, 326, 327, 328,
    329, 330–31, 331–2, 332–3, 333–4
    photograph 326
    White Baptist Abba Fan 329
    see also Pecan Summer
Cherney, Lawrence 281, 289, 292
Cheyfitz, Eric 27
Chi, Jimmy
    Bran Nue Dae 85, 88

Index

Corrugation Road 85, 88
The Sunshine Club 85, 88
Cicero, *De inventione* 27
citizenship
    Cairns' paradigm 212–13, 221
    musical, and Canadian opera 213–14,
        220–30
    semiotic theory 221
Clappé, Arthur A., *Canada's Welcome* 216,
    222, 225, 226
    cultural signifiers 224
Clément, Catherine 127
Coast Salish *see Magic Flute, The*
Coetzee, J.M., *Waiting for the Barbarians*
    (novel) 7, 57, 63
    opera, comparison 59, 64, 66–7
    see also Waiting for the Barbarians
Cohen, Hart 108
colonialism
    linguistic 29
    and mimesis 74–5
    and opera 16
    and Orpheus myth 25–6, 27, 28, 29
colonization
    aesthetic, *Tzinquaw* 231–2
    internal 3fn5
    see also decolonization
Columbus, Christopher 22–3, 24
composers, Indianists 174
Connerton, Paul 149, 154
conquistadores, *Requerimiento*
    proclamation 29
Conrad, Joseph, *Heart of Darkness* 7
Cooper, James Fenimore 187
Copernicus 24
corroboree 94, 98
    Antill's *Corroboree* 97, 98–9
Cort, John 193
Cortés, Hernando, mindset 24
Cowan, Isobel 81
Cree language 280, 286, 291
Crosby, Marcia 236
Cruikshank, Julie 54–5

Daedalus *see* Icarus
dance
    Buck on 4
    operas 5

Darwin, Charles 74
Darwin Theatre Group 106
Dawson, Neville 118–19
De Certeau, Michel 26
de Léry, Jean 29
decolonization
    and *Louis Riel* 260
    of the mind 31, 56, 140, 142
    and reinhabitation 142
    see also colonization
Deleary, David 31, 45, 49
Deloria, Philip 33–4, 54, 175
Dénommé-Welch, Spy & Catherine
    Magowan, *Giiwedin* 11
Densmore, Frances 202
Deseret News 201, 206
Diamond, Beverley 7
didjeridu
    and Aboriginality 87
    appropriation of 97
    characteristics
        in *Journey to Horseshoe Bend* 112
        in *Tonic Continent* 112
        in *One Night the Moon* 87
        in Sculthorpe's *Requiem* 100
        in *The Young Kabbarli* 101
discovery, and science 20–21, 23
Donington, Robert 23
Douglas, Clive 101
    Kaditcha: A Bush Legend 78
Duff, Wilson 11
Dunbar-Hall, Peter 85
Durão, Santa Rita, *Caramuru* 164, 165
    Moema, comparison 169
Dusatko, Thomas 12

Edwards, Gale, librettist, *Eureka* 88
Eighth Wonder, The (John) 8, 141–55
    Alex's story 149–53, 154
        Alex's arias **151**, **153**
        buried alive motif **150**, 152
    Aztec
        scene 144, 145–6, 147–8, 150,
            154–5
        symbolism 8, 155
    Bennelong Point 143–4
    chronology 145
    design 145–6

350   *Opera Indigene: Re/presenting First Nations and Indigenous Cultures*

Earth and Sky 144, 146
    music examples **147, 150, 151**
    narratives 146
    Opera House story 146–8
    Quetzlcoatl story 144, 148
    social memory 154
Elliott, Robin 5, 10, 11
Estacio, John, *Frobisher* 245

Farwell, Arthur 33, 174
    American Music movement 190
Featherstone, Mike 141
Feld, Steven 176
Ficino, Marsilio 17
Fillmore, John Comfort 174, 175
    Indian Fantasia Number One for Full
       Orchestra 176
First Peoples
    cultural suppression 236
    Okanagan 245, 246, 257
    opera creation 1, 7
Fjellheim, Frode 35
    Arctic Mass 37
    see also Skuvle Nejla
Fletcher, Alice Cunningham 174
    A Study of Omaha Indian Music 175,
       176
    Indian Story and Song from North
       America 175–6
Foucault, Jacques 23, 24
Francis, Daniel 215, 217
Freeman, Cathy 86

Galle, Theodore, *Amerigo Vespucci*
    discovers America **22**
gamelan music, transcriptions 297–8
Gatti-Casazza, Giulio 179
Gibson, Chris 85
Gilbert & Sullivan, influences, *Tzinquaw* 5,
    231, 238
Gilbert, Helen 85
Gilbert, Henry, *Dance in Place Congo*
    177fn8
Ginzburg, Carlo 19, 20
Glass, Philip
    minimalism 65
    operas 65–6
    see also Waiting for the Barbarians

Goldsworthy, Kerryn 118, 130
Goosens, Eugene, Sir 99
Greenblatt, Stephen 26
    Marvellous Possessions 307
Greene, Alison 10
Greyeyes, Michael *see Pimooteewin*
Gruenewald, David 142, 155
Guimarães, Bernardo, *Juypra* 166
    novel, comparison 169–71
Gustlin, Clarence 197

Haida Gwaii (Queen Charlotte Islands) 11
haka 78, 82
Halliwell, Michael 7, 83
Halpern, Ida 235, 236, 241, 242
Hamlet, ironic encomium on human spirit 17
Hampton, Christopher *see Waiting for the*
    Barbarians
Hannan, Mairead 86
Hanson, William F. 197–8
    see also Sun Dance Opera, The
Harris, Ross, *Waituhi* 81
Harvey, Michael Maurice, music, *Eureka* 88
Henderson, Ian 76, 134
Henderson, Moya *see Lindy*
Herbert, Tracey 311–12, 321
Highway, Tomson
    Caribou Song 281
    Dry Lips Oughta Move to Kapuskasing
       283
    Kiss of the Fur Queen 282
    The Rez Sisters 282, 283
    The Sage, the Dancer and the Fool 282
    see also Pimooteewin
Hill, Elizabeth 11
Holo Mai Pele 35
Holt, Lillian 140
House in Bali, A (Ziporyn/Schick) 11,
    295–308
    cloud fabric 306, **307**
    House, character of 300, 303
    languages 306
    McPhee character 295, 296, 303
    music
       examples **300, 301, 302**
       gamelan 301, 302
    origins 299
    premier 299

Index

351

production issues 306
Sampih character 304–5
Spies character 303–4
synopsis 296–7
time variations 299
video design 306
Howe, Adrian 124, 127, 130, 134
Hudson's Bay Company 191
Hui, Melissa, *The Cellar Door* 287
see also Pimooteewin
Hul'q'umi'num language 314
Hunter, Ruby 86
Hutcheon, Linda 263, 264
Hutcheon, Linda & Michael 262

Icarus 18, 19
Bacon on 20
changing interpretations 20
Columbus, comparison 20
ideology, and opera 211
Il Guarany (Gomes) 159, 160, 171
archetypal characters 166–7
myths 165
narrative structure 167
O Guarany (novel), comparison 167–8
sacrificial myth 167
Indian String Quartet 33
Indianismo
Brazilian literature 164, 165
Brazilian opera 8, 9, 159, 165
and myth 160–64
Indianist school, USA 33
Indigene, meaning 2fn3
Indigeneity, representations of 5, 97
Indigenous identity 1
performing 80
Indigenous opera
Australia 83–8
Canada 216, 220–29
New Zealand 81–3
performativity 87
research 2–3
Indigenous peoples, operas about 78
Ingamells, Rex 98
Ingraham, Mary 9, 10, 35fn18, 215fn11,
216, 262, 286
Irigaray, Luce 149
Irish, the, Bacon on 26

Italy, French invasion 17

Jackson, Helen Hunt, *Ramona* 177
Jason story, changing interpretations 19–20
jazz, and Indianist music 184
Jeffrey, Gordon 246–7
Jenkins, Keith 263
Jindyworobak movement 7, 77–8, 94,
97–8, 101
Johnson, Diane 117, 121
Johnson, Pauline 11
Johnston, Peter Wyllie 88
joiks, *Skuvle Nejla* 40, 41, 42, **42**, 44
Journey to Horseshoe Bend (Williams/
Schultz) 5, 8, 94, 95, 96, 97,
106–13
Aboriginalization of Lutheran liturgy
112
Aranda language 106
Bach's "Wachet Auf", use **107**, 111–12
chorales 109
didjeridu characteristics 112
Indigenous choir 109–10, 110–11
instruments 108
orchestration 108–9
structure 109
"Two Ways" thinking 112–13
Jupyra (Braga) 159, 160, 171
Indianismo 170
Jupyra novel, comparison 169–71
myths 165

Kaplan, E. Ann 89
Karantonis, Pamela 7, 325
Keeshig-Tobias, Lenore 283
Kelly, Paul 86, 87
Klondike Gold Rush 191
Kouvaras, Linda 8

La Flesche, Francis 174, 176, 181
The Osage Tribe 180
LaCapra, Dominick 261
Lake, The (Pentland/Livesay) 10, 216, 222,
225, 245–57
accounting aria, Susan's 250–51, 252,
252–3, 255
Allison, John & Susan, story 245–6,
247, 248–9, 257

atonality 248
cultural signifiers 224
duet, Susan/Marie 255–6
music examples **252, 256**
Na'aitka monster 247–8, 255
narrative ambiguity 250–51
non-staging of 247, 257
Okanagan First Nations people,
portrayal 257
possession allusions 251, 252, 253–4
radio broadcast 248
settlers, unfavourable view of 249,
255, 257
Langton, Marcia 74, 75, 87, 88, 89
Lavallée, Calixa, *The Indian Question* 216,
222, 225
cultural signifiers 224
identity issues 227
Leichhardt, Ludwig 7
Levin, David 276
Lieurance, Thurlow 174
Lindenberger, Herbert, *Opera the
Extravagant Art* 264
Lindy (Henderson) 6, 8, 116–40
binary oppositions 116–17, 124–5
black/white divide 127
catharsis 134
CD recording 116fn4
Dingo music 126, **128–9**, 138
expert evidence 123–5
Indigenous culture, awareness of
122–3, 135
and Indigenous knowledge 138
Lindy's music 130, **131–3, 136, 137**
realism 138–9
reviews 135, 138
sexuality 117–18
"trespass" 120–21
"witch hunt" 117–19, 121
Little, Jimmy 84
Livesay, Dorothy 242
see also Lake, The
Lockyer Steel, Deborah 53–4
Longfellow, Henry 187
Hiawatha 183
Louis Riel (Somers/Moore) 10, 11, 216,
225, 230, 245, 259–76
Canada as anti-hero 263

cultural signifiers 224, 228
and decolonization 260
electronic music 270–71
intertextuality 264–5
Métis characters, atonal representation
272
music examples **266, 267, 269, 273**
musical
eclecticism 228
quotations 264–8
sources 222–3, 226
and national unity 261–2
and operatic convention 263–4
origins 261
Prime Minister Macdonald's aria **275**
Riel's arias 268, 269–70, **269, 274**
Lowe, Greg 119
Lowe, Sally 119
Lowinsky, Edward 15–16

McClary, Susan 130
MacDonald, Flora 139
MacDowell, Edward 33
McGrance, Bernard 26
MacLeod, Margaret Arnett, *Songs of Old
Manitoba* 265
McNally, Michael 184
McPhee, Colin 11
biography 295–6, 297–8
gamelan transcriptions 297–8
Kinesis 299, 300, **300**
see also House in Bali, A
McQueen, Robert 11, 309, 310, 312–13,
313–14, 315–16, 316–17, 318–19,
320, 321–2
Magic Flute, The (Vancouver Opera/Coast
Salish) 4, 11, 309–24
achievement 322
choreography 315–16
costumes
creation 317, 318
Queen of the Night **318**
Sarastro and his men **317**
critique of 320–21
cultural issues 314–15
Hul'q'umi'num language 314
interview about 309–24
locations, multiple 319

music 315
  origins 309–10
  reception 319–20
  set design 318–19
  Snowbird dance 316
Magowan, Fiona 79
Malouf, David *see Voss*
Marcus, Julie, on Chamberlain case 119–20
Marino, Giambattisto, *L'Adone*, encomium
  on Galileo 18–19
Martines, Lauro 17
Mason, Tina, *Diva Ojibway* 34
Mead, Margaret 296, 303, 305
Meale, Richard *see Voss*
Medici, Cosimo de', Prince 23
memory, collective 141
Merola, Gaetano 183
Métis people 10
  uprisings 260
Mexico, conquest of 24
mimesis
  and colonialism 74–5
  meaning 74, 75
  model 79–80
  Taussig on 74
minimalism
  definition 65
  Glass 65
modernity, and Lutheran Reformation 24
Moema (Carvalho) 159, 160, 168–9, 171
  Caramuru epic, comparison 169
  Caramuru myth 168
  myth of the outcast 168
  myths 165
  plot 168
  sources 165
Monteverdi, Claudio, *Orfeo* 6, 16–17
  encomium on human spirit 17, 18
  Infernal Spirits, as Other 27
  and modern episteme 24
  portents of doom 18
Moore, Mary Carr, career 190
  see also Narcissa: Or, The Cost of
    Empire
Morgan, George 155
Morrison, Frank *see Tzinquaw*
Morrison, Howard 81
Moses, Daniel David 283

multiculturalism, Canada 10, 212
Munslow, Alun 263
Munyarryun, Djakapurra 86
Murray, Alexander Hunt 265
music
  Indianist
    and jazz 184
    popularity 176–7, 185
    Ramona Pageant 185
  Native American
    recordings 174–5
    transcriptions 174, 175
  and native encounters 28
Musical America 206
musicians, on seafaring expeditions 28
myth
  Brazilian opera 165
  captivity 163
  of conquest 163
  diluvian 163
  Edenic 162–3
  frontier 161–2, 166
  of the good Indian 163
  and *Indianismo* 160–64
  of national foundation 161, 165, 171
    phases 164
  of national origins 163
  outcast 164
  sacrificial 163
    Il Guarany 167

Nakai Theatre 34
Narcissa: Or, The Cost of Empire (Moore)
    9, 190, 207
  authenticity 193, 196
  music examples **194–5**
  plot summary 192
  reception 196–7
  revivals 196, 197
  sources 191
Native Americans
  attribution of demonology 26–7
  ballet dancers 33
  musicians 33
  representations 188
  vanishing race theory 193
  see also operas, Indianist; Wild West
    shows

Native Earth Performing Arts 34
Native Theater School 34
nature, mastery of 23
Nawalowalo, Nina & Gareth Farr, *Vula* 82–3
Nelson, N.L. 201, 202, 206
Nevin, Robyn 125
New Zealand, Indigenous opera 81–3
New Zealand Opera Company, *Porgy and Bess* 81
Newman, Marion 322–4
Nowra, Louis, *Radiance* 85

Okanagan First Peoples 245, 246
  in *The Lake* opera 257
opera
  Brazilian, myth 165
  Canadian, and musical citizenship 213–14, 220–30
  and colonialism 16
  as "contact zone" 32
  embodiment 37
  European tradition 284–5
  genre shifts 36–7
  houses 188
  hula 35
  and ideology 211
  and Indigenous performers 32
  joik 35
  language choice 36
  and postcolonialism 57
  and tonality 15–16
  see also Indigenous opera
operas
  about Indigenous peoples 78
  Canadian, about First Nations characters 215–16
  Indianist 177–8, 188, 189
oratorio, definition 289
Orpheus myth
  Bacon on 24, 25–6
  and colonialism 25–6, 27, 28, 29
  and Otherness 28
  and science 16–17, 27
Oskenonton 33, 183
Other, Infernal Spirits as (*Orfeo*) 27
Otherness, and the Orpheus myth 28

Page, Stephen 86
Pecan Summer (Cheetham) 5, 6, 11, 36, 85
  making of, interview 325–36
  pecan, relevance of 327–8
  Sydney Olympics, performance 86
  Yorta Yorta story 5, 36, 325
Pedro II, Dom, Emperor of Brazil 159
Pell, Kelton 86, 87
Pemberthy, James
  Dalgerie 78
  Larry 78
  The Earth Mother 78
Pentland, Barbara 235, 241
  Ice Age 246
  News 246
  Tellus 246
  see also Lake, The
performance studies 73
performativity 73
  Black River 83–4
  Indigenous opera 87
  meaning 75
Perkins, Rachel, *One Night the Moon*
  authenticity 87
  didjeridu use 87
  musical styles 87
  narrative 86
Persson, Cecilia *see Skuvle Nejla*
Petrone, Penny 242
Pico della Mirandola 17
Pillars of Hercules 19, 21
Pimooteewin (Highway/Hui/Greyeyes) 5, 6, 10, 279–93
  audience workshops 279
  cast members 290–91
  as contested opera/oratorio 287, 288–91
  costumes 287
  Cree language 280, 286, 291
  humor 284
  instruments 285
  kuroko figures 287, **288**, 292
  music 285–6
  narrative 284–5
  Narrator, role 284
  origins 281
  personal narratives about 279–80
  re-creation of 291–3
  singers 285

Index

staging 286–7
story 280
touring production 279, 292–3
Trickster figure 285
workshops 288, 292
Pisani, Michael 271
place, concept 141
and narratives 142
postcolonialism, and opera 57
Power, Anne 8, 134
Pratt, Mary Louise 32
Pucci, Idanna 307, 308
Puccini, Giacomo, *Madama Butterfly* 85
Putnam, Frederic Ward 174

Rangatira Maori Opera Group 32
Rare Earth Arias 34
Reade, Charles
Gold! 76
It's Never too Late to Mend 76
Redfeather, Tsianina 33, 177, 178, 182, 183
see also Shanewis
Reece, Skeena 1, 12
Reformation, Lutheran, and modernity 24
Reid, Bill 11
Reid, Jennifer 276
reinhabitation 155
and decolonization 142
Renihan, Colleen 10
Richler, Noah 282
Riel, Louis, in Canadian history 260–61
see also Louis Riel
Rimsky-Korsakov, Nikolai, *Scheherazade*
183
*Robin Woman, The see Shanewis: The
Robin Woman*
Robinson, Dylan 10, 309, 312
Rodriguez, Judith 122, 127, 130
Rome, Sack of 17
Romero, Silvio 169
Ronceria, Alejandro, choreographer,
BONES 31, 45
Rudd, Kevin, apology to Indigenous
inhabitants 93, 105
Ryan, Robin 86

Sa, Zitkala (Gertrude Simmons Bonnin) 9,
178, 182, 184, 189, 197, 201, 207

education 198–9
see also Sun Dance Opera, The
Said, Edward 7, 16
Culture and Imperialism 15
Saint Clare, Andrish, *Trepang* 35–6
Sámi renaissance 34–5
Sara, Johan Jr. 35
Schafer, R. Murray 260, 264
Schechner, Richard 73
Schultz, Andrew 8, 106
Black River 83, 84, 106
performativity 83–4
Tonic Continent, didjeridu
characteristics 112
see also Journey to Horseshoe Bend
science
Bacon on 24, 25
and discovery 20–21, 23
and Orpheus myth 16–17, 27
Sculthorpe, Peter 94, 152
Djilile 100
Requiem, didjeridu 100
Rites of Passage 8
Aranda language 100–101
sources 100
Senczuk, John, librettist, *Eureka* 88
Seneca, *Medea* 19
September 11 (2001) events 63
Shanewis: The Robin Woman (Cadman/
Redfeather) 9, 33, 174, 178–82
instruments 180
music example **181**
plot 178
powwow song 179–80, 182
premiers 178, 179
Hollywood Bowl 183
revivals 179, 184
staging 179–80
stationery heading **183**
Shea Murphy, Jacqueline 34, 53
Skuvle Nejla (Fjellheim/Persson) 5, 7, 31,
36, 37–8, 39–40
bilingualism 38, 39–41
BONES, comparison 55–6
embodiment 44, 45
genres 41, 42
joiks 40, 41, 42, **42**, 44
music examples **41**, **42**, **43**

356   *Opera Indigene: Re/presenting First Nations and Indigenous Cultures*

plot 37–8
production process 41, 42, 44
scenes **39, 45**
staging 38
vocables 40
Smith, Catherine Parsons 9
Indianist opera, taxonomy 177
Smith, Sherry 178
social memory, in *The Eighth Wonder* 154
Somerville, Margaret 141
Stravinsky, Igor, *The Rite of Spring* 99
Streep, Meryl, *Evil Angels/A Cry in the
    Dark* 116
Strehlow, Carl 96, 110
Strehlow, T.G.H.
    Journey to Horseshoe Bend (novel) 96,
        106, 108
    Songs of Central Australia 96
Striggio, Alessandro, librettist, *L'Orfeo*
        6–7, 16, 23, 24
Sun Dance Opera, The (Hanson/Sa) 9, 182,
        197, 207
    authenticity 203
    Hanson on 201
    music examples **204, 205**
    ownership issue 203, 204
    reception 206
    Sun Dance ceremony 200–201, 202
    Ute-derived melodies 203
    versions 199–201
Sutherland, Margaret 8, 96
    Haunted Hills 105
    see also Young Kabbarli, The
Sydney Metropolitan Opera 83
Sydney Olympics (2000), ceremony,
        Indigenous participation 86
Sydney Opera House 8, 78, 143
    see also Eighth Wonder, The
Symons, David 78, 101
Syron, Brian 78, 79
Syron, Liza-Mare 78–9, 80

Tacey, David 155
Talking Stick Festival 1
Tallchief, Maria 33
Taussig, Michael 75
    on mimesis 74
    Mimesis and Alterity 74

Taylor, Timothy 16, 31–2
Te Kanawa, Kiri, Dame 32, 81
Te Puhi Kai Ariki Brennan-Doyle, Timua 32
Te Wiata, Inia 32, 81
Thring, Frank
    Collitt's Inn 77
    The Highwayman 77
Till, Nicholas 6
Todd, Loretta 291
Todorov, Tzvetan 24
Tomlinson, Gary 23
    on vocables 48
tonality, and opera 15–16
Trickster figure
    in First Nations culture 282–4
    in *Pimooteewin* 285
Troyer, Carlos 174
Turino, Tom 50
Turner, Victor 73
Turrbal people 83
"Two Ways" thinking 94, 96, 101
    Journey to Horseshoe Bend 112–13
    Young Kabbarli 104–5
Tzinquaw (Morrison/Abel Joe) 5, 10,
        231–43, 311
    aesthetic colonization 231–2
    authenticity 242–3
    Cowichan songs 231, 233–4, 237–8,
        240, 242
    design 240–41
    and First Nations rights 235–6
    Gilbert & Sullivan influences 5, 231,
        238
    music styles 231, 238
    narrative 233
    origins 232–3
    premier 232
    reception 234–5, 241–2
    revival 243
    and salvage paradigm 236–7
    stage production 240–41
    structure 233–4
    text 239–40

Uluru, Chamberlain baby disappearance
        115, 122, 139
Utzon, Jørn 8, 143, 153

Valkeapää, Nils-Aslak, *Bird Symphony* 35
van der Straet, Jan 21
Vancouver Opera *see Magic Flute, The*
Vaughan, Victoria 11
Vespucci, Amerigo, discovery of America
    21, **22**, 23
Vézina,Joseph, *Le Fétiche* 216, 222
    cultural signifiers 224
vocables 1
    in *BONES* 48
    in *Skuvle Nejla* 40
    Tomlinson on 48
Volpe, Maria 9
Voss (Meale/Malouf) 5, 6, 7, 57–63
    dance 60, 61–2
    music, significance of 59–60, 62–3
    naming 59
    non-verbal communication 60–61
    novel, comparison 59, 60
    Waiting for the Barbarians,
        comparison 70–71

Wai Kapohe, Deborah 32
Waiata Maori Choir 32
Waitangi, Treaty (1841) 81
Waiting for the Barbarians (Glass/
    Hampton) 6, 63–71
    Dreamscapes 69
    language 67–8
    naming 69
    novel, comparison 59, 64, 66–7
    repetition 64–5
    torture scene 68–9
    Voss, comparison 70–71
    writing trope 69, 70–71
Wallace, Russell 31, 45, 49
Warrington, Lisa 81
Watkins, Dennis, librettist, *The Eighth
    Wonder* 142

West, Cecil, designer, *Tzinquaw* 234, 240–41
Westen, Thomas von 37
    opera character 38, 39, 44
Westwood, Matthew 138
Wherry, Cathi Charles 311–12, 321
White, Hayden 259, 263
White, Patrick, *Voss* (novel) 7, 57
    opera, comparison 59, 60
Whitehead, Gillian, *Outrageous Fortune*,
    instruments 82
Whitman, Marcus & Narcissa 190, 191, 193
Wild West shows 184, 187
Willan, Healy, *The Life and Death of Jean
    de Brébeuf* 245
Williams, Gordon Kalton 96, 106, 110–11,
    112
    see also Journey to Horseshoe Bend
Williams, Lorna 310–11
Williams, Toni 81
Williamson, Malcolm 152
Wright, Judith 155

Yorta Yorta
    in *Pecan Summer* 5, 36, 325
    storytelling 5
Young Kabbarli, The (Sutherland) 6, 8, 94,
    95, 96, 101–5
    basis 95
    didjeridu use 101, 104
    instruments 102
    music example **103**
    neo-Classical influences 104
    structure 102
    "Two Ways" thinking 104–5
Young uluKabbarli, The (Sutherland),
    premier 102

Zapf, Donna 270
Ziporyn, Evan, *see also House in Bali, A*

T - #0002 - 040324 - C0 - 234/156/21 [23] - CB - 9780754669890 - Gloss Lamination